Americanism and Americanization

Americanism and Americanization

A Critical History of Domestic and Global Influence

MEL VAN ELTEREN

McFarland & Company, Inc., Publishers

Jefferson, North Carolina, and London

LIBRARY OF CONGRESS CATALOGUING-IN-PUBLICATION DATA

Elteren, Mel van.
Americanism and Americanization : a critical history of domestic
and global influence / Mel van Elteren.
p.   cm.
Includes bibliographical references and index.

ISBN-13: 978-0-7864-2785-7
ISBN-10: 0-7864-2785-X
(softcover : 50# alkaline paper) ∞

1. United States — Relations — Foreign countries.   2. Europe — Civilization —
American influences.   3. Americanization.   I. Title.
E744.5.E58   2006   303.48'27304 — dc22   2006023500

British Library cataloguing data are available

Cover art ©2006 Photodisc

Manufactured in the United States of America

*McFarland & Company, Inc., Publishers
Box 611, Jefferson, North Carolina 28640
www.mcfarlandpub.com*

For Nancy, my soulmate
through thick and thin

Acknowledgments

I want to acknowledge the help of several people who contributed either directly or indirectly to the writing of this book and deserve my heartfelt thanks.

My wife, sociologist/Americanist Nancy A. Schaefer, challenged me to sharpen my thinking and express my ideas and findings more clearly at every stage of the project — I am deeply indebted to her.

Arie de Ruijter, professor of social sciences and dean of the Faculty of Behavioral and Social Sciences of Tilburg University, offered me the necessary institutional support and space to carry the project to fruition. The staff at Tilburg University library were always professional and pleasant in processing the steady stream of interlibrary requests.

I am also indebted to the editors of the *Journal of American Culture*, the *Journal of Popular Culture* and *Popular Music and Society*, as well as several other members of the related American Culture Association and Popular Culture Association (especially Ray B. Browne, Marshall Fishwick, Gary Burns, George H. Lewis, Kathy Merlock Jackson, Gary Hoppenstand, Don Cusic, Seymour Leventman, and Hai Ren) for allowing me to test out some of my ideas.

The same applies to my fellow board members of the Netherlands American Studies Association (Kees van Minnen, Jaap Verheul, Wil Verhoeven, Joke Kardux, Hans Bak, Ruud Janssens, Marja Roholl), Hans Krabbendam and other co-organizers of the relevant annual conferences at the Roosevelt Study Center, Middelburg, the Netherlands.

I have also benefited from earlier discussions with Kaspar Maase (then at the Institut für Sozialforschung in Hamburg), John Dean, George McKay and others at conferences of the European Association for American Studies, and my fellow participants in the 1991–1992 Theme group on the Reception of American Mass Culture in Europe (Rob Kroes, Mick Gidley, David Ellwood, David Nye, Robert Rydell, Hans Bertens, Doeko Bosscher) at the Netherlands Institute for Advanced Study in the Humanities and Social Sciences, as well as from my invitation to the international conference "American Culture in Global Perspective," hosted by Michael Kammen at the Woodrow Wilson International Center, Washington, DC, from October 8 to 10, 1998.

Of course, I am solely responsible for the book's content and central argument.

Contents

Introduction

"Americanization" is an umbrella term under which many features and different processes have been lumped together since it first appeared in the early nineteenth century. Over the past few decades several critics have insisted that the concept of "Americanization" should be jettisoned altogether, arguing that it is little more than a catchphrase with dubious analytical value, even sometimes used by non-Americans as a term of abuse. Yet the term continues to play a central role in many descriptions and discussions of specific change processes in local settings outside the United States that are in some way related (or at least attributed) to American influence. In general, the purpose of this book is to demonstrate that the concept still has value today, if used thoughtfully and accompanied by clear demarcations and qualifications when applied to specific cases. This study also takes account of power relations — including structural and cultural impositions on the part of the United States — that have been either neglected or downplayed by many students of American influence abroad during the past quarter century.

The interest in Americanization as it evolved among international scholars in the late twentieth century focused mostly on America's cultural influence abroad, which was in line with the traditional preoccupations of European intellectual elites.[1] This restriction of the multipronged phenomenon that is behind the label Americanization is not unproblematic and may even prevent a good understanding of the cultural aspects themselves. Moreover, as will be explained in Chapter 5, a number of publications have appeared in which the notion of cultural imperialism, and more particularly American cultural imperialism, has been thoroughly deconstructed and severely contested to the point that nothing is left of its critical charge. Influenced by a prevailing tendency within cultural studies and postmodern anthropology to put much emphasis on the selective borrowing and active appropriation by local recipients of cultural forms coming from elsewhere, the indigenization, hybridization or creolization of global cultural flows has become the main focus. From this perspective, Americanization is seen as the local interpretation of U.S. culture traveling abroad, as manifested, for example, in the Europeanization, or more specifically the Frenchification, Germanification, Dutchification, Italification and so forth of American culture as it reaches the Old World, or the Australianization, Japanization, Brazilianization or whatever localization of American models and imports in other parts of the world. In short, the research interest is first of all focused on how recipients turn American culture into something of their own by incorporating the imported components into the local culture.

By the same token, the accepted view among leading theorists of cultural globalization, practitioners of cultural studies and kindred scholars in other fields within the humanities and social sciences is that globalization rules out Americanization in the sense of a relatively more powerful influence exerted by the United States, or specific U.S. agents or institutions, upon other regions, nations and peoples of the world. It is more or less taken for granted that in the many forms of "glocalization" — that is, the numerous inter-

1

plays between global tendencies of cultural homogenization and local tendencies of cultural heterogenization and differentiation — hybrid forms of culture predominate to such an extent that it has become virtually impossible anywhere to recognize a domineering, let alone hegemonic, American influence. Although this approach does have its merits in emphasizing the active involvement of recipients of American culture (thus countering a crude notion of U.S. cultural imperialism), it also has serious shortcomings, as I hope to demonstrate in this book, which is written from a critical, social-emancipatory perspective that emphasizes the value of self-determination by human beings in societal contexts from a radical Enlightenment perspective.[2] The aim is to offer a more adequate conceptualization of Americanization than is commonly available in the relevant literature.

At this point it is necessary to explain and defend my use of the terms "America" and "American." I readily admit that there is a problem in using "America" to refer exclusively to the United States. Strictly speaking, the word designates the entire landmass of the New World, which comprises North, Central, and South America as well as the Caribbean islands. Geographically, America extends from Canada to Patagonia, but its name has been co-opted by the United States and reconstructed as a term to indicate only that nation. Some would say it has even been narrowed to a national English-only category, often excluding those of Latin American ancestry, no matter how long they have resided in the United States and no matter how substantial their contributions to the economic and cultural fabric have been (Pacini Hernadez 2001: 63) — a tendency still apparent. As Mark Berger stated in his history of Latin American studies and U.S. hegemony in the Americas: "The historical appropriation of the words 'America' and 'American' by the U.S. symbolizes and reinforces the way in which the U.S. has presumed to speak for and lay claim to common values with the rest of the hemisphere" (Berger 1995: 18). This imperial gesture was for Octavio Paz a reason to state that "the United States of America is an abuse of language" (Paz 1993: 11, qtd. in Ceaser 1997: 15). The name stirred controversy during the commemoration (some insisted on the term "remembrance") of the 500th anniversary of Christopher Columbus's discovery (some called it "invasion") of the New World in 1992. Many opponents declared that its appropriation by the predominantly white and Anglo-American (respectively Euro-American) population of the United States reflected a Eurocentric bias against indigenous peoples and marginalized groups living in the Americas.

Indeed, "America" by right should refer to the whole of the Americas, not just to one part of it. Yet, there is a significant reason why it is legitimate to suspend our scruples on this issue in the present study. Its subject matter entails the actual, purported or imagined impact of one or more forms of "Americanism" that are inherent to the USA (or at least believed to be so by the observers involved), and *not* such influences of the other Americas. When I speak of "Americanization" in the following, I refer specifically to the impacts of the United States for which "United Statesianization" (Hannerz 1992a: 9) or "USAmericanization" (Robertson 2003: 257) would have been more precise descriptions. But neither of these awkward terms (or similar ones that express a clear reference to the United States) has been widely accepted. Therefore I want to retain the term Americanization here, which will be defined more precisely in Chapter 5. Likewise, throughout this book the terms "America" and "American" are used as conventional shorthand references to the United States of America. I do remain cognizant, however, that the United States is but one nation in the Americas and that the use of "America," "American," and, indeed, Americanization is not intended to attribute to the United States characteristics that would hold for all of the Americas, and then overlook the vast differences of societies and peoples in North, Central, and South America.

I take as starting point that Americanization, in all of its manifestations and interpretations, refers to the real or purported influence of one or more forms of Americanism on some social entity, material object or cultural practice. Processes of this kind have taken (and are still taking) place inside and outside the United States. The social entity can be a group of people or social category, a region, a nation or a transnational world or culture that goes beyond this geographic scale — a specific cultural area, civilization or even "the globe" as a whole. The object in question can be any good, product or artifact and its associated technology or practice. Americanism is provisionally, and therefore less accurately, defined for the purpose of this book as a characteristic feature of the United States, and refers to principles and practices believed to be essential or inherent to the American "national culture."

In what follows I consistently approach the local appropriation and processing of American influences abroad in relation to the projection of diverse forms of American power. Moreover, the theoretical framework elaborated in this book is not confined to the cultural sphere, which would mean running the risk of missing the bigger picture of the process, even though culture is understood here in a much broader sense than tends to be the case in the existing literature on the subject. Besides a wide variety of cultural forms, low and high — disseminated by the cultural industries and mass media — it also encompasses cultural influences implicated in capitalist globalization, such as the transnationalization of the state and corporate business, management and labor practices, strategies of private and semi-private international relations forums and think tanks, cultural and political development policies regarding "less advanced" countries, academic and professional associations and so forth. Alongside the cultural, my approach includes economic, military, social, political, and sociopsychological dimensions of Americanization as well as their interrelationships. This means that if we look at a particular instance of cultural Americanization, its links with other forms of Americanization will also be theorized and taken into account empirically to the extent deemed necessary for an adequate understanding of the phenomenon in question. Similar implications will be obvious with regard to instances of economic, military, social or sociopsychological Americanization that necessitate further explorations of connections with other dimensions. To be sure, this conceptualization also includes positive and ambivalent discourses on Americanization and recognition of American influences that possibly have beneficial effects on receiving cultures in that they inspire, rejuvenate, revitalize/spiritually renew or liberate locals in various ways, and may even be helpful in certain cases in emancipating subaltern groups.

My approach does not detail the effects of Americanization on its recipients, which would involve describing myriads of different cultural interchanges and social transitions (Rosenberg 1982: 13). This study aims to offer a differentiated analytical perspective for a deeper understanding of the plurality of processes of Americanization through a closer look at the basic processes involved in a wide variety of empirical cases and a critical rethinking of the theoretical and methodological issues that are at stake. In this I am fully aware that the key components, driving forces, and implications of specific instances of Americanization can only be assessed more precisely through empirical research on a case-by-case basis.

The book has the following structure. The first two chapters offer a historical survey of the usages of the terms "Americanism" and "Americanization" in Europe (the major locus of initial interest in American influences abroad) against the background of diverse images of America. The first chapter addresses the origins of the preoccupation with Americanization in the context of political and philosophical debates on Euro-American exchanges, beginning in Britain in the 1830s and then turning towards France and Germany as the other two main sites of contestation of American influence since the 1850s. It considers not only the discourses of conservative intellectuals and politicians, but also those of businessmen, trade union leaders and other working-class leaders, political liberals, social radicals, and ordinary people until the interwar years. The second chapter outlines the debates on Americanization in Western Europe after World War II, which leads to a schematic overview of the major discourses at the turn of twenty-first century. In addition, this chapter throws light on the parallels between the various discourses of cultural Americanization — historically the predominant interest of foreign elites — and different visions on mass/popular culture in Europe and other parts of the world within the European orbit.

The next two chapters take a closer look at the American scene and chart the various usages of the terms "Americanism" and "Americanization" in American history. Chapter 3 traces the exclusionary political meanings of Americanism in the mid-nineteenth century and examines the Americanization movement with regard to the new immigrants from the late 1890s until the 1920s, as well as the critiques of its ideals of Americanism by adherents of ethnic pluralism. It further covers the forced assimilation campaigns regarding Native Americans from the late 1880s until the early 1930s and the Americanization programs specifically aimed at Mexican immigrants. Finally, this chapter scrutinizes the appropriations of Americanism among labor and the left in the work setting and in politics prior to the New Deal era. Chapter 4 analyzes first the various interpretations of Americanism and Americanization within the New Deal context and Popular Front culture until World War II. Secondly, it highlights the crucial role of Americanism regarding U.S. citizenship as a political issue at the peak of the Cold War. Then the focus shifts to the contestations of Americanism during the 1960s and after, when various new social movements emerged, along with multiculturalism and its attendant identity politics. A major point of interest are the political struggles revolving around preferred meanings of Americanism and Americanization in relation to questions of immigration (regarding the influx from Latin America in particular) against the backdrop of a new conservative Americanism that emerged in the 1980s. Finally, attention is paid to the exclusionist Americanism vis-à-vis Arabs and Muslims and Americans of Arabic descent, as well as political dissidents of various stripes in the "war on terrorism" after September 11, 2001. The chapter ends with a section about the more specific phrase "Americanization of the South" (and a related one: "Southernization of America") that came in use during the second half of the twentieth century.

Historically informed by this wide-ranging overview, Chapter 5 presents a systematic approach of the subject matter and defines the key terms more precisely. It examines the major approaches that are in vogue and indicates the problematic sides of each. The latter discussion is continued in the next chapter, where the pitfalls of an extreme social constructionism are explained and the necessity is argued of partly undoing the deconstructions of Americanization that have taken place in the past few decades. More generally, this means recapturing the critical elements in the notion of Americanization that have gotten lost in the approaches at issue. Thus Chapter 6 lays the foundations of an interpretive framework that I believe is more helpful in comprehending processes of Americanization than the paradigms that are prevalent today.

Chapter 7 elaborates the theoretical framework for analyzing Americanization abroad and conceptualizes the processes concerned in terms of power relations, distinguishing various units of analysis and charting the major avenues through which American influences are conveyed abroad, introduced into foreign contexts, and acted upon by local recipients.

It concentrates on the export side of Americanization and historicizes the framework by offering a periodization of American influence abroad. Chapter 8 completes the framework by going into more conceptual detail regarding the reception of American influence. It also considers possible functions and effects of Americanization when trying to make assessments of specific cases.

The final chapter offers an in-depth analysis of the intertwinement of Americanization and corporate globalization at the turn of the twenty-first century. First it examines current theorizing on globalization, which is characterized by an overriding tendency to reject the whole notion of Americanization. It is argued that these theorists have thrown the proverbial baby out with the bath water, namely an interest in America's persisting strong influence in many domains globally. Yet, it is also recognized that one has to move beyond a state-centrist approach in order to adequately grasp the significantly increased influence of transnational corporations over the past few decades. Therefore next this chapter explores the major ways in which transnational corporations — in relation to U.S.-dominated, international governance — spread capitalist modernity worldwide. An attempt is made to explain how U.S. business leaders and affiliated political power-holders still manage to set the agenda of much of the global economy and why many of their foreign counterparts have adopted similar neoliberal policies. The chapter concludes with a discussion of the historical contingency of the American face of much of corporate globalization and then also looks at possible transformations by a transnational coalition of countervailing powers.

1

Early European Preoccupations with Americanism and Americanization

Originally the terms "Americanism" and "Americanization" derive from the realm of cultural-political discourse both in Europe and the United States. They have been used as slogans and battle cries by opponents in various ideological struggles and culture wars, and are therefore burdened with ideological connotations and emotional associations. The latter are part and parcel of their working history — that is, the history of their various *modi operandi* and societal impacts — and may offer important indications of relevant developments that lie behind the phenomena observed. If employed as analytical concepts, as is the purpose of this book, one must determine their meanings both historically and systematically, and examine the tensions between their usage by historical actors in political and cultural critiques and their deployment as conceptual abstractions in contemporary scientific discourse (Jarausch and Siegrist 1997: 21). Therefore the focus will first be on the working history of Americanization in Europe (chapters 1 and 2) and America (chapters 3 and 4) respectively, before approaching the subject systematically.

Next the origins of "Americanism" and "Americanization" will be traced in the context of political and philosophical debates on Euro-American exchanges in the nineteenth century, beginning in Britain during the 1830s and then turning towards France and Germany as the two other main sites of contestation of American influence since the 1850s. The interwar years were a heyday of intellectual and political reflections on Americanization in Europe, and get due coverage as well.

Origins and developments in usage of the terms "Americanism" and "Americanization" in Europe

The term "Americanization" arose within the context of cultural exchanges between the United States and Europe, particularly Britain, France and Germany, during the first period of modern globalism which began around 1800 (Hopkins 2002: 6). Local elites, often educated and well versed in European high culture, were concerned about the phenomena it referred to. This notion was later also applied to settings outside of Europe where America's influence was felt. We must keep in mind here that England was "the most direct source of colonial cultural patterns" and that France thought of itself as representing universal ideals, like America, and "provided the most obvious source of alternative models for the early United States" (Blair 1988: 6). The elites of both countries were therefore especially interested in how the new nation developed artifacts, technologies, production techniques and cultural practices that differed from theirs, and in its turn influenced those in Europe. This occurred against the background of a long-standing tradition of European representations of America, from the beginning "a curious mixture of science and mythology" (Schulte Nordholt 1986: 7; Cunliffe 1961; Bradbury 1995: 5–6, 88–89).

THE BRITISH SCENE

In the nineteenth century both the ideal and the reality of America became highly relevant for the debates and political struggles in Europe. This was nowhere more so than in Britain where the rise of Chartism and reform, of radicalism and protest, threatened the existing political order. In the eyes of Chartists and reformists, America represented the Land of Liberty, a Beacon of Freedom, the place for the regeneration of man. Following Tom Paine, radicals and republicans knew they could find a safe haven here. It was a place known for social experiments and utopian communities, Owenites and Fourierites — a liberal paradise in many respects.

It was in the 1830s that the issue of Americanization became most prominent on the public agenda of Britain. With Chartist and Corn law agitation, and pressure for universal male suffrage, the decade was one of severe political conflicts. In the United States this was the age of Jacksonian democracy with its aggressive, populist-egalitarian tendency, which drew the attention of many British observers who were also closely watching developments at home. Jean-Philippe Mathy poignantly describes these conservative British perceptions:

> The British, of course, especially those of Tory persuasion, were among the fiercest critics of the barbaric egalitarianism of the Jacksonian era. How could such a boorish, unrefined sample of humanity ever have come out of English civilization? The problem was not so much that America was full of common folks, for there were lots of these in Britain, too, but that they were so unashamedly conspicuous, bent on running things and conquering positions of power and leadership [Mathy 1993: 25].

Major scapegoats in this regard were the two American heroes of European democratic and revolutionary circles, Franklin and Washington, who were both derided for their petty middle-class thriftiness (Cunliffe 1963: 508).

In the eyes of these British conservatives, radical movements on both sides of the Atlantic seemed to be joining hands; the anti-slavery movement, communitarian movements of Robert Owen and others, and a wide variety of other radical causes like universal male suffrage, republicanism, socialism, and feminism were traveling back and forth between the two continents. It was at this time of transatlantic political turbulence, in 1831–32, that the French aristocrat Alexis de Tocqueville — following in the track of earlier French observers like Crèvecour, Condorcet, Volney and Chateaubriand — went to America to "see more than America." His official mission was to examine the American prison system, but (like other European visitors) his aim was to inspect and analyze the actual workings of democracy itself. De Tocqueville used his personal observations to chart the trends and possible dangers of democracy, and to explore the potential future of other European societies. He wanted first and foremost to find out why the efforts at establishing a democracy in his native country, starting with the French Revolution, had failed, while the American Revolution had apparently brought forth a stable liberal democratic republic. The comparison, of course, extended more generally to "Europe." No other country in Europe, with the partial exception of Britain, was a democracy then.

De Tocqueville studied the United States from a perspective informed by his thorough knowledge of other countries, particularly France, but also, to a significant degree, Great Britain. In his remarkable study *De la Démocratie en Amérique*, published in Europe in two volumes in 1835 and 1840, he reached the conclusion that "equality of condition" and "sovereignty of the people" were the two essential American characteristics from which all others derived.[1] His depiction of a new democratic order of life — the age of the masses, what he called the "Anglo-American condition" of the human being lost in the crowd — was differentially received. Contingent upon people's political attitudes, it confirmed some readers in their political hopes and others in their pessimist views. The latter group took at heart that de Tocqueville (as other French liberals such as Stendhal or Jacquemont) admired America's political achievements but came to distrust the cultural constraints of a democratic society, thereby signaling the risk of the "tyranny of the majority" as a result of the emphasis on consensus and uniformity in the New World (Mathy 1993: 31; Bradbury 1995: 90; Lipset 1996: 17; Ceaser 1997: 16). This response pattern should be located in the broader context of the relationship between politics and culture in the discourse on America that was forged in the political and philosophical debates over the French Revolution in Europe, further elaborated in the next section.

De Tocqueville's book was immediately translated into English, and had a strong impact on English social thought in the nineteenth century through the works of the poet and cultural critic Matthew Arnold (1822–1883) and the philosopher John Stuart Mill (1806–1873). Due largely to de Tocqueville's influence, "America" or "Americanization" in English thought often epitomized what were considered to be perilous tendencies in the development of modern industrial society, or what came to be called "mass society." In Arnold's book *Culture and Anarchy* (1869), he wrote: "in things of the mind, and in culture and totality, America, instead of surpassing us all, falls short." He depicted America as the prototype of the traditionless, the land of the material not the cultural. In Arnold's view, culture should involve "the pursuit of our total perfection by means of getting to know, on all the matters which most concern us, the best which has been thought and said in the world" (Arnold 1962: 6). Arnold's fears of Americanization were part of his overall concern about the sociocultural implications of the rise of mass democracy. In his work, "anarchy" was in fact synonymous with popular culture defined as working-class culture. He used the term to refer both to the lived culture of the new urban and industrial working class, and to its entrance into formal politics.

For Arnold, the increasing influence of working-class culture, epitomized by the suffrage campaign of 1866–67, meant social and cultural decline — a breakdown in social and cultural authority. Arnold believed that enfranchising the anarchic "populace" had dire consequences for the middle classes, if the former was not kept in check. But he was also critical of the middle classes. They, after all, were the "Philistines" who equated greatness with wealth or with industrialization. The function of culture was to produce a cultured middle class with the necessary cultural authority to exercise a hegemonic cultural influence in the society. The working class would always be on the side of "anarchy," always in a relation of binary opposition to "culture." What was required of its members was that they recognized their cultural difference and acknowledged cultural deference. The work of the educated elite was to know the best and then to make the best prevail. Such knowledge was the result of "disinterested and active use of reading, reflection, and observation." Once this was achieved, it was the men and women of culture's duty to get their countrymen to seek culture. However, in his perspective, culture, as the best that has been thought and said, was not there to be embraced by all. Where possible, Arnold recommended the dissemination of "sweetness and light," especially a secular religion of "English literature," through education and cultural policy to "the raw and uncultivated masses," with the aim of tempering their vulgar and dangerous inclinations. In this conception, cultural education of the lower classes had thus two social functions: first, to enable middle-class hegemony, and, second, to police, through strategies of difference and deference, the unruly and disruptive forces of "the populace" and their culture (Shiach 1989: 82–86; McGuigan 1992: 21; Storey 1998: 3–4).

Lionel Trilling has noted that Arnold's fear about Americanization was in fact a fear of vulgarity, a loss of distinction, and above all, a concern that "eccentricity of thought" would be crowded out by the democratic mainstream (Trilling 1963). According to Leslie Johnson, Americanization meant two forces especially for Arnold: "a tendency towards fragmentariness" due to the absence of a powerful central authority, be it an aristocracy or the state, to guide, educate, establish standards, and "an addiction to the banal," that is, the absence of standards of excellence leading to the cultural and moral degeneration of society that could only be halted by the inculcation of a properly constituted culture through education (Johnson 1979: 21; Strinati 1995: 24). The cultural agenda that Arnold established, would remain dominant in Britain from the 1860s to the 1950s.

John Stuart Mill was worried that democratic emancipation, which as a liberal (in terms of his time) he supported in principle, would lower standards of culture and of political discourse. Mill would, on the basis of de Tocqueville's warnings about "the tyranny of the majority," have changed his faith in democracy. In Mill's review of de Tocqueville's first volume on *Democracy in America*, he argued that the criticisms leveled at democracy in this work were really only criticisms of America (Mill 1963: 200–201). But five years later, in his review of de Tocqueville's second volume, Mills was far less critical, now suggesting that de Tocqueville's fear of the tyranny of the majority was probably well based, arguing that the American people were merely an exaggerated version of the English middle class. The English were to catch up with the Americans: the spirit becoming ascendant amongst the English was American. Then Mill also expressed his anxieties about democracy and the "growing insignificance of individuals in comparison with the mass" (Mill 1963: 260).[2]

In this context it is noteworthy that much of the traffic of translations went the other way: most of the British accounts of America were immediately translated into French and exerted an important influence on "the cultivated readership's perception of the young republic," as Mathy reminds us: "In those days, French critics usually deferred to the judgment of their British counterparts; the latter were believed to possess, by virtue of the commonality of language and cultural origins, a privileged insight into things American" (Mathy 1993: 26). And in the first half of the nineteenth century, critical reports on American society by conservative British soldiers and explorers, such as Basil Hall and Thomas Hamilton, outnumbered sympathetic accounts, such as those of Frances Wright and Harriet Martineau (*Society in America*, 1837). These criticisms reinforced and fueled the negative views about America held by the French readers also.

In addition, world's fairs on both sides of the Atlantic were also significant in the popularization of the terms "Americanism" and "Americanization." From the London Great Exhibition of 1851 onward, America and modernity became closely associated, and evoked different responses among observers, depending on their particular backgrounds and interests. It was especially in the context of these and similar public displays that the word Americanization was used to refer to America's technological modernity, that is, its mechanical inventions and technical ingenuity, which both intrigued and repelled Europe's political elites and intellectuals (Pells 1997: 7). While those who held on to tradition or feared cultural leveling denounced America's modernity, modernizing elites welcomed America's involvement in a project that paralleled theirs. They associated America with democracy, modernity, rationality and science. The British biologist and philosopher Thomas Henry Huxley (1825–1895), for example, saw America as representing the promise of a scientific and rational future. Huxley was heavily influenced by Darwin's evolutionism and optimistic about the way in which society was developing. He thought it was useless to try to preserve social and cultural forms that were in decline. Instead, he envisioned immense possibilities being opened up for everybody by the forward movement of a progressive and scientific modernity, in which America was leading the way (Johnson 1979: 50).

After the recession of the 1870s, U.S. corporations made substantial investments in Europe — at that time the biggest consumer market outside the United States — with Britain as most important destination. U.S. overseas investments, from a very early stage, tended to concentrate on the newer, technologically more advanced sectors in both producer and consumer goods. Thus, it was the new industries of the Second Industrial Revolution that U.S. corporate businesses took abroad in the form of branded and packaged foodstuff (canned goods and beer), consumer chemicals (soaps, paints, and drugs), mass-produced light machinery (sewing machines, office machinery, and cameras), standardized machinery such as boilers, pumps, and printing presses, as well as electrical equipment, metals, and industrial chemicals (Wilkins 1974: 214; Dicken 1999: 36; Taylor 1999: 52–54). By the turn of the twentieth century, the penetration of the British and continental-European economies by American firms had become so substantial in local people's experience that a British observer, Frederick McKenzie, felt obliged to write a book entitled *The American Invaders* (published in 1902). In this he described the unceasing "American invasion" with manufactured goods in Europe that had a profound effect on numerous aspects of the everyday lives of the masses all over Europe. It was clear to him that the "many factories built by American firms in this country are today supplying not only England but also a large part of the world outside of America with goods which otherwise would have come from the U.S." (McKenzie 1902: 240; qtd. in Dicken 1999: 46).

At about the same time, the British journalist William T. Stead used the word "Americanization" in his book *The Americanization of the World* (1901) to designate a cultural practice through which the social and, even more, the ethnic pluralities of people living in the United States were transformed into a homogeneous nation. This concerned the assimilation of immigrants in the U.S. to the predominant culture, and intervention strategies of U.S. political or business leaders aimed at political and sociocultural modification of American citizens' behavior into a collective American identity that was considered as normative and therefore imperative by these elites. In this process America was supposed to be leading the rest of world, working towards a U.S.-dominated world culture. At the background was the shift of world economic leadership from Britain to the United States between 1870 and 1914 (Dicken 1999: 36–37).[3]

This corporate-led "Americanization" also drew the attention of the left. During most of the first century of American independence, the British left regarded the U.S. as the "best poor man's country." But as the years went by and corporate capitalism won or secured a strong foothold in the United States, America obtained another meaning, and turned into the land of robber barons, trusts, conglomerates and union-busting by the end of the century. The "American invasion" of Britain and continental Europe only made things worse in this regard. For conservatives and many of the rising, entrepreneurial middle class, America looked more like a dangerous example than a future paradise during most of the nineteenth century. The right tended to take a patronizing, if not overtly hostile stance towards America. This tendency reversed in the late nineteenth century, however, when it was conservatives who admired America, particularly for its "wonderful contrivances" (Anthony Trollope), and saw a common Anglo-Saxon destiny in the fortunes of the two nations (Bradbury 1995: 88). Then it was the right who celebrated American political, economic and military power, while the left saw American strength as monop-olistic, oligarchic, and hegemonic (Cunliffe 1986: 26). Yet the Arnoldian strain of cultural conservativism persisted. In an essay written in the late 1880s, published in *Questions at Issue* in 1893, literary critic Edmund Gosse retook Arnold's rhetoric of anarchy and Amer-ican materialism, and he admonished against the spread of the democratic sentiment reach-ing the realm of culture, whereby the traditions of literary taste, the canons of literature, were successfully being reversed by a popular vote (Gosse qtd. in Leavis 1979: 154).

THE FRENCH SCENE

France is characterized by a long-standing fascination with America as emblematic of fundamental developments of modernity such as cultural homogenization or vulgar-ization, one-dimensional democratization, and degeneration, from an enduring anti–Americanism discourse (with different emphases by various groupings in the course of time). This was partly countered by versions of pro-Americanism, increasingly so in the late twentieth century; indeed, neutral views were hard to find.

Politics and culture became strongly intertwined in the discourse on America as a result of the political and philosophical debates over the French Revolution. On the left, defenders of the French Revolution initially hailed the American Revolution as a precur-sor of the French Revolution. During the first stages of the Revolution, the group that pushed the process forward was sometimes referred to as *américanistes*; it included famous persons such as Marquis de Condorcet, Baron d'Aulne Turgot, and Emmanuel-Joseph Sieyès. Even at that time, however, this group did not consider either American's revo-lutionary principles or the way its founders practiced "political science" in designing the political institutions of the new nation to represent the most advanced strain of the rev-olutionary cause. Over time, their qualified endorsement gave way to growing opposi-tion as those on the left (with regard to the French Revolution) began to recognize more to despise than to admire in America. They accused the United States of having coopted the modern revolutionary cause and bringing it to a halt before it could achieve its higher goals. In seeking to distinguish the French Revolution from the American Revolution, they argued that the latter was grounded on the principle of self-interest rather than basic values and ideals, as well as on an inadequate understanding of modern thought. Given this defective foundation, America must inevitably produce a "low," or inauthentic, form of politics and culture (Ceaser 1997: 11–12).

However, there was a current of pro-Americanism that persisted. During the Empire and the Restoration (1804–1830) a number of liberals, republicans, and democrats retained eighteenth-century idealized images of America as the land of happiness, an agrarian par-adise peopled by good savages, altruistic Quakers, modern-day equivalents of Cato and Cincinnati, and freedom-loving farmers who shared an ethos dominated by the stoic virtues of the ancient world and the tolerant, enlightened rationalism of Thomas Jefferson. Most intellectuals in the political opposition during those years, from the Idéologues (around Destutt de Tracy) to the small, but active, liberal circles of Benjamin Constant and Ger-maine de Staël, were strong admirers of the new republic (Rémont 1962; Mathy 1993: 26).

The major purveyors of anti–Americanism before 1830 were the *ultras*, hard-line roy-alists with Joseph de Maistre (1754–1821) as leading exponent. He launched one of the most virulent, and influential, attacks on rationalism and the "political science" approach of establishing government by "reflection and choice" as employed by America's founders. In de Maistre's view, reason itself (not just metaphysical thinking) was suspect, and, at the deepest level, society was subject to God's plan or Providence. In his conception, each nation or people developed within God's plan according to its own organic path of evolution. A nation could never be constructed by willful reconstitution on a rational foundation of abstract ideas such as natural rights and contract philosophy. Instead its bearings should be found in the preexisting historical whole of a nation, that is, in faith, custom, tradition. From this perspective, even people's prejudice fulfills a positive social function by unifying certain groups and also increasing their sense of security. De Maistre, Louis de Bonald, and other representatives of the conservative reaction to the French and American Revolutions saw a nation as a cultural unity characterized by a common consciousness, a common soul, and a common language. A society's continuity demanded as much moral unity, even unanimity, as possible. For some of them, including de Maistre and de Bonald, the ideal of this unity was most closely approximated in the Middle Ages. They wanted to preserve the older religious forms — Catholicism, not Protestantism — and to restore the religious unity of medieval Europe. This means that their conservatism was reactionary; its aim was to regress to the *status quo ante* rather than to conserve the existing order (Zeitlin 1968; 50–55; Ceaser 1997: 80–83).

The *ultras* saw the American Revolution as the source of the French Revolution and both as embodiments of modern rationalist thought. What was true of France must also hold true for America; they were both a threat to civilization. Their vision of the United States, strongly influenced by translated Tory pamphlets, was both political and cultural in character. Political considerations on the powerlessness and dull demeanor of the executive government, the weakness of the military, and the abstract rationalism underlying the U.S. Constitution and the institutions of the new regime went hand in hand with criticisms of the boredom, utilitarianism, and lack of refinement of American life (Mathy 1993: 26). This assimilation of the two Revolutions became the dominant conservative position on the European Continent. But America posed a special problem to these conservatives in that it belied their claim, confirmed by the French case, that no orderly and successful society could be based on reason and liberal democracy. Still, many of them maintained that the excesses of the Revolution in France or other evils — such as a lowering of standards or a homogenization of society — would appear at some point in the United States.

There was (and remains) another strain within conservative thinking, however, that distinguished between the two Revolutions and held that America was not an expression of the new rationalist philosophy but a special case with a primarily conservative outlook. Thus this conservatism could claim the American Revolution as being part of its own tradition. This view was represented by certain elements of Edmund Burke's thought and his partial defense of the American cause in political speeches and writings in England, as well as by one strain of American conservatism, seeking to link Continental conservatism to the American founding, led by the historian Russell Kirk, the major American disciple of Burke in the post–World War II era.[4] Yet most nineteenth-century European conservative thinkers always saw America through the prism of the French Revolution. Gradually, when the French Revolution receded in memory, America became the active symbol of revolutionary thought for many on the right and served as a living reminder of the devastating ramifications of rationalism and of democracy.

Ironically, the conservative vision of the French Tories, contested and often ridiculed while they ruled the country, gradually was adopted by the French elites when the liberals took power. There was a short outburst of enthusiasm for the United States as the "model republic" after the upheaval of the Trois Glorieuses (27–29 July 1830) and Lafayette and his "American school" were briefly in the limelight again. But the younger generation of liberals were less impressed by America's virtues than their seniors, men, who, like Saint-Simon, had fought alongside Lafayette for American freedom and still hung on to the republican idealism of their youth. The establishment of a constitutional regime in France after 1830 made it less necessary to praise the United States as an alternative to the absolute monarchy. Evils such as slavery and the growth of a suffering industrial working class became more evident now that it was no longer politically expedient to downplay their existence. The image of the United States as agrarian myth and the most perfect form of republican government gradually lost support among the liberal and democratic left when the French public noticed the rapid urbanization of the country, the growing political role of the uncivilized, plebeian West (exemplified by Jackson's America), and the expansionist implications of the Monroe Doctrine. A theme that also repeatedly drew attention was the discrepancy between the tolerance guaranteed in the laws and the religious fanaticism of the American sects (Tillett 1961; Mathy 1993: 27, 29, 32–33).

It was against this backdrop that an array of cultural-political attacks on the United States came to be launched in the nineteenth century and after. The left viewed America as backward and in the end reactionary, whereas the right saw America as a revolutionary menace to their organic concept of society. But eventually both parties agreed on America's vulgar characteristics. America may not be anarchic, but it was, at any rate, banal, superficial. It lacked creative art, good taste, depth. According to this politically mixed group of critics, the societal structures built on America's shaky ground of reason and natural rights would never be able to erect and sustain a cultural edifice of significance. Over the years, descendants on both sides of the political spectrum would express essentially the same criticisms of American culture, notwithstanding notable differences of opinion in their problem diagnoses and recommendations for reform. The symbolic America, although differently conceptualized, could expediently be used to both parties' benefit and on occasion served as a common ground to forge unholy alliances targeting "Americanisms" of various kind (Ceaser 1997: 11–12, 66–67, 79–85).

What most of these thinkers' views of America had in common was that they were rooted in a humanistic and aristocratic ethos derived from intellectual standards and critical practice originating in the Renaissance and further developed in the age of French classicism. Although the French literati differed widely in political and ideological commitments, they occupied similar positions in the social structure, equidistant from the lower classes and the business and professional elites, and held on to the model of cultural excellence that had persisted for centuries among the cultivated elites. As Mathy suggests, the traditional emphasis on intellectualist, universal categories of judgment, on abstraction rather than empirically grounded reasoning, and the rejection, on moral and political grounds, of economic and financial activities as being inappropriate for men of letters, helps explain the widespread denouncement of the "materialism" and "pragmatism" of American culture. The further penetration of market capitalism into society undermined the traditional intelligentsia's position. Which is ironic, because the progressive fractions of the Western European secularized clerisy had played a major role in the legitimation of modern political and economic structures, and had often help bring these about by direct political action.

What happened however, is that in gaining power the bourgeoisie not only threw off the fetters of dogmatic church authority and absolute monarchy, but it also emancipated itself, to a degree, from the authority of the traditional guardians of knowledge and arbiters of cultural taste. More often, and to an ever greater extent, the middle classes relied on the verdict of the market rather than the authority of the scholarly elites, in making cultural appraisals. Gradually losing their monopoly on aesthetic tastemaking and intellectual trendsetting, the cultivated elites reacted strongly against the nouveaux riches' tendencies to set the standards of truth, morality, and beauty independently (Mathy 1993: 7–8). Thus, in the late nineteenth century, high modernist writers and artists expressed their disdain for petty bourgeois aesthetic categories, which they branded as "vulgar" and "philistine." Baudelaire and Zola, for example, scorned the Parisian public for completely misreading the achievements of Delacroix or Manet. It was the autonomy of artistic judgment involved in popular tastes vis-à-vis the artistic judgments of the cultural elite that evoked their rage and condemnation.

In addition, the literati's authority was threatened by certain cultural aspects of the new social order associated with science and technology. Autonomous institutions of specialized research and learning, funded by the state and staffed with professional experts, took control over the discourses of truth, judgment, and taste that define and orient social practices. Generalist intellectuals who still proclaimed to legislate and uphold standards for the whole of society in matters of aesthetics, ethics or politics, were prone to lose the most in this process. They were the ones who felt the whole process of modernity had gone out of hand (Bauman 1987: 136, 158). However, in France, more than anywhere else in Europe, until well into the twentieth century, the intelligentsia retained some cultural power due to the strong influence over educated people's minds of a century-old literary culture, the prestige of *ancien régime* models of taste and behavior among the bourgeoisie and a centralized school system with the capacity to inculcate in the middle classes a quasi-religious respect for the sanctity of elite classical culture. By contrast, the United States represented to French intellectuals the perfect expression of what they had such a hard time to come to grips with at home: the triumph of expert knowledge, petty bourgeois taste, and the disenchantment of the world (Mathy 1993: 8–9).

The word "américanisation" originates from the same period as the first world exhibitions in London and Paris: the Second Empire, a time of intense modernization in France. It was Baudelaire who introduced the expression in 1855, when the poet gave a depiction of America as a technical civilization from a discourse of cultural anti–Americanism. Like other highly devoted proponents and practitioners of aesthetic modernity Baudelaire was also a very determined opponent of technological modernity. This ambivalent attitude manifested itself too in his admiration of American literature (especially Edgard Allan Poe's tales) on the one hand and his denigration of the cultural climate from which it originated on the other (Mathy 1993: 274 n. 1). Modern humanity was set on a downhill course of technical materialism leading to moral and spiritual corruption: "The poor man is so Americanized by the zoocratic industrial philosophers that he has lost all notion of the difference between the phenomena of the physical and moral worlds, and those of the natural and supernatural" (qtd. in Ory 1990: 46).[5] Two years later, in the preface to his translation of Edgar Allan Poe's *More Tales of the Grotesque and Arabesque* (1857), Baudelaire condemned an epoch in which "Americanomania has virtually become a socially accepted fad" and described America as a "great hunk of barbarism illuminated by gas." His criticism was not only aimed at American culture, but more widely at the vulgarity that he thought was inherent to any commercially-minded democracy (qtd. in Ory 1990: 46; Ceaser 1997: 11). This criticism originated from de Maistre whom Baudelaire quoted.

The context of Baudelaire's first citation is important; it was a reference to the first *Exposition Universelle de Paris* in 1855, which was a triumphant celebration of the technical and industrialist scenarios for the human society of the future. The Second Empire's technocratic elite with its Saint-Simonian, productivist worldview enraged *les gens de lettres*. It is therefore not surprising that the noun "Americanization" derived from Baudelaire's verb appeared at the time of the second Exposition, in 1867, when the Concourt brothers wrote in their *Journal* of January 16 that it was "the last blow in what amounts to the Americanisation of France — Industry outdoing Art, steam threshing machines in place of paintings ... in a word, the Material Federation." In the same period Pierre Larousse's *Grand Dictionnaire universel du XIX siècle* (first part appearing in 1863 and the complete volume in 1866) defined the new word "américanisme" as "unbounded and exclusive admiration of the government, laws, and customs of the Americans, and chiefly of the inhabitants of the United States" (both quotes in Ory 1990: 46).

In the eyes of the abovementioned critics industrial progress would replace quality with quantity, and bring about a mass culture based on standardization that would lead to a "leveling-down" of Culture and erosion of established taste hierarchies. Kroes signals that "[t]here are echoes of de Tocqueville here, but the eroding factor is no longer the egalitarian logic of industrial progress. In both cases, though, whatever the precise link, America had become the metonym for modernity" (Kroes 2000: 207).

This preoccupation with modernity, particularly as related to political democracy, was also the driving force of a campaign to have the Catholic Church declare "Americanism" an official heresy (to be ranked alongside such past great heresies as Albigensianism and Jansenism), that a number of French clergymen began near the end of the nineteenth century, echoing de Maistre's critique of America a hundred years earlier. The target was a strain in American Catholicism that tried to reconcile the Catholic faith with liberal democratic principles. This concerned a reformist tendency among American Catholics who generally had begun to be more assertive in church circles on behalf of a more progressive or liberal Catholicism. The French clergy sympathetic to this strain called themselves *américanistes*, replaying the politics of the French Revolution, when a group on the left, identified by the same name, manifested itself especially in the Revolution's first phases. Ultimately, however, Pope Leo XIII did not follow the line of the diehard protagonists in their crusade against American Catholicism. In a papal letter of 1899, the pope condemned the excesses of certain radical modern ideas known as Americanism, but he did not directly accuse the leaders of American Catholicism of promoting such doctrines. American Catholics seemed to have considered themselves warned rather than reprimanded. Thus ended this odd attempt to forge a connection between a national identity and a religious heresy (Skard 1961: 53–54; Portes 1990: 258–268; Ceaser 1997: 164–165).

THE GERMAN SCENE

In Germany, the third major country of relevance here, the public discourse on Americanism and Americanization developed partly along different lines and was very pronounced because of its much stronger embeddedness in Romantic thinking. Therefore the strains of Romanticism that informed the German elites' stances toward "America" will be discussed first. One current developed from the longing for something new, for a release from the burdens of history and for a chance to start over. In 1827 Goethe gave expression to this theme in his poem "To America," which opens with the well-known line "Amerika du hast es besser / Als unser Kontinent, das alte" [America, you're better off / Than our Continent, the old] (Goethe 1948: 655, qtd. in Gemünden 1998: 18). Better here means to be free of the past, with its "ruined castles," "useless memories," and "unrewarding strife." A variant of this optimistic theme was the idea of America as a young people or a young race, robust and full of vitality, a place where history might start all over again (Ceaser 1997: 167–168, 16). But in the Romantic period few European minds tended to agree with the sage of Weimar in this regard. Most considered the youth of the new nation to be a liability rather than an asset, since for them it meant a lack of culture and manners — vulgarity (Schulte Nordholt 1986: 12).

Much more influential was the other strand of German Romantic thinking, that offered a very different, almost opposite, picture of America, and became dominant by the middle of the nineteenth century. This view (and attendant structure of feeling) reflected the working out of the philosophical and political implications of Romanticism as it developed in Germany in reaction against universalist and Enlightenment ideas. Its protagonists, feeling that the French Revolution had left mostly "desiccated cultural forms" in its wake, sought to develop a new way of life out of the ruins. Their movement ran counter to the cult of reason and scientific objectivity arising from the eighteenth-century Enlightenment (Benjamin 2005: 38). Instead of societies "artificially" created by reason or contract, the Romantics preferred social formations that grew organically in the course of history. They opposed the calculative rationality of individuals, and favored the deeper bonding and solidarity in a historical community. America in its founding political principles came to be seen as the prototype par excellence of a society with the despised Enlightenment characteristics. This political element was crucial in Germany, where the Romantic writers played a major role in defining the idea of the nation in the countermovement against the Napoleonic occupation, which was interpreted as an imposition of Enlightenment ideas. Thus, popular ("völkisch") and nationalist ideas emerged in opposition to rationalism. The blame for representing and spreading Enlightenment ideas and practices was soon transferred from France to America. As Caeser puts it: "America was treated and interpreted mainly in the light of the French Revolution" (Ceaser 1997: 271 n 8).

Most of the stereotypical views of America had already been formed before 1860. It comes as no surprise that a country like the United States, born and bred in the Enlightenment, was precisely for this reason the object of Romantic criticism. The Romantic writers built on existing anti–American themes, articulated them more sharply and gave them a special cultural emphasis. Despite their strong inclination to condemn American society, the Romantic critics had, on the other hand, a genuine admiration for what they supposed to be the continent's unspoiled wilderness. With only a few exceptions, these writers did not share Buffon's rigid assertions about the backwardness of American nature — so popular among European elites at the time — but rather admired the great American wilderness.[6] They were fascinated by images of wild and unspoiled nature, untarnished by any kind of convention (Schulte Nordholt 1986: 9–11).

Importantly, the Romantic view of America became the foundation for the abstract negative notion of Americanism as it developed in the later part of the nineteenth century. Even the great historian of the Renaissance, Jacob Burckhardt, concluded in his *Weltgeschichtliche Betrachtungen* [*Worldhistorical Considerations*] (posthumously published in 1905) that barbarians and Americans have no culture because they have no history. It was mostly the conservative thinkers who elaborated the theme of America as a threat to European life, and especially to its higher cultural achievements. As the historian Fritz Stern points out, "From the 1870s on, conservative writers in imperial Germany expressed fear that the German soul would be destroyed by 'Americanization,' that is, by mammonism, materialism, mechanization and mass society" (Stern 1961: 131). This cultural elite saw the protection of the "German soul" as its sacred mission, aimed at protecting Germany if not against all forms of democratization, than at least against its liberal form, Americanism, whereby the tastes of ordinary people came to rule cultural affairs (Ceaser 1997: 171). Thus, the responses to America's real or purported influence in Germany can be seen as a late nineteenth/early twentieth century equivalent of cultural opposition to French "civilization" by an emerging German bourgeoisie in the eighteenth century, in which case American culture had replaced that of France (Kroes 1986: 39–40).

Conservative thinking about America in Germany was not entirely negative though. Next to the traditional conservatives who defended an older, more aristocratic order — and for whom America seemed hostile to high culture — there was a group of thinkers referred to as the "revolutionary conservatives" or the "reactionary moderns." The latter put all emphasis on the need to be realistic and forward-looking. They adopted a social Darwinistic-like mindset, assuming that whatever loses, simply because it has lost, is untrue, and whatever emerges as victorious should likewise be considered true. Americanism as the dominant force in the world therefore held a strong appeal for these thinkers, since it managed to achieve a dominant position in the struggle between nations that took place in the only reality that counted: the actual historical world.

Despite its attraction, however, some revolutionary conservatives such as Arthur Moeller van den Bruck, Oswald Spengler, and Ernst Jünger found reason to be highly critical of Americanism — they even came to see it as the main threat to sustaining civilization. In their eyes Americanism lacked spiritual depth and self-understanding because it was tied to the shallow materialist, universalistic, and liberal democratic ideas of the Enlightenment. Moreover, when allowed to spread its ideas and practices, it would ultimately destroy civilization. Thus, in order to survive, civilization's foundations needed to be renewed and transformed. Only a nation endowed with spiritual depth and philosophic awareness would be able to accomplish this. Only a reformed Germany would be capable of subduing the forces of technology and letting them be governed by the political principle that could meet the demands of a new era. This reactionary modernism took its most extreme form in Nazism, which emphasized the power of myth (of blood and soil, of race and fatherland, of destiny and place) while simultaneously mobilizing all the accomplishments of "social progress," in which major compromises were made with the advances of science and technology in practical affairs. All of which occurred for the sake of a sinister and gargantuan project of "sublime" national achievement (Ceaser 1997: 171–172; Harvey 1989: 209).

These reactionary moderns were all in some way influenced by Nietzsche's philosophical thinking and his discussions of America. In *Menschliches, Allzumenschliches* [*Human, All too Human*] (1878), Nietzsche depicted America as an extension of Europe and a "daughterland" of European culture. America simultaneously epitomized certain of its most worrisome elements too, in intense form. Modern European culture was characterized by a restlessness that one found more extremely in America. This agitation was a threat to higher culture, which, above all, needed contemplation. Modern culture, in the way of life manifested foremost in America, threatened to lead us into a new barbarism (Nietzsche 1986: 132, 365, as summarized in Ceaser 1997: 172). In Nietzsche's subsequent discussion of America, in *Fröhliche Wissenschaft* [*The Gay Science*] (1882), the New World appears as more distant and alien, sending its powerful influences back to Europe. America represents the coming future in its most dystopian form, an obsession with the material and a total systematization of work and production. Its culture is driven by a constant chase after profit, seeking to reduce everything to numeric calculation, whereby the finer things of life are crowded out or else "enjoyed" under the calculus of quick consumption. Everything is reduced to efficiency and work. These features were already beginning to infect old Europe and were spreading a spiritual emptiness (*Geist-losigkeit*) over the continent (Nietzsche 1974: 258–259, qtd. in Ceaser 1997: 173).

Until the mid-nineteenth century, America was discussed as a geographic place or country, although its perceived qualities often featured in argumentations serving political and philosophical purposes. We noted earlier that by the second half of the nineteenth century "America" was also being seen as a process or a worldview that could be detached from its physical home location and moved elsewhere. Thus America became part of a symbolic universe. The initial meaning of the word *Amerikanisierung* (Americanization) developed out of a more concrete usage, however. The earliest references can be found among German immigrants in the United States in the 1850s, who lamented the "Americanization" of the German community, referring to its loss of identification with the homeland and its wholehearted adoption of the ways in the new country. At about the same time (1852) one finds the first historical registration of the same use of the verb "Americanize" with regard to Swedish immigrants, to describe the rapidity with which they adopted the customs of the communities they moved to in the United States. In this discourse Americanization referred to an individual phenomenon that occurred in particular instances in local contexts. It was an aspect of emigration that was linked to the immigrant and was in this sense not referring to a transnational process or flow. People were Americanized *after* they moved to America, and this process was perceived more in terms of sociopsychological factors than cultural processes (O'Dell 1997: 19).

Like elsewhere in Europe, in Germany, the American way of life had a strong appeal to ordinary people, the "common man." But the radiation of America's modernity in Europe was influential in the discourse among some German intellectuals as well. In 1877, the renowned physiologist, Emil Dubois-Reymond, extended this notion of Americanization to the "overrunning of European culture with realism and the growing preponderance of technology" (Basler 1930: 144, qtd. in Ceaser 1997: 163). In this view, push factors were emphasized, America was fostering these developments, indirectly at least, by the mere force of its economic power. In addition, Dubois-Reymond also referred to pull factors in suggesting that the American way of life struck a natural chord among the European masses. Americanization was a powerful and attractive influence in stirring deep-felt desires for political, economic, and cultural democratization among these people.

It was the writer Paul Dehns, however, who in an article, "Die Amerikanisierung der Welt," published in 1904, offered one of the first explicit definitions of the process in the German world: "Americanization in an economic sense means the modernization of the methods of industry, exchange and agriculture as well as all other areas of practical life. Americanization in its widest sense, including the societal and the political, means the uninterrupted, exclusive, and relentless striving after gain, riches, and influence" (Basler 1930: 144, qtd. in Ceaser 1997: 163).[7] Others elaborated this definition to include the related idea of a rationalization and standardization of the processes of production, carried out in order to reach the mass of consumers where the greatest buying power was expected to rest now. Thus, well before World War I Americanism in Germany had become a crucial symbol in the public discourse.

The America of the turn of the twentieth century was perceived as a powerful, almost irresistible force that was considered to be degenerate in the sense of being grotesque and often blindly destructive. Leading thinkers in Germany attributed this degenerate force to intellectual or spiritual causes. "America" represented the political idea of a constructed (rather than organically-grown) political order based on individual freedom and democ-

racy, the economic principle of the pursuit of well-being, and the idea of cultural populism in which ordinary people's tastes were of great influence on society's artistic boundaries. More generally, America came to symbolize the technological and scientific project
of modernity. These developments were also reflected in certain linguistic changes in the
meaning of America, as the German philologist Otto Basler elucidated in an influential
essay, published in 1930. Instead of the simple name "America" of the nineteenth-century discourse the abstractions "Americanism," "Americanization," and "Americanness"
came in use (Basler 1930).

Interestingly enough, it was in this context that, in the early twentieth century, sociologist Georg Simmel anticipated all the major themes that the American sociologist George
Ritzer has recently discussed in several books on what the latter calls the "new means of
consumption." These include fast-food chains, credit card systems, and similar rationalized consumption systems, which have drawn the interest of scholars studying America's
cultural impact abroad. Simmel was concerned with the growing Americanism in his time,
which for him stood for the "enormous desire for happiness of modern man" and, more
negatively, for modern "covetousness" (Simmel 1991: 27, qtd. in Ritzer 2001: 96).[8] Also
relevant here is the striking image of the "iron cage"[9] that Max Weber added to the symbolic America at the end of *The Protestant Ethic and the Spirit of Capitalism* (Weber 1958,
orig. 1904–1905).[10] This metaphor referred to the modern human condition, as the famous
sociologist-economist saw it. The modern economic order is bound to the technical and
economic conditions of machine production, which determine the lives of individuals who
were born into this constellation, "with irresistible force," including those not directly
involved in economic acquisition. This "cage of the future" is a "mechanism" and not controlled by an internal human motivation but by an external force, and can be found in its
fullest form in the United States. Weber's well-known, pessimistic judgment on life in the
cage for the "last men" at this stage of cultural development is clearly written with this
symbolic America[11] in mind: "Specialists without spirit, sensualists without heart; this
nullity [sic!] imagines that it has attained a level of civilization never before achieved"
(Weber 1922, 1: 204). Weber portrays a cold, disenchanted world where the overriding
process of rationalization has culminated in a social system that no one controls, a system
that has us in its tyrannical grip. The means have become the end of the process, which
is according to Weber the "fate of our time" (Ceaser 1997: 183–185).

ORDINARY PEOPLE, POLITICAL LIBERALS,
AND SOCIAL RADICALS IN EUROPE

The abovementioned fears of the American menace among British, French, and German conservatives were not shared by Europe's lower classes and a substantial number of
political liberals and social radicals. For various reasons, European workers, craftsmen,
peasants, liberal and leftist activists[12] found the United States appealing, and many eventually emigrated to the United States. It seemed to be a haven of opportunities for common folks, a "workers' paradise," and the site par excellence — an open air laboratory, so
to speak — to test and try to practice libertarian and egalitarian ideals (Pells 1997: 5).

Until the late nineteenth century many European socialists, anarchists, and Marxists saw America as a continent that would offer ample opportunities for the development
of the kind of society they envisioned (Moore 1970). To them the United States embodied goodness, opportunity, prosperity, and equality, and gave people a reason to believe
in a better future. They saw the same promise in America that attracted political liberals

and non-socialist radicals to the New World — its freedom from European influences that hindered them in realizing their societal ideals. All shared the vision of America as the land of liberty and the living exemplar of egalitarianism (Cunliffe 1961: 21). But these leftists were not uncritical of life there; America's image was badly tarnished by slavery before the Civil War and by persisting racism afterwards. Later in the nineteenth century, Tammany Hall (municipal political control by methods associated with corruption and bossism) and excesses of corporate capitalism made them feel uneasy as well. Nevertheless, these reform-minded people found much to admire too, especially America's political institutions that offered important guides to help Europe out of its own social disorders. Whatever its flaws, America was still "the freest and most blessed republic" yet operating on earth. Workers in Europe sought to escape their problems by moving to the U.S., whereas reformers developed plans for the remodeling of Europe based on American examples (Moore 1970: xiii).

This consensus in European political opinion among social radicals was disrupted from time to time in the nineteenth century, but only Marxist interventions after 1880 finally shattered it. Then a number of Marxists distanced themselves from the traditional admiration of the United States shared by most parties of the European left. As R. Laurence Moore put it in his history of European socialists' visions of America,

> ... if "Americanism" were accepted as a surrogate for militant Marxism, then the Marxists' own special program for world revolution would be a dead letter. Marxist stalwarts might just as well emigrate (as many, so it was sadly noted, did) or join with those working to remodel Europe according to America's specifications [*ibid.*: xiii-xiv].

They agreed with members of the European right that America offered no viable alternatives to life in Europe. Accepting the views of America's severest critics, they ridiculed the idea that regeneration might be accomplished simply by physical relocation to the United States and that European class struggles would end with the adoption of American ways. Thus, in both respects they turned against "Americanization." Yet many other Europeans continued to see America as if nothing had changed since the 1840s. In the 1880s, republicans, democrats, parliamentarians, and other representatives of European liberalism still held on to the promise of America. Leading European republicans like Georges Clemenceau still saw the solution for Europe's societal problems in the imitation of existing American institutions, but most European Marxists no longer did so (*ibid.*: 34–35).

A number of prominent European Marxists including Eduard Bernstein (before he became a revisionist socialist), Karl Kautsky, Wilhelm Liebknecht, August Bebel and Jules Guesde, came up with their own revised versions of the American promised land, rejecting the old promise of America that liberals and social radicals had formulated regarding the difference between the New World and the Old. They integrated the sharpest criticism of American life advanced by European conservatives with their own dialectical view of history in terms of a stage theory of history. Hence they envisioned a sudden transition of the American capitalist order into a socialist society, as Marx himself began to proclaim a few years before his death in 1883. As Moore summarized, "It was the unfolding of capitalism with its inhumanity, its inequities, and its inevitable crisis which pushed mankind into the socialist era. The very same process with the very same underlying forces was at work in Europe. What was different in America was not the process, but the state of its development" (*ibid.*: 81).

Formulations of this view — containing the idea of a unique destiny for the American nation — had begun in the 1880s and were most popular in the years from 1895 to

1905. Strongly inspired by the intense capital accumulation, economic integration and centralization of power brought about by U.S. corporate capitalism — embodied first and foremost by the American trusts (and later holding companies)— the way seemed clear for government appropriation of the means of production as envisioned in the Marxist dream of the transition to socialism. After 1905, Marxist pronouncements about any kind of American promised land underwent a steady decline, because developments in the United States posed explanatory questions[13] that European Marxists found increasingly difficult to answer from a belief in a future socialist America to be attained after passing through the necessary stage of advanced capitalism. Revisionist socialists, especially after 1900, challenged Marxists by critical revisits to the "old" promise of America. By 1917, the United States had become a large stumbling block for Marxist theorists who still believed in economic determinism. Following the Russian Revolution, fear and disgust came to replace their hopes for a strong capitalist America that would contain the seeds of both its own destruction and a future socialist society (*ibid.*: xvii).

By the late nineteenth century, the attitudes of Europe's political and economic leaders toward the United States were changing too. Businessmen began to admire American technology and industrial efficiency. The growing international presence of American power, and the emergence in the early twentieth century of Theodore Roosevelt — with his disdain for pacificism and faith in the destiny of strong nations — struck a chord among the elites of Germany, Britain, and France. Yet at the same time, Roosevelt's foreign policy was branded as "American imperialism" and severely criticized by European politicians both on the left and the right. The late nineteenth century was also a period during which the influence of America's popular culture came to be felt in Europe. Various types of popular entertainment evolved then on both sides of the Atlantic, including tabloid newspapers, popular novels, circuses, amusement parks, world's fairs, and black minstrel shows. The Wild West show was America's unique contribution that introduced Europeans to a simplified version of America's founding myth (Pells 1997: 6, 12).

THE INTERWAR YEARS AND EUROPEAN PREOCCUPATIONS WITH AMERICA'S MODERNITY

The philosophical writings and discussions among nineteenth-century Europeans mentioned above were the foreshadowings of a much stronger and wider preoccupation with America's modernity among Europeans in the 1920s, when America's presence became more pronounced in Europe due to a combined effect of exports, investments and tourism. After 1917, the American Expeditionary Force initiated post-war cultural exchange by introducing Europeans to American inventiveness, practicality, efficiency and energy through its demonstrative display and use of machines and methods, and by having American soldiers ("doughboys") also taste the attractive sides of the Old World. Many Europeans were so impressed by the ideas and methods brought by the U.S. army that they began to think of adopting these themselves. After the war, a large number of the former soldiers returned to Europe as tourists, artists, or businessmen, thereby spreading U.S. culture in various ways.

A second strong impetus to U.S. influence was given by the Dawes Plan (1924), the international peace conference of Locarno (1925), and the "financial stabilization" programs resulting from a U.S.-led peaceful change and reconstruction policy, opening Europe up further to American business and economic and cultural penetration. The most significant commodity exported to Europe was popular culture (particularly movies and popular music) through which Europeans experienced America vicariously on a larger scale. American fads were brought to Europe when boxers and dance troupes toured the continent. There was also the conspicuous consumption culture of the well-do-to, specifically among middle- and upper-class youths living in and round the big cities (with Berlin as prototype). There a thriving subculture emerged around "Americanism" in the form of roaring twenties fashion, dance crazes, jazz music, modern "Americanized" sports and games, and, to a more limited degree, speeding in fast cars or on motorbikes (Schäfer 1986; van Elteren 1991).

As the United States emerged from the Great War as a rich and buoyant country, gradually attaining a dominant position in international relations, American society and culture became a major issue in domestic ideological debates throughout Europe. Contemporaries employed the term "Americanization" to refer both to America's influence on Europe and the overlapping process of modernization indigenous to both continents but more advanced in America. More than ever, America became a metaphor and a symbol for modernization, thus testifying to the nation's rise to a leading position in Western civilization (Costigliola 1984: 22, 167–168). Understandably, conflicting views of America mirrored the ideological and political divisions among the intelligentsia and the educated public at large. There was a general tendency to interpret virtually all manifestations of American culture as the product of a society dominated by technology and the machine. It was America's technological superiority that made other aspects of its culture more attractive to these Europeans. This turned into a true fad for Americana that waned only during the Great Depression, although the admiration for America's technological superiority still persisted.

To war-weary economic and political elites, struggling to cope with the problems of modern mass society, the United States seemed to have the answers; therefore they tried to emulate American models in European practices. In Germany, for example, from around 1923/24, for many of the owners and managers of big companies, the United States became the model country par excellence regarding modern technology, management practices, and work methods. This also holds true for parts of the trade unions and labor movements, especially their social-democratic variants. The Soviet Union, on the other hand, represented an alternative model for economic and social modernity at the time. But Bolshevism and Americanism were seldom posited as simple opposing alternatives. Except for the communist left, even for those most critical of capitalism, Americanism appeared to provide technological and organizational innovations that were compatible with socialism and that were more pertinent to the German economy of the 1920s than developments in backward (but communist) Russia (Hermand and Trommeler 1988: 49–85, 68–69, 313–322, 401–407; Nolan 1994: 8).

To deal with the problems of modernization, these Europeans looked at America's institutions and values for inspiration. For them, according to Frank Costigliola, "Americanism" stood for:

> a pragmatist, optimist outlook on life; a peaceful, rational compromise of political differences; an efficient, modern way of organizing work that emphasized machines and mass assembly production; rising standards of living with declining class antagonisms; scientific use of statistics and other information; and the predominance of mass society (this meant democratic politics, widespread consumption, and popular entertainment) [Costigliola 1984: 20].

Usually, "Fordism," the more specific technological-organizational system and economic ideology embodied in the Ford automobile company, also figured prominently as an area of interest here.

The "Americanism" these Europeans saw, epitomized by the U.S. economic-industrial model, was couched in terms of contradictory understandings of the secrets of American economic-technological success. And it was the word "rationalization"[14] (rather than the American term "efficiency") that was almost always linked to the term "Americanization" in the European literature and debates. This was because the United States was seen as the basic ideal and exemplary embodiment of the rationalization of production. From this perspective, it is also understandable that even the Russian Bolsheviks, despite sustained resistance against capitalism, attempted to adopt many of America's technological innovations and production techniques, creating their own version of "scientific management" (Taylorism), called "Stachanovism," in factory work. Although the Europeans who took part in these debates tended to see Americanism and rationalization as inevitable and economically progressive, bitter disputes often arose about the ways in which they fostered social emancipation of workers.

Probably the most important site of such discussions was Weimar Germany. Here, from their separate vantage points, manufacturers, economists, engineers, industrial sociologists and psychologists, reactionary modernists, adherents of the German People's Party and other right-wing politicians, liberals within the Democratic Party, social democrats, communists (only sporadically represented), Christian and socialist trade unionists, and ordinary workers recognized different merits and disadvantages in the American model, and proposed dramatically different reforms. Because these debates about economic-industrial reform were couched in terms of Americanism, they automatically became debates about culture, society, and human nature, as much as about technology and economy (Nolan 1994).

While many Europeans welcomed Americanism more generally, others turned against it or were ambivalent. Yet, nearly all shared the belief that it was an integral part of Europe's future; the United States was leading the way which Europeans would have to follow. In the 1920s and early 1930s a number of European intellectuals, including the Frenchmen André Siegfried and Georges Duhamel, the Englishmen F.R. and Q.D. Leavis, and the Dutchmen Menno ter Braak and Johan Huizinga, wrote their verdicts of specific characteristics of American life they denounced, trying to salvage Europe's, or more specifically their own society's, declining power and prestige (Siegfried 1927; Duhamel 1931; Leavis 1930, 1979; Ter Braak 1949–1951: 261–262; Huizinga 1972a, 1972b; cf. De Graaff 1986; Krul 1990). They drew a broad readership (at least among the educated public) and people often referred to their critical judgments about certain tendencies in the United States they disliked: urbanization, the dominance of finance capitalism, Taylorization and the monotony of the assembly line, racial conflicts, the omnipresence of advertising, and the mass media. America was seen as the great antipode of Europe, and European intellectuals contended that the United States and Europe stood for opposite ideals in various regards: atomism versus holism, mechanicistic aggregates versus organic wholes, *Gesellschaft* versus *Gemeinschaft*, homelessness and uprootedness versus rootedness and place-boundedness, commercialism versus Culture, spiritual depth versus materialistic shallowness, the ahistorical predisposition versus the capacity to be situated meaningfully in time, and so forth.

Many educated people in Germany continued to express their problems with America in terms of a materialist "unculture" (or merely practical-technical *Zivilisation*) versus a genuine *Kultur*, with its connotations of deep reflective capacity, communal rootedness, idealistic self-transcendence, and a strong sense of tradition — all features that America allegedly lacked (Ermarth 1993a: 16). Kindred spirits in Britain, France and elsewhere in Europe did the same. These European intellectuals were fervent critics but not "irrationalists." They questioned modernity and contrasted the technical rationality of industrial civilization with a humanistic definition of reason inspired by classical and Renaissance ideals of moderation and genteel culture. They saw American civilization as the destroyer of Western intellectual values, which were replaced by a mass culture consisting of technological hubris, positivism, and the unbridled pursuit of pleasure and profit. Their critical accounts were part of a traditional humanist discourse that opposed the American technological nightmare with a highly idealized version of European culture based on moderation, refinement, and the disinterested cultivation of aesthetic and spiritual values. There were others, however, like Ernst Jünger in Germany and Louis-Ferdinand Céline or Pierre Drieu la Rochelle in France, who "favored a more radical response to the decadence of the West: an appeal to nationalistic pride, a call for action, a celebration of efforts and self-mastery, a rejection of materialism in the name of pagan, anti–'Judaeo-Christian' spiritual values" (Mathy 1993: 11, 19–20).

Whereas members of smaller nations usually tended to identify with Europe as a whole (Wilterdink 1991: 23), those of larger nations such as France, Britain and Germany often depicted European traits as if they were a collection of their own national virtues; for example, British or French regard for individualism or, especially after the rise of Nazism, the German glorification of the collective spirit of the *Volk* (Pells 1997: 21). In the case of France, one should recall that French intellectuals not only felt threatened in their long-established national identity, but also in their role as self-proclaimed leaders of a *universal* republic of letters. This would turn them into potential victims of America's cultural and ideological leadership with its rise to superpower after 1945 (Mathy 1993: 35). It should also be noted that in so far as they saw "America" as the threat of an homogenized and standardized culture, the tendency among intellectuals of smaller nations to identify with "European culture" contained a paradox. Thus, they chose to go beyond the national variety of cultures to reach the higher level of "European culture," thereby homogenizing Europe's internal diversity (Kroes 1991: 7).

A leitmotiv among conservatives in the 1920s and 1930s was that Soviet Russia and America as two empires rising on either side of Western Europe were partly responsible for the crisis and forthcoming collapse of civilization. The most pessimistic of European minds would soon equate the reign of modern technology and its gradual "planetarization" (Heidegger's term to indicate globalization) with, and hold responsible for, the moral decadence of the Western world. This tendency became most prominent in Weimar Germany. The country had only reached political unity as a nation after a long struggle during a large part of the nineteenth century. Its future destiny was now threatened by the arrival on the international scene of the two nations which were seen as hostile and alien to German identity and the culture of *Mitteleuropa* (Mathy 1993: 33–35).

As Martin Heidegger wrote in the 1959 edition of his *Introduction to Metaphysics* (a series of lectures he gave in German in 1935),

> This Europe, in its ruinous blindness forever on the point of cutting its own throat, lies today in a great pincer, squeezed between Russia on one side and America on the other. From a metaphysical point of view, Russia and America are the same; the same dreary technological frenzy, the same unrestricted organization of the average man [Heidegger 1959: 37].

For Heidegger, Americanism and Bolshevism both indiscriminately applied the driving principle of modernity, technology and its controlling and calculative mindset vis-à-vis reality. Although he continued to note the essential "metaphysical" similarity of these two nations and two regimes, America emerged as the sole symbol of the crisis of modernity, with Bolshevism a mere variant of Americanism. The closest thing to a definition of Americanism that Heidegger gave was: "The primacy of sheer quantity is itself a quality, i.e., an essential characteristic, which is that of boundlessness. This principle we call Americanism." In his view, it was "the emerging monstruousness of modern times; America was "the site of catastrophe" (*katastrophenhaft*) (Heidegger qtd. in Ceaser 1997: 9, 192, 196).

Importantly, in Heidegger's thought America was less a geographical place than a temporal situation: America was a moment in history; the spatial manifestation of the temporal fact of the "darkening of the world" and the "forgetting of Being" that was the basic feature of the modern age. In light of its influence on a wide variety of later thinkers, and striking resemblances with specific elements of some of today's views on Americanization (even though their precise meaning may be very different in given cases), his thinking demands more attention here.[15] For this I rely on James W. Ceaser's valuable distillation from Heidegger's scattered writings.

In the Heideggerian worldview, Americanization represents first the transformation of language into nonlanguage, which results from the flatness or thinness of mass communications carried by modern technology that enables information (including news) to flow increasingly faster across space, but when it reaches people it is delivered out of any context or grounding in authentic experience. This dissemination of information is either leveling or without meaning. "American" (or sometimes "English-American") is the term Heidegger uses, in a metaphorical sense, to indicate the more general deformation of all the advanced modern languages, which entails a transformation from a medium with a poetic function able to capture the particular and the distinctive into a bland vehicle for technical communication, whatever the language one is supposedly using. Even though we may think we speak our native tongue, we actually talk "American." This is a true disaster from Heidegger's perspective, because for this philosopher language is the "house of Being," the means by which people grasp their life-world. Therefore this deformation of language automatically implies a deformation of thought. To be able to practice reflective thinking, one must be able to use language poetically, in such a way that it is grounded in the particular. This is impossible in America, which stands for the triumph of the uniform over the particular.

Second, Americanism represents consumerism, which is more than a mere desire for material convenience or security but epitomizes a fundamental attitude to reality. In modern technological society, life is characterized by the "reign of the ersatz," in which everything and everybody is replaceable. In some way anticipating critiques on the detrimental effects of planned obscelescence from the 1950s onwards, Heidegger points out that we as modern consumers do not replace goods because they are worn out or defective, but because we value them only temporarily, constantly waiting for something new to thrill us. This we do to fill a void in our lives. The artificial in modern consumption is characteristic of America, although the American element (technology) arrived much earlier in Europe. The American way of life does not only threaten us today; "the way of technology" was already a threat to our ancestors and their material culture, embodied by housing, clothing, and product designs. In short, Heidegger targets the homogeneity of mass-produced articles in America and the standardization of culture.

Third, in Heidegger's view, America is the site where developments in philosophy, the humanities, and social sciences have moved furthest towards specialization. This segmentation (or fragmentation) of knowledge into different specialties reflects the governing thought that knowledge is meant to master reality and to make objects calculable. Each discipline is assigned its own domain and objects to study and discover how to use or control these. Man himself is approached as such an object, not only in biology but also in psychology and economics. Modern psychology will soon enable Americans to establish what man is and how he can most efficiently be brought into a position of most effective use. Heidegger calls such understanding of man "pseudo-philosophy" (*Schein-philosophie*), which already came to dominate American universities and was increasingly being emulated by German science. Like consumerism, however, American science is a deformation, leading us away from genuine thought and toward the situation of "home-lessness." Here we arrive at the final feature of Americanism.

America also symbolizes the ahistorical, the inability to situate oneself meaningfully in time. The relation of ahistorical man to time parallels that of the consumer to things. Both relationships share homelessness as a metaphor. To be homeless is to be uprooted, lacking a place, either in a physical accommodation or inside a genuine tradition. The absence of a sense of history leads to an attitude in which nothing is seen as permanent, and nothing exists to be transmitted or handed down to later generations. Those trapped in this position live in a perpetual present, and, paradoxically, the only permanent con-dition is the continual quest for the "always new of permanent change." This problem-atic is even more damaging to the collective than it is to the individual. Since a shared history is what makes a group of persons into a larger whole, the absence of such a his-tory means that there can be no *Volk*. America is the example par excellence of a collec-tivity of persons that is not a true people/nation. Writing at the time of America's entry into World War II, Heidegger, made this explicit. The United States, spiritually repre-senting the ahistorical attitude, was waging war on the historical sense (apparently best represented by Nazi Germany), and thereby following a path to self-destruction. Amer-ica was now the enemy of Germany, and by implication also of Europe and of all valu-able things in the West (Ceaser 1997: 197–200; 274–276). Although this may suggest a strict dichotomy between Americanism and Europeanism, Heidegger actually viewed Americanism also as something European, representing a working out of modern Euro-pean thought that was the culmination of the entire Western metaphysical tradition. Amer-icanism stood for homogenization, one-dimensional life, and the elimination of difference.

Yet, as indicated earlier, not all intellectuals entertained a position of "absolute cul-tural discontinuity" as the likes of Heidegger and other conservative thinkers tended to do. There were those who "refused to throw the baby of modernity out with the bath-water of corporate or state bureaucracy or to equate the liberal rationalist tradition of the Enlightenment with the development of mass production and collectivization," and rejected a black and white view of the relationship between America and Europe (Mathy 1993: 20). We should also remember that the glittering American Dream — with its entic-ing rags-to-riches stories — kept many among the working classes of Europe enthralled. But nineteenth-century dreams about America as a haven for common folks had largely faded by now among the left.

Nonetheless some saw positive elements in the new developments. Marxists were now inclined to see the transformations of the process of production induced by further mech-anization or "automation" as a decisive step in the evolution of capitalist society toward communism. The new forms of the rationalization of labor, they argued, would acceler-ate industrial concentration and turn more and more workers into proletarians, which would enhance the revolutionary consciousness of the masses and augment the existing societal contradictions. In Italy, Marxists opposed the conservative intellectuals and oth-ers who detested the "Americanization" of Europe. In his *Prison Notebooks*, the philoso-pher and communist party leader Antonio Gramsci ridiculed the traditional elites, who felt themselves threatened by the rise of the new social relations. In his essay "Americanism and Fordism," written in the 1920s, he foresaw that the introduction of American-style mass production into Italy would intensify economic exploitation and extend the realm of the state across private and public life. But he refused to denounce the cultural changes that accompanied such structural changes.

Foreshadowing a view of historical changes in the social position of intellectuals within the cultural field that Pierre Bourdieu would develop some fifty years later, Gramsci considered the critique of the "new culture" of Americanism as an expression of the moral and intellectual reaction of declining social strata to the rise of the modern that was inevitable in his eyes: "In Europe it is the passive residues that resist Americanism (they represent 'quality' etc.) because they have the instinctive feeling that the new forms of production and work would sweep them away implacably" (Gramsci 1971: 305). Gramsci contended that "what is today called 'Americanism' is to a large extent an advance criticism of old strata which will in fact be crushed by any eventual new order and which are already in the grips of a wave of social panic, dissolution and despair" (*ibid.*: 317). To him, the essence of Americanism was rationalism unhibited by the existence of social classes and values derived from a feudal past. America was characterized by the complete ideological hegemony of bourgeois values, unaffected by feudalism. Gramsci also contended that before Italy could become socialist it had to go through a stage in which it would Americanize both socially and economically, a development he welcomed. Like earlier Marxists, he saw the United States as the embodiment of a bourgeois democratic society, which lacked the traditional pre-capitalist elements still evident in Italy and other European cultures (*ibid.*: 21–22, 272, 318).

Liberal interpreters of America, such as Alexandre Kojève and André Maurois in France, "underscored the philosophical and political continuities between both cultures and usually downplayed the demonic side of the modern" (Mathy 1993: 20). There were significant liberal minorities among the cultural elites who held an open-minded, positive attitude towards various kinds of modernity, among which those conveyed by cultural forms as borrowed from America. Most moderns in the sphere of culture and art were enchanted by the cultural artifacts and the spiritual and youthful energy that America exported. Other moderns were ambivalent towards "America," while most traditionalist artists fervently opposed American influences (Berg 1963; van Elteren 1991).

American artists who had taken refuge in Europe in the early 1920s, looking for new inspiration and low costs of living, were astonished to find many European writers, painters, and architects searching for aesthetic themes in America's technologically-dominated culture that they themelves denounced. This became especially manifest in Germany (with Berlin as the major site of modernity), where people, eager to put behind Germany's recent military past, were enthralled by American cinema, jazz, the Charleston, boxing, and spectator sports. They appreciated the movies that celebrated modern ideas of consumption and material abundance, and among writers during the Weimar Republic Charlie Chaplin became the icon of a truly democratic and egalitarian culture. U.S. popular culture thrilled many German artists, particularly members of the *neue Sachlichkeit*, or new objectivity school, who were looking for modern cultural models to replace imperial styles no longer in favor. In designing new structures, some built with American loans, German architects of this strain incorporated efficient design elements borrowed from the United States (Schäfer 1986).

Despite a fear of domination by the machine that many of these intellectuals and artists shared with other Europeans, they nevertheless embraced Americanism as a way to increase Europe's economic productivity, thinking that it would resolve local social and ideological conflicts. To them, America's mass culture seemed democratic and progressive, the wave of the future, highly appropriate for the machine age. They understood American mass culture "as a modern folk culture that grew out of the needs of large urban masses ... the Berlin avant-garde saw American mass culture as a vehicle for the radical modernization and democratization of both German culture and life" (Kaes 1985: 323, qtd. in Gemünden 1998: 21). And they pitted American mass culture against the traditional bourgeois notion of a German *Kulturnation* (cultural nation).

Initially, many of these new objectivity modernists were simultaneously loyal to Bolshevism and Americanism, both promising a democratic, technocratic, peaceful, and abundant future. Especially during the years of the quasi-capitalist New Economic Policy in Soviet Russia, these two paths appeared to these Europeans to merge into a single road. In their view both creeds promised popular sovereignty, a common culture of the masses, and technological development for the sake of progress and social justice. In the early twenties, seeing the contrast between Russia's distress and America's success, some left-wing German artists like Bertold Brecht came to the conclusion that Americanism was a surer and more comfortable road to these ends than Bolshevism. (Brecht already began shifting from Americanism to Bolshevism before the stock market crash in 1929, however.) Others, including the members of Piscator's communist theater group "Epic Theater," with its Brechtian dramaturgical approach, hung on to Bolshevism, while simultaneously reaching for the American Dream. Although these intellectuals and artists all embraced the technocratic vision of Americanism, their vision differed from that of industrialists though. The businessmen aimed for greater productivity and profits, the benefits of which they were unwilling to share with their workers. The intellectuals and artists of the *neue Sachlichkeit*, on the other hand, saw increased efficiency and productivity in U.S. style as a vehicle towards greater social justice.

At the same time some intellectuals and members of the middle class sided with small entrepreneurs struggling to survive in a rapidly changing world increasingly dominated by corporate capitalism, while defending the virtues of *Volk, Kultur,* and *Heimat* against the invasion of foreign products and people, functionalism, and modernity. This brought them into sharp conflict, of course, with the members of the new objectivity school — a clash between *völkisch* traditionalism and Americanist modernity. The Americanism vogue in Germany lasted until the Depression when European artists became disillusioned with their American dreams of everlasting prosperity and progress, and American expatriates went home. Yet at an earlier stage already, when American investors penetrated the German economy following the precedent of the Dawes loan in 1924, the America cult of a number of intellectuals had turned into a critique of U.S. capitalism. The avant-garde then became disenchanted with the mass culture of jazz, sports, and cinema as its progressive potential became, in their eyes, increasingly streamlined according to the laws of capitalist production. America now stood first of all for modern technology and industrial rationalization, which appealed to those other Germans bent on emulating American models in the German industry (Costigliola 1984: 22–23, 168, 178–180, 221; Gemünden 1998: 21). Thus Americanism remained a highly contested area in Germany.

2

European Concerns about American Influence After World War II

This chapter charts the further development of European preoccupations with Americanization since the mid-twentieth century. This culminates in a schematic overview of the major discourses on the United States and Americanization among Western Europeans at the turn of the twenty-first century. The final section shows the close parallels between the different discourses on cultural Americanization and different views of mass culture/popular culture.

POST–WORLD WAR II WORRIES IN EUROPE

Anxieties expressed about Americanization in the post–World War II era in Western Europe were to a great extent a repeat of those in the interwar period, now tied to further democratization of society and culture, the rise of the modern welfare state, and more affluence for working-class people. However, among large segments of the working and lower-middle classes a discourse of positive dreams about America persisted. A mythologized America was their dreamland of abundance and consumerism. "Freedom," "equality," and "America" stood for many ordinary people for the enlargement of their personal room to maneuver. Freedom as liberation from recognizable discomforts and equality in the access to ease and joy, were always included in their dreams about the good life. Through the consumption of goods, images and sounds from America, and attendant vicarious experiences of America, along with personal contacts with Americans at home or even through visits to the U.S., as well as local imitations and derivations of things American, the American way of life was for these people constantly reaffirmed as the materialization of their vision of the good life (Maase 1992: 186–190).

In the first post-war period "Americanization" was also strongly articulated by American economic aid and political and cultural interventions in relation to the Marshall Plan. One of the main concerns among cultural critics was the "leveling-down" or the lowering of standards, in areas such as the quality of life and aesthetic taste, the negative sides of greater economic and cultural equality represented by "Americanization." In Britain, where the debate over Americanization became more salient and more contentious after 1945, the work of the literary and social critics F.R. and Q.D. Leavis was very influential. Although their work spanned a forty-year period, their attitude towards popular culture and Americanization was formed in the 1930s already. In *Mass Civilisation and Minority Culture* (1930) F.R. Leavis had announced that "it is a commonplace that we are

30

being Americanised," a commonplace, however "that seems, as a rule to carry little understanding with it…" evidenced by the fact that "those who are most defiant of America do not propose to reverse the processes consequent upon the machine." More than forty years later the critique would be essentially the same, as Leavis discredited in *Nor Shall My Sword* (1972) "American conditions" in terms of "the rootlessness, the vacuity, the inhuman scale, the failure of organic cultural life, the anti-human reductivism that favours the American neo-imperialism of the computer" (Leavis, qtd. in Bigsby 1975: 10).

Strictly speaking, F.R. Leavis did not blame America for the process of what he too called Americanization. For him, Americanization epitomized the industrialism, materialism, and fragmentation of modern industrial society that threatened the very existence of traditional culture. America was the archetypical example of what Leavis called the "technological-Benthamite" society. He saw American conditions as those of modern civilization; America had gone further along the trajectory of modernization, and was assumed to represent the future that lay ahead for other comparable societies, including Britain (Johnson 1979: 95–96, 202).

In *Fiction and the Reading Public* (1932) Q.D. Leavis turned against popular fiction and other modern forms of popular culture being used as a source of easy stimuli and passive pleasure, and she repeatedly compared this to a drug: "The temptation to accept the cheap and easy pleasures offered by the cinema, the circulating library, the magazine, the newspaper, the dance-hall, and the loud-speaker is too much for almost every one" (Leavis 1979: 214). Her work manifested a clear distrust of pleasure, and she continued to worry about the need for self-discipline now that the new diversions were replacing a Protestant tradition of reading as self-improvement.

In trying to combat what they saw as the morally debilitating effects of modern mass communication, F.R. Leavis and Denys Thompson published a seminal guidebook for teachers of English and history, *Culture and Environment* (1933), in which they gave instructions of how to train students to discriminate between various cultural expressions in terms of quality and to resist mass-popular culture. Like Matthew Arnold, the Leavisites believed that culture had always been a minority affair. The problem, however, was that the cultured minority could no longer command deference for their values and judgments. The minority found themselves in "a hostile environment," in which the Arnoldian project had failed due to the subversive challenge posed by "mass civilisation" and its "mass culture" (McGuigan 1992: 46; Storey 1998: 4).

The Leavisites' campaign against the "mass" and the "Americanized" built on points of resistance where elitist minority culture might take a stand. In this the pastoral was mobilized against the popular, and the organic community of an idealized good old England against mass society. "English rusticity" was "raised in a gesture combining nostalgia and criticism but … [it was] detached from politics, a refuge rather than a site of opposition" (Webster 1988: 181). The Leavisites' influence was apparent in the cultural program of the literary magazine *Scrutiny*, that exerted considerable influence on higher education, the training of teachers, the teaching of English in schools, and so forth. Even though *Scrutiny* still made critical judgments in terms of binary oppositions such as Culture versus *kitsch* or mass, it cultivated a more complex attitude towards America. Its contributors broadened and problematized the debate. For example, Denys Thompson wrote that if "England is less Americanized than America, it is in the discreditable sense that less resistance to the advance of civilization has been developed: no English university has yet produced a *Middletown*" (Thompson qtd. in Webster 1988: 182). (The latter was a reference to Robert and Helen Lynds' two successive studies of Muncie, Indiana in the mid–1920s and 1935 (Lynd and Lynd 1929, 1937), that entailed an "anthropological" critique of the industrialized culture of a Midwestern town, also drawn on by Q.D. Leavis.)

Paradoxically, America provided *Scrutiny* with a comparison that could advance their project of building a critical, professional intelligentsia. And one of the most powerful uses of American writing as critical resource was precisely Q.D. Leavis's borrowing from Thorstein Veblen's work on American higher education in her critique of English literary and academic circles. In 1939 she had written that literary criticism in England was deformed by its dilettante disregard for values and by its class basis. She then compared the educational and social background as depicted in her book with that of the United States, and saw advantages in the fact that the United States did not have a public school system, no ancient universities and no tradition of a closed literary society run on civil service lines. There was an intriguing doubleness at work here. "For *Scrutiny,*" according to Francis Mulhern, "the United States was both the homeland of modern 'machine civilization' and the advance post of opposition to it" (Mulhern 1981: 77, 126, 125).

In addition, a left-Leavisite approach[1] evolved that held a more nuanced view of popular culture in relation to high culture and showed a clear commitment to working-class culture, giving a different emphasis in its critical view of Americanization. Leftist writers and literary critics such as George Orwell and Richard Hoggart wanted to preserve the "texture" of the traditional working-class community against the homogenizing allure of post-war affluence — television, high wages, and consumerism (Hebdige 1988: 51; Strinati 1995: 28). In his well-known book *The Uses of Literacy* (1957) Hoggart was concerned about the manipulative and exploitative influence exercised by American mass culture over the working-class community — especially its vulnerable youth — by the "America" of Hollywood films, cheap and brutal crime novels, milk bars and their blaring juke boxes. He feared that working-class people would be seduced to lose themselves and their culture in a mindless "candy-floss world," the "hollow brightness" of a "shiny barbarism," imported from America. Hoggart did not attack a "moral decline" in the working class as such, but he saw a decline in the "moral seriousness" of the culture that was provided for them. Yet he was not totally negative about the value and influence of American culture, acknowledging, for example, the merits of the more realistic and straightforward qualities of the "tough-guy" American crime novel in its appeal to working-class readers. More importantly, Hoggart recognized that working-class people were not merely passive recipients of mass-cultural influence. The idea of an audience appropriating, to some extent, for its own purposes the products offered to it by the cultural industries is apparent in his thinking — particularly in relation to popular songs in the 1930s — but never fully explored (Storey 1997: 47–49; Strinati 1995: 28–29).

For critical observers such as cultural studies scholar Dick Hebdige, the preoccupations with "the spectre of Americanisation" in the debates from the mid–1930s to the early 1960s revolved around a "negative consensus of cultural if not political conservativism" that linked such diverse writers as Evelyn Waugh, Orwell, T.S. Eliot (American expatriate), Leavis, and Hoggart. For Eliot and Leavis it was elitist minority culture and for Orwell and Hoggart the working-class community that needed protection against the affluence and inauthenticity of mass culture. This negative consensus solidified around a shared interpretive response towards what was seen as American cultural imperialism. Whenever the "leveling-down" process was discussed, automatically references to the noxious influence of American popular culture appeared that were phrased in the existing vocabulary of the "Culture and Society" tradition (where the term Americanization initially came from). However, representations of America-as-threat now operated in a public, explicitly populist discourse and were circulated in a wider variety of publication and broadcast contexts since the war years. This broader "official" resistance to American influence emanated from a "covert hostily" to the American military presence in Britain from the early 1940s onwards and Britain's increasing dependence on American military and economic aid. This transformed into a more generalized anti–Americanism after the war due to worries on the part of the British establishment over Britain's loss of Empire and decline as a world power and America's increasingly dominant role. Increasing working-class affluence and consumption threatened the intellectual arbitration of taste and middle class consumption as forms of symbolic and positional power (Hebdige 1982).

In this context Hebdige referred to Gramsci's critique of the prevailing response among Italian intellectuals to the emergence of "Americanism" mentioned earlier. Similarly, English cultural conservatives, irrespective of their political affiliations, saw in the influx of American popular culture an attack on the cultural heritage they chose to defend. They perceived correctly that their future as cultural arbiters was at stake. In contrast, Hebdige pointed to "alternative definitions of America and American influence at the time" that contradicted the fears about the homogenizing influence of American culture in the British context. It was youth culture in particular that found the diversity of difference by an active appropriation of elements from American popular culture, imposing meanings and attempting to articulate self-identities through particular signifying practices — forms of resistance through rituals against middle-class and upper-class culture.

The profusion of youth-cultural options then available, most of which were associated (however indirectly) with a "mythical America," suggested that American culture did not have the homogenizing influence that its critics assumed. The positive images of America that did persist throughout the period, operated outside the public discourse of Americanization. They were being constructed and maintained underneath and in spite of the "official" authorized discourses of school and state. These "Americanizing" tendencies in working-class culture and youth culture found their literary stronghold in marginalized genres such as crime fiction and comics. It is no coincidence that the close relationship that often existed between "moral panic" and "Americanization" became manifest in the 1950s campaign against American horror comics, next to the public outrage about juvenile delinquency associated with "teddy boys" (Hebdige 1982, 1988: 58; cf. Webster 1988: 24–25, 183–184; Strinati 1995: 34).

The debate about Americanization was prolonged into the 1970s and 1980s and focused, for example, upon the threats posed to national cultural identities by popular American television programs such as *Dallas* and *Dynasty*. However, the rise of Thatcherism entailed a number of issues that generated specific political questions that went beyond earlier anxieties about America in Britain, as Duncan Webster has pointed out in an insightful overview of the various positions (Webster 1988: 174–247). Several critics suggested that the special relationship between Britain and America had been replaced by one that resembled colonization rather than partnership; in their eyes Britain had become a U.S. client state or even worse: America's 51st state. Thatcherism was seen as complicit in the Americanization of Britain. But the left's rhetoric about American encroachment on British sovereignty was also part of a strategy to challenge the Iron Lady's patriotic image by focusing on her subservience to American military, political and economic interests.

The 1980s witnessed several points of conflict between British and American interests: Reagan's invasion of Grenada, and American policy in Central America and the Middle East. The American nuclear and military presence in Britain linked anti-nuclear protest to questions of sovereignty around images about American military occupation and worries about the extent to which the British government would be consulted in any nuclear confrontation, which transcended some political divisions among the British public. The political opposition would point to the Conservative government's tendency to suggest that Britain could learn from American (neoliberal) models of health care, welfare, arts funding and so forth. Right-wing think tanks played a significant mediating role in this, acting as a bridge between the American new right and Thatcherism (Harvey 2005: 57–62). British industrial independence had been undermined, according to the opposition, by the Conservatives' willingness to let companies be taken over or sold off to American competitors. Moreover, the implications of "Star Wars" research for British scientists and the extension of U.S. licensing regulations to British high-tech companies were seen to be overriding British scientific and technological development.

Under these circumstances the notion of U.S. cultural imperialism gained significant influence again in public debates about Britain's condition. Critiques of the influence of American culture and opposition to U.S. foreign policy were linked to each other in such ways that this blocked effective political analysis according to Webster. Conservative worries about the national cultural heritage based on "little Englander" assumptions were entwined with political opposition to American policies across the political spectrum, whereas American popular culture could have been mobilized in a variety of fields against the established conservative English consensus. The latter refers to the potential radical charge of American popular culture, in which certain elements may be used as a cultural resource for local resistance and opposition to the national-popular culture or a specific part thereof (Webster 1988: 179, 209–210, 245–246).

In Germany the debates about Americanization obtained a special character because of the United States' grip on the American occupation zones in the immediate postwar period and deliberate attempts at "re-educating" the German population, as well as the sustained presence of Americans and American institutions on U.S. army bases and their environs (Jarausch and Siegrist 1997). Other important factors were the continuing occupation of many positions of power by conservative elites (including a significant number of ex-Nazis) and the long-standing tradition in secondary and higher education of Humboldtian *Bildung* through participating in elitist forms of culture with little room for expressions of popular culture. Based on pessimistic cultural diagnoses of the present, and deeply dismayed that venerable traditions of the educated middle class were in decline, losing their binding validity, these conservatives feared inundation by "vulgar" U.S. mass culture. But because German ideas and culture (both high and "folk") had been perverted by Nazism, younger Germans tended to indict their nation's cultural heritage while gravitating towards a very different sort of culture to fill the vacuum (Ermarth 1993a: 16).

Although there were certain continuities between the 1920s and the late 1940s and 1950s, "Americanization" became laden with extra complexities in the latter period. A crucial factor was that an entirely new generation was raised with American popular culture from earliest childhood onward, in a specific political-psychological context. They grew up in a "fatherless society," having lost their fathers in the war — either literally or figuratively, the latter having lost their moral authority by participating in Hitler's army — and America provided ersatz fathers.[2] Since it was the Americans who liberated Germany from Nazism — which Germans had failed to do — many Germans had internalized the American liberators/invaders (and more generally U.S. exemplars) "to the point of siding with them against themselves." This predicament would be comparable to what psychologists call the Stockholm Syndrome, in which "hostages become grateful to their captors for not exercising their power over life and death...." (Elsaesser 1985: 32). This situation produced among those youths very complex and highly ambivalent attitudes toward the culture and politics of the United States. These complexities only became manifest when this generation came of age in the late 1960s, and a similar development took place in Austria (Gemünden 1998: 23, 32).

The clashes over Americanization in relation to youth in the 1950s should also be seen as part of the postwar struggles for cultural hegemony in the Federal Republic of Germany. As Kaspar Maase has pointed out in his analysis of the rise of U.S.-influenced popular culture in West Germany during the 1950s, "the acceptance of mass arts which represented popular taste and popular attitudes had to be accomplished against the resistance and the snobbery of the traditional cultural elites, against teachers, critics, representatives of the churches, political campaigns against 'filth and trash' and so on. The conflict about Americanisation was the focus of this struggle" (Maase 1993: 169). He attributes to the *Halbstarke* (German version of the "greasers" or "teddy boys") the role of the avant garde of innovation: "these proletarian youths strengthened their positions by the symbolic alliance with 'America'" (*ibid.*: Maase 1996a). I would add that American high culture (especially literature and the visual arts) was also a significant site of contestation in struggles for cultural hegemony in West Germany, in this case between modernist and traditional cultural elites. Further, besides conservative and traditionalist opposition, other critical voices resounded in the same period, as part of a polemical political discourse. Some proponents and sympathizers of socialism (including repatriates from the United States who had gone into exile there, escaping from the Nazis) referred to "Americanization" to explain the "loss of utopia" and the diminishing resonance of their anti-capitalist ideology among the German population (Schildt 1991, qtd. in Sywottek 1993: 132).[3]

After 1968, the student protest movement initiated in Germany a tense debate about issues of German identity, its past, capitalism, and the relation of arts to politics. In this debate it became clear that "America" had become intertwined with specifically German problems in complex ways. Leading figures in this debate displayed a paradoxical attitude toward American politics and U.S. popular culture. On the one hand, they were attracted to a culture that had been decisive during their formative years in shaping an eagerness to identify with American culture and society, while, on the other hand, they rejected American politics and the colonizing effect of its mass culture (Gemünden 1998: 23–24). Increasingly disillusioned with American policy, values, and lifestyles, writers and cultural critics such as Hans Magnus Enzensberger, Eberhard Schmidt, Robert Jungk, and younger members of the Frankfurt School signaled the emergence of a "one-dimensional society" inhabited by consumerist conformists, for which the United States was the archetype, pointing to Germany's and Europe's own future.

A strong political anti–Americanism emerged among the German New Left, for which the Vietnam War was the major catalyst. It was then that the American model of freedom and democracy that had permeated the culture from the 1950s onwards, became the focus of attention. This movement targeted U.S. imperialism across the world, and more particularly the Americanization of Germany by the American military, U.S.-dominated political institutions, and U.S. corporations and their affiliates in Europe. Yet at the same time the German New Left borrowed ideas, symbols, expressive styles and strategies from its American counterpart,[4] and more generally Germany's *Subkultur* drew inspiration from the American counterculture, importing many of its musical and other cultural expressions that were considered "authentic"— not part of phony U.S. "mass culture."

However, this dual approach to America could also be found among similar movements in other Western European societies. It was part of a larger transnational sphere in which other national inflections also made their contributions to the processes of change concerned: from France, Great Britain, the Netherlands and Sweden to Vietnam, Angola, and Chile. In other words, America affected Germany, not only directly in a one to one relationship, but also through events that took place in other settings; for example through feelings of sympathy for the American civil rights movement, the shared concerns of the peace movement/anti-nuclear weapons movements (active throughout Europe and the United States) and the actions of the student protest movements in Berkeley, New York, Paris, London, Stockholm, Amsterdam and other places. But ultimately it was America — a dominant focal point that could hardly be ignored — that was most instrumental in setting the terms and defining the content of the transnational within this context. And its symbolic significance was probably never more important throughout most of Europe than in connection with the Vietnam War (O'Dell 1997: 195, 197–198).

The fall of the Wall in 1989 and German unification the following year initially instilled in many Germans a euphoric sense of national pride, but also gave rise to heated discussions about German's national and cultural identity among intellectuals from both the East and the West. For many, 1989 came to represent yet another "Stunde Null" (Zero Hour) that called for a taking stock of German history at the threshold of a new beginning. East German intellectuals were apprehensive about the import of American consumer culture, which for them seemed new and threatening. Some saw unification as a takeover in which Americanization would displace a "genuine" (East) German culture. GDR's "old ideological kitsch" that most people just ignored, was expected to be replaced by "commercial kitsch" that would draw larger and more eager audiences, and therefore was a menace. Yet in the West, too, unification led to a profound questioning among intellectuals about the role American culture would play in a German national identity yet to be molded. The so-called "neutral nationalism" and "national revolution" movements that emerged then targeted Americanization as a prime source of German sociocultural inertia and decay, again upholding an alternative in a "third way" between the communist East and capitalist West (Ermarth 1993b: 129).

An odd coalition of people from the right and the left (including filmmakers Hans Jürgen Syberberg and Wim Wenders, and playwright and novelist Botho Strauss) aimed to lay the groundwork for the future unified country, where the negative effects of Westernization, more particularly Americanization, could be reversed through a recovery of German art, culture, and language. The rhetorical specter of cultural imperialism resurfaced as the American, or rather the Americanized German cultural industry, once again became a powerful *Feindbild* (projected image of the enemy) against which a German identity should be resurrected and upheld. This occurred at a time when American productions were dominating German television screens and movie theaters more than ever. Wim Wenders, whose work until the late 1980s reflected an ambiguous and highly self-conscious love-hate relationship with the U.S., now tended to define German culture exclusively in terms of an opposition to American popular culture, endowing German cultural identity with rootedness, authenticity, and purity, qualities that were supposedly located outside of history. Wenders in fact invoked the eighteenth-century notion of *Kulturnation*— that is, the idea of a shared literature, music, art, and philosophy — that provides a certain cultural identity in lieu of nationhood (Gemünden 1998: 195–204). In the early 1990s, Wenders manifested his new position politically as a leading figure in the French-dominated European opposition to U.S. cultural imperialism, particularly the purported threat of Hollywood's worldwide supremacy, in defending European audiovisual industries. In September 1993, he was among the more than 4,000 European intellectuals, artists, and producers who published a petition in six major European newspapers for "cultural works" to be excluded from the new GATT agreement that was being negotiated at the time (van Elteren 1996c).

The theme of anti–Americanism remained at the basis of much of the national discourse in France, since French intellectuals clung to their long-standing tendency to perceive American society as either model or *bête noire*, "utopia attained" or dystopia come true, invoking de Tocqueville's famous remark: "I admit that in America I saw more than just America." Across the spectrum of intellectual positions, the same question was asked over and over again: Is what is happening over there a premonition of what will happen over here? Is American society and culture now what France will be like in two or three decades? What matters for us here is that the French — just like the Americans — have the pretension of having constructed a universal model of society, and that both models end up being compared to each other. "If one of them weakens," however, "it ceases to inspire the men and women of the planet, and that can only benefit the other" (Kaspi 1990: 238). This has led to a competition between two world missions that were structurally in essence the same, but took others forms when the international balance of power changed at mid-century. As Richard Pells explains,

> Both the Americans and the French saw themselves as model societies, each with a mission to transport the ideals of their respective revolutions to the corners of the planet. The Americans spoke in the name of "democracy" and the French defended "civilization," but their global ambitions were similarly grandiose. By the postwar years, however, France and America were no longer well-matched rivals, economically or militarily. The French continued to compete with the United States in the cultural arena. The Americans, preoccupied with the Soviet threat, appeared not to notice that they were also in contest with France for the world's affection. No doubt this obliviousness was infuriating to French intellectuals and politicians [Pells 1997: 184].

Whether the U.S. inattention was deliberate or not, the French set out to turn the tide of American "cultural imperialism" in relation to the spread of American words, business practices, products (including Coca-Cola, McDonaldized fast food etc.), and more generally U.S. popular culture forms, especially film and music. For the latter we should recall two examples in particular. First, the Blum-Byrnes agreement of May 1946 gave the Americans access to France's protected markets in return for a U.S. loan to France, leading, among other things, to a massive influx of American films when France eliminated its prewar import quotas on American movies. Second, the struggle over the cultural exemption clause that was finally added to the GATT agreement of December 1993 (through the efforts of the French government backed by a group of prominent European film directors) excluded audiovisual products from the market liberalization agreement between the European Union and the United States (Winock 1990: 71; van Elteren 1996c; Pells 1997: 217, 274–277).

An anti–American sentiment was prevalent in most French intellectual circles until the mid–1970s. The strong position of the communist left during the heyday of the Cold War was of special significance in the debates and political struggles about Americanization. Another important factor was the diminishing authority of French literary intellectuals as guardians of knowledge and good taste vis-à-vis the rise of economic and technological elites, the triumph of expert knowledge over generalist insights, and the disenchantment of the world due to modernization. In the eyes of these intellectuals, American civilization was the quintessential embodiment of modernity. Their critical accounts had what Mathy calls "a paradigm of discontinuity" between the two civilizations in common. Nevertheless, this binary framework pitting the United States against France always included a fascination with the innovative and energizing rather than the alienating aspects of American modernity as well (Mathy 1993: 2, 5, 8–9).

The discourse of the intellectual left of the 1950s and 1960s entailed critical reflections on economic, political and racial issues in the context of American capitalism and imperialism. To this discourse belong the works of Jean-Paul Sartre, as well as the existentialist left's contestations of the hegemonic claims of the United States, from the Cold War to Vietnam (*ibid.*: 11–12). This discourse was also reflected in the debates about Coca-colonization in the 1950s and the discussions about U.S. cultural imperialism in relation to films and other audiovisual materials at various occasions since 1945. This discourse was being marginalized from the late 1970s onwards, although one could then still find isolated intellectuals on the left such as Régis Debray[5] and Jean-Pierre Chevènement who attacked the mediocrity of the "pan-Atlantic discourse" and "the alignment of French ideology on American ideology," or even "the American Left," whose persistent aim was thought to be the rapid Americanization of French society and the avoidance of any revolutionary outcome of the crisis of advanced capitalism (Lacorne and Rupnik 1990: 9, 20).

Until the 1960s, positive accounts of American culture and society came mainly from the liberal right and from the side of the Christian-Democrats (the Atlanticist camp). Liberal is here meant in the European sense of the term, that is, opposed to authoritarian, state-centered political regimes (whether monarchist, fascist, communist, or otherwise) as against liberal in its American meaning, that is, progressive, in favor of state intervention in economic and social matters, and left of center. The works of the sociologist Raymond Aron, although at times critical, are exemplary for this position.

The worldwide diffusion of the American counterculture in the 1960s and 1970s and the decline of Marxism as the dominant frame of reference of the French left gave rise to a new kind of pro-Americanism (although it had its precursors within a strain of Romanticism of the nineteenth century). This libertarian or countercultural discourse focused on the social and cultural diversity and the political experimentalism of America at the time (including attempts at building communes), which was perceived as the alternative par excellence to statist socialism or European moral and political decadence. The writings of Jean-François Revel and Edgar Morin best exemplify this position (Mathy 1993: 12; Lacorne and Rupnik 1990: 8).[6]

From the late 1970s onwards a postmodern version of American culture gained much influence among French intellectuals. In the wake of a strong reaction to the "totalizing grand narratives" of Hegelian-Marxist thinking in philosophical circles after May 1968, postmodern thinkers developed ironic, ambiguous and sometimes contradictory notions of contemporary culture and society. Although they often entertained a pessimistic view on the dehumanizing and standardizing aspects of life in modern bureaucratic societies, they nevertheless celebrated the liberating effects of the information revolution (Lyotard) or the pragmatic and egalitarian "realized utopia" of America as the reign of the simulacrum (Baudrillard). Once again America was seen as the land of the future which leads the way, this time in the era of postmodernity and the United States as the "end of history" (Mathy 1993: 12–13).

CURRENT STATE OF AFFAIRS

To complete this overview, I mention the discourses on America and Americanization here that became more prominent in Western Europe in the late twentieth century. One important discourse is that among those businessmen, managers, groups of professionals and academics, governmental officials and so forth who are proponents of neoliberalism and U.S.-style capitalism and managerialism. They want to adopt a "free-market" orientation in virtually all domains of life through emulation of and adherence to American-style practices including the "deregulation" (or rather reregulation) deemed necessary for this. These people are inclined to model local practices after U.S. exemplars and to mimic their American counterparts' work habits and lifestyles. Remarkably, this category also includes to a degree, since the early 1990s, New Labour and its Third Way in Britain and similar strains among Social Democrats elsewhere in Europe for whom America, or rather "an inspirational version of the United States," fulfills a significant role as role model and challenge (Ellwood 2004: 20; Nolan 2004).

The extreme right, which maintained a virulent strain of anti–Americanism, had lost much of its respectability in the mid-twentieth century and had been able to win influence only with difficulty — sometimes by disguising its views and/or joining the left *incognito*, sometimes by making tactical alliances with centrist or moderate rightist forces. However, in the 1980s a radical right reemerged in countries like France,[7] Italy, Germany, Austria and Belgium, among which were movements expressing anti–American views. The European New Right, whose leading theorist is France's Alain de Benoist, borrows heavily from radical conservatism in the Weimar era — embodied by figures like Ernst Jünger, Carl Schmitt, and Martin Heidegger — and ventilates sharp critiques of neoliberal globalization. New Right adherents attack economism, rationalism, multiculturalism, and the idea of universal human rights. They embrace Carl Schmitt's view that Anglo-American economics, rationalism, liberal institutions, and individualism destroy the cultural bases for coherent identity, social cohesion/community, and political unity, and let global capitalism wipe out cultural differences, culminating in a world of total cultural homogenization (Schmitt 1996). The New Right revives this tradition, couched in a postmodern racial identity politics that claims to defend the "right to difference" and resists cultural homogenization. The ideology of so-called "ethnopluralism" that its members hold is predicated on the idea that sending immigrants home counters globalization and saves indigenous cultures. The leading idea is that cultural survival depends on reclaiming governmental dominance over markets and empowering ethnic particularities as sites of resistance against homogenizing neoliberal globalization. From this perspective, European radical conservatives have called for federated ethnic states, with ethnically-based citizenship, trying to forge an authoritarian order that does away with liberal civil rights and excludes ethnic others. In extreme cases, they may even take recourse to reactionary tribalism and ethnic cleansing as happened in former Yugoslavia (Antonio and Bonanno 2000: 63–64).

At the turn of the millennium there was a sudden uprising of right-populist movements with some momentum even in Western European countries like Denmark, Sweden, and the Netherlands, moderate consensus democracies and welfare states assumed to be immune to such political extremism. Yet these movements do not tend to be anti–American but anti–Islamic and xenophobic towards immigrants and asylum seekers from developing countries. Some strains are even pro-American in some ways, cultivating a mixture of positive views of Americanization, including American dreams of ordinary people and those of neoliberals positively attuned to U.S. capitalism and managerialism. At the other end of the political spectrum we find leftist anticapitalist groups in Europe that are part of the "anti-globalization" movement (more adequately called "alternative globalization" movement) that emerged in the 1990s and are critical of America's dominance in globalizing corporate capitalism.

Last but not least, there is a growing group among the center-left after the cessation of the Cold War, that opposes political, military, and economic Americanization in response to conflicts about multilateralism, international law, and international institutions, about the use of force and the limits of sovereignty, about controlling arms and regulating the environment, and about varieties of capitalism and models of modernity. These disagreements, especially between Germany, France and the United States, predated the end of the Cold War, but the latter disciplined and contained such disputes (Nolan 2004: 30). This strain with negative views on Americanization became more pronounced in response to the more blatant unilateralism that the United States has demonstrated since September 11, 2001 and the "new American imperialism" driven by the blend of neoconservatism and radical neoliberalism espoused by the George W. Bush administration.

The following scheme represents the various discourses as they exist today, including some that were more influential at an earlier stage and are marginalized now. To be sure, these ideal types do not fit neatly in a political grid constructed in terms of right and left, revolutionary or reactionary. A humanistic approach, for example, is compatible with progressive or conservative views on a particular topic, although it usually excludes any kind of extremist or collectivist ideology.

Postmodernism is a special case, as its ideological and political significance has been much debated in relation to the nature of the Enlightenment project, as manifested in particular by the polemical exchange between Lyotard and Habermas (McLennan 1992). It has been suggested to distinguish between various postmodernisms (conservative and progressive or "constructive" versions), each with different aims and consequences in terms of historical agency, collective mobilization or transformative impact on social structures (Thompson 1992). Some of the discourses may overlap. Specific strains of postmodernism entail liberal-democratic elements, others are clearly of a radical libertarian bent. The recent center-left discourse includes liberal-democratic components, while defenders of a "culture nation" ideal may adhere to a nationalist extreme right discourse. Moreover, as with individuals, a particular group can at various moments in its "life history," or even simultaneously, hold conflicting views on the United States.

Today, discussions about Americanization are no longer restricted to Western Europe. From its origins in Britain, France and Germany, interest has spread to Eastern Europe, Australia, Canada, and to Latin America, the formerly colonized nations of Africa, and most noticeably in recent years, to parts of the Islamic world where America is seen as the diabolic opponent of everything that is good and valuable in life (Lewis 1990). The worldwide resurgence of movements and networks with a mission to pursue various kinds of Jihad — the Islamic version of a holy war — can be seen as direct responses by diverse groups who perceive Americanization and its attendant religion, Christianity, as a threat to unique ancient cultures and the revealed truths originating in divine inspiration (Cohen and Kennedy 2000: 363).

European intellectual ideas of America have also resounded in the United States itself, which is not something new but reaches back to the Republic's beginning and became almost an art form in the works of literary figures such as T.S. Eliot and Ezra Pound. But it is in the late twentieth century that such America discourse reached its

Major discourses on America in Western Europe
at the turn of the twenty-first century

Positive views

utopian (*libertarian*)	*postmodern*	*dreams of ordinary people*	*pro-U.S. capitalism and manager-ialism*	*liberal-democratic* (*Atlanticist*)

Negative views

(neo-)Marxist	*humanist*		*nationalist extreme right*
leftist strains in "*anti-globalization*" *movement*		*center-left against U.S. unilateralism, radical neoliberalism and neo-conservatism*	*defenders of* "*culture nation*" *ideal*

(author's elaboration of scheme in Mathy 1993: 9).

peak in the New World, when European thinking about America—particularly that of Heidegger as filtered through French philosophers such as Foucault, Baudrillard, Derrida and the like—became influential in the fields of literary and cultural studies and philosophy, as well as in cultural studies-inflected American studies (Ceaser 1997: 5–6).

DIFFERENT DISCOURSES ON CULTURAL AMERICANIZATION AND VIEWS OF MASS CULTURE/POPULAR CULTURE

In the European discourses about American influence abroad we can discern positive, negative, or ambivalent perspectives, and sometimes, albeit rarely, complete indifference. The historical record shows two extremes with regard to cultural Americanization: on the one hand a pessimistic perspective (America as dystopia) that suggests cultural imperialism and/or cultural leveling at work; and on the other, a libratory (utopian) perspective, often associated with an "Americanophile" tendency, that sees increased room to maneuver and psychological space for those involved in the process of change. Between these extremes lies a highly ambivalent discourse, in which both oppressive and liberating forces are recognized in America's impact overseas, whose exponents are differently attuned to various imports from the United States.[8]

The division between positive and negative discourses on cultural Americanization runs partly parallel with the distinction between mass culture and popular culture. Another way to think about this issue is to recognize the ambiguity, what Stuart Hall calls "the double stake," in popular culture, "the double movement of containment and resistance, which is always inevitably inside it. The study of popular culture has tended to oscillate wildly between the two alternative poles of that dialectic—containment/resistance" (Hall 1981: 228).[9] Those who refer to popular culture as mass culture want to indicate that popular culture is a highly commercial culture, which is mass-produced for mass consumption by a mass of non-discriminating consumers. They suppose it is a culture that is consumed passively and thoughtlessly. The term "mass culture" is being used in both political right and left versions of this cultural critique, and refers to the purported threat to the traditional aesthetic values of high culture in the first case and to the traditional way of life of a working class enthralled by mass culture's appeal (reinforcing or even raising "false consciousness") in the second. For many (but not all) critics of mass culture, it also often represents a threat to the national culture itself.

These fears and anxieties among critics of mass culture in Europe have been likewise triggered by the specter of Americanization, because American popular culture is seen to embody all that is wrong with mass culture. Mass culture is thought to be related to the mass production and consumption of cultural commodities and the United States tends to be identified as the cradle and home base of mass culture since this capitalist society is most closely associated with these processes. Because so much mass culture hails from America, Americanization is perceived as a threat as well. But, as we have seen earlier, concerns about the harmful effects of American cultural influence can already be found in the nineteenth century, before the arrival of mass production and consumption of culture on a massive scale (Strinati 1995: 22; Storey 1997: 10–12).

Aversion to mass culture was always greater among intellectuals, government officials, and members of the upper classes. However, representatives of European high culture have sometimes been more appreciative of American mass culture/popular culture than their counterparts in America. Illustrative examples abound including Picasso's affection for the Katzenjammer Kids cartoon strip; the celebration of American modernity by leftist German intellectuals such as Grosz and Brecht in their early careers; the veneration of the Hollywood film among French filmcritics and filmmakers that inspired the *nouvelle vague* in French films during the 1950s and '60s; the impact of Hollywood *film noir* on the French "new novel"; as well as the appreciation of modern fiction (particularly hard-boiled detective stories and "realistic" American novels à la Steinbeck)[10] by French writers such as Jean-Paul Sartre and Claude-Edmonde Magny (Ellwood et al. 1993: 331; Pells 1997: 243–258). Yet in the era of globalizing postmodernism, in which distinctions between high and popular culture are blurred and the recycling of earlier popular styles has accelerated, such cultural taste differences between European and American intellectuals seem to have evaporated.

At times, foreign critics of American mass-cultural influence have also been careful to acknowledge that there was much to admire in American culture, such as the passion for education, political idealism (at least in the ages of Wilson, Roosevelt and Kennedy), a spirit of self-help and patriotism, and a philanthropically-supported system of high-culture institutions. In Australia, for example, in the period before high culture was institutionalized in the form of permanently established orchestras, opera and ballet companies with the help of governmental subsidies, representatives of high culture would look enviously to America's philanthropically funded orchestras and art galleries (Waterhouse 1998: 52–53). In some respects, this is happening again today in several modern welfare states where the subsidized arts are suffering from cutbacks in governmental funding and some policymakers see American-style philanthropic support and corporate sponsorship as a possible way out of the financial problems they are faced with.

(American) *mass* culture is no mere chimera but to some extent a reality that must be seen in its appropriate time-place perspective. Foreigners within the U.S. cultural orbit tend to understand and consume "America" as a grand narrative of some kind — be it positive, negative, or otherwise — which they construct from available bits and pieces. This applies to the narrative about mass culture as well. Rather than from ignorance or lack of interest in the diversities of American culture, this tendency of representational homogenization may very well stem from the popular culture actually on offer at a given time, as John Clarke explains in a critical exposé on cultures of consumption in America. He refers to a recurrent theme in many studies of the relationship between class and ethnicity in the late nineteenth- and early twentieth-century formation of the American working class, which entailed the transition from localized class-ethnic cultural formations to a national mass culture embodied in the creation of mass media of entertainment (film and radio) and in the growth of systems of mass production, distribution and consumption (for example in clothing and food). These changes eroded the collective practices and identities of class-ethnic cultures and "created the overarching social identity of the American consumer" (Clarke 1991: 74). In other words, a certain "massification" of Americans and American society took place, suggesting salience regarding the notions of "mass culture" and "mass society," which should not be rejected out of hand as most critics of classic theories of mass culture tend to do.

In this connection, the distinction made by Michael Kammen between popular culture and mass culture is useful. He takes the basically participatory and social interactive character of the former as decisive criterion, locating the arrival of a national mass culture a few decades later than in Clarke's reconstruction. On the basis of his historical investigation, Kammen sees a development in the United States in which popular culture, that existed from the early colonial days in many forms, enjoyed its heyday during the half century after the mid–1880s, and then rapidly declined as its participatory and sociability elements diminished. Thus it turned into mass culture with a transitional period when both types of culture coexisted and were partly overlapping. He gives the following reasons why he considers the period from about 1885 to 1935 as an era when U.S. popular culture as defined here was most influential:

> First, because it was during this period that a notable growth of leisure time occurred. Second, because the commercialization of organized entertainment reached a whole new plateau previously unknown. Third, because innovations in transportation and technology made it possible for entrepreneurial amusements to reach audiences on an expanded scale. Fourth, because a gradual repudiation of the genteel tradition created opportunities for modes of social behavior and interaction that would have been unthinkable to most middle-class Americans in the age of Victorian polite culture. Fifth, because the distinctiveness of regional and local lifestyles still retained enough strength to resist the powerful surge of homogenization that accompanied what so many people in the later 1920 referred to as "standardization." And sixth, because the pervasive manifestations of popular culture in that era remained largely participatory and interactive, based upon certain modes of sociability that began to fade in the decades following World War II when mass culture as we know it emerged fully and subordinated popular culture by supplanting or else overwhelming much of it and then replicating it for audiences on a numerical scale previously unimagined [Kammen 2000: 70–71].

But Kammen rejects a neat evolutionary progression and allows for the simultaneous existence of both types of culture during certain periods. In his view, popular and mass culture overlapped by as much as a generation, and was "most notable and therefore difficult to disentangle" during the 1930s and '40s, a time of transition that he designates as "the pivotal era of proto-mass culture" (*ibid.*: 71). Particularly relevant for our purpose is, of course, that the forms of non-elitist culture exported abroad during Kammen's popular culture's heyday (1885–1935) were more likely to belong to mass culture than to popular culture (again as defined by Kammen). An important reason, in my view, is that through intensive interventions of cultural industries (especially from the 1920s onwards) these cultural goods and manifestations were then relatively more packaged, homogenized and divested of their vestiges of regional and local backgrounds. Thus most of the participatory character of U.S. popular culture forms were lost when they became detached from their roots during the transfer abroad. Although local people might create their own participatory forms in relation to the cultural imports (for example, indigenous subcultures around the stars of Hollywood films and other American celebrities, and around popular music such as Charleston and swing), these did not fully compensate the loss. The appearance of U.S. popular culture as "mass culture" abroad may also have been enhanced by the fact that, with the obvious exception of such phenomena as the reception of African-American jazz performers in Paris, foreigners did not always recognize the class, ethnic, and other specific origins of popular culture from the USA — they simply considered it all "American" (Ellwood et al. 1993: 331).

Whereas *a mass-cultural analysis* (in the conventional sense) sees cultural leveling (or "dumbing down," a more recent term), cultural imposition and in some versions, cultural imperialism at stake, *a popular-cultural analysis* tends to be more concerned with the ways in which the reception of American culture might provide a positive — a democratizing, libratory, pleasant or even utopian — frame of reference (McKay 1997: 20).[11] More generally this entails an approach in which, as John Storey puts it: "Texts and practices of popular culture are seen as forms of public fantasy. Popular culture is understood as a collective dream world" (Storey 1997: 12). Referring to Richard Maltby's claim that popular culture provides "escapism that is not an escape from or to anywhere, but an escape of our utopian selves" (Maltby 1989: 14), he suggests that, in this sense, popular culture practices such as Christmas and the seaside holiday "function in much the same way as dreams: they articulate in a disguised form collective (but suppressed and repressed) wishes and desires." Storey calls this "a benign version of the mass-cultural perspective" because, as Maltby has pointed out: "If it is the crime of popular culture that it has taken our dreams and packaged them and sold them back to us, it is also the achievement of popular culture that it has brought us more and more varied dreams than we could otherwise ever have known" (Maltby 1989: 14, qtd. in Storey 1997: 12).

This fits with the central argument — commonplace in critical cultural studies and history now — that popular culture is a contested terrain entailing a dialectic of containment and resistance, as outlined earlier, and that mass-cultural artifacts are simultaneously ideological and utopian. In the same vein, cultural Americanization possibly amounts to "coerseduction," a neologism coined by P.J. Ravault, used to indicate that this is a process involving both coercion and seduction. It introduces an ambiguous assessment of American influences as having both damaging and subversive, as well as progressive, potential. At stake are issues of "translation," which encompass processes of mediation, appropriation, and adaptation that determine the actual outcome of the process (Minganti 2000: 151).[12] As Fredric Jameson contended in his influential formulation of 1979,

> ... the works of mass culture cannot be ideological without at one and the same time being implicitly Utopian as well: they cannot manipulate unless they offer some genuine shred of content as a fantasy bribe to the public about to be so manipulated ... [E]ven if their function lies in the legitimation of the existing order — or some worse one — [they] cannot do their job without deflecting in the latter's service the deepest and most fundamental hopes and fantasies of the collectivity, to which they can therefore, no matter in how distorted a fashion, be found to have given voice [Jameson 1979: 144].

Referring to the appeal value of mass/popular culture, Stuart Hall wrote in a seminal essay published two years later: "If the forms of provided commercial popular culture are not purely manipulative, then it is because, alongside the false appeals, the foreshortenings, the trivialisations and shortcircuits, there are also elements of recognition and identification, something approaching a recreation of recognisable experiences and attitudes, to which people are responding" (Hall 1981: 233).[13]

Concerning the positive discourse on Americanization, and the implied appeal of American (popular) culture to foreigners, there are according to George McKay three ways in which the United States presents itself to or is constructed by people abroad: America is seen 1) as zone of liberation or democracy; 2) as locus of pleasure; and 3) as utopia — the construction of America as utopian space or fantasy zone. Of course, these are analytical distinctions — the representations/constructions in question overlap and interpenetrate in everyday life. The first variant concerns America's attraction to certain groups that is located in its cultural politics and democratizing impulse, which appear to offer more room to maneuver for non-elites than elsewhere. This includes a long-standing tendency among "ordinary people" abroad to consider U.S. society as a site of democracy that does not accept and even challenges the Eurocentric tradition of social and cultural hierarchy. Their perceptions also refer to an American tradition of creolization, a pervasive tendency to borrow freely, to dissect and mix all kinds of culture — in other words, a widespread freewheeling in the cultural domain, released from genteel control (Kroes 1993: 310; Ellwood et al. 1993: 323). This tradition is distinguished by a celebration of the vernacular, a recognition of higher meanings in plain cultural forms, moments of transcendence, of silent exaltation about its own creative capacity — for instance, with regard to political constructions such as the U.S. Republic or the American Constitution, technical miracles like the Brooklyn Bridge, the illumination of the Niagara waterfalls and similar encounters with the sublime. Another prime example is the poetry of Walt Whitman that honored ordinary men and women, celebrating their speech and manners. The attractiveness of these features to foreign popular culture audiences has been even greater at critical historical moments when democracy was at risk, or when social or cultural hierarchies were contested as happened in many European countries after World War II.

American popular culture's (perceived) "crudeness" in several of its variants and manifestations has added to its appeal abroad because of its stronger and more articulated challenge to cultural hierarchy (Kroes 1996a; McKay 1997: 36–37). A significant part of the export hits of American culture drew its appeal from popular traditions which were, and still to a degree are marginalized or even considered "non-culture" by the cultural elites of the United States. American popular culture in Europe, to a great extent, thrived on its "vulgarity" (Pattison 1987) and "primitiveness," "its indifference to the pretensions of art and philosophy" (Pells 1997: 241). Next to this "vulgar" tendency, there has been another important line of influence in popular culture, of course — that of mainstream entertainment carried by the American middle class: positive, smooth, family-oriented, morally beyond reproach. This characterizes, for example, most of the Hollywood films and the family sitcoms of the 1950s and early 1960s, as well as the neat teenage idols of the time who were in the musical tradition of Tin Pan Alley. Examples in the late twentieth century include TV series such as the *Bill Cosby Show* for a broader audience and *Beverly Hills 90210* for teenagers. The latter cultural expressions appealed to similar groups overseas as well.

Especially for youth, the "zone of liberation" of American popular culture was attractive precisely because its pleasures were unauthorized, and because its expressive forms were experienced as sensually expressive, shrill, unvarnished, enthralling and overwhelming — which could also be employed to articulate class and generational conflicts. Beginning in the 1920s (on a small scale), and from the 1940s onwards on a much larger scale, young people (and youthful middle-aged people) in Europe and elsewhere have identified with those elements in American society that appeared marginal, alienated, and tended to be linked to the taste preferences and the behavior repertoires of lower social classes and marginalized cultures in the United States itself. These included black jazz musicians, Beat writers, rock stars, "juvenile delinquents" (with iconic film actors like Marlon Brando and James Dean and their latter-day descendents), hippies and New Leftists in the 1960s, Native Americans in the 1970s, black rappers and members of hiphop culture in the 1980s and 1990s, black baseball players and so forth. What they had in common was that they differed culturally and stylistically from the "complacent" European middle class, and embodied the adolescent spirit of disaffection and imprudence expressed through provocative casualness and dress styles.

At the background here is the fact that, in the multicultural society of the United States cultural exchange continuously took place between the dominant white, Anglo-Saxon, mainly Protestant Americans (since the mid-twentieth century a broader Euro-American, Christian population) and the various ethnic and regional minorities. These exchanges occurred most intensely with the African-American population, although increasingly during the past few decades with the Latino populations too (Maase 1992: 29; van Elteren 1996b: 70–71; Pells 1997: 241–242). As Hannerz rightfully contends, "The subcultures of young and liminal white Americans during much of the twentieth century could hardly have taken the forms they did without a notion of Black culture, understood as involving a fundamentally, existentially superior approach to life; the hardline culture of poverty concept turned upside down" (Hannerz 1992b: 79). Consequently, Maase's assertion is much to the point when he suggests that "Afro-Americanization [or rather African-Americanization] of popular culture" might be a better term than "Americanization" for these particular processes in Europe (Maase 1992: 23) and, I would add, elsewhere in the world.

In the second variant of constructions of America sounds, images and presentations of America do not just give pleasure, they *signify pleasure*. The attractiveness of American rock music in postwar Europe, for example, was to a great part predicated on its transmission of an "aesthetics of sensuousness," a secondary system of meaning that implied physical and symbolic deciphering, and evoked the utopia of a distant America (Wicke 1990: 48). As Simon Frith has pointed out, "America, as experienced in films and music, has itself become the object of consumption, a symbol of pleasure" (Frith 1983: 46). Accordingly, as Duncan Webster has indicated, audiences who are familiar with these audiovisual materials and American *mises-en-scène*, recognize the scenes and images, and derive visual pleasure from them, "implying a narrative promise of excitement and suspense" (Webster 1988: 200). Also relevant is that much talk about American popular music revolves around visions of an imaginary America, as so much of this music relates to cinema as well as landscape. Reference to films is part of American music's resonance, whether that is through associations with an American landscape, or direct allusion, or even actual involvement. Webster also mentions a further link between American songwriting that lies in the economy of genre, or what is gained from revisiting similar characters, settings and themes though their accumulated connotations (*ibid.*: 162–163).[14] One important current of representation of America of course is the (misconceived) history of the West. In advertising, for example, America is represented through an appeal to popular myths of its own Western history, and through the iconography of its Western landscapes (Farber 1994). Through visual advertising, people abroad "are invited to consume not just an American product but 'America' itself" (Webster 1988: 228). In *Watching Dallas* (1985), Ien Ang suggested that these signs of American pleasure are so dominant in today's globalizing world that they more or less function as signs of *universal* visual pleasure. But this view is problematic because it overlooks variations in America's appeal value abroad including dislikes and outright rejections, of course. Furthermore, its attraction may obtain a distinctive character because of specific local conditions.

The picaresque theme in all kinds of American popular culture is of particular relevance here. As I have argued elsewhere (with regard to citizens of old-style welfare states in Northwestern Europe at the time), the strain of limitless, expressive individualism in American society (Bellah et al. 1985) and the "loose-boundedness" embedded in much of U.S. popular culture (Merelman 1984) have been irresistible to particular audiences in societies that they see and experience as too regulated and over organized.[15] For locals under its spell, "America" then represents the antipode of a predictable, dull and boring society. In this mythological reality of "the land of unlimited opportunities" one feels free from everyday worries, from restrictions set by existing societal structures. We are likely to find an Americanophilia here that is the expression of a yearning for wide open spaces (physically and mentally), novelty, vital energy, and freedom of action (van Elteren 1996a: 143–144).[16] This is — among other things — well illustrated by the *imaginary Americas* cultivated by members of various European youth subcultures in the 1950s and 1960s and beyond. The images, fantasies and myths about a more exciting reality and a life full of "kicks"— which might be quite differently framed and interpreted by teddy boys, middle-of-the-road teenagers, beatniks, mods,[17] hippies — offered them starting-points to escape from (in their eyes) the triviality and monotony of everyday life, at least in their imagination, allowing them to enjoy life more intensively. Given the constraints and opportunities of their specific youth culture, thus they all tried to practice a version of the adage: "I'm free and I do what I want" (van Elteren 1989).

The last variant concerns the attraction of U.S. (popular) culture in terms of the construction of America as an utopian space, or fantasy zone, in which any of our desires would be fulfilled. People then use "America" positively as a projection screen for their own images and fantasies: "['America'] becomes what we are not, what we want it to be, what *we* want to be. It does not matter whether this bears any similarity to *the real thing*" (McKay 1997: 40, italics in original). This concerns "America" as represented and experienced in people's utopian fantasies, a projection of their imaginings that hardly corresponds with the "real" America, whatever that may be. This goes beyond the obvious point that the versions of America on offer to foreign audiences contain misrepresentations; in fact we are dealing with "America" as constructed by producers and consumers of U.S. culture which entails myths, fantasies, and other ascriptions and projections. It is a space that non-Americans design in the image of their own subjective desires. This happened very pronouncedly, for example, in Soviet Russia where there was a lack of information and authentic experience of America because of the Iron Curtain. Russians had to satisfy their curiosity with an imagined America (Ostrovsky 1993: 71). But even in places such as Western Europe where such information and experience was (and remains) more widespread, America was (is) constructed and imagined.

In recent history, the counterculture of the 1960s and early 1970s is one of the most obvious "clusters of cultural moments and movements" to come to mind when thinking of Americanization as constituting a discourse of liberation (McKay 1997: 41).[18] Considering the postwar period leading up to the sixties and the counterculture, the overseas influence and inspiration of expressive and social movements in America is evident. A

wide range of social and cultural ideas and practices that were emulated abroad originated in the alternative values and worldviews of these U.S. countermovements. These
include the aesthetics and cultural politics of the Popular Front of the 1930s and 1940s
that lived on as a subterranean culture (including folk music, blues and jazz) after its defeat
as a political movement by 1948, partly overlapping with the subculture of the Beats; the
civil rights movement and the struggle for racial equality; leftist student activism; the
anti–Vietnam War movement; second-wave feminism; environmental concerns and action;
gay rights (Aronowitz 1993: 131–166; Denning 1996: 110–114; van Elteren 1999). Concepts of an "other" or "alternative" America thus received much attention in those years.
An intriguing example is the European student movement of the sixties, insofar as this
was a counterpart of the American New Left. Ironically, these rebellious students,
influenced by the alternative America concerned, often considered themselves "anti–
American," a term that the mainstream media also used to label them. Strictly speaking,
this was an inappropriate term that obscured the fact that many of these Europeans
protesting against the war in Vietnam and American imperialism were inspired by the
ideals and cultural expressions of the American New Left and counterculture. What was
considered anti–American should rather have been called anti the American political
establishment. The concept of anti–Americanism rested on assumptions about U.S. culture as a monolith — assumptions plainly contradicted by the protestors' own U.S.-inflected
lifestyles (Schou 1992: 143–145).

Yet we must be aware that the broad, heterogeneous movement toward "liberation"
only partly originated in the United States and as a radical project was only partly brought
to fruition there. Moreover, much of the "underground" culture of rock festivals and
"alternative" lifestyles was soon commodified and incorporated into mainstream American culture as a form of hip consumerism (Frank 1997). In the 1960s, European youth
embraced (progressive) American causes by holding local anti–Vietnam and anti–U.S.
imperialism protests outside American embassies or consulates. But they also extended
the progressive student movement by linking up to student radicalism elsewhere, particularly in France in 1968. Nevertheless, the orientation on the American discourse of liberation, couched in the *lingua franca* of globalizing U.S. popular culture, persisted. The
1980s peace movement in Europe employed American symbols and strategies against
America, or rather the military and nuclear presence of the United States on European
territories, thereby also drawing inspiration from earlier Civil Rights rhetoric and practice. This dualistic attitude towards America among foreign audiences — simultaneously
embracing its popular culture and criticizing the United States as an imperialist, oppressive power — was enforced, among other things, by American movies about the Vietnam
war in a complex way. For instance, foreign publics turned the new icon Rambo into a
symbol of anti–American demonstrations at the time of the Cruisile missile debate in
Europe, and these films also inspired first or renewed discussions of war atrocities perpe-
trated by European powers in their own colonial eras. Similarly, non-violent direct action
by 1990s eco-warriors in Britain was in part an emulation and then extension of activist
groups like Earth First! from the United States in this country (Ellwood et al. 1993: 329;
McKay 1997: 43–44).

Among intellectuals, late-twentieth century European visions of America as an
utopian (or rather dual utopian/dystopian) space can be found in the works of the Italian semiologist Umberto Eco (1986) and the French post-structuralist philosopher Jean
Baudrillard (1986) that depict America as the pre-eminent embodiment of postmodernity and future of the rest of the world. "Once more," as Bradbury contended, "it is pos-

sible to go to America in order to see more than America, to travel in hyper-reality." And again, this — now "postmodern" — America "is not so much different as exemplary — the ultimate case of that state of multiplied simulacra, semiotic excess, virtual reality, extravagant fantasy in which much of the world thinks it now lives" (Bradbury 1995: 463–464).

Ultimately, all three variants of constructions of America entail a search by foreigners for a social and/or cultural space of their own by imaginations of, and selective borrowings from, a foreign entity: "America." Later in this book I shall return to this fundamental paradox and consider its implications regarding structural determination, cultural imposition and disempowerment on the one hand and agency, liberation, and empowerment on the other.

3

U.S. Engagements with Americanism and Americanization Until the Early 1930s

This chapter focuses on the working history of the relevant concepts in the domains of politics, labor, immigration and assimilation in America prior to the New Deal Era. It aims to unpack the variegated usage of the term "Americanism" as a discursive term to indicate a specific patriotic notion about the nation's identity and ideals. Important in this context are the diverse deployments of the term "Americanization" with regard to assimilation of both new immigrants during successive periods of American history and, ironically enough, Native Americans in the late nineteenth and early twentieth centuries. The mainstream Americanization programs in the first two decades of the century get due attention, as do the critics of these programs, adherents of various forms of ethnic pluralism and cultural cosmopolitanism. Finally, the preoccupations with Americanism and "becoming American" among labor and the left until the early 1930s are examined.

EARLY USAGES OF THE TERMS "AMERICA" AND "AMERICANIZATION"

During most of the time the European debates about Americanism and Americanization took place in relative isolation of those in the United States. Within the U.S. context, "Americanism" usually referred to a patriotic political philosophy. The term has been in use from the very beginning of the nation. In a letter he wrote in 1797, Thomas Jefferson referred to "parties" who "have in debate mutually charged each other ... with being governed by attachment to this or that of the belligerent nations, rather than the dictates of reason and pure Americanism" (*A Dictionary of Americanisms* 1966: 27). This is Americanism in the sense of "a love of America and preference of her interests," as defined in Webster's 1906 Dictionary, which, in Jefferson's time, of course, meant the interests of the American colonists who had revolted against Britain (Wilson 1957: 29).

Americanism in its populist version meant principally understanding and obeying the will of the people. "Whether asserting the claims of a putatively egalitarian community or the rights of individuals against the state, it was the majority with its love of liberty that must decide. To mock the opinions and/or oppose the interests of the majority was more than foolish politics; it was un-American" (Kazin 1998: 12). Thus, American politicians, leaders of trade unions, social and religious movements, and other movers and shakers were obliged to make "populism" an integral part of their strategies if they wanted to become and remain successful. As historian Michael Kazin has pointed out in his depiction of the populist heritage in the antebellum years, Americanism was the first element in the shared language of politics:

> This was the creed for which independence had been won and that all genuine patriots would fight to preserve. it was breathtakingly idealistic: in this unique nation, all men were created equal, deserved the same chance to improve their lot, and were citizens of a self-governing republic that enshrined the liberty of the individual. It was also proudly defensive: America was an isolated land of virtue whose people were on constant guard against the depredations of aristocrats, empire builders, and self-agrandizing officeholders both within and outside its borders [Kazin 1998: 12].

But "Americanism" did not always have this aura of Republican reason and the connotation of America as a democratic beacon to the world. Its meaning has been contested at various times — particularly during periods of crisis and severe societal conflicts — and it was sometimes abused by chauvinist, xenophobic or racialist groupings.

"Americanization" in the United States originates from a context of domestic pressures towards a consensual society and shared cultural-political identity. The label "Americanization" was originally applied to the anticipated assimilation of immigrants and racial minorities to the dominant culture or, more formally, to qualities demanded of territories seeking statehood. In each of those contexts, Americanization concerned broadly "a process by which an alien acquires our language, citizenship, customs and ideals," as a contemporary analyst of the Americanization movement of the early twentieth century put it (Hill 1919: 612). Initially, the term "Americanization" referred to "the acquisition of American mores by individual European immigrants," which also remains the standard usage in the United States today (White 1983: 109), but it now pertains to immigrants coming from all parts of the world. Although the term has been used in a rather neutral way, it often obtained assimilationist overtones, at times of a very directive nature.

"Americanization" gained a pronouncedly coercive meaning in the context of campaigns of forced assimilation of Native Americans to Euro-American values and lifestyles. Furthermore, as America's continental expansion progressed, territories seeking statehood were accepted at least ostensibly because they were permeated with American traditions and ideals (Bell and Bell 1998: 1–2). But the further spread of Americanization did not halt at the nation's continental borders. Especially since the 1890s, ideals of national mission and economic self-interest drove the United States further outwards. "Americanization" then came to refer to America's influence abroad (first debated by Europeans), which from America's leading perspective entailed a "universalization" of its Americanization mission. Let us now look at the major developments in Americanization at home.

EXCLUSIONARY POLITICAL MEANING
DURING THE MID–NINETEENTH CENTURY

During the 1840s and 1850s, Americanism took on a highly restrictive political meaning. This occurred in the context of nativist moral panics evoked by massive immigration and the sudden growth of the Catholic population beginning in the 1830s, which was experienced as eroding the Protestant religion — an integral part of American identity. The American or Know-Nothing party was organized in the 1850s to exclude all foreign-born citizens from office, to discourage immigration, and to "keep America pure." It employed the term "Americanism" to indicate its own policy, on the East Coast, of fighting the Roman Catholicism of German and Irish immigrants, and trying to prevent persons of foreign birth from exercising political rights until they had lived in the United States for twenty-one years. On the West Coast, the Know-Nothing Party usually targeted the Chinese (Ong Hing 1997: 17).

In those years, the words "Americanize," "Americanizing," and "Americanization" were commonly used to refer to the recognized urgent need that the immigrants become assimilated to American life. The word "Americanization" in this sense appeared first (sometime after 1854) in a published article in *Brownson's Quarterly* by Orestes A. Brownson (a Vermon Yankee by birth, himself the most prominent of a group of notable American converts to Catholicism), who opened the first Catholic debate on Americanization, and took a strongly assimilationist position. However, there was disagreement as to precisely what the process entailed. The Irish, being called on by Brownson to Americanize, retorted by publicly asking what pattern of Americanism they should conform to — that of New England, Virginia, or Kentucky. They also asserted that some forms of Americanization, such as indulging in heedless materialism and "mammon-worship," were unwholesome.

More generally, the ultimate goal of Americanization has always been a site of contestation. Of course, the central question that looms at the background here concerns national identity, just what it means to become or to be an American. Some have interpreted true Americanism strictly, as requiring close conformity to the dominant culture in terms of language, religion, and manners, while others have taken a more liberal position about the range of variation that could be accommodated within the national identity. In the late nineteenth century, along with rising controversies about the melting pot, the former view obtained the upper hand, as more Americans became convinced that the nation's declining level of social cohesion and solidarity demanded social intervention.

This shift was partly instigated by the increasingly visible presence of the "new immigrants" from Eastern and Southern Europe who crowded into the cities. They were seen as more alien than earlier immigrants in their language and cultural patterns, and easily associated with social unrest, strikes, and urban problems such as crime and slum housing. Established groups, whose self-definition was based on an Anglo-Saxon (or at best, Northern and Western European) line-of-descent narrative, feared that the nation would fall apart because these new immigrants threatened the dominant culture of America. At issue was also an increasingly influential Anglo-Saxon racialism among the elites that entailed a more ethnically restrictive, Anglo-Saxon version of the American national identity.

Thus it became easier to persuade the general public that the newcomers needed more systematic assistance in adopting the beliefs and values of the "old-stock" Americans. Those with ethnocentrist, if not racist beliefs interpreted Americanism in narrow terms and saw a need for Americanization to protect the national identity from the dangers posed by the massive immigration at the time. Others, however, were driven by a more positive motivation to assist the immigrants in adjusting to the unfamiliar and often harsh conditions of life they encountered in America. This group represented a continuation of an older tradition of cosmopolitanism in American culture. The Americanization movement contained both of these strains, but as it developed from the late 1890s to the early 1920s the former emphasis became much more influential, eventually giving the whole movement a predominantly repressive and nativistic character (Gleason 1982: 77, 84–85; Kaufmann 2004: 18–19, 24–29). This movement coincided partly with the assimilation movement regarding Native Americans that started around 1880 and lasted until the early 1930s, to which we turn first.

"Civilizing the Indians"

During the first several hundred years of Euro-American presence on the continent, whites treated the Native Americans as a problem, to be resolved, at least temporarily, by separation rather than assimilation. The Western frontier, which served more generally as an outlet or safety valve for societal energies and problems, served as repository for the displaced tribes. A benevolent rhetoric of blending in the sense of close physical interaction and mixing between Euro-Americans and Indians also already existed at an early stage of the nation's development. It figured prominently in Jefferson's view of future America that he outlined in 1803, prior to the Lewis and Clark expedition (1804–1806), meant to find the fabled Northwest Passage. But so did the idea of forced relocation to barren lands and mountain areas in the far West of those Native Americans who would hold out (Gilman 2003: 60–61). The policy towards Native Americans that Jefferson conceived was carried to ruthless extremes by President Andrew Jackson; eastern Indian tribes that stood in the way of western settlement were coaxed or forced to migrate to territories west of the "Permanent Indian Frontier," marked by a line of military posts that had been erected after Jefferson's Louisiana Purchase (Utley 1994: 40, 42). This Indian relocation was primarily designed to open Indian lands and secure state jurisdiction, but, at least in theory, it was also designed to provide a working basis for inculcating the tribes with the essentials of white civilization. The missionary efforts at education, Christianization and economic transformation being made then were interrupted by the Manifest Destiny of the 1840s and beyond.

By the 1870s, the frontier, in the sense of good, rich, available and cheap public lands, was closing. The presence of the tribes concentrated on reserved land then became a major problem for the white American society, especially when the lands that Indians were living on appeared valuable, of vital logistic importance and under-utilized from the perspective of mining companies and white settlers. Despite the fact that Native Americans were born on lands over which the United States claimed sovereignty, an 1884 Supreme Court ruling declared that Native Americans were not native-born U.S. citizens. Instead they were juridicially considered to be "wards" inhabiting "domestic dependent nations." In those years, the federal government embarked on endeavors to make them U.S. citizens.[1] This led to the assimilation movement that in theory sought to induce a blending of the cultures but whose actual practice was quite different — certainly not the mixing of equals. Rather, in following coercive assimilation strategies, the movement aimed first to shatter the tribal societies, then incorporate the reduced components of Native-American cultures, into the alleged melting pot of the mainstream American society. This "Americanization" comprised a comprehensive assault on every aspect of Indian culture — property, economic structure, language, appearance, religion, political forms, values, and Indian world view (Ragsdale 1989: 399–400; Wolfley 1991, qtd. in Smith 1993: 562).

Conquests in the West coincided with the rise of the Indian reform groups in the East. By the end of the 1880s, their ideas about the Indians' salvation had been largely incorporated into federal policy. Their programs, for the most part, were not new; some went back to colonial times, others to president Ulysses S. Grant's (1869–1876) Peace Policy, but a new element was that the conquest was by now so complete that the reservations offered enclosed laboratories to carry out the intended social experiments without serious challenge, because unceded territories or independent tribes roaming across the prairies no longer complicated the process (Utley 1994: 254). The 1887 Dawes General Allotment Act gave the crucial impetus to these efforts. It reassigned tribal lands — that is, reservations were broken up and the land allocated in severalty and in acreage amounts that paralleled those available under the various U.S. homesteading provisions — and extended U.S. citizenship to individual Native Americans, with the proviso, however, that they could only acquire full land rights (and hence obtain full citizenship) after a 25-year period of federal trusteeship. It was certainly no coincidence that the act, typically allotting families 160 acres and single adults 80 acres, also made huge areas of "surplus" tribal lands (two-thirds of the area in question) available to white settlers, gold or silver diggers, and others, soon to be followed by mining and other extractive industries.

The assimilation movement was not monolithic in ideology or constituency. It consisted of a blend of motivations and philosophies, including ethnocentrism and racism, self-interest and greed for Indian lands, expediency and pragmatism, a need to proselytize, altruism, paternalism and moral uplift, and a corresponding mixture of proponents. The overall tendency was clear, however. To U.S. officials, humanitarian reformers, and most other Euro-Americans active in this domain, preparing Native Americans for citizenship meant Americanization in the sense of "civilizing" them, that is, "displacing their traditional religions, family structures, and systems of subsistence, landholding, and tribal governance with Christianity, heterosexual monogamy, and self-sufficient farming on individually held lands, thereby ending tribal existences" (Ragsdale 1989: 412–413; cf. Smith 1993: 561–562; Utley 1994: 244, 254).

In short, this assimilation aimed to replace the central beliefs and practices of a tribal society with Euro-American societal and religious values and practices attuned to their situation. The white reformers sought to instill the mentality of competitive individualism in Native Americans, casting out the communalistic, cooperative orientation of tribal life. They emphasized respect for private property, especially land. The assimilationist movement, spearheaded by Christian reformers, held the view that tribal deities had to be replaced with the Christian God. American evangelicals distinguished themselves in part by an emphasis on individual salvation, which paralleled, in theory and practice, the concepts of economic individualism. At the end of the nineteenth century evangelical Protestantism and the policies of the national government — social, economic, political and legal — had almost completely merged, to the point that it entailed a "Protestant hegemony" as Francis Paul Prucha, a Catholic historian and Jesuit Priest, has called it (Prucha 1985: 59). This front of institutionalized Christian individualism contrasted sharply with tribal religions harboring the belief that there was no salvation except for the continuance of the tribe itself (Ragsdale 1989: 404–405).

The Americanization movement also aimed at a substitution of a growth-oriented orientation — with its emphasis on progress, speed, efficiency and profit — for native values geared to the subsistence societies of the New World and ecological balance. It included the attempt to turn Native Americans into modern consumers, coupled with an emphasis on the veneration of private ownership, as the underlying component of the competitive ideal. The leader of an American reform group, the Friends of Indians, Merrill Gates, proclaimed in 1896 that, as reformers addressing the "uncivilized Indian," they would have to induce in him the necessary psychological condition: "We have, to begin with, the absolute need of awakening in the savage Indian broad desires and ampler wants. To bring him out of savagery into citizenship we must make the Indian more intelligently selfish before we can make him unselfishly intelligent" (qtd. in Ragsdale 1989: 404). But to evoke such wants and then to offer for sale the commodities to satisfy those wants was, of course, not a strategy of Americanization addressed only to the relatively small number of Native Americans. On a much broader basis, in the first several decades of the twentieth century, it was a strategy that, according to many commentators, had emerged as the central dynamic of a process that would lead to the "Americanization of the world." This entailed more generally a psychological, cultural, and commercial approach, aimed at inculcating in the individual desires for pleasure and happiness to be satisfied in the capitalist marketplace (Matthews 1998: 15–16).

Tribal cultures were suppressed by direct regulation of certain aspects of Native American behavior. The Department of the Interior, the Commissioner of Indian Affairs, Bureau of Indian Affairs administrators and Reservation agents restricted hair length, limited funeral practices, meat slaughtering techniques, Indian dances, plural marriages and certain sexual customs, as well as religious practices. Moreover, Indian police and Indian courts, installed to maintain order on the reservations, were also influential in rooting out features of the old ways of life judged "barbarous" or "heathenish" or otherwise at odds with civilized life. These institutions, staffed by tribal members, did not enforce indigenous tribal law, but instead implemented codes of Indian offenses that prohibited many traditional cultural and religious practices (Ragsdale 1989: 407–409; Utley 1994: 254).

Federal authorities targeted young Native Americans for a thorough modification of their values in a ferocious attempt to destroy the "inferior" Native American cultures at their roots. Forced assimilation of youths through highly disciplinary education at reservation day schools and reservation boarding schools played a pivotal role. This education was aimed at learning (better) English at the expense of one's native language, acquiring white manners, gender-bound vocational skills and work habits deemed necessary for the Indians' societal adjustment, as well as inculcating patriotic American citizenship. For the same purpose, beginning in the late 1870s with the small Indian Division at the Normal and Agricultural Institute (founded in 1868, originally an all-black school) in Hampton, Virginia and the Carlisle School for Indians in Pennsylvania, opened in 1879, numerous Indian children were placed in white-led, off-reservation boarding schools. These were set up — often by religious denominations — under government contract to remove these children from the influence of their families in order to disrupt the traditional process of cultural transmission from generation to generation (Gilman 2003: 331).

By 1900, ten percent of Native American children were placed in 307 industrial boarding schools modeled on Carlisle, and spread across the country. More pupils went to day schools than to boarding schools, but the boarding-school ethos to remove children from their families and communities influenced both. The ethic of Native American kinship, based on extended families and physical proximity, was at right angles with the individualism promoted in the Americanizing education process. Native American parents were pressured and coerced into sending their children away to boarding schools under threat of withholding food, clothing, or money. Some children would have come willingly and with the approval of their parents though. There were also children who may have entered these schools to escape intolerable conditions at home — for them the school environment may have offered a relatively safe haven from parents who threatened to harm their children, but their numbers are undetermined. Reluctant children were hunted down and physically transported to schools against their will. At these schools they were isolated for up to eight years and not permitted to see their families. They were not allowed to wear native clothing, speak their own languages, practice native customs, or even keep their own names. They were punished and even beaten for transgressions (Ragsdale 1989: 409–410; Trennert 1990: 224–230; King 2005: 27). The latter was, however, how children in orphanages in general were treated — "spare the rod and spoil the child."

These policies were defended by the same racialist theories that legitimated patronizing Anglo-Saxon governance of "lower races" abroad. In the minds of many politicians and legislators, Native American assimilation and imperialist policies (such as those regarding the Philippines) were closely linked, therefore they usually gave support to both (Williams 1980). In their eyes the process of Americanization assumed relevance too for the annexed peoples of Puerto Rico and the Philippines (a result of victory in the Spanish-American War of 1898), just as it did for new immigrants from Europe. While the expectation with regard to Native Americans and European immigrants was that education would provide a smooth route to assimilation (though actual practice was very different for the former), African Americans were considered to be unassimilable to the dominant polity and therefore excluded from any Americanization efforts. The annexed peoples were placed in an intermediary position and subjected to actions, justified as "benevolent assimilation" by U.S. nation-builders, in the form of "a halfhearted regime of Americanizing education" (King 2005: 22, 25, 32–36).

With the emergence of centralized federal management and the gradual closing of the public domain for further settlement, leading to a decline of private access to Native American lands, the impetus for the assimilation programs diminished accordingly. The movement also stagnated in part because of the emergence of a racist perspective in the early twentieth century, which assumed that Native Americans could not attain the levels of accomplishment of the white race. (This view was partly inspired by new scientific studies that challenged the concept of social evolution and seemed to bolster a thesis of variations in the inherent capabilities of different races.) Probably more important factors that contributed to the abandonment of the assimilation programs were the waning of religious transcendent ethics along with an increasing secularization of society, and a greater tolerance for cultural pluralism. The rise of cultural relativism in anthropology, at right angles with the abovementioned racist view, conceived of tribalism as a significant cultural form that could and should be preserved. Anthropological field studies of Indian life and customs became popular among the general public and contributed to a broader awareness of the depth, complexity, and uniqueness of the Native American cultures and the threat posed by the ongoing policies of assimilation. This created a constituency for the preservation of living cultures instead of their eradication.

The assimilation campaigns would last until the New Deal era, when laws were passed that ended most assimilation policies, at least for the time being, and began, instead, a period of preservation and promotion of tribalism (Ragsdale 1989: 422–427).[2]

THE MAINSTREAM AMERICANIZATION MOVEMENT AT THE TURN OF THE TWENTIETH CENTURY

At the end of the nineteenth century, cultural pressure to conform to the manners and mores of the dominant culture was intensified by new patriotic rituals of Americanization. For example, to celebrate the Columbus quadricentennial in 1892, President Benjamin Harrison declared October 12 a national holiday and instituted the Pledge of Allegiance. And in 1898, one day after the United States declared war on Spain, New York decided that students must recite the pledge daily — soon followed by other states (Gitlin 1995: 52, 247 n 52). All across the nation a practice evolved of playing the national anthem at sports and school events and the reciting of the Pledge of Allegiance in schools. Self-conscious efforts of "self-Americanization" emerged, which were driven by a nationalist longing for an authentic indigenous culture, often accompanied by national cultural protectionism — even though such endeavors could not do without borrowing from foreign sources altogether. Such attempts were made, for example, in the field of classical music within the broader context of the nationalistic Americanization movement in the first two decades of the twentieth century (see further below). This happened after U.S. cultural critics had for decades exposed the "Teutonization" (Germanification) of the American musical scene, while regretting American people's seeming inability to come up with their own artistic creations. Their resistance was part of a larger-scale rejection of European culture, if not European cultural imperialism, which reflected a growing weariness of universalist, transnational and internationalist movements and ideals among American journalists, politicians, trade unionists and intellectuals. At precisely the time when people elsewhere began feeling threatened by the "Americanization of the world," with European intellectuals leading the way, Americans themselves were just as obsessed if not more so about national cultural identity (Gienow-Hecht 2004: 35–36, 49–50).

Powerful pressures for "Americanization" of Americans were articulated publicly by intellectuals, presidents and high-ranking government officials. It was Theodore Roosevelt who most strongly popularized the term "Americanism" at the turn of the twentieth century. He coined and propagated the expressions "100 Percent Americanism" (as normative ideal) and "hyphenated Americans" (a category of people to be denounced if they did not melt into the American crucible) and returned to the subject time and again. Taking the motto *E Pluribus Unum* (one out of many) as the organizing principle of nation-building quite literally, he phrased it in a most coercive way: "There can be no fifty-fifty Americanism in this country ... there is room here only for 100 per cent Americanism, only for those who are American or nothing else" (qtd. in Toinet 1990: 219).While his Progressivism expanded and enriched American civic nationalism, Roosevelt's conception of American nationhood was also racialist. He celebrated racial hybridity, believing that what he saw as the world's "most accomplished races"— the British, the Americans, and the Australians — derived their strength from the blending of diverse and complementary racial strains. Roosevelt was constantly in search of situations in which different ethnic groups of Americans could be brought together in crucibles, mixed with each other, and molded into one people. In his eyes, war was the most important crucible, for the stress and dangers of combat generated pressures to unify and solidarize that no peacetime endeavor could attain. Yet Roosevelt's conception of the melting pot was racially inflected. His exemplary crucibles concerned the uniting of disparate groups of Euro-Americans into one American people and always excluded one or more non-Caucasian races — usually blacks, often Asians and Native Americans (Gerstle 2001: 6, 15–16).

Thus Roosevelt combined a relatively inclusive concept of whiteness with an aggressive commitment to a white supremacist nation. At least publicly, Roosevelt did not view Southern and Eastern Europeans as racially separate and inferior.[3] But like most other right-leaning Progressives, Roosevelt had a low regard for the immigrants' cultural heritages, and had a strong desire to inculcate in them the allegedly superior mores of his conception of America's hybridized lead culture. In exchange for inclusion and equal treatment as native-born Americans, European immigrants had to become Americanized. They should give up their names, native languages, cultural traits, and any political views that were at odds with U.S. patriotic loyalty. Many other Progressives did not publicly express severe racial stereotypes or endorse coercive Americanization, but nevertheless saw the dissolution of ethnic cultures and their replacement by a thoroughly American identity as one of the most important tasks of Progressivism (Roosevelt 1923; Gerstle 1994: 1051; Berlet and Lyons 2000: 81–82).

The Americanization movement in the first two decades of the twentieth century developed in three stages. The first extended from around 1900 to 1914; the second covered the years of World War I, and the third the years immediately afterwards. In the first phase, the more parochial nationalist strain was represented by such patriotic groups as the Daughters of the American Revolution (DAR) and by the Boston-based North American League for Immigrants. This kind of Americanization implied forced assimilation to one cultural pattern, that of the dominant Anglo-Saxon whites. The more cosmopolitan strain included settlement-house workers, advocates of the Social Gospel, and others committed to Progressivism and its preoccupation with individual virtue and vice. Progressives were bent on reforming individuals and improving character. While immigrants were to be educated in the ways of American democracy, civil servants were to be made honest and efficient; young women were to be saved from prostitution and young men from drink. These character-building goals gave rise to crusades for Americanization, "good government," social hygiene, and Prohibition, which were considered to be necessary stepping stones to creating the unified moral community that Progressives aimed for (Gerstle 1994: 1044). All progressive Americanizers stressed the need for protective legislation for immigrants and looked positively upon the cultural contributions the new immigrants could make to American life.

Differences in approach and shifts in emphasis became especially manifest in the area of education. "Americanization" as practiced, for example, in New York City public schools entailed a deliberate intervention strategy to prevent recent immigrants from identifying with those of similar national origin — including their families (*sic*) — and to encourage them to identify instead with American ideals. But the problem was that these ideals had to be formulated on the spot, specifically for the project of Americanization, against the presumed ideals and characteristics of the new immigrants (Gleason 1982: 85–86, 106–107; Bérubé 1994: 226). As Marcus Klein writes in *Foreigners*, "immigration prompted invention of 'Americanization,' and Americanization in turn prompted the invention of a set of terms by which America could be regarded as having some kind of predefinition. The terms of the predefinition were potentially meaningful, obviously, by the amount that they distinguished Americans from immigrants" (Klein 1981: 28, qtd. in Bérubé 1994: 226). The Americanness implied in this Americanization was a fiction, as even its most fervent proponents — cultural leaders from the East Coast with the power to set the national agenda — had to acknowledge. They knew full well that the nation was a social construction and that no single national character formed the basis of it. A significant part of this project of "inventing" a national character to be imprinted on immigrants was the institutionalization of American literature in public schools as a narrative of Puritan origins and high moral destiny. Nina Baym has called this a "Whig project of installing New England as the original site of the American nation (...) designed to unify the unformed and scattered American people under the aegis of New England by creating a national history anchored in that region" (Baym 1989: 460, qtd. in Bérubé 1994: 227).

One must realize, however, that this Americanization strategy was, at least for its time, a liberal (and liberating) project. It operated in the public sphere as a counter-movement to nativism and Know-Nothingness, which considered immigrants to be unassimilable to American society. On the other hand there was the racialist view, as expressed, among others, by the well-known educational historian Ellwood P. Cubberley in *Changing Conceptions of Education*, that aimed at inculcating into the immigrants' children the restrictive Anglo-Saxon conception of righteousness, law and order, and popular government, as well as to install in them a reverence for America's democratic institutions and for all other matters of purported national relevance for the American people (Cubberley 1909: 15–16). However, Anglo-Saxon racialism basically did not believe in the possibility of assimilation, unless the immigrants had the right kind of racial characteristics to begin with. Racialism implied exclusion of all who did not already fit that pattern. Americanization in its cosmopolitan version, with philosopher John Dewey as its leading representative, implied that it was the schools' responsibility to teach children of various ethnic groups mutual respect, and to enlighten all involved about the great contributions of every strain to the composite social fabric. In proclaiming a common culture, this educational Americanization also fostered the liberal ideal of equal opportunity of chances — whether immigrants subject to Americanization agreed with this intervention practice or not (Gleason 1982: 86, 107; Bérubé 1994: 227–228).

The outbreak of the war in Europe in 1914 triggered ethnic confrontations that ushered in a much more intensified phase of the Americanization movement. Many Americans were appalled by the return to Europe of thousands of immigrants who were reservists in the armies of the belligerents and the eruption of ethnic nationalisms on the part of immigrants groups with ties to the warring parties. They had not realized how strong the nationalist sentiments and attachments of these foreign-born Americans to their countries of origin were. Sensational reports of German propaganda and sabotage efforts in the United States in the popular press and other media reinforced anti–German sentiment and gave rise to a widescale campaign against "hyphenation" more generally. The test of Americanness became opposition to the "Hun," and Americans were now to be shaped into Kaiser-hating, English-speaking liberators (Gitlin 1995: 54). Initially, the activities of the Americanizers aroused opposition from the side of organized labor. Some of the labor leaders (including Samuel Gompers, head of the American Federation of Labor, and Frank P. Walsh of the United Mine Workers) expressed their doubts about the motives of certain Americanizers and demanded that the movement, in order to be successful, should be accompanied by reforms in labor conditions, unionization, and increases in wages. This criticism ceased as the Americanization movement gained momentum after 1916 (Hartmann 1948: 144–146).

The wartime Americanization campaign reached its climax during the years of U.S. involvement in the war (from April 1917 onwards). Political and cultural authorities insisted that all ethnic groups demonstrate their political loyalty to America and its "War for Democracy" through cultural conformity — "100 percent Americanism." Government organizations such as George Creel's Committee on Public Information and the National Americanization Committee (NAC) orchestrated the massive campaign in which many local public and private institutions took an active part. Elementary schools and adult education programs, patriotic societies like the Daughters of the American Revolution, fraternal organizations like the Knights of Columbus, as well as Chambers of Commerce, the General Federation of Women's Clubs, the prowar National Security League, and employers like Henry Ford all made Americanization into a top priority of their policies. The Americanization endeavors commonly included courses in English, civics, and American history, vigorous promotion of naturalization, and exorbitant celebrations of patriotic holidays — especially the Fourth of July. As employers joined the Americanization crusade, Americanization also began to aim at making immigrants into productive and compliant workers/adjusted American citizens (Gleason 1982: 86–87; Gerstle 1986: 85).

By the time the United States joined the Great War its civilizing mission had also become "universal"—spreading democracy abroad was simply seen as synonymous with Americanism. The Cleveland Americanization Committee, for example, after having defined Americanization as "the co-operative process by means of which 'many peoples' in our city and in America become 'One Nation' united in language, work, home ties, and citizenship, with one flag above all flags, and only one allegiance to that flag," proclaimed unhesitatingly: "Americanization is a co-operative movement bigger than America. It is a world-wide movement that all peoples may be united in a 'world brotherhood.' (...) Americanization is carrying democracy to *all peoples*, first, within the boundaries of America, and second, to all peoples without the boundaries of America, in order that the world may have great industrial, educational, economic and political freedom" (Hill 1919: 630, italics in original). Apparently there was no recognition here of possible conflicts between a globalizing Americanization of this kind and the needs, aims, and interests of foreign peoples under its influence.

Americanization became most sharply articulated in the third phase of the movement, in the context of postwar fear of social revolution, triggered by the 1917 Communist Revolution in Russia. To Americanizers, tests of political loyalty now became more important than ever. During the red scare that then spread across the country, immigrants were pressured to give unqualified support to "quintessentially American" political beliefs, such as the sanctity of private property and free enterprise, and had to renounce explicitly any affinity for "un-American" ideologies such as socialism or communism. Patriotic groups intensified their Americanization programs, as they saw it, to inoculate the great mass of the immigrants against the revolutionary contagion being spread by radical leftists. Two of the nine subdefinitions of "Americanization" mentioned in a brochure, entitled *What You Can Do for Americanization*, aimed at the general public and published by the National Americanization Committee in March 1918, were explicitly formulated in terms of "The combating of anti–American propaganda activities and schemes and the stamping out of sedition and disloyalty wherever found" and "The elimination of causes of disorder, unrest, and disloyalty which make fruitful soil for un-American propagandists and disloyal agitators" (qtd. in Hill 1919: 630). Various of the constituent unions of the AFL as well as the United Mine Workers actively supported the Americanization drive in 1918–1920. This may also have reflected the fear on the part of the more conservative unions of the Industrial Workers of the World (IWW) and their call for an all inclusive "one big union" and other radical leftist trends (Hartmann 1948: 261–264).

The war and its aftermath produced severe restrictions on free expression. The federal Espionage Act of 1917 provided sentences of up to twenty years imprisonment and a $10,000 fine for making false reports with intent to interfere with the war or for attempting to obstruct enlistment or to cause insubordination in the military. It also authorized the post office to exclude mail that violated the law. In 1918, the law was amended and enlarged, and came to be called the Espionage and Sedition Act. From now on virtually all criticism of the war or the government was outlawed, and the act's coverage included people whose language was supposed to "wilfully utter, write, or publish any disloyal, profane, scurrilous, or abusive language about the form of government of the United States, or the Constitution, ... the flag ... or the uniform of the Army or Navy" (Goldstein 1978: 113). Criticizing the form of government or the Constitution and advocating any restriction of production of anything necessary or essential to the persecution of the war were also illegal according to the act.

The Woodrow Wilson Administration used the act to prosecute individuals or organizations considered to be subversive through the deployment of federal troops and zealous U.S. district attorneys, in a combination of random terror and carefully directed prosecutions, aimed at destroying the IWW and the Socialist Party. This resulted in over 2,100 indictments, over 1,000 convictions, and over 100 sentences to prison terms of ten years or more, including the imprisonment of Socialist Party leader Eugene Debs and kindred spirits. In many cases, American citizens were sentenced to prison for up to twenty years for merely verbal opposition to the war. Many states (especially in the West) enacted even more draconic laws than the federal legislation during the war years. Seven states and territories passed criminal syndicalist laws (targeted mainly at the IWW), and eleven states outlawed various forms of opposition to the war. Moreover, the American Protective League (APL), a *private* volunteer group operating with Justice Department sanction and counting some 350,000 members by the war's end, carried out a broad range of intelligence-gathering and vigilante activities. Also active were "councils of defense," private patriotic organizations resembling the APL, which were organized on state, county, and town levels throughout the country. In addition there were many mob attacks, including lynching, tarring and feathering, whipping, and "deportations" to distant places, which increased during the war and continued afterwards. The victims were mainly African Americans, "Wobblies" (members of the IWW), Non-Partisan Leaguers, "pro-Germans," and radicals (Sexton 1991: 126–129).

The change is clear: patriotism became exclusionary and rhetorically aggressive. Strongly nativistic groups, such as the National Security League and the American Legion (founded by Theodore Roosevelt Jr. in 1919, to carry on the political work of his father) demonstrated their vigilance in identifying subversive groups and activities, called for the deportation of "alien radicals" and took recourse to fierce propaganda tactics (Gerstle 1994: 1053). Many state and local authorities restricted the use of languages other than English in the schools and required public school teachers to be American citizens. Employers who employed immigrants joined the campaign against "subversion," and Henry Ford was in the forefront. Thus, Americanization became closely identified with welfare capitalism and antiunionism (Gleason 1982: 88–89; Gerstle 1986: 85). The nativism and populist xenophobia of these years was also reflected in racist, anti–Semitic and anti–Catholic campaigns, as well as in the very restrictive Immigration Act of 1924. During the bloody Red Summer of 1919 major race riots took place in many cities (Levine 1993: 91). Telling is the revival of the Ku Klux Klan with its traditions and ideals of white supremacy (to be exercised by "white male persons, native-born gentile citizens of the United States of America") and its appropriation of the term Americanism, advocating a "pure Americanism." This was not a fringe movement. With a peak of four and a half million members by 1924 it became for a time the dominant political power in Oregon, Oklahoma, Texas, Arkansas, Indiana, Ohio, and California (Pfaff 1993: 186–187). Importantly, the American Legion, the fundamentalist crusade to restore Christian faith and "biblical truth" in education, and even the Ku Klux Klan, drew support among those who, some ten years earlier, had considered themselves Progressives (Gerstle 1994: 1053). What happened in the 1920s, was what John Lukacs has called the transformation of Americanism from "an ideology of becoming" (focused on the assimilation of immigrants) into "an ideology of being" — evolving around being "true Americans" (Lukacs 1984, qtd. in Pfaff 1993: 185–186).

Contrary to a view held by many historians, the restrictions on immigration set by the immigration act of 1924 did not bring an end to the Americanization movement. As labor historian Gary Gerstle has emphasized, one should not overlook the fact that by then Americanizers had to a large degree institutionalized their programs. These programs also included Americanization training that most universities and teachers' colleges had made an integral part of their curricula by 1921. Also important regarding the social-ization of American citizens was the fact that from 1917 to 1927 each state passed laws requiring citizenship classes for all schoolchildren, and that by 1922 the Federal Bureau of Education had distributed the *Federal Textbook on Citizenship Training* to more than 3,500 communities to aid local projects of Americanization (Gerstle 1986: 85–86). Given the panics among authorities about "un-American" groupings, organizations and activi-ties, it comes as no surprise that this citizenship training was politically biased, and often was deployed to legitimate the existing political and social order by defending "the ide-ology of the propertied group against that of the Communist or other radical propa-ganda" (Merriam 1931: 119, qtd. in Gerstle 1986: 86).

AMERICANIZING THE MEXICAN IMMIGRANT WOMAN

One type of government-sponsored Americanization program that ran from 1915 to 1929, was aimed specifically at Mexican immigrants, and has been studied in depth by George J. Sanchez on whose account I rely heavily here (Sanchez 1990). More than one million Mexicans entered the United States from 1910 to 1930 (with a temporary slow-down of this migration during the recession of 1920–22), leading to heavier concentra-tions in the urban centers of the Southwest and Midwest and putting heavy pressures on the barrios there. Restrictionists, consisting primarily of organized labor and nativists, sought to limit the influx of Mexican immigrants. In contrast, Southwestern employers, particularly railroad, agricultural, and mining companies, who claimed to need cheap labor, defended unrestricted Mexican immigration. Most of them were no less racist in their attitudes but emphasized the economic advantages of Mexican labor. To counteract the arguments of restrictionists, they stressed that the undesirable traits outlined by nativists actually benefited American society, arguing that the Mexican worker provided the perfect, docile employee, had no interest in intermixing with Americans, and would, in fact, return to Mexico as soon as he/she became redundant as laborer.

While these employers fought with restrictionists over future Mexican immigration, a third group sought to assimilate Mexican immigrants. Initially, support for this posi-tion came from Progressive social reformers, many of whom were middle-class Anglo-American women committed to the social settlement movement and the Social Gospel tradition. They held the view that society had an obligation to assimilate the Mexican immigrants, like other groups, and they hoped to improve societal treatment of immi-grants in general. However, as World War I heightened anxieties concerning immigrants, nativist sentiments that began to affect Americanization efforts through the "100 Per Cent American" movement became relatively more influential.

In California, the "Americanizers" first became powerful with the election of a Pro-gressive governor, Hiram Johnson, in 1910. By 1913, Johnson had established a perma-nent Commission on Immigration and Housing, that investigated the working and living conditions of all immigrants in the state and directed efforts to teach English to foreign-ers and have them take part in Americanization programs. Through governmental and private organizations other states also sought to Americanize Mexicans, but California's program was the most complete attempt to bring together government, business, and pri-vate citizens to deal with the "problem of the immigrant" in a scientific and rational man-ner according to the prevailing standards of the day. The Commission successfully recruited university professors, religious social workers, government officials, and middle-class volunteers.

These Californian reformers considered the Mexicans similar to Southern and Eastern European immigrants in principle. Although Mexicans might present a greater challenge than did Italians or Jews, they did not think there was something in the Mexican character that would make them unassimilable to the American way of life. But a major difference with the Americanization efforts of the social-settlement response to European immigrants before World War I was that there was no longer a focus on "immigrants gifts" (that is, their cultural enrichments) to American society. In the 1920s little value was given to Mexican culture — as with immigrant cultures more generally in Americanization programs

As the Commission expanded its Americanization programs, its members began to center their attention on Mexican immigrant women and their potential role in the cultural transformation of their families. School districts set up special classes and employed "home teachers," who, according to a Commission's report of 1916, were to instruct "children and adults [read: women] in matters relating to school attendance, ... in sanitation, in the English language, in household duties, ... and in the fundamental principles of the American system of government and the rights and duties of citizenship" (qtd. in Sanchez 1990: 254). During World War I, the home teacher became the central medium of the Americanization efforts aimed at the Mexican family.

Mexican immigrant women were believed to be primarily responsible for the transmission of values in the home. The expectation was that if the Mexican woman adopted the new values, they would pass them on to their children and husbands. By focusing on the strategic role of the mother in the Mexican family, the "Americanizers" hoped to affect the second generation of Mexicans in the United States, even if the first generation would turn out to be less malleable than they hoped for. Since the father's role in parenting was assumed to be minimal, it all came down to the cooperation of the Mexican mother. In this regard the Americanization ideology at issue was in line with the traditional American belief in an exalted role of motherhood in shaping the future political citizenry of the republic.

Yet, besides creating a home environment that fit the given industrial circumstances, the Americanization of Mexican women was valued for the direct benefits American society might gain from participation of female immigrants in the labor force. Mexican women were seen as a prime target group for reducing the shortage of domestic servants, seamstresses, laundresses, and service workers in the Southwest. However, as was more generally the case in Americanization programs, the conflict between the private responsibilities of American women to their homes and families and the public roles they began to play as workers and citizens in the 1920s were not addressed. Because the Southwest lagged behind the rest of the nation in industrialization, local reformers aimed to accommodate Mexican women and men as rapidly as possible to a growing industrial society and inculcate Mexican families with the necessary work ethic. To achieve these ends, the public and private responsibilities of women were blurred, and the "Americanizers" thought to take care of both issues at once. By encouraging Mexican immigrant women to wash, sew, cook, budget, and mother happily and efficiently, they would be prepared for entering the labor market, while at the same time running a household that nurtured American values of economy. Encouraging Mexican women to engage in hard work was also seen as an important facet in "curing" the habits of the stereotypically "lazy Mexican." It would have the effect of promoting discipline, which in turn would foster the inclination to instill a similar level of self-control in their children.

Much of the program was based on highly stereotypical beliefs about Mexicans. High priority was given to getting Mexican women out of their homes, because this was seen as the only avenue through which the Americanization efforts could succeed in altering their values. This was deemed necessary in order to overcome the alleged limitations placed upon them by Mexican husbands thought to be traditional, unwilling to adopt modern manners that were compatible with the new industrial order. The Americanization programs, however, were not intended to undermine the traditional Mexican family structure. Rather, these programs built on the cohesiveness of the Mexican family to achieve their goal of assimilation. It was these reformers' conscious strategy to use the Mexican woman as a conduit for creating a home environment well suited to the demands of an industrial economy.

Diet and health were two areas in which the Mexican female was regarded as a pivotal figure in transforming outdated practices in the home. To counter "malnourishment," Mexican women were encouraged to give up their penchant for fried goods, the too-frequent consumption of rice and beans, and their custom of serving all members of the family — from infants to grandparents — the same meal. According to these reformers, tortillas had to be replaced with bread, beans with lettuce, and the food should be broiled instead of fried. A healthy diet was also seen as fundamental for creating productive members of society. Cleanliness was likewise emphasized since program directors believed that Mexicans could not easily learn sanitation and hygiene "because" they found remaining dirty less strenuous than cleaning themselves. At the background was a fear among Anglo-Americans that their childrens would catch a contagious disease when in the presence of Mexican children at school, which was also one of the reasons given in objecting to mixed education (Sanchez 1990: 250–258; Ong Hing 1997: 18–20, n 13, 194–195).

These efforts to Americanize Mexican immigrants ended abruptly in 1929 as economic recession reduced the demand for migrant labor. Predictably, Mexican immigrants were (newly) characterized as unfit for citizenship and unassimilable in a tense socioeconomic climate. Some Mexican-American citizens were even expelled from Los Angeles (King 2005: 31).

DISSENTING VIEWS OF ETHNIC PLURALISTS

The Americanization movement offended two small but highly articulate groups: the intellectuals among the "new immigrant" communities, who resented the pressure to give up their long-standing culture and conform to what seemed an inferior, impoverished way of life; and the native-born rebels, who saw in the transplanted immigrant cultures chances for a more colorful, varied and creative national life in the future — if these cultures could be protected from the tyranny of the longer-settled "Anglo-Saxon" majority. A well-known representative of the first group was Horace M. Kallen. The case for cultural pluralism, for the active preservation of cultural difference rather than gradual, let alone rapid, forced assimilation, was put most brilliantly by this philosopher and student of Jewish culture. His experience of the earlier phase of the Americanization campaign in the Midwest, where he taught at the University of Wisconsin from 1911 to 1918, may have intensified the fervor of his famous article "Democracy versus the Melting-Pot," published in *The Nation* in 1915, which was an explicit attack on sociologist Edward A. Ross's nativist tract, *The Old World in the New* (1914). Kallen suggested that America was composed of a wide variety of cultural traditions of national communities that were primary and interacted and related with one another, forming a heterogeneous and fundamentally unmeltable whole. Like other early twentieth- century cultural pluralists (including sociologists Robert Park and Robert McIver), Kallen found intrinsic value in difference and diversity. His theory, too, was based on the idea that cultural difference derived from descent, that is, it was a primary and irreducible attribute or condition, ingrained in man's ethnic disposition ("sown in the seeds of man"). He argued that the inner cultural identity of the immigrant that he carried with him into his new land, remained an "inward" experience, regardless of how one's life course evolved and external relations changed.

According to Kallen, the cultural traditions of immigrants could not and should not be abolished since the price paid for individual "liberation" was spiritual poverty. Only membership in a historical national community could provide fundamental meaning and protection against the devastating psychological effects of alienation. Since a living culture could only develop over a long period, a distinctively American culture was hard to find. America had only been able to develop minor regional variations of British culture thus far.[4] New England in particular had produced a vigorous offshoot of Anglo-Saxon culture, but had by now exhausted its creative potential, as evidenced by a decline of religious fervor and self-scrutiny from Jonathan Edwards to Mary Baker Eddy. Nothing but an impoverished tradition was left, the shallow individualism (or "thin Yankee-ism") of the modern business society, in which economic greed set the standard, so that the working ideal of ordinary people was to get rich and to live and to think as the rich. It would be a disaster if the rich cultural heritage of many recent immigrant groups were rejected and replaced by a meager imitation of this way of life. The very characteristics that triggered nativist responses, the national and religious beliefs of the immigrants, were perhaps their greatest spiritual assets, since it enabled them to develop and retain self-respect by participating in the culture of their European homelands even to an extent that their own peasant ancestors often had not done.

Kallen also argued that even if America had offered a richer life for imitation, thorough and creative acculturation would not be an option that could be realized. Only superficial conformity to the dominant culture was possible, but human beings could not change their ingrained cultural habits at will. And they certainly could not quickly be assimilated so as to be able to make active contributions to the new culture rather than paying mere lip service to it. The forces of ancestry and history were too strong for such change in the short term. Given this tenacity of inherited culture, reinforced by the ethnic segregation of the great cities, a homogeneous America could only be achieved through terror and intimidation. As Kallen pointed out in the early twenties, the Ku Klux Klan was the logical outcome of the melting pot philosophy, not a perversion of it. The conformity thus created would only ensure that America continued to lack a culture in the narrower sense of creative art. For this the seedbed of a historically organized web of values and institutions was required. A positive program of cultural pluralism needed to be adopted that would give room to maneuver and equal dignity to all the diverse communities present in the nation. Democracy should be made to apply to groups as well as individuals, guaranteeing groups the right to exist, so that immigrants could retain and enjoy their essential, irreducible cultural identities even while participating fully in the civic affairs of the new land. Importantly, Kallen's pluralism did not really subvert Anglo-Saxon hegemony, nor question the rules of democratic participation. Rather it sought to preserve ethnic and cultural differences within the given body politic, nothing more (Kallen 1915, 1924; Matthews 1970: 9–10; Vaughan 1991: 450–451).

The second group of critics of the Americanization movement included radical dissenters like the literary and cultural critic Randolph Bourne and socialist Elizabeth Gurley Flynn, both opponents too of the war. They took a distinct minority stance by calling for a combination of cultural patriotism (loyalty to the ethnic culture one belonged to) and internationalism as the best — that is, least chauvinistic — definition of patriotism. Their goal was the prevention of assimilation, at least under duress and perhaps even under any circumstance. They saw Americanism as a kind of public religion imposed on the American people by Anglophile elites rooted in the genteel New England tradition, who were obsessed by the problems of immigration. To most native-born citizens Americanism meant compliant assimilation to the hegemonic culture, the "tame flabbiness," as Bourne called it, that was accepted as "Americanization" (Bourne 1916a, 1916b, 1918; cf. Lasch 1991: 356–357).

As an alternative to Kallen's cultural pluralism and a direct challenge to the assimilation paradigm, Bourne espoused a notion of cultural identity, based partly on descent and partly on consent, along with a view of American nationalism that was explicitly pacifistic and internationalist. Like Kallen, he believed that identity was a product of the given national, regional, familial, ethnic origins of a people (descent), but he also recognized that identity was articulated in voluntary affiliations, "willed attachments" to others (consent), leading to "communities of sentiments." Bourne, one of the most influential prewar critics who also had great posthumous influence after his untimely death in 1918 (he became a cultural hero to many young intellectuals), cherished a high ideal of cosmopolitanism, driven by the desire to use ethnic difference to deprovincialize politics and culture in America (Bender 1988: 61). The group of leftist intellectuals he belonged to had traveled in Europe, where they had studied multilingual Switzerland and the ethnic pluralism of the Austro-Hungarian Empire. They had then also become enamored with the theory of nationalities in terms of a transnational federacy developed by Austro-Marxist thinkers (Leggewie 2000: 185).

In his seminal essay, "Trans-National America," published in the *Atlantic Monthly* in 1916, Bourne proposed a cosmopolitan ideal that combined an acceptance of sustained particularisms with a commitment to creating a common or public culture. He offered this cultural vision, further derived from the social experience of New York, as a vision for the whole of America. He saw in New York City in particular an exemplary model of a multi-ethnic, polycentric culture, in which a vibrant modern cosmopolitanism was emerging, where immigrants lived side by side with artists, bohemians with suffragists, students with workers. Groups of producers and aficionados of culture with similar tastes were springing up in neighborhood theaters, artists' collectives, progressive and anarchist education centers, and in the editorial offices of the "little magazines" and the immigrant presses. Here Bourne found a viable countercultural alternative to the commercial world of corporate capitalism and the ward politics of the urban machine. It was in the city's working and living communities that a federated, trans-national democratic culture was developing outside the world of Puritan America and outside the state. For Bourne the immigrants who were transforming New York City were his chosen allies against the constraints of Anglo-Saxon provincialism. These immigrants, in turn, were experiencing a transformation as well, in that contact with Anglo-Saxons expanded their cultural horizons. A process of cultural cross-fertilization was taking place, especially among young people. This process seemed especially productive when young Jewish intellectuals were involved — Bourne explicitly praised the contributions of Felix Frankfurter, Horace Kallen, Morris R. Cohen, and Walter Lippmann. The juxtapositions of difference in the metropolis meant neither chaos or conflict; instead it offered freedom from narrow orthodoxies.

The diversity of the metropolis was a solvent that worked against a tendency to make one's own, usually limited, interpretation of reality universal.

Bourne shared the European-style critique of American mass culture as being "leveled-down," catering to the lowest common denominator of popular tastes as Kallen too had stressed as one objection to Americanization. Bourne adhered to a firm belief in art as a realization of spiritual values and an agent of social improvement. He was worried about the negative role of mass entertainments in the shaping of the emerging society and contended that they represented a "lowbrow snobbery," "as tyrannical and arrogant as the other culture of universities and millionaires and museums," and threatened the vital diversity of cultures within America (Bourne 1916c, qtd. in Gorman 1996: 62–63). In search for what he called a "third alternative," Bourne saw a strategic usage of ethnic traditions — based on an appreciation of the nation's multiplicity of folkways and traditions — as a defense against standardization, a counterpoint to the pull of the corporate commercialism of the movies, dance halls, and amusement parks with their formulaic entertainments. In his modernist transnationalist conception, the metropolis revitalized and reshaped the possibilities of the arts, in group pageants, community festivals and neighborhood theater productions. There was a crucial difference, however, between the positions of Bourne and Kallen. The latter tended to favor the preservation of parochial loyalties almost for their own sake. He was not so much for cultural cross-fertilization as for the harmonious cooperation and mutual enrichment of clearly defined, contrasting, persisting ethnic units. Bourne shared some of Kallen's hope that a plurality of particularistic interests could function as countervailing forces in American society in general, but his view had a more limited scope. Bourne was enthralled by the idea of a community of intellectuals, a complex, yet unified, life-world to which a variety of particularisms would make their distinctive contributions. He was more willing than Kallen to have the immigrants undergo cultural changes. Particular cultures and subcultures were repositories for insights and experiences that could be drawn on in the interests of a more comprehensive outlook on the world. To the extent that a particular ethnic heritage was an inhibition to the enlargement of cosmopolitan experience, it was to be left behind. Insofar as it was an avenue toward the enrichment of experience and expanding of understanding, access to it was to be preserved. In other words, immigrants should retain enough of their own cultural heritage to enrich American life (Hollinger 1971: 133–135, 142).

With this goal in mind, Bourne was in favor of a kind of "dual citizenship," an institutionalization of divided loyalties. He maintained that individuality had to be based on early instruction in a definite, particular set of cultural practices. In addition, he wanted "tribal minorities" to expose themselves to wider currents of thought without acquiring the mental habits of "cultural half-breeds."[5] To Bourne, the "Zionist idea" epitomized the ideal of modern cosmopolitanism, the most inspiring conception of trans-nationalism. (He considered Kallen — a German-born immigrant, an organic intellectual, a student of William James and an active and ardent Zionist — as an exemplar of this ideal.) As he saw it, the Zionist did not believe that there was a necessary conflict between cultural allegiance to the Jewish center and political allegiance to a state. Rather, he enjoyed a "dual citizenship"; he was at one and the same time "a complete Jew" and "a complete citizen" of any modern political state where he happened to live and work and where his interests lay. Moreover, early Zionism also pointed the way to the sort of nationalism Bourne advocated, one that was pacifistic and internationalist. The Zionist state (at least, I would emphasize, in its idealistic conception at the time) was non-military and non-chauvinistic and imposed limits on the role political loyalty should play in the modern world. As Bourne understood it, Palestine was to be built as a Jewish center on purely religious and cultural foundations. It was not to be the home of all the Jewish people, nor did Zionism propose to keep Jews from living in full citizenship in other countries.

Bourne, reversing the usual conclusion then, insisted that Jews in America were proving every day the possibilities of the dual life he envisioned. For him and many second-generation American Jews, Zionism represented freedom from both ethnocentrism and 100 percent Americanism. The cosmopolitan individual who enjoyed a dual citizenship with divided loyalties and multiple perspectives, represented not so much alienation as a healthy fluid self-identity "at home" in several worlds. Alienation of this sort, or what Bourne referred to as the unintegrated self, was the most advantageous position for the marginalized, the outsider or the hyphenate-American. In thus reversing the conventional depiction of Jews and other immigrants as marginalized, Bourne revaluated the meaning of marginality itself. Marginality, in this light, was a form of embeddedness, an anchor that kept one from either being sucked into the "centripetal" forces of the city, or thrown into atomized isolation by the centrifugal forces of liberal society (Vaughan 1991: 452–456).

Bourne's rejection of contemporary chauvinism was of virtually no importance in the national political context, where public policy was dominated by attempts to forcedly assimilate American immigrants into a preexisting set of American values, beliefs and attitudes. But in giving ideological expression to the cosmopolitan ideal that in his view decisively distinguished New York from the provincial values of America, Bourne made a significant contribution to the emergence of a national, secular, ethnically-diverse, left-of-center intelligentsia in the interwar period (Hollinger 1971). For our purpose it is important to note that, ironically, in his 1916 essay "Trans-National America," Bourne also argued that an exceptionalist United States would lead the way to an internationalist future in which Americans accepted one another in their diversity and nations lived peaceably together. As McGerr has pointed out:

> Bourne believed in the singularity of the United States and the glory of its destiny. America composed of so many immigrants from around the world, was "a novel international nation, the first the world has seen ... [I]t bespeaks a poverty of imagination not to be thrilled at the incalculable potentialities of so novel a union of men." In particular, the United States would set an example of peaceable heterogeneity. "Only America," Bourne claimed, "by reason of the unique liberty of opportunity and traditional isolation for which she seems to stand, can lead in this cosmopolitan enterprise." For Bourne, exceptionalism could lead to transnationalism; the two were not antithetical..." [McGerr 1991: 1063, quoting Bourne [1916] 1964: 114, 120–121].

McGerr rightly concluded that such transnationalism can very well entail a form of imperialism: "the transnational world may well emerge from such unlovely phenomena as American power and American exceptionalism" (*ibid.*: 1064). This insight is pertinent in the context of U.S.-led transnationalization or globalization, as we will see later.

Bourne's teacher, John Dewey, America's leading philosopher of democracy, was also opposed to racist and nativist varieties of nationalism, but defended a democratic version of Americanism. His pluralism was one of individual choice, based upon a model of the good society as a mosaic of voluntary associations similar to de Tocqueville's depiction of Jacksonian America. In retrospect, Dewey's position seems closer to the optimist environmentalism of the proponents of Americanization than to the strong historical sense and fear of American conformity that Kallen, Bourne and others brought to the debate. And in Dewey's popular view, the war should be supported because it was designed, in accordance with the Wilsonian idea, to "make the world safe for democracy," and would lead to an invigorated ideal of Americanism. This democratic Americanism required the extension of political rights to all citizens, but for the time being only women's suffrage — an historical milestone after decades of agitation — was to follow (Matthews 1970: 12; Gitlin 1995: 56).

Influential in this theorizing about ethnicity were the cultural relativist explanations of human behavior by the school of anthropology that developed at Columbia University under the direction of the German immigrant scholar Franz Boas. In the 1890s, he had begun his attacks on the dominant evolutionary school of anthropology with its assumption of a universal law of stages of unilinear progressive development through which all cultures had to pass from simple to complex. Boas also spoke out against the Nordicist theories of race and intelligence and racial interpretation of cultures expressed by authors like Madison Grant and Lothrop Stoddard. Randolph Bourne came under Boas's influence when he attended Columbia University after 1909. Bourne's Bohemian lifestyle, "career," and writing in turn inspired younger anthropologists. Ruth Benedict, one of Boas's most famous students of the next generation was influenced by the example of Bourne's cultural-political rebellion and his efforts to achieve disinterested understanding of immigrant cultures and other civilizations. The students trained by Boas in the 1920s (also including Margaret Mead) would join with colleagues from other anthropological centers to employ anthropology as a weapon in the attack upon the highly restrictive versions of "Americanism" in vogue at the time. For those young recruits to the discipline, anthropology in the 1920s would be a means to "internal expatriation" (or migration in the mind), a respectable alternative to physical migration, which allowed for "escape" to cultural milieux far more exotic than the Left Bank or Greenwich Village, while offering the opportunity for social criticism (Matthews 1970: 16–23; Stocking 1974: 202–218, 307–330).

AMERICANIZATION, LABOR AND THE LEFT UNTIL THE EARLY 1930S

The leadership of the American Federation of Labor (AFL), founded in 1886 (which became the leading trade union in the late 1890s), responded to the massive influx of new immigrants by emphasizing its allegiance to an American sense of identity rather than solidarity among all members of a transnational or even domestic working-class alliance. In AFL's view of the model citizen-worker who stood for "the average man," American citizenship was held up against working-class identity. This occurred through an ideology that reinforced the political and national consensus, although the rhetorics were often laced with a defiant Americanism that defined the enemy as the holders of corporate wealth and those government officials who were their lackeys. Samuel Gompers and his allies also strengthened a sense of craft unionism (with notable exceptions, such as the United Mine Workers and the International Ladies Garment Workers Union, which were not confined to craft and skilled workers) by distinguishing the "legitimate working class" from the rest, thereby contributing to a wider gap between skilled and unskilled (mostly immigrant and African-American) workers than in other countries (Kazin 1998: 55–60; Voss 1993: 2, 242).

The ideological struggles between management and industrial unionists evolved around different versions of "Americanism," which also changed in the course of time.

The Ford Motor Company is an exemplary case as an in-depth study by political scientist Mark Rupert has made clear. Management and industrialist unionists at this company both attempted to win the allegiance of rank-and-file autoworkers through rhetoric and symbols of "Americanism." In a series of struggles stretching over decades, the meaning of "Americanism" was defined, challenged and redefined — although the core meanings of Americanism were tied to the liberal tradition in America, and how this was to be interpreted, reproduced or transformed. Since the introduction of the moving assembly line and true mass production in 1913–14, the everyday culture[6] of industrial workers at Ford was a site of contestation, first between the company and unorganized workers, and later involving the United Automobile Workers. Already before World War I, Ford's management had begun endeavors to "Americanize" its largely immigrant workforce as part of a systematic strategy to foster an industrial culture based upon what Rupert calls "abstract individualism." This entailed "a vision of the wage relation as a contractual arrangement between an individual worker and his employer, voluntarily entered into for mutual benefit. This, in turn, implied that workers should accept a responsibility to managerial authority, and a work ethic, in the interest of their own economic self-betterment" (Rupert 1995: 164).

But Ford's ideological campaign was a double-edged sword. On the one hand Ford workers seem to have internalized the cultural norms of abstract individualism to the extent that they increasingly tended to act in terms of market rationality and accumulation of property (particularly house-ownership). On the other hand, this campaign also borrowed the political language of individual rights and liberties to frame protests against Ford's labor policies of highly intrusive paternalism — as exemplified par excellence by the activities of Ford's Sociological Department (later renamed Department of Education) that actively meddled in the workers' private lives (*ibid.*: 164–165). Ford also tried to dissolve the ethnic and national identities of its immigrant workers through their forced attendance in the Americanization classes at the Ford English School, founded in 1914. This school would become a model for Americanization programs across the country. Ford's Americanization project was part of the large-scale wartime movement of manufacturers who employed immigrants. Courses in English and citizenship were usually added to existing programs of welfare work or industrial betterment that had been gaining ground at large industrial corporations since the turn of the century. They were likewise products of the emerging professional area of personnel management. The addition of Americanization classes was seen as a more explicit, self-conscious recognition of the linkage between assimilation to American culture and the acclimation of preindustrial immigrants to factory discipline, a recurrent phenomenon in American social history (Gleason 1982: 88).

In constructing new identities as "Americans" for immigrant Ford workers the aim was to integrate them into the culture of liberal capitalism, "to get them to see themselves as autonomous individuals who could find liberty and success in their new land by severing ties of dependence with ethnic communities and institutions, and casting their lot with Ford Motor Company" (Rupert 1995: 119). In an elaborate graduation ritual at the Ford English School, the transformation of immigrants with various ethnic/national backgrounds into American citizens — understood as abstract individuals — was theatrically symbolized as follows:

> On a stage was represented the side of a steamship, from which a gangplank descended into a large cauldron labeled "Ford English School Melting Pot." A stream of immigrant workers came down the gangplank variously dressed "in the poor garments of their native lands." As they poured

into the melting pot, the mixture was stirred by Ford English School instructors. Through this process, their concrete distinctions were dissolved and there upon they emerged dressed in "American clothes" [suits and ties], faces eager with the stimulus of the new opportunities and responsibilities opening out before them. Every man carried a small American flag in his hand [*ibid.*: 122].

Between 1915 and 1920, more than 16,000 workers graduated from the Ford English School with its one-nation ideology and symbolism (King 2005: 29).

Thus, Americanization programs taught immigrants to abandon the habits, family patterns, traditions, and loyalties of the agricultural and handicraft societies they originated from in favor of industrial discipline, "rationality," and wage labor. It meant learning to be a "good citizen," and to reject the "un-American" doctrines of socialism, communism, and anarchism. This form of managed Americanization helped immigrants to take on the social and material privileges of whiteness — to become white American citizens. And, in accordance with Ford's direct economic interests, it meant becoming part of the new consumer society. Which brings us to an evident truth, namely, that Americanization was not just a consciously directed campaign. The everyday pressures of the workplace and the marketplace, as well as the rapidly expanding advertising and film industries, also pushed immigrants to assimilate (Ewen and Ewen 1992: 33; Berlet and Lyons 2000: 116–117).

Since the late nineteenth century with the rise of a modern consumer society, adoption of consumerism had been a significant factor in the assimilation of immigrants into the modernizing American society — like it was for many native-born Americans (Gross 2000: 18–19, 30). The new culture of consumer capitalism that, according to a leading expert, "became over time the very culture of America" (Leach 1993: 12), was indeed a crucial site of contestation with regard to the Americanization of immigrants. This undeliberate cultural assimilation did not occur smoothly, but often entailed a painful transition. Older immigrants lamented the loss of culture, religious faith, family ties, and friendships that they experienced upon settling in American cities. There were also tensions between the older and younger generations. Immigrant parents might feel intimidated by their children's education and work career, sometimes demanding their son's or daughter's salary payments for family support. The second generation often ridiculed parents for their lack of capacities in speaking and writing good English, and demonstrated their Americanness with new clothes and entertainment (Gross 2000: 38).

The Americanization programs in corporate industries also had a direct political impact on workers. In order to secure the consent of its regular workforce, the Ford Motor Company used a liberal rhetoric during World War I to identify as loyal Americans those workers who most closely identified their own interests with those of the company. Workers who resisted the authority of Ford's management and the power of capital were stigmatized as "enemies." For this purpose, Ford employed spies in his factories from the American Protective League, a private espionage organization endorsed by the Justice Department, to trace unionists and labor radicals among the foreign-born workers. Nuclei of unionists were infiltrated and nipped in the bud; many radicals were summarily fired (Gerstle 1986: 85; Rupert 1995: 165). Ford's efforts to shape a compliant work force were not very successful, however, evidenced by the surge of unionism and radicalism immediately after the war, particularly as manifested in the nationwide steel strike and the Seattle general strike of 1919. A Senate committee that investigated the steel strike attributed the insubordinate and radical tendencies among so many workers to their foreign background and called for a renewed Americanization campaign.

Employers from all over the country held a national meeting in Massachusetts in

1919 to further enhance the Americanization of their workers, which culminated in revitalized Americanization programs in the next decade (Cohen 1990), in tandem with employers' efforts to eliminate unions, described as the "American Plan," a term that entered the vocabulary of industrial relations in the early 1920s. In addition, the government deprived radicals of their civil liberties, and hunted the members of "un-American" organizations such as the Industrial Workers of the World, the Socialist Party, and the brand-new Communist Party and Communist Labor Party (both split-offs from the Socialist Party in 1919) during the Palmer raids of 1919–1920. Throughout most of the next decade radicals were treated as true pariahs in American society, well symbolized by the seven-year ordeal of the anarchists Sacco and Vanzetti, culminating in their 1927 execution. Faced with rising inflation, stronger competition, and renewed restiveness among auto workers, Ford took recourse to a much more coercive workplace regime whereby explicit ideological appeals to workers were dropped, for the time being. The policy would change again with the rise of the UAW in the 1930s (Rupert 1995: 165).

The Americanization campaigns of the 1910s and 1920s had a deep and pervasive influence on the culture and politics of American workers. This was manifested, among other things, in a steep rise in the percentage of naturalized citizens among Eastern and Southern European immigrants[7] — which was also partly the regular second-generation effect among immigrants, of course — and a severe drop in trade-union membership in the 1920s, even in industries such as coal and textiles that did not share in the prosperity at the time. These campaigns disseminated a conservative Americanism all over the country. It was an Americanism that fostered conformity and allegiance to conservative political values and promised economic prosperity to all those willing to make the necessary efforts for it.

Yet, to Americanize at the time did not necessarily mean to assimilate wholeheartedly or accept the status quo. Conservative Americanism did not fully monopolize the political culture. Significant numbers of ethnic Americans remained relatively insulated from the dominant culture within their ethnic enclaves in the cities, especially those of the Northeast and Midwest. Many among the second generation of new immigrants rebelled against their education; they usually did not come up against civics education as such but resisted the disciplinary function of their schooling. Some of them became more self-consciously political, however, and took their American civics lessons seriously, seeking to link these with their own social experience. They began to realize (and point out publicly), that poverty and social inequality were at odds with the promise of American life, and they found in American political traditions the ideals and language to legitimate liberal and radical politics. Thus they reinterpreted Americanism in a politically progressive rather than conservative way.

Still, in the 1920s, many trade unionists felt obligated to dodge the stigma of "un-Americanism," and even tried to prove their organizations' allegiance to "God and country" by taking a distance from radical unions and political parties. A trade union leader like John L. Lewis of the United Mine Workers of America stated that "knee-jerk radicalism" could not solve labor's problems, and suggested that progressive social movements in America only demanded a return to first principles, a mere reassertion in practice of the rules already spelled out by the Founders of the Republic. Lewis went even so far as to suggest that his union, if allowed to put these thoughts into action, would strengthen American capitalism and the conservative Republican party of Harding and Coolidge (Gerstle 1986: 86–87). But a book written by an important member of Lewis's own staff hints at the development in the union's higher ranks of a much more creative interpretation of the first principles of the Republic. Jeff Lauck claimed in *Political and Industrial Democracy, 1776–1926* that in order to preserve the political achievements of 1776 and to counter the enormous influence that the big corporations had developed in the past 150 years beyond the control of the nation's democratic institutions, democracy had to be extended to the realm of the workplace (Lauck 1926). This work contributed to the elaboration of an alternative civic consciousness, one that challenged the conservative Americanism that dominated the political discourse at the time.

Left-leaning populists (or "liberals" as they increasingly called themselves) in the 1920s also took an active part in the construction of this other, progressive Americanism through popularizing the phrase "industrial democracy" as part of an Americanist discourse. Initially, they had been inclined to look sympathetically at the new forms of democratic governance that seemed to be arising in revolutionary Russia. These liberals thought they had found an exciting version of extra-parliamentary, direct democracy in the form of "workers' control" in the "soviet." And they began calling for a similar extension of the principles of political democracy to economic life in America. However, when the iron grip of Bolshevik control made the soviets increasingly appear too great a risk to experiment with in American circumstances, these liberals (spearheaded by Herbert Croly and his *New Republic* intellectual circle) turned towards the less radical form of industrial democracy advocated by British guild socialists such as Harold Laski and G.D.H. Cole and, from 1918 onwards, by the British Labour Party itself. A series of strikes by American workers in 1919 struck these liberals with fear and made them ever more enthusiast about the British way, as it seemed to them the only option that could possibly prevent a Bolshevik-style revolution in the United States (Gerstle 1994: 1053–1054).

Many socialists, too, increasingly took recourse to this concept of industrial democracy as a substitute for socialism, a way of promoting their vision in an extremely conservative age. In 1919, for example, the Intercollegiate Socialist Society (ISS) changed its name to the League for Industrial Democracy (LID). This change reflected its leaders' awareness that the term "socialism" had by then obtained highly negative connotations in American political discourse. The word "socialist" was also dropped from the title of its chief publication; *The Socialist Review* was renamed *Labor Age* in 1921 (Gerstle 1986: 87–88). However, translating the concept of industrial democracy into a concrete political program without evoking a whole world of socialist meaning proved to be difficult. When IDL's leader, Norman Thomas, publicized his definition of industrial democracy in 1925, he laid out a complete program for the transformation of society, including unionization, nationalization of major industries, farmer and consumer cooperatives, a workers' party, democratic control of the worlds of finance and credit, and so on. This hurt his cause, however, because Thomas and other socialists were thus prevented from offering an alternative conception of industrial democracy with sufficient distinctiveness to compete with ones that were less (or not at all) socialistic in orientation. This clearly shows the pressures put on socialists to redefine their political vision in language that would allow it to be articulated in American political discourse.

Attempts to fit into the American mold were also apparent in strategies aimed at developing a working-class radicalism that went further than giving lip service to an Americanist discourse. While retaining a European-style socialist tendency, they sought to develop a leftist radicalism that would be truly in the American grain. Some radical labor organizers in the 1920s and early 1930s began arguing that American working-class radicalism had to free itself from all the "isms" that permeated European radical movements and address American workers and farmers in the language of the Founding Fathers.

This course of action was taken, for example, by Louis Budenz, a radical labor organizer and editor of *Labor Age,* whose "American approach" deeply influenced A.J. Muste, a pacifist minister who had been radicalized during the 1919 textile strike in Lawrence, Massachusetts. Since his days as an immigrant youth in Michigan, Muste had been enthralled by the American Dream, especially as associated with Abraham Lincoln. He saw his radicalism as an attempt to make American society live up to the (Lincoln-like) American Dream. Together, Budenz and Muste built an American radical movement, first in the Conference on Progressive Labor Action (CPLA) organized in 1929 and subsequently in the American Workers' party founded in 1933, and led by Muste. The leitmotiv was that "the labor movement in America must grow up out of the American soil; it must face the realities of American life; it must be built and controlled by the workers of America," as a CPLA Statement of Principles, in May 1932, declared (*ibid.*: 89).

Similarly, Norman Thomas's Socialist Party tried to Americanize its socialism. After socialists had organized workers, farmers and the unemployed across the country into "committees of correspondence" in the course of 1932, 4,000 delegates from these committees held a Continental Congress for Economic Reconstruction in Washington, in May 1933, shortly after Franklin D. Roosevelt had taken office. Like the CPLA had done the year before, they too wrote a new Declaration, declaring independence from "the profit system of business, industry and finance," that had "enthroned economic and financial kings ... more powerful, more irresponsible, and more dangerous to human rights than the political kings whom the fathers overthrew" (Shannon 1955: 227–228, qtd. in Gerstle 1986: 89). The resolutions that were then passed were modeled after the Socialist Party program and called for the abolition of America's capitalist system and its replacement with a cooperative commonwealth.

Until 1932, these activities occurred against the background of modes of repression during Herbert Hoover's presidency which were aimed against what was believed to be the red-instigated unrest of the unemployed and included deportations of political "undesirables," the restriction of "alien movement" within the country, and banning radical papers from the mails. When some 10,000 veterans (many of them unemployed) bivouacked in Washington, D.C., in 1932, and demanded veterans' bonuses, 600 soldiers, commanded by General Douglas MacArthur, teargassed over 1,000 protestors and burned their Anacostia encampment. However, most armed repression was a local police matter. In the early 1930s, police attacked, shot, and teargassed unemployed demonstrators in various places and made many "free speech" arrests. The network of secret police expanded, and the enforcement of state syndicalist, insurrection, and sedition laws increased significantly (Sexton 1991: 142). The New Deal Era would give the labor-left new life and initially offer relief from federal repression.

4

Relevant Developments
During the New Deal and Beyond

This chapter first continues the working history of domestic usages of "Americanism" and "Americanization" within the New Deal context until World War II. Thereafter the focus shifts to the crucial role of Americanism regarding U.S. citizenship as a hot political issue at the peak of the Cold War. This is followed by an analysis of the contestations of Americanism during the 1960s and after, when various new social movements emerged, along with multiculturalism and its attendant identity politics. A major point of interest are the political struggles revolving around preferred meanings of Americanism and Americanization in relation to questions of immigration (regarding the Latin American influx especially) against the backdrop of a new conservative Americanism that emerged in the 1980s. The next section highlights the exclusionist Americanism vis-à-vis Arabs and Muslims, and Americans of Arabic descent (or others perceived as such), as well as political dissidents of various stripes in the "war on terrorism" after September 11, 2001. To complete the picture, the phrases "Americanization of the South" and "Southernization of America," that came in vogue after mid-century, are discussed as well.

THE NEW DEAL AND THE POPULAR FRONT

With the arrival of Franklin D. Roosevelt in office in March 1933, democratic Americanism was linked to the New Deal. This Americanism was a mixture of populism, Progressivism, militant industrial unionism, and a broadly based leftism that united the New Deal and the Communist Party into the Popular Front. Songs and stories celebrated the virtues of the "common folk" vis-à-vis the wheelings and dealings of hardheaded bankers and corrupt politicians. The photography of Dorothea Lange and Walker Evans celebrated the unfamous and downtrodden. True patriotism was now first of all a love of equality, and this nationalism was highly inclusive, inviting entry into an open Americanness, in a land that "was made for you and me," as folk singer Woody Guthry put it. In his exploration of American exceptionalism, *Toward a United Front: A Philosophy for American Workers* (1933), Leon Samson must have had this form of Americanism — with its utopianism, theatricalism, and pragmatism — in mind to explain why a socialist revolution failed to materialize in American society. This independent Marxist, dissident from the Communist Party, wrote:

> Americanism is to the American not a tradition or a territory, not what France is to a Frenchman or England to an Englishman, but a doctrine — what socialism is to a socialist ... a solemn assent to a handful of final notions — democracy, liberty, opportunity, to all of which the American adheres rationalistically much as a socialist adheres to his socialism — because it does him good,

because it gives him work, because, so he thinks, it guarantees him happiness. Americanism has thus served as a substitute for socialism.[1] Every concept in socialism has its substitutive counter-concept in Americanism, and that is why the socialist argument falls so fruitlessly on the American ear [Samson 1933: 5, 16].

The popular idiom that there are no classes in America expressed an unconscious wish, Samson suggested. It was unconscious because the American's "socialistic instincts," conflicting with the capitalist institutions and ideas surrounding him, were repressed. Americanism as substitute socialism was a double-edged sword; it was both the main obstacle to the coming of socialism and its peculiarly American opportunity. Since Americanism was basically a case of massive false consciousness, socialists' main task in the United States was to try to make people aware of the basic conflict between their essentially socialist cast of mind and society's capitalist structure. Samson thought the battle should therefore focus on the ideological domain. The American mind was essentially "classless" and would no longer tolerate a class society if it was perceived in fact as a class society. Hence, making Americans aware of the class system was synonymous with abolishing classes in American society. Once the workers saw that the failures of the American dream could be directly attributed to capitalism, they would move toward socialism precisely because of their deeply ingrained Americanism (previously a barrier to socialism). Samson's book, which was driven by the idea of Americanizing socialism and symptomatic of a broader stream of attempts to Americanize Marxism, concluded with a call for the creation of an American labor party in order to weaken the grip of Americanism's false consciousness on the American working class (Denning 1996: 431).

The strain of trade unionists and labor organizers giving an insurgent interpretation of American patriotism (that had remained weak throughout the 1920s and early 1930s) gained in strength during the Depression when the discrepancies between the promise of American capitalism and the dismal reality of American society became so obvious. During a strike against Toledo Auto-Lite in 1934 — the first of the major clashes between labor and capital in that decade — thousands of workers inspired by organizers for the American Workers' party, carried banners that proclaimed "1776–1865–1934." In 1936, CIO's leader John L. Lewis spread a version of the idea of industrial democracy over a nationwide network, challenging all who would oppose the movement for it embodied in the Congress of Industrial Organizations. Early in the next year, symbols and rhetorics of this insurgent Americanism were at the heart of the most important CIO victory of the decade — union recognition conceded by General Motors after a sit-down action by workers who had occupied GM plants in Flint, Michigan, for six weeks. The strikers emerged from the plants, proudly waving American flags. Their favorite song, like CIO unionists everywhere, was *Solidarity Forever*, sung to the tune of the *Battle Hymn of the Republic*.

Importantly, this CIO Americanism of the 1930s was ambiguous and not by definition identical with radicalism. Under its banner went a variety of political strains, ranging from socialism to corporatism,[2] and even to business unionism. And for fifteen years there would be battles among and between CIO leadership and shopfloor representatives of various political persuasions about the CIO's political character as well as the leading concept of Americanism. Nevertheless, CIO's Americanism brought together workers of very different political, ethnic, and religious backgrounds in one large movement for industrial unionism. It also spread the idea among unionists that American workers rather than American capitalists were the major bearers of American civilization, and that the success of organized labor in reaching its goal was crucial for the future of the Republic (Gerstle 1986: 90–91).

A leftist articulation of Americanism and nationalism lay at the center of the Popular Front social movement, and was expressed especially in the cultural works of the artists and intellectuals from working-class families associated with this movement. It consisted of what Michael Denning, in his comprehensive history of the Cultural Front of the 1930s and 1940s, has called "a paradoxical synthesis of competing nationalisms and internationalism — pride in ethnic heritage and identity combined with an assertive Americanism and a popular internationalism" (Denning 1996: 130). This Americanism had its seedbeds in the immigrant and black working-class neighborhoods of the modern metropolis (New York, Chicago, Los Angeles, San Francisco and other cities such as Philadelphia, Minneapolis and Boston), inhabited by the second generation of the Southern and Eastern European immigrants who arrived in the late nineteenth and early twentieth centuries: ethnic Italians, Jews, Poles, Serbians, Croatians, Slovaks, as well as Mexicans, Japanese, Chinese, and Filipinos, along with African Americans who had migrated north. Denning thinks this "pan-ethnic Americanism" may have been "the most powerful working-class ideology of the age of the CIO which significantly reshaped the contours of official U.S. nationalism" (*ibid.*). He also emphasizes that the politics and poetics of Americanism at the heart of the Popular Front social movement was *not* simply a "politics of patriotism," rhetorically employed by politicians and trade unionists to evoke unity and harmony by inculcating among workers a deep reverence for the United States' political heritage, values and institutions (Denning 1996: 129). In fact, the figure of "America" became a site of contestation over the trajectory of U.S. history, including the meaning of race, ethnicity, and region in the United States, and the relations between ethnic nationalism, Americanism, and internationalism.

It cannot be denied, however, that the "politics of patriotism" mentioned above *did* play a significant role in tactical strategies deployed by a number of politicians and union leaders in trying to mobilize and retain a mass following (Gerstle 1986: 85). The obvious example here is the American Communist Party, which became the dominant organization of the American left in the late 1930s. The Party markedly grew in popularity after 1935, when its leaders, following a Comintern's order, abandoned the ultra-revolutionary politics of the "third period," and sought alliances with a broad range of progressive forces in American society. This enhanced appeal was particularly due to the communists' ability to turn their party's image into the most "American" of all the leftist parties by seeking to demonstrate in all kinds of ways that "Communism was Twentieth-Century Americanism" (*ibid.*: 90). This seems to indicate that many Party's constituents were true believers in democratic Americanism, just like many other members of the Popular Front were.

Due to its variegated sources and political influences from within the left, the variant of Americanism that was expressed in many of the new forms and styles of Popular Front culture was a complex and contradictory mixture of three tendencies. It included first of all a fascination with the grand narratives of the American past in leftist terms and an appropriation of American mythologies with a radical edge. However, this attraction to American mythologies was yoked to an accentuation of nationality and ethnicity as expressed by the writers and artists of the Cultural Front and further manifested in the federal structure (in terms of nationalities) of the International Workers Order (IWO), a fraternal benefit society that developed alongside the CIO and, together with other, smaller organizations of this kind, made up the other half of the Popular Front movement culture. As an insurance organization, it offered sickness, disability, and death benefits, and served as a base from which a network emerged of lodges, vacation camps, and schools that were centers of culture and entertainment.

Nonetheless, there was a significant decline in ethnic cohesion during the age of the CIO, and many Popular Front figures took a distance from forms of racial or ethnic nationalism, while challenging conservative religious and entrepreneurial leaders in ethnic communities and calling for a renewed "ethnicism" that would transcend the prevalent forms. Thus, this racial or ethnic nationalism was inflected by a third tendency, that is a popular internationalism that upheld a pan-ethnic ideal of a federation of nationalities both within the United States and across the world from the perspective of the internationalist proletariat (Denning 1996: 73–77; 131–133). But this pan-ethnic internationalism remained an unstable constellation, challenged by persistent racial and ethnic divisions, official Americanism, and conservative anti-communist ethnic nationalisms.

An official mainstream Americanism emerged in the New Deal state and in the culture industries, carried by Roosevelt's historical bloc that came in power in 1933, and represented par excellence by the fireside chats of Franklin Roosevelt and Frank Capra's famous populist film trilogy *Mr. Deeds Goes to Town* (1936), *Mr. Smith Goes to Washington* (1939), and *Meet John Doe* (1941) in which this filmmaker honored small-town heroes fighting corruption in the big city and Washington politics. "Capra ... won the hearts of millions of Americans with movies extolling America's golden small town past, when life was simple, people were honest, and morally upright individuals commanded respect" (Gerstle 1989: 191).[3] Here Americanism meant "the rewards of social stability — wealth, success and the girl for the hero; fellowship, happiness and trustworthy leaders for the rest of us. It was a religious faith in a secular social myth that found its embodiment in patriotism and American democracy" (Sklar 1975: 212, qtd. in Kammen 2000: 68). This mainstream Americanism had its limits, as Denning points out: "This populism might well be called sentimental, for, unlike the populisms of the right and the left, its narratives avoided the depiction of enemies, villains, or scapegoats. The people were not oppressed or exploited, they were merely 'forgotten.' They had only fear itself to fear; with confidence and faith, adversity could be conquered" (Denning 1996: 127–128). It was also less inclusive, especially with regard to African Americans.

The Americanisms on the right were certainly not insignificant. After a brief honeymoon, by 1934 a major part of corporate business had turned against Roosevelt's New Deal. With the support of General Motors and Du Pont, the American Liberty League was set up to provide the disorientated Republican Party with a program to counter the New Deal. Against the intrusion of statist, collectivist and socialist conceptions under the banner of the New Deal, it was to uphold the "fundamental Americanism," embodied in the Constitution and in the American business tradition. On the extreme right were the modern Ku Klux Klan, fringe movements such as William Dudley Pelley's Silver Shirts, the American Order of Fascisti (or Black Shirts), and the German-American Bund, as well as several quasi-secret vigilante groups, organized to combat unions in industrial cities, like the Black Legion in Detroit.

Then there were several grass-roots movements of national significance that are less easy to classify because they belong to the ambiguous tradition of American populism. These included Louisiana governor/U.S. Senator Huey Pierce Long Jr.'s "Share Our Wealth" movement (led by Gerald L.K. Smith after Long's assassination in 1935), Father Charles E. Coughlin's National Union for Social Justice, and Dr. Francis Townsend's Old Age Revolving Pension organization. These movements were alike in their defense of an Americanism of Middle America in economic distress. Scholars of the postwar "liberal consensus school" like historian Richard Hofstadter and sociologist Seymour M. Lipset, in line with their general view of populism in American history, recognized here right-wing movements dominated by the politics of status-anxiety, resentment, bigotry, racism, and more generally, irrationalism (Hofstadter 1972; Lipset and Raab 1978). Later analysts, however, have come to different conclusions. For example, Alan Brinkley downplayed the threat of fascism in his historical study of Long and Coughlin. He pointed out how their railing against distant, powerful and rich evildoers evoked individual autonomy, decentralization, and independence, which appealed in particular to a middle class whose status and community position were under threat by both an economic crisis and an emerging mass society (Brinkley 1982). Recently historian James Weinstein characterized Long as "a consummate, and sometimes ruthless politician" who was "by far the most successful" of all the 1930s radical politicians operating on behalf of working people. In this he came much closer to traditional populism — with its radical defense of small, largely agrarian, capitalists — than to socialism. But, as Weinstein explained, he had also absorbed much of the socialist movement, which was manifested in differences from the populists in his political practices: an avoidance of virulent racism; an emphasis on propertyless workers' rights and needs; and an emphasis on universal access to higher education and health care as basic rights (Weinstein 2003: 157–168; cf. Williams 1981).

Contrary to the image of the 1930s as "the red decade," these years also saw prosecutions of leftists on the local or state level, instigated by the powerful Hearst Press and the business-sponsored American Liberty League, fierce defenders of "100 percent Americanism." The late 1930s witnessed the beginning of congressional investigations, purges, and blacklists aimed at repressing the political opinions of people who had violated no laws. States began to demand loyalty oaths by law or established investigating committees. The practice of taking "loyalty probes" (investigations of people's "political patriotism"), usually inspired and monitored by the FBI (led by J. Edgar Hoover), spread into unions, government, the media, and education. Most importantly, the House Special Committee on Un-American Activities, chaired by conservative Democratic Congressman Martin Dies of Texas, began hearings on charges that the LaFollette Committee — which, in 1936, had held hearings on violations of the civil liberties of unionists and employer attacks on the CIO — had been penetrated by communists, like the CIO, and that it had called as witnesses "certain well-known communists" to attack businessmen. These congressional hearings led, as early as 1938, to the public stigmatization of loyalty suspects and, consequently, of much of left-of-center opinion. Notwithstanding FDR's support, the LaFollette Committee, that had allowed organized labor to testify to a broad audience about violations of its civil liberties, was terminated in 1940, after only four years of operation. But the Dies Committee (later known as the House Un-American Activities Committee, HUAC) would thrive for about a quarter of a century, mainly under Republican direction. After America's entry into the war in alliance with the Soviet Union, the red hunts were halted or suspended, but not before the procedures and methods had been established that McCarthyism would deploy for its postwar anti-communist drive (Sexton 1991: 144–145; Denning 1996: 126–127).

THE AMERICAN DREAM AND
CONTESTATIONS OF AMERICANISM

It was in the context of mainstream Americanism of the 1930s that the vision of the American Dream became articulated more clearly in the public arena. In print, this occurred first of all through the best-selling popular history *The Epic of America*, written by James Truslow Adams and published in 1931. The American Dream he articulated resonated so well among Americans that today it seems as if this was there from the very outset of the nation. Adam's description persisted, and has apparently been used for the current definition of the American Dream in *Merriam-Webster's Collegiate Dictionary*: "(1931): an American social ideal that stresses egalitarianism and especially material prosperity" (2001: 37). Adams, a member of a patrician white Anglo-Saxon family, was close to the Progressive tradition and deeply suspicious of business as well as enamored by immigrants. He did not coin the phrase "the American Dream," though, as he himself acknowledged, stating that it was a "concept" that was generally considered as being "typically American" (Adams 1931: vii–viii, qtd. in Gitlin 1995: 249 n 57). Nevertheless, it was only after the publication of Adam's book that the phrase began to circulate in the speeches of politicians and the titles of plays and novels (Brandt 1981: 24).

In his book, Adams wrote enthusiastically about "that American Dream of a better, richer, and happier life for all our citizens of every rank which is the greatest contribution we have as yet made to the thought and welfare of the world. Ever since we became an independent nation, each generation has seen an uprising of the ordinary Americans to save that dream from the forces which appeared to be overwhelming and dispelling it." This dream was of "a land in which the life could be better and richer and fuller for every man, with opportunity for each according to his ability or achievement." It entailed not only opportunity but also social equality. Adams furthermore recognized that the dream was tarnished by "three centuries of exploitation and conquest." Although the dream of freedom from the heel of dominant classes, that attracted so many immigrants, had been realized more fully in actual life in America than elsewhere, this was still imperfectly the case. Denouncing the greed of big businessmen and proposing a more equitable distribution of wealth, Adams suggested that such reforms were necessary to truly realize the dream (Adams 1931: viii, 404–405, 416–417, qtd. in Gitlin 1995: 57–58). But there was another, more fundamental shortcoming to this concept of the American Dream: the celebration of this American merging into a national collectivity was almost exclusively premised on the whiteness of all the merging parties. Not all Americans were the descendants of voluntary immigrants; Indians, most African Americans, and some Mexican Americans were not, of course. Therefore Todd Gitlin does not hesitate to call this democratic Americanism "a sort of ethnocentrism from below" (Gitlin 1995: 57).

Adams's notion of the American Dream, which came close to being the religion of patriotism, also caught the attention of historians, sociologists, and other scholars. As early as 1938 the sociologist Robert K. Merton referred to the American Dream in an important essay on social anomie (normlessness) in American society.[4] He associated the Dream first of all with success, especially monetary success, and indicated that this was the principal goal of American culture, deeply inculcated into all members of this society (although more so among some groups than others). Those citizens who could not obtain such success through regular, socially accepted routes resorted to other means to reach the same end, that were considered anomic by mainstream society. Thus, such "aberrant behavior" might "be regarded sociologically as a symptom of dissociation between culturally prescribed aspirations and socially structured avenues for realizing these aspirations" (Merton 1968: 188). In other words, this concerned a discrepancy between widely shared cultural goals and the institutionally sanctioned means to achieve these ends, which were not available to the "deviant groups" involved. A significant number of scholars subsequently elaborated on this interpretation, equating the American Dream with the achievement of the sort of success dramatized in the Horatio Alger "rags-to-riches" stories and in the vast body of how-to-succeed literature produced in America during the late nineteenth century and continued into the twentieth century. This literature still flourishes today, in more up-to-date narratives about men (and occasionally women) of ordinary backgrounds rising to the top as CEOs in the corporate world of mass media or computer technology and software.

Yet there were other scholars who took another road, not so much disagreeing with Merton's interpretation as simply ignoring it. For them, the Dream was essentially a utopian vision of a better society, held by all dreamers, from Sir Thomas More on down, for whom America was the last, best hope of humankind, a place not meant for the achievement of individual success but for the realization of a good, if not perfect, society. There has indeed never been such a thing as *the* American Dream, but it did and still does refer to something that the various versions have in common. It is first of all a myth of the future. The meaning of America lies not in what its citizens are at a certain point but in who they shall become, which means that the myth is necessarily vague and without specific content: "the governing idea is that [Americans] are — America is — all possibility" (Brandt 1981: 25), or as Merton wrote, "...in the American Dream there is no final stopping point" (Merton 1968: 190). Still a good case can be made that the American Dream, as the concept entered the public domain in the 1930s, basically always entailed either one of the two aforementioned strains: the materialistic success story of the hegemonic culture or a reformist/utopian dream of some kind, carried by a countervailing tendency. This manifested itself in contestations about the meaning of Americanism.

During the late 1930s, when the United Automobile Workers fought a battle to unionize Ford, the ideological theme of "Americanism versus Fordism" was central to the union's appeal to Ford workers. Fordism, depicted as a tyrannical regime in which one wealthy man's power and privilege enabled him to violate the rights of his workers, was counterpoised to unionism as an alternative organizing principle that implied the construction of "industrial democracy" in which the rights of workers would be protected and they would be allowed some degree of participation in their work place. Thus the UAW managed to counter employers' anti-union propaganda and give voice to the aspirations of large segments of the industrial working class. The unionists branded Ford's open shop regime as "un-American" and contrasted this with their own vision of Americanism in which the rights of labor were to be legally safeguarded alongside those of capital. This presupposed an American way of life in which basic values such as self-determination and equality were extended into the workplace, and in which workers would be enabled to secure an "American standard of living" for themselves and their families. Importantly, this mixture of' "Americanism" and "industrial democracy," and their unresolved ambiguities, allowed the union to be very inclusive and to reach workers at every position along an ideological spectrum ranging from communism and Trotskyism to Catholic corporatism (Rupert 1995: 165–166).

At any one time Americanism had its defenders as well as its opponents in the United States, their positions taking a different character, of course, depending on the prevailing version of Americanism. World War II revived a unifying Americanism that was on the brink of extinction. The war evoked xenophobia and uniformity, but also the democratic values of the Popular Front. Government propaganda tended to discourage the expression of difference, and popular culture was used as a weapon in the war effort. Movies and radio, books and pamphlets, popular artists and social scientists — a large number of the propagandists were liberals and leftists — portrayed a unified, finally fused America. Americans took refuge within a collective identity that gained coherence from the fact that the country was under assault. Yet throughout the 1940s anti–Semitic attitudes and practices (including university quotas and job discrimination) also flourished, and during the war Japanese Americans were interned and their property confiscated, while Italian and German Americans were occasionally suspected of fascist or Nazi sympathies. Furthermore, restrictions on Chinese and Filipinos — both American allies — were maintained throughout the war and after (Gitlin 1995: 59–60). The war also set in motion processes that would further strengthen the darker side of Ford's Americanism, leading from an industrial culture of individualism and shared prosperity to a repressive conformity in which dissidence was equated with disloyalty, and the covert operations of industrial secret police replaced the intrusive, but relatively open, interventions by investigators and "advisors" of the Ford Sociological Department as a primary instrument of labor control (Rupert 1995: 124–125).

The Cold War and Americanism

With the rise of anti-communism after the war, the remainders of the Popular Front Americanism of the 1930s quickly fell into disarray. By collaborating with conservative Democrats and Republicans in the transformation of "socialism" into a pejorative term, liberals helped create the repressive Cold War climate in America. In this process "Americanism" proved to be a flexible ideological framework, an expedient means to delegitimate radical, nonconformist and professedly internationalist ideas. The House Un-American Activities Committee (HUAC) returned to its prewar preoccupation: the communist penetration of the CIO and the Democratic Party. One of its new activities that drew much media attention was an inquiry into subversion in the film industry. Fearing a public revolt at the box office, the film industry's top management announced they would not employ anyone accused of communism who refused to deny the accusation, which signaled the beginning of the firing and blacklisting of hundreds of HUAC witnesses.

In 1947 President Truman issued Executive Order no. 9835, under which more than two million federal employees were made subject to loyalty checks. The Justice Department compiled official lists of "subversive" organizations and "fronts" and prosecuted communist leaders under the Smith Act of 1940, which, even in peacetime, criminalized membership of designated "subversive" groups or advocacy of their programs. This act required all resident aliens to register and be fingerprinted and made it a criminal act to advocate or belong to organizations that advocated the overthrow of the government by force or to incite disloyalty or interfere with the morale or discipline in the armed forces. Penalties included prison, heavy fines, and deportation of foreigners, even if the offending beliefs had long been discarded. The victims were imprisoned ultimately not for espionage but for a thought crime — they were proven guilty of formally adhering to Marx and Lenin.

An all-time low in the postwar communist hunt by the HUAC was the passing of the draconian Internal Security Act (ISA), known as the McCarran Act after its sponsor, the Democratic Senator Pat McCarran, by Congress in September 1950. This act required designated communist groups — that is, the Communist Party and all communist "front" organizations — to register with the government and reveal the sources of funds, the names of officers, and in many cases the names of members. It deprived their targets of their right to hold passports, government or defense jobs, and prevented foreigners who had once been members of the Communist Party from entering the country. It also limited picketing of federal courts, and even gave the President powers to intern "potential subversives" in concentration camps during security emergencies. This "preventive detention" provision remained on the statute books for no less than twenty years, although it was never implemented. The main outcomes of the act were harassment and exclusion of suspect aliens and the denial of government jobs. Like its precursor in the late 1930s, state legislatures played a significant role in the postwar red scare. From 1945 to 1954, forty-five states passed laws aimed at suppressing the Communist Party and "subversive organizations." These laws required "seditious" organizations to register, barred them and their members from the ballot and public employment, and required disclaimer oaths for everyone listed on a ballot. Throughout the country, free assembly was curtailed, and injunctions often prohibited assemblies (Sexton 1991: 149–150; Marqusee 2004: 30, 32; Ybarra 2004).

From 1945 to 1957, HUAC called 3,000 witnesses and cited 135 of them for contempt, next to 91 of such citations issued by all other investigating committees conducting hearings on un-Americanism, which also included the Senate Internal Security Subcommittee (SISS) and the House committees on Immigration and Naturalization, Public Works, Military Affairs, Education and Labor, District of Columbia, and Veterans Affairs; as well as Senate committees on the Judiciary, Labor and Public Welfare, and Interstate and Foreign Commerce. Congressional hearings, which reached their peak with the televised Senate hearings of the 1950s led by McCarthy backed by the FBI (still headed by J. Edgar Hoover) and the new Central Intelligence Agency (CIA), established in 1947, led to many job dismissals and ruined careers and reputations. Some 13.5 million people, or about one in five people in the labor force, were affected by loyalty-security programs as a condition of employment, and some 10,000 were fired from their jobs — about 3,900 federal, 5,400 private, and 1,000 state and local employees. In addition, over 20,000 were formally charged between 1947 and 1953 with disloyalty under the federal program alone; most charges involved association with a suspect person, often a family member. Penalties could also include denial of voting rights and loss of such benefits as unemployment compensation, public housing and loans, welfare, veterans benefits, and disability and old age benefits. Loyalty suspects were barred from practicing law or obtaining radio and television licenses. Suspect foreigners were deported or denied entry into the country, and naturalization was revoked in many cases. Such penalties were applied by the often dubious standards of various public agencies without the victims having the benefit of legal safeguards established by the criminal justice system (Sexton 1991: 146–148, 152–153).

As the Cold War emerged, radical leftists and their liberal sympathizers at the Ford Motor Company were excluded from the domain of legitimate Americanism, and alternative versions of industrial democracy that entailed a critical potential and challenges to liberal capitalism, were marginalized. Rupert sees the unionization struggles at Ford, and the ideological theme of "Americanism versus Fordism" that both facilitated and constrained the triumph of unionism, as being representative of the ideological struggle that ultimately led to the post-World War II cultural consensus and hegemony of a form of embedded liberalism[5] in America. In his reconstruction, liberal capitalism — modified to accommodate collective bargaining and a more interventionist government — constituted the consensual basis of the mass industrial society of the postwar era by promising mass prosperity and a "democratic" alternative to totalitarianism: "It was on the basis of such an ideological framework — with an ontology of abstract individualism residing at its center — that industrial labor could reach an accommodation with corporate capital in America, and both could work together to reconstruct the core of the world economy along liberal capitalist lines" (Rupert 1995: 165–166).

At the height of the Cold War, when jingoist variants of Americanism reigned supreme, critic Edmund Wilson defined Americanism as an affection for, and partiality toward, the United States, and he suggested that "it has been made to serve some very bad causes, and is now a word to avoid" (Wilson 1957: 31). In this connection it is noteworthy that McCarthyism, and its demonization and prosecution of real or purported leftists, was carried out by recently assimilated immigrants, often Catholics, "intent on demonstrating that the purity of their "Americanism" was superior to that of the old-established but liberal and cosmopolitan Anglophile Protestants" (Pfaff 1993: 187). Thus, prime targets were individuals and groups at the State Department, the established institutions of private Eastern education, the Eastern press, and those in public service who were accused of practicing "un-American" activities. However, it should also be noted that traditional conservatives at the elite level in both major parties (but mostly Republicans) were among McCarthy's most avid supporters and activists of his movement. McCarthyism's roots in an already-existing conservative faction inside the Republican Party must not be underestimated. It was right-wing Republicans, bitterly hostile to the New Deal and appalled by Truman's 1948 victory, who actually launched the postwar red scare, as they worked their way toward power. Especially the long-established Republican political and economic elites in the Midwest were disturbed about cosmopolitanism and about the prestige given to the well-educated and the established families and businesses in the East (similar targets as those of McCarthy). On the other hand, McCarthy and other Midwestern conservatives never went beyond rhetorical attacks on Eastern corporate elites; they never made real attempts to injure the vital interests of Eastern businessmen, who, with their Midwestern counterparts, were all members of the moneyed classes (Rogin 1967: 223–226, 230–231; Griffith 1970: ix; Fried 1990: 9).

According to Gitlin, McCarthyism was of limited importance for shaping popular identity. In the eyes of many Americans it was first of all the rising standard of living and "the prospect of an unceasing improvement in private life" that showed that "Americanism *worked*," given the fact that the major criterion for success in the culture was economic advancement (Gitlin 1995: 62, emphasis in original). Moreover, support for Eisenhower, no less than for McCarthy, could express conformity to Americanism, and cater to the needs of those ridden with a "compulsive Americanism" (Rogin 1967: 246). However, when the excesses of McCarthyism eventually were over, its assumptions still remained in place. Ultimately, McCarthyism understood in its broader sense (including the everyday consequences of the McCarran Act) was not so much about the prosecution of communist spies or celebrities by grand inquisitors, but rather about the political domestication and containment of factories and offices, schools, local libraries, radio stations, as well as popular culture forms such as comic books, TV series and advertisements. In this regard McCarthyism certainly did influence popular identity. Suspicion of "subversiveness" was extended from communists to socialists, liberals, progressive Democrats, labor activists, and New Dealers more generally.

The "new loyalty" and prevailing conformity, which entailed an uncritical and unquestioned acceptance of the status quo in America, is also responsible for the disappearance from the public agenda of the issues of fair distribution, concentration of corporate power, and class conflict during most of the postwar period until the mid–1960s. The crusade against un-Americanism expanded the province of conservatism and achieved a national acceptance of its version of Americanism. It strengthened the ability of employers to repress unionism, through the passage of the Taft-Hartley Act of 1947 (adopted over Truman's veto), considered to be the most severe antilabor legislation of all English-speaking nations — if not of all advanced western democracies — in the postwar era. Among its many provisions was the requirement that union officers must sign a non-communist loyalty oath in order to use the National Labor Relations Board (NLRB), a requirement that turned out to be unenforceable, but nevertheless caused much trouble to the labor-left.

In the labor movement the purge of leftists (or those labeled as such) led to mass expulsions, splits, internecine struggles and an historic depoliticization from which the U.S. trade unions would never fully recover. About 80 percent of the country's one million public school teachers underwent some form of loyalty screening by state and local governments. Higher education was also affected, leaving little room for intellectuals of the radical left. It concerned the revenge of big business on organized labor, and of the right on the New Deal. This modern-day witch hunt was intertwined with international developments — at the background were anti-colonial struggles in Indochina, Indonesia, the Philippines and West Africa, many in which U.S. corporate interests had a major stake. McCarthyism's defining legacy was not its procedural abuses of the judiciary but, most of all, the foreclosure of radical options in general. Any politics that did not accommodate to the hegemonic version of Americanism was demonized, and the political center pushed to the right (Sexton 1991: 154–157; Marqusee 2004: 32, 34).

MULTICULTURALISM, IDENTITY POLITICS, AND THE RISE OF A NEW CONSERVATIVE AMERICANISM

The Americanness held together by the Cold War and economic prosperity gave way in the 1960s, when growing numbers of Americans involved in civil rights and antiwar movements repudiated American practices and questioned American ideals. From the late 1960s onwards, a separatist urge around the issues of ethnicity, "race," and gender began to dominate the agenda of radical activists, and the idea of a common culture of Americanness was left far behind. "For the first time since 1919, significant groups of Americans refused to speak the language of Americanism. Black nationalists and student radicals turned their earlier reverence for American ideals into their hatred of a 'totalitarian' *AmeriKKKa*" (Gerstle 1989: 334). The idea of a common American identity, if there ever was one, was seen as either a hoax or a menace by these radical opponents of the dominant version of the American Dream, and was in fact ceded to the right, who would later reclaim this identity during the Reagan restoration. As Gitlin indicated in *The Twilight of Common Dreams*:

> On the model of black demands came those of feminists, Chicanos, American Indians, gays, lesbians. One grouping after another insisted on the recognition of difference and the protection of their separate and distinct spheres. Initiative, energy, intellectual ingenuity went into the elevation of differences. The very language of commonality came to be perceived by the new movements as a colonialist smothering — an ideology to rationalize white male domination. The time for reunification would come later, so it was said — much later, at some unspecified time [Gitlin 1995: 100].

The rise and further expansion of this identity politics was also mirrored in American studies: by the 1970s and 1980s it was no longer fashionable to write about America as a large community with common beliefs and values, or an "American identity" as had been the case previously, particularly in the consensual myth- symbol-image school of explanation of the 1950s and early 1960s. The prevailing trend among U.S. Americanists now was to focus on fragments of the American experience, on local particularities, on micro-history, and the differentiating effects of class, gender, race and ethnicity (Pells 1997: 105, 107).

In public debates the terms "Americanism" and "Americanization" were seldom explicitly employed, due to the fact that with the revival of ethnicity from the mid–1960s onwards, these very words tended to be associated historically with abuse (a major legacy of the Americanization movement of the turn of the twentieth century) and were therefore discredited (Gleason 1982: 89, 142). But these terms did constitute a clear subtext and reclaimed their conservative meanings in the assimilationist discourse. The liberal establishment saw the traditional, hegemonic center in disarray and the overarching political commitment of the population under pressure; a leading representative like Arthur Schlesinger Jr. signaled a crisis of national identity and complained about failing assimilation and lack of social cohesion, thereby taking a resolutely modernist position. He insisted that American unity presupposes a common culture, and depends on the repudiation or marginalization of group difference (Schlesinger 1991a). A conservative thinker like Samuel P. Huntington, lamenting the existing multiculturalist condition, emphasized the need to re-Americanize the United States, in line with earlier nativist campaigns of this kind (Huntington 1996: 305–37). He did so while according to nearly every opinion poll, and by common consent, Americans are one of the most patriotic peoples in the world. New Christian fundamentalists embraced American exceptionalism more passionately than any other religious or secular group, thus re-establishing a belief in America's special place among nations. This "fundamentalist Americanism," "the faith that God's plan for the United States and its individual citizens is one of superiority, unending growth, and prosperity," also helped them to proselytize aggressively outside the United States, since they were convinced that America had something superior to offer the rest of the world and that other peoples should be guided and ruled by American principles (Brouwer et al. 1996: 13–14).

Other Americans took a very different, cosmopolitan stance. Postmodernists acknowledged, tolerated, or even celebrated individual and group difference, upholding the decomposition of the nation-state as main frame of reference (Schlesinger 1991b: 68, 98). A multiculturalist platform of progressive-liberal reformists and leftist activists acknowledged the need for some commonality or unity among people who share a de facto national identity, but which is not identical per se with a homogeneous common culture and is also recognized as time-bound. Its members asserted an American multiculturalism that is something more than a discourse and practice of ethnic inclusion in the sense of living-apart-together (Bérubé 1994: 234–235, 238). They tried to come up with creative answers to the basic question: "What *kind* of national unity is necessary to the functioning of a putatively democratic and nominally egalitarian society?" (*ibid.*: 225), to which there was no easy answer in an era of accelerated globalization and its pervasive ramifications for ethnic, religious, and national identities.

Controversies over multiculturalism in America since the 1980s remind one of those in the early twentieth century, insofar as they continue to revolve around the argument that American citizens should get rid of their ethnic particularities in order to participate fully in the imagined community of the nation. Even dissenters from this argument have taken this as their starting point in attempts to come to a new common sense about multiculturalism in America today — as something that goes beyond the politics of ethnic inclusion — and to formulate what multiculturalism will consequently mean in the realm of public schooling and other forms of public policy (Bérubé 1994: 225–241). In 1986, historian Gary Gerstle even saw striking resemblances between the ideological climate of the 1980s and that of the 1920s, and discerned a conservative Americanism gathering force, in which patriotism, like in the earlier period, was "a tool used by the right to bludgeon labor and the left" (Gerstle 1986: 84, 92).

By the turn of the twenty-first century, conservative Americanism had become much more powerful. Several conservatives, who correlated race/ethnicity and immigration, expressed the need for the "Americanization" of newcomers, in a nation allegedly in multicultural disarray. Since they clung to a Euro-conformity paradigm of what constitutes an American, they meant in fact "Euro-Americanization." However, with an official vision of a multicultural society in place, the government was no longer involved in Americanization programs aimed at supplanting immigrants' cultures, nor was it planning to do so (Ong Hing 1997: 174–177).[6] A broadly based resistance movement had developed against the fast-growing, huge Latino immigrant populations in the Southwest, as manifested in repeated calls for "appropriate" immigration restrictions, coupled with the Official English movement that emerged in the early 1980s.

The latter movement developed as a backlash against federally mandated initiatives to promote bilingual and multicultural education in public schools — initiatives that sought to implement the provisions of the Bilingual Education Act of 1968. In reaction to the bilingualism that had become reality to some extent during 1981–1990, ten states in the South and Midwest adopted Official English by statute, which was contrived by conservative political elites in state legislatures. Meanwhile, in 1983, a grassroots organization, "U.S. English," sprang up to defend the cause of Official English in states with less sympathetic political elites. The movement seeks the establishment of English as the nation's only official language and promotes the enactment of legislation that restricts or prohibits the use of languages other than English by government agencies and, in some cases, by private businesses as well.

Needless to say, English Only campaigns primarily target Latinos and Asians, who make up the majority of recent immigrants. Most language-minority residents are Spanish-speaking, a result of the sharp increase in immigration from Latin America. In 1996, the House of Representatives passed an Official English bill that would have mandated all federal and state governmental agencies to operate using only the English language, but the Senate failed to act on it. A revised 1998 bill that still would have made English the official language of the United States, was defeated 238 to 182 in the House in favor of a bipartisan amendment that would merely "promote the teaching of English." Yet in 2001, U.S. English (that enrolled almost 1.2 million members then) launched a new drive to force Congress to pass a bill making English America's "common language." Thus far these efforts have failed at the federal level. But at the time of writing, 27 states have adopted English as their official language, while several more are considering similar legislation. Passage of an English Only ordinance has likewise resulted in the cancellation of multicultural events and bilingual services, ranging from direction signs in public transit systems or the use of foreign languages on private business signs to medical services at public hospitals. This all occurred notwithstanding the fact that, according to the American Civil Liberties Union (ACLU) and other defenders of American civil rights, English Only laws are evidently inconsistent with the Equal Protection Clause of the Fourteenth Amendment.[7]

Ironically, many of the leading figures in the counterattack against multiculturalism are from ethnic minority backgrounds. For example, U.S. English president Mauro Mujica is an architect-businessman and Hispanic immigrant from Chile and its founder, Senator S.I. Hayakawa (R–CA), is a Canadian immigrant of Japanese descent. To some degree this is a symbolic strategy, allowing such organizations to maintain respectability through successful immigrants as representatives. But it is also the case that, though more whites support English Only than nonwhites, Official English legislation is backed by a significant proportion of ethnic minorities.[8] If the movement were to adopt a more ethnically exclusivist position, it would jeopardize the legislative progress it has made thus far. For this reason it has been argued that while many Official English activists may support the notion of an Anglo-American nation, this does not imply that Official English is a dominant ethnic tendency. According to Eric Kaufmann it should be seen as a civic rather than an ethnic nationalist movement. On the other hand, as this political scientist readily admits, there are important links between Official English proponents and immigration restrictionist organizations, including more extreme groups who hold eugenicist or racist beliefs (Kaufmann 2003: 461–462; 2004: 265–266). Therefore this view appears to be problematic — one should at least depict the Official English movement as a heterogeneous group with both civic and ethnic nationalist tendencies, whose relative impact differs according to context. Moreover, on closer inspection the dichotomy between ethnic and civic nationalism arguably does not fit the American case. Despite a prevailing rhetoric of one-people nationhood and its concomitant melting-pot metaphor, American nationality is built on a community of groups, with outsider groups continually demanding inclusion and challenging groups already included (King 2005: 5, 178 n. 5). This means that civic nationalism in America rests on ethnic foundations, even though civic nationalists tend to stress their belief in an ideological rather than a genealogical (Anglo- or broader ethno-)Americanism.

More generally, a new wave of white minority politics against what is considered to be a Latino takeover by its proponents is cresting in the beginning of the twenty-first century, with California again leading the way. Its participants, mostly conservative white Republicans, accuse their enemy of "race hatred," aiming to undermine the very foundations of Anglo-American civilization. But this new politics of fear does not remain confined to this Southwestern state and is emerging across the country as its promoters redefine and invert who is racial victim and who is racial oppressor. This has been manifested in a campaign (including ralleys on various university campuses in the Southwest, beginning with the UCLA campus, March 2004) against the Movimiento Estudiantil Chicano de Aztlán, known as Mecha, a national Chicano student group founded during the identity and power movements of the early 1970s. Several leading Latino politicians have also come under attack for association with Mecha. Their opponents point to references in Mecha's founding documents to "La Raza," a concept popularized by the early twentieth-century Mexican intellectual José Vasconcelos, which literally means "the race" but refers figuratively to Latinos born of the Spanish conquest of Indians. While serving as an expression of ethnic solidarity among these Latinos, the new nativists interpret this vocabulary as a pernicious ideology of racial supremacy. Several other groups of white ethnocentrists across the country are just as obsessed by the growing Latino influence they see confirmed by new census data. (According to a census report released in March 2004, one of every four Americans is expected to be of Latino descent by 2050. In California whites are just 47 percent of the population and will be outnumbered by Latinos within twenty years.)

The European American Issues Forum (EAIF), founded in 1996, has been involved in organizing "campus chapters" in the form of Caucasian Clubs at high schools and colleges in California. Even a bulwark of mainstream environmentalism, the Sierra Club, has come under attack. Recently a group of well-heeled, anti-immigrant, anti–Latino activists tried to take over the Sierra Club, in order to use this as a medium for further dissemination of their belief that they are defending American civilization against the barbarian invaders from the South. They were defeated by the Club's management, however. Scholars like Victor Davis Hanson, author of the bestseller *Mexifornia*, have provided intellectual backing to this hate-based movement, with frequent appearances on television, radio, lecture circuits and on the Internet.[9] *Mexifornia* is replete with Spenglerian phrases like "decline," "balkanized enclaves," "the fiction of cultural equality" and other "pathologies" brought by Mexicans and other Latinos to the "West." It proposes an "assimilationist program," that reminds us of the Americanization programs with regard to Mexican immigrants directed by the Commission established by Progressive Era California Governor Hiram W. Johnson mentioned earlier. But contrary to these Progressives' unease, to some degree, with the excesses of corporate capitalism, there is no recognition by Hanson and kindred conservatives of the glaring disparity between rich and poor surrounding Hanson's San Joaquin Valley home base, nor of the extremely high number of reported hate crimes in the area between Bakersfield and Stockton in recent years (Lovato 2004). Even more intellectual authority has been conferred on this movement by establishment political scientist Samuel P. Huntington, who calls U.S. Latinos "the single most immediate and most serious challenge to America's national identity" in *Who Are We? The Challenges to America's National Identity* (2004). In Huntington's view "The Hispanic Challenge" is the major cause of a "clash of civilizations" at home.[10]

On the other hand, however, several politicians and policymakers both on the left and the right have come to realize that the border and immigration policy over the past decade (including the many crackdowns on illegals crossing the Southern border since President Clinton's 1994 Operation Gatekeeper) has ultimately failed and that there is a pressing need for immigration reform. Whereas traditionally the business lobby and its Republican allies only want a bracero-like guest-worker program, Democrats, labor and liberals have emphasized legalization, if not amnesty for the undocumented. There is a movement to attain liberalized immigration reform that would meet the needs and preferences of both sides. The groups involved range from immigrant rights' groups, the U.S. Conference of Catholic Bishops, the National Council of Churches and organized labor to farmers, growers and fast-food franchises up to the U.S. Chamber of Commerce. Conservative Idaho Senator Larry Craig and the American Farm Bureau have joined hands with Democratic Senator Ted Kennedy and the AFL-CIO. Republican Senator John McCain has teamed up with Kennedy to sponsor legislation that has been strongly endorsed by both corporate businesses and working America. The Kennedy-McCain bill, introduced in May 2005, would create a separate program that would allow immigrants to reside in the United States as long as they could provide evidence of employment. The bill would allow foreign workers to enter the country and fill job vacancies requiring few or no skills. Applicants would have to show that they had a job waiting in the United States, pay a fine of $500 in addition to application fees, and clear all security, medical, and other checks. A visa would be valid for three years, and renewable once for an additional three years. After six years the worker would either have to return home or have begun the application procedure for a green card. However, if the worker would lose his or her job, he/she would have to find another one within 60 days or face deportation. Undocumented immigrants too would be eligible to register for a temporary visa, valid for six years. In order to qualify for permanent resident status (and thus to obtain a green card), they would have to meet certain work requirements, pass criminal and security background checks, pay substantial fines and application fees ($2000 or more per adult), demonstrate knowledge of English and civics, and register for military service.

Ironically, in 2004 President Bush, with an eye on both the growing Latino vote and his big-business supporters, called for a new massive guest-worker program. He then backed the program advocated by the Essential Worker Immigration Coalition (an alliance of the nation's forty-three largest employer associations). Many Democratic liberals and some immigrant advocacy groups were against any such plan, since they saw it as similar to the bracero schemes of the 1950s. A coalition stretching from pro-business Republicans to liberal Democrats agreed on the broad outlines of legislation as formulated in the Kennedy-McCain bill, that would tighten border controls but also create a legal way for Mexican workers to come to the United States and, most important, provide for eventual legalization of the estimated 11 to 12 million undocumented immigrants already living in America. While the AFL-CIO, expressing its fear of the creation of an undemocratic, two-tiered society, withdrew its support for the idea of a guest-worker plan, one of the country's biggest unions, the Service Employees International, which has been focusing on organizing immigrant workers, supports the plan.

But in 2005 the power balance began to shift toward the anti-immigrant right that seized the political initiative in the legislative domain. It started a campaign against Kennedy-McCain calling the bill a general amnesty and a "pay to stay" scheme. Anti-immigration drives have been (and are being) held in about a dozen states — not just in the Southwest but also in Washington, Colorado, Virginia, Georgia, Alabama, Arkansas, Florida, Utah and even far-away "liberal" Massachusetts. A citizens' group called the Minuteman Project began vigilante patrols of the Mexican border. Prominent Democrats have been competing with Republicans in seeking to appeal to anti-immigrant sentiments, particularly in the Southwestern states, among those who worry that illegal immigrants are unfairly taking jobs and social services.[11] Much of this activity is inspired by the passage (in November 2004) of Proposition 200 in Arizona, the state that is most adversely affected by illegal immigration. This law requires that legal residency be demonstrated before certain public services are offered. The fact that 47 percent of Latinos voted for Proposition 200 was seen as a clear message to the federal government to take appropriate anti-immigration action by local restrictionist Republicans who opposed fellow Republicans like McCain and Arizona Representative Jim Kolbe who are in favor of immigration liberalization (Cooper 2005).

On December 16, 2005 the House of Representatives passed the Border Protection, Antiterrorism, and Illegal Immigrant Control Act. This draconian anti-immigrant bill (sponsored by Republican James Sensenbrenner Jr. of Wisconsin) would make it a federal misdemeanor crime rather than merely a civil violation to break immigration laws. This would have the effect of criminalizing the millions of undocumented immigrants in the United States. The bill would require low-level immigrant officials to expel (without a hearing) anyone found within 100 miles of the border believed to be a recently arrived undocumented immigrant, except for citizens of Mexico and Canada. Moreover, it would severely undermine due process rights for anyone accused of being in the country illegally. This bill (House Resolution 4437) also calls for a vast expansion of policing along the U.S. border, including the coordination of activities between local authorities, the Department of Homeland Security and the Department of Defense. It would require a new, 700-mile wall along the Mexican border, which stretches for 2,000 miles. Absent from the Sensenbrenner bill is any guest-worker program or procedure to legalize those already in the United States.[12] The bill was intended to torpedo any liberalization of immigration. The President, under pressure of militant anti-immigrant groups on the right of his constituency and worried about splitting the Republican Party in an election year, has retreated, thereby giving more leeway to xenophobic fringe groups (Cooper 2006: 20).

On the other hand, recent demonstrations of primarily Latinos (and smaller numbers of allies in other ethnic communities), organized with the Catholic Church's active support, have articulated strong pro-immigrant worker sentiments. Triggered by anger about the Sensenbrenner bill, many immigrant workers showed up at protest meetings and marches in cities and suburbs across the nation on March 25 and April 10, 2006. An immigrants' rights movement with a growing social and electoral clout has emerged out of a network of labor and community organizations, hometown associations and Spanish-language radio, TV and newspapers. Its leaders merge traditional labor and civil rights strategies and tactics with more transnational, networked — and personalized — organizing to meet the challenges of the global issue of immigration. The new *movimiento* pushes for comprehensive reform of immigration policy that is not expected to come from the current Congress. Its demands concern family reunification, a solution to the visa backlog, by April 2006 at 6.2 million; and a "path to citizenship" that allows immigrant workers to build lives in the United States with a future. Spanish-language media continue to push the idea that although the Sensenbrenner bill has stalled in Congress, the fight over immigrant rights is not over. They played a significant role in a day of national protest on May 1, 2006, a boycott designated A Day Without an Immigrant, during which children and workers walked out of schools or their jobs (Editorial *The Nation* 2006; Meeus 2006; Morales 2006).

However, according to investigative journalist Roberto Lovato this movement should not be framed as a "new civil rights movement," which risks overlooking its roots in Latin American struggles and history. The *movimiento* (some of whose older leaders include former students and political activists who were persecuted in Latin America during the late 1970s and 1980s) is as much the northernmost expression of a resurgent Latin American left as it is a revived, more globalized, human rights-centered continuation of the Chicano civil rights movement and other previous struggles to improve immigrant rights in America. This is reflected, among other things, in the response to the globalization of labor by a major participating organization, the Farm Labor Organizing Committee (FLOC), through the creation of a "migrating union," whose organizers have followed migrant workers to Mexico (where the organization has an office) and then back to the United States over several months.

One should also not overemphasize the role of the local Spanish-language media — it is the organizers of the *movimiento*, nationally and locally — who have indeed built strong relationships with those media — who are leading the charge as they organize and lobby around the immigration debate in Congress, around the anti-immigrant backlash at the national, state and local levels and around a more proactive agenda. Among local and regional activists who do not belong to the inner circle of immigrant rights advocates in Washington focused on elections and legislation, people are more inclined to look beyond elections and even the pending immigration bill, aiming for a strong power base in the longer run through constant organizing. Organizations like Centro Hispano Cuz-catlán, which organizes around worker rights, housing and immigration, also play significant roles in the construction of broader local networks like the Immigrant Communities in Action coalition. Through this coalition, Indian, Pakistani, Korean, Filipino, Bangladeshi, Indonesian and other immigrant groups have co-organized some of the country's most diverse protest marches (Lovato 2006).

Outbursts of anti-immigrant discourse historically leave African Americans ambivalent. Earlier waves of (primarily European) immigration diminished their job prospects, and many black leaders openly opposed unchecked immigration. But African Americans also felt empathy for those immigrants, who were victims of colonial domination in their home countries and were fellow targets of discrimination in the United States. That ambivalence is apparent again in this latest immigration debate. Most African-American leaders back the aims of immigration activists, and several national polls show that black citizens are more than other groups inclined to support liberal immigration measures.

But there is also considerable opposition to such measures within the black community. This revolves largely around issues of employment and is driven by fears that immigration issues and Latino concerns will suspend efforts to redress the injustices of the legacy of slavery. Some activists within this counter-movement argue that, given the high unemployment and incarceration figures of black communities across the nation, ex-prisoners and inner-city victims of chronic education failures are especially vulnerable. It is from this segment of the black community that much of the African-American opposition to the immigration movement is emerging. Critics on the left have pointed out, however, that black unemployment rates in cities like Cincinnati, Indianapolis, Pittsburgh and Memphis, which have relatively small numbers of immigrant workers, are just as high as elsewhere. They contend that focusing on undocumented immigrants as a cause of unemployment of unskilled workers distracts from the real causes, that is, racial discrimination, the decline of the trade union movement and the deindustrialization of the economy. In their eyes the most useful strategy to attain better conditions for all workers is to join forces with the new Latino-led immigrant movement struggling to improve labor conditions. This also means linking up to the broader counter-strain against neoliberalism that has become influential in various Latin American countries. The current political leaders of Argentina, Bolivia, Brazil, Chile, Uruguay and Venezuela recognize that the policies of the IMF, the World Bank and other carriers of the "Washington Consensus" have helped cause the economic distress that fostered emigration to the United States in the first place. These Latin American nations are demanding new economic arrangements expected to provide sustainable solutions (Muwakkil 2006).

EXCLUSIONIST AMERICANISM AFTER 9/11

After September 11, 2001, however, Americanist exclusiveness has been most strongly articulated vis-à-vis Arabs and Muslims, and Americans of Arabic descent (or others perceived as such) both at home and abroad, in the context of the ongoing "war on terrorism." The 9/11 events spawned a true panic regarding conspiring terrorists and opponents of the George W. Bush Administration's war in Iraq and foreign policy, along with others considered to be a threat to the government. The USA Patriot Act, which was passed through Congress and signed by President Bush only six weeks after the September 11 terrorist attacks, authorizes law enforcement officials to carry out electronic surveillance and wiretaps more widely, and allows the president, when the nation is under attack, to confiscate any property within U.S. jurisdiction of anyone believed to be involved in such attacks. The Act also makes tighter oversight possible of financial activities, to prevent money laundering, and diminishes bank secrecy in an effort to disrupt terrorist activities. Furthermore, the USA Patriot Act allows the Federal Bureau of Investigation to share information gathered in terrorism investigations under the "foreign intelligence" standard with local law enforcement agencies, which, in essence, nullifies the higher standard of oversight that applied to domestic investigations as defined in provisions of the Foreign Intelligence Surveillance Act of 1978.[13] Moreover, the Act authorizes the government to deny entry to foreigners because of speech rather than actions, to deport even permanent residents who innocently supported disfavored political groups, and to imprison foreign nationals without charges. It exposes immigrants to the risk of extended, and in some cases, even "indefinite" detention, based solely on the Attorney General's untested certification that he has "reasonable grounds to believe" that a non-citizen is engaged in terrorist activities. This in fact implies suspending the Due Process Clause, which applies to all persons within the United States, including aliens, whether their presence is lawful, unlawful, temporary, or permanent.

In May 2005, the Senate Intelligence Committee introduced a bill that aimed to reauthorize provisions of the Patriot Act that would otherwise expire by the end of the year. This legislation would make all of the Act permanent, with one exception — Section 223 protects privacy by giving victims of unlawful government surveillance a court remedy; the bill would allow that section to expire. But the proposed bill actually went further than that, and significantly expanded a number of Patriot Act powers. The expansions included proposals, such as allowing the FBI to obtain personal records (from medical facilities, libraries, hotels, gun dealers, banks and other businesses) in terrorism cases without prior court review. This would severely undermine the Fourth Amendment's protections against unreasonable searches and seizures. The proposed bill also added an entire new section that would allow intelligence investigators to track, without probable cause, the outside of any sealed mail sent or received or the contents of any unsealed mail. It also greatly expanded the amount of information obtained without probable cause through extensive surveillance of so-called "routing information" through the Internet.[14]

Building on a growing nationwide discontent with the Patriot Act, this reauthorization act led to a new wave of public outcry and severe criticism of the Patriot Act by the ACLU and other defenders of civil liberties. However, as legal affairs expert David Cole has pointed out, the disputes that arose around the decision whether to reauthorize sixteen "sunsetted" provisions of the Act often ignored fundamental issues having to do with the rights of foreign nationals. Moreover, outside of the province of these debates were the civil liberties abuses since 9/11 that took place without reliance on the Act, since they were based on executive initiatives that had not been challenged by Congress. The battles focused primarily on two of the proposed new sections of the Patriot Act, one popularly known as the "libraries provision" that would allow the government secretly to obtain records of any person from any business, regardless of wrongdoing, and the other authoritizes secret "sneak and peak" searches of homes without promptly informing the home owner. Among the most troubling provisions that were not subject to attempts to "sunsetting" were those on immigration mentioned earlier. This is in line with the fact that practices like torture and rendition, which have been largely reserved for foreign nationals ("them," not "us"), did not generate the grassroots concern that the library provision had done. This double standard was due to two major factors. The immigrant provisions affected foreign nationals nearly exclusively and the only issues that offered some leverage to liberals in the prevailing political climate were those of mutual concern to conservatives — and the latter had not championed the mentioned immigrant issues (Cole 2005).

In July 2005 a majority of the House voted to block the Justice Department and the FBI from using the Patriot Act as legitimation to review library and bookstore records (in other words, it rejected the libraries provisions). An important conducive factor was that many members of Congress represented districts where local anti–Patriot Act resolutions had been enacted. However, the remainder of the proposed reauthorization act passed the House without any significant amendments ("In Fact..." 2005). In the following months there was also increasing pressure on the Senate by the White House and its allies to adopt this revised bill. But a "cloture motion" to limit debate on legislation to reauthorize the Patriotic Act was rejected by the Senate on December 16, 2005, which meant that efforts to make substantive changes to the law deemed necessary by its critics could continue. This motion failed only hours after the *New York Times* revealed that the President had directed the National Security Agency (NSA) to spy on people in the United States in clear violation of the Foreign Intelligence Surveillance Act (FISA). Congress had passed this law in 1978, in response to revelations that former President Nixon was using "national security" claims to spy on U.S. citizens he considered his "enemies," which was undoubtedly in contravention of Fourth Amendment rights.[15] However, just before the Christmas break, after repeated calls from the White House that this antiterrorism law was indispensable to homeland security, Congress voted to extend the Patriot Act for just one month. Early in February 2006, the expiration date was further extended to March 10. This meant that Congress had to reconsider the bill's reauthorization yet again.[16] The final result was that in early March 2006 Congress passed the USA Patriot Act Reauthorization Act with a small number of minor amendments, which failed to protect the liberty and privacy of ordinary Americans according to the ACLU and many other critics from across the political spectrum.[17]

Importantly, in May 2005 Congress passed immigration provisions as part of the Iraq War appropriations bill that go much further than the Patriot Act. These allow for the deportation of foreign nationals who ever joined or made a donation to any organization that ever used, or threatened to use, a weapon. Accordingly, foreign nationals who ever donated to the African National Congress, the Israeli military, Afghanistan's Northern Alliance, the Nicaraguan *contras* or the Irish Republican Army can in principle be deported. To prove that one's support or membership was not intended to further terrorism or violence is no defense. Critics charge that this legislation resurrects the "guilt by association" approach of the 1952 McCarran-Walter Act that codified immigration laws during McCarthyism.

Civil liberties abuses committed by U.S. law enforcement agencies or the military outside of the Patriot Act include: the incommunicado detention and inhumane treatment of hundreds of "enemy combatants" from around the world without charges or hearings at America's military base, Guantánamo Bay, Cuba; torture at Abu Ghraib and other U.S. prisons in Iraq, Afghanistan, Guantánamo Bay, and anywhere touched by the "war on terrorism"; the use of immigration law to launch a nationwide campaign of ethnic profiling; the detention of more than 5,000 foreign nationals, virtually all Arabs or Muslims (none of whom have been convicted of a terrorist crime) on the mere basis of suspicion of terrorist links or activities; the development and application of computer data-mining programs that offer the U.S. government access to a wealth of private information about U.S. citizens (again without any grounds for suspicion); the FBI's monitoring of public meetings and religious services without grounds for suspecting criminal activities; and the use of "coercive interrogation" to extract information from suspects in "the war on terrorism" (Cole 2005).

After the summer of 2004, when the Supreme Court ruled that prisoners at Guantánamo Bay have habeas corpus rights to contest their detention in U.S. courts, there has been a significant increase of the number of kidnappings and "extraordinary renditions" of suspected terrorists to foreign countries (including Poland, Romania, Jordan, Egypt, and Syria) where they were or are extralegally detained in secret prisons and subjected to torture by the U.S. military, contract interrogators (employees of U.S. for-profit organizations involved through outsourcing), CIA employees, as well as foreign nationals from the respective host countries. Allegations about these practices were first raised in the *Washington Post* in early November 2005, and have led to public outrage expressed by human rights groups in America, Canada and Europe, as well various governments. These kidnappings and "renditions" have spawned critical inquiries in Spain, Italy, Sweden, Iceland and Canada, while the European Union and Council of Europe (COE)[18] are investigating the CIA "black sites" (Smith 2005; Editorial *The Nation* 2005). An interim COE report published on January 24, 2006 confirmed the "rendition" of more than 100 prisoners "affecting Europe." Its author, the Swiss MP Dick Marty, suggested that "some European governments actively collaborated, some tolerated while others simply looked away" from the CIA's clandestine operations on their countries' soil over the past two or three years. He insisted that it would be unfair to single out any EU member, however, because governments across Europe had been "willingly silent" on the issue. But the report concluded that there was no firm evidence so far of the existence in any European country of secret CIA detention centers allegedly set up after the terrorist attacks of 9/11. Despite denials expressed by the new U.S. Secretary of State, Condoleezza Rice, during a trip to Europe in early December 2005, the Swiss MP and some critics have suggested that such centers had been installed at several locations in Europe but were moved to North Africa after the *Washington Post* broke the story.[19] A draft interim European Parliament report dated April 24, 2006 included pronouncements that were more definite about the involvement or complicity of various European governments in the illegal abductions, extraordinary renditions and secret detentions of alleged terrorists on the territory of member states carried out by the CIA or other third-country security services on several occasions. The research committee considered it "implausible, on the basis of the testimonies and documents received to date, that certain European governments were not aware of the extraordinary rendition activities taking place on their territory and in their airspace or airports...."[20] The report mentioned Germany, the United Kingdom, Spain, Ireland, Italy, Sweden, and Bosnia explicitly as sites where detainees were thus secretly transferred to countries like Egypt, Jordan, Syria and Afghanistan, known for their frequent use of torture during interrogations. May 9–12, 2006 a delegation from the European Parliament traveled to Washington to report on these preliminary findings, and then also met representatives of the ACLU.

On December 14, 2005, the House of Representatives passed an anti-torture amendment to the Defense Department spending bill (with Senator John McCain as the major driving force), despite calls from the White House that the president would veto such a measure. It never came to that, however, because key lawmakers and the White House made a back-room deal that undermined the very principles that the House had affirmed through its amendment. The changes allow government officials to treat suspected terrorists cruelly under special circumstances. This could also limit liability for government officials violating prohibitions against abuse and torture, even in cases involving U.S. citizens in federal custody held on U.S. soil. The new revisions could likewise allow evidence obtained by abuse and torture to be used to detain a person indefinitely, and sever access to the courts by individuals detained at Guantánamo Bay, except for very limited appeals, thus undermining the legislation's provisions for applying the Constitution to government actions while at this prison (Meeus 2005).[21]

Attempts at immigration control in relation to border security (identified with national security) also affected regular U.S. citizens. The Sensenbrenner bill would create a federally mandated requirement for everyone — U.S. citizens and non-U.S. citizens alike — to obtain a "permission slip" from the federal government before they could take a job. This legislation would create a sea change in federal employment rules since all workers in the country would be required to participate in a national employment eligibility verification program, which would use an Internet-based system to check the names and social security numbers of all employees against a Department of Homeland Security Database.[22] This legislation would allow individuals who are deemed to be "dangerous aliens" to be detained under the order of the Secretary of Homeland Security pending deportation. The initial period of such a detention would be 90 days, but this could be extended indefinitely.[23]

However, American business groups, including the U.S. Chamber of Commerce, have vigorously opposed this legislation, because it would severely diminish a principal source of cheap labor and place onerous demands on American businesses to screen all of their workers, while bearing the brunt financially of the high costs of implementation (Bacon 2005: 5). And millions of legal, eligible American workers could have their right to work seriously delayed or denied, while fighting bureaucratic red tape to have administrative errors resolved. Nevertheless, on May 25, 2006, the Senate passed the so-called "Compromise Bill"[24] that holds on to the proposed Employment Verification system, which requires that all employers check all new hires, regardless of citizenship or immigration status, against a federal government database. But the Senate has added worker protection, due process and privacy protections to the employment verification provisions. Under the Senate's bill as amended workers would have real administrative and judicial opportunities to challenge erroneous government data that result in denial of work and could recover payback if that happens.[25] The bill offers some form of legal status for an estimated 4 million undocumented immigrants. This legislation divides the undocumented into four categories, with exacting waiting periods for green cards and up to sixteen years for citizenship for those eligible; no long-term legalization provisions for most; increased means of criminalizing, detaining and deporting all immigrants. Overall, however, amendments have brought the Senate bill closer to the approach taken by the House. These include, for example, funding for the building of a 370-mile militarized fence and 500 miles of vehicle barriers along the Mexican border and an amendment to make English the official "national" language. The final legislative product of a possible compromise with the more draconian House (Sensenbrenner) bill is most likely to be even worse from the perspective of immigrant rights (Sarkar 2006: 18).

In addition to tightening national security in the ways mentioned above, the George W. Bush Administration also appears to condone the monitoring of political dissent as an integral part of the "war on terrorism." This dissent has taken three principal forms since 9/11: mass protests and rallies, messages on signs or clothing, and other acts of defiance by communities and individuals, ranging from silent vigils in parks to the passage of resolutions by local governments protesting federal measures that threaten fundamental freedoms. By December 2005, the legislatures of seven states and 400 communities had passed resolutions condemning the Patriot Act's civil liberties abuses and calling for appropriate changes to be made. Some government officials, including local police, have done their utmost to suppress dissent wherever it has sprung up, drawing on a wide variety of tactics — from censorship and surveillance to detention, denial of due process and excessive force. The Pentagon has been monitoring peaceful organizations such as Greenpeace, Food Not Bombs, Veterans for Peace and United for Peace and Justice, as well as other anti-war and anti-military recruiting protesters throughout the United States (including local peace groups in Florida, Georgia, Rhode Island, Maine, Pennsylvania, California and Washington).[26] Protesters in Missouri were beaten and teargassed, demonstrators in California were even fired on, while campus police have helped FBI agents spy on professors and students in Massachusetts. Government officials have even compiled political dossiers on protesters arrested in New York (as has been exposed and challenged by the American Civil Liberties Union). According to the Patriot Act, domestic terrorism includes any crimes that "involve violent acts or acts dangerous to human life" and "appear to be intended" to influence government or a civilian population by "intimidation or coercion." The ACLU has warned that this definition is so broad that it could cover the civil disobedience activities of diverse protest organizations, including Operation Rescue, Greenpeace, and the anti-globalization movement.[27]

All of these governmental interventions were deployed on behalf of a highly restrictive Americanism that excludes and marginalizes foreign nationals, almost all Arabs and Muslims suspected of being involved in terrorism in one way or another, as well as dissidents of various political stripes and many other American protesters upholding constitutional rights that should protect U.S. citizens' fundamental freedoms.

"AMERICANIZATION OF THE SOUTH"
—"SOUTHERNIZATION OF AMERICA"

In the domestic context, the term "Americanization" has also been employed to refer to changes in the regional culture and identity of the South that incorporated the region further into the nation. In this case, the term relates to those processes of national integration particularly involving the South. The term came into usage after the election of Woodrow Wilson, a Southerner by heritage and training, to the White House in 1912 — along with the election of a Democratic Party-controlled Congress — which marked the reemergence of Southern political influence on the national scene and the beginning of a stronger integration of the South with the rest of the nation. The Americanization of the South was a major theme during the years from 1910 to 1985, when the South made the transition from a predominantly agricultural society to a modern industrial society and thus came to look more like the nation as a whole. This happened as a result of federal interventions (New Deal programs, governmental investments etc.), war-related changes during both world wars (fostering national patriotism in the South, building military bases and training armies in the South), further industrialization and socioeconomic advancement, as well as higher geographic mobility, both of Southerners to the cities in and outside the region, and migrants from elsewhere to the South (Wilson 1989: 591).

During the years from 1920 to 1945, the Americanization of the South wrought a

severe crisis in the Southern identity, which also fostered much cultural creativity, especially among the region's intellectuals and artists who felt the impact of the region's transition from a traditional to a modern society. The leading question was what the regional
identity — being Southern — meant in the context of world wars and international, modernist intellectual and literary currents. During the 1920s the South appeared to the nation
as a region plagued by the Ku Klux Klan, hookworm and pellagra, lynchings, the Scopes
Trial and the excesses of religious fundamentalism, whereas the political leadership of the
South demonstrated nothing but a booster mentality. Intellectuals realized they could no
longer take the Southern identity for granted. In the 1930 Southern Agrarians' manifesto
I'll Take My Stand, this group of conservative intellectuals asserted an identity of the
South as an organic culture representing the last hope of the Western world to contain
industrialization and the forces of modernization and dehumanization. They suggested
that the spiritual strength gained from many generations of material deprivation should
be used productively, while the romantic and sentimental view of Southern culture was
questioned and rejected. From this transition period the Southern Literary Renaissance
and a wealth of studies in the social sciences emerged. Journalism, literary criticism, history, fiction, and poetry all benefited from the new spirit of self-criticism. The arrival of
new industrial corporations and service industries in a weakly unionized South, in the
1960s and after, the rise of the Sunbelt, further integration in transcontinental transporta-
tions and communications networks, as well as the migration of substantial numbers of
middle-class whites from the Northeast and Midwest to the South and Southwest, fostered a further Americanization of the South (*ibid.*: 592–595).

On the other hand, social and political changes since the mid–1950s allowed the
South to put a stronger stamp on the rest of the nation. Religious cultures and movements originating in the South grew rapidly and became much more influential in the
North. The same applies to Southern music such as rhythm and blues, country and
western, and the mix of rockabilly that dominated post-war American music (Malone
1979). Southern political figures from Martin Luther King Jr. to George Wallace became
national figures. The wartime migration of black and white Southerners to the defense
plants of the North and West in the 1940s played a major role in this development. It
was the largest internal migration in U.S. history, which "remade the American working class" (Denning 1996: 36) and deeply affected the course of post-war American culture and politics. Inextricably linked to the South-North movement, the relations
between black and white Americans became a much more pronounced issue in the
national culture as a whole. Due to on the one hand urban disinvestment, slum clear-
ance in neighborhoods adjoining white neighborhoods, and the construction of high-
density public housing especially for the black population and, on the other hand,
government subsidies of mortgages and highways to build new suburbs, de facto segregation along color lines became a dominant social fact of American social life in the second half of the twentieth century. The second-generation "new immigrant" working
class that had built the CIO and the Popular Front was replaced by a new working class,
which consisted of a populist mix in which the descendants of the turn-of-the-century
immigrants blended, together with Southern migrants and their offspring. This would
thoroughly change the character of working-class politics and culture, and offer a very
different landscape for national politics (*ibid.*: 36–37).

The phrases "Southernization of America" and "Southernization of American politics" entered the vocabulary of political scientists and journalists in the 1970s (Denning
1996: 35–37, 467). John Egerton used the term "Southernization" to describe the impact

of Southern culture, ideas, and values on the United States as a whole. As he suggested, the North (that is, the non-Southern states), having lost the Vietnam War and finding the Southern ills of poverty and racism alive in its own community, had shown itself more like the South in its political, racial, social, and religious inclinations (Egerton 1974: xix). As a result, the South and the American mainstream began to converge (Cobb 1984: 119–120). The political transformations in American society during the period 1964 to 1972 in parts of the North is evidenced by the appeal of the Southern conservative presidential candidate George Wallace, who gave voice to a growing national white backlash in the mid–1960s. Even more telling was Richard Nixon's "Southern Strategy" (adopting part of Wallace's agenda) and victory in 1968, which resulted in the political and social union of the conservative Republican North with conservative Sunbelt States, with the Deep South at its core. An economic union was involved too, the effects of which would not be seen until well after the social and political repercussions were apparent. James Cobb underlined these effects in *The Selling of the South* (1982), pointing out that the forces that induced the nationalization of the South also triggered the Southernization of the national economy as economic globalization obligated companies to adopt "a more cost-related approach" regarding workers and government (Cobb 1982, 1993). In the late 1990s, Stephen Cummings coined the term "Dixification of America," to refer to the destruction of trade unions and the deregulation of both capital and labor markets due, in large part, to Southern-originated economic policies (Cummings 1998). This "Dixification" of politics cannot be attributed solely to Southern influence, of course, given the ideological influence of the Chicago School of monetarist economics and the strong involvement of economic, financial, and political interest groups in the North defending the neoliberal supply-side economics (with its tax, spending, and regulation cuts). As Cummings himself acknowledged, "Since Dixification also includes the economic impact of conservative Republican economic politics as well, it is not a true subset of Southernization" (*ibid.*: 10).

The "Southernization" of American politics is more generally evident in presidential election results in the past few decades. Sun Belt Republicans have won no less than seven of the ten last presidential elections: two Californians (Nixon and Reagan, each twice) and two Texans (Bush Sr.[28] and Bush Jr., the latter twice). After 1960, the only Democrats who won the presidency were white Southerners: Carter (self-professed "born-again Christian," backed by a majority of Christian Evangelicals during the 1976 election, but rapidly losing their support when they saw a leftward move of the Carter Administration)[29]; and Clinton (the latter twice; yet as a New Democrat he acted as a de facto modern-day "Eisenhower Republican" in his second term, hemmed in on all sides by a predominantly Republican Congress (Micklethwait and Wooldridge 2004: 119–121). A recent book on the emergence of the Bush Jr. Administration's politics carries the ominous phrase "the Southern takeover of American politics" in its title. Its author even speaks more specifically of the "Texanization" of American politics, taking hold concurrently with the collapse of communist systems in Eastern Europe. Deep-rooted Southern militarism, unregulated market ideology, and religious fundamentalism combined to bolster the Republican right's triumphalism in the post-Cold War era (Lind 2003).

We can see that the terms "Americanization of the South" and "Southernization of America" refer to different sides of processes of further national integration occurring in the post-World War II years, that includes the move towards highly conservative politics (but is more than a mere Southern takeover). In this book, the issue of the Americanization of the South will not be explored further, since our interest is first of all focused on American influence abroad and, second, on domestic Americanization — the indigenization of foreign imports and exemplars, and the assimilation of immigrants to American society.

5

Mapping the Field of Americanization Systematically

This chapter offers a conceptual overview of Americanization in its various manifestations, drawing on the previous working histories of relevant terms on both sides of the Atlantic. It also lays the foundation of an interpretative framework that befits the intended critical approach. First the major terms will be discussed, taking the historical context of their varying meanings into account, offering definitions that suit the book's purpose. Then follows an analysis of the prevailing ways in which Americanization abroad has been conceptualized more recently, in terms of local assimilation and transculturalization.

DEFINING THE TERMS "AMERICANISM" AND "AMERICANIZATION" MORE PRECISELY

The first key concept that we deal with here, Americanism, is defined in *Merriam-Webster's Collegiate Dictionary* (2001) as: "n (1781) 1: a characteristic feature of American English especially as contrasted with British English; 2: attachment or allegiance to the traditions, interests, or ideals of the U.S.; 3 a: a custom or trait peculiar to America; b: the political principles and practices essential to American culture." Similarly, the *Dictionary of Americanisms* (1966) mentions four definitions of Americanism: "1. A word or expression originating in the U.S.... 2. 'A love of America and preference of her interests' (quoting from *The Webster* 1906 edition) ... 3. Adoption or display of American ideas, habits, etc. A peculiarity in manners, views, conduct, etc., thought to be typically American ... b. Also applied to typically American things ... 4. The principles of the American party." *The New Oxford Dictionary of English* (2001) gives a more restricted definition of Americanism: "a word or phrase peculiar to or originating in the United States," which remains fully within the domain of language usage. It is particularly the second and third part of the *Merriam-Webster's* definition that interest us here, because they refer to America's guiding ideals and distinctive features that may be of influence and subject of debate both at home and overseas.

"Americanism" is a dual phenomenon. In its positive sense it refers to "America's hallowed repertoire of guiding ideals, explaining its course and destiny to the American nation, while at the same time providing an aspiration to non-Americans abroad." In its negative sense it is the antithesis of Europeanism, "everything that European intellectuals conceived of as their common cultural heritage" (Kroes 1993: 303). Anti-Americanism in Europe has always targeted an Americanism in this latter, noxious sense. I would add that this also concerns non-Europeans elsewhere who were (or are) within the European cultural orbit. Furthermore, we find meanings of Americanism in a negative sense that employ different opposites, such as that between America's globalizing modernity embodied by the individualistic, materialistic hedonism of U.S. capitalist consumerism, "McWorld," and the cultural heritage of ethnic, religious, and national groups as well as local democracy around the globe (Barber 1995).

"Americanization," the other key notion here, traditionally meant something different to Americans and those outside the United States. Non-Americans used the term, often negatively, to refer to American influence abroad, while Americans tended to call this process by other names. To them, "Americanization" meant assimilation to the dominant American way of life by newcomers and other residents who were not yet fully integrated. For those Americans who wished to criticize aspects of American life, other labels were needed in distancing themselves from the tendencies in question. Their vocabulary included terms such as commercialization, vulgarization, trivialization, leveling-down, degeneracy, modernity, Hollywood, mass culture, or sometimes even foreign, meaning non-local (Matthews 1998: 17, 20).[1]

These different meanings and usages of the term Americanization are reflected in the definitions given in *Merriam-Webster's Collegiate Dictionary* (2001): "n (1858) 1: the act or process of Americanizing 2: instruction of foreigners (as immigrants) in English and in U.S. history, government and culture," whereby "to Americanize" is circumscribed as "1: to cause to acquire or conform to American characteristics; 2: to bring (as an area) under the political, cultural or commercial influence of the U.S."[2] It is the first part of the definition of Americanization as well as both meanings of the verb "to Americanize" that have our primary interest here. The former refers to both American influences overseas and what I call domestic Americanization, that is, the indigenization of foreign imports and assimilation of immigrants in America itself. As noted in Chapter 3, the term Americanization has also been employed to refer to the forced assimilation of Native Americans and annexed peoples of Puerto Rico and the Philippines to the dominant Anglo-Protestant culture. This area, although highly interesting in itself, will not be explored further in this book. Needless to say, however, most of the conceptualizations of Americanization that will be presented here are (with appropriate adaptations) applicable in these contexts as well.

First I shall discuss my preliminary definition of Americanization abroad and then turn to domestic Americanization. Basically, there are two distinct tendencies in the ways Americanization has been defined, studied and discussed. This fits with the idea that Americanization is multifaceted, with economic and cultural factors being of prime importance — analogous to the way in which Robertson (2001) sees globalization. First there is the tendency for Americanization to be studied in terms of its cultural manifestations (for example, appropriations of U.S. popular culture by diverse youth subcultures in other countries). By contrast, there is the tendency for the economic dimensions of Americanization (for example, the economic influence of America in consumer good markets and over consumption patterns, or in the communication industries) to be discussed at the cost of the cultural forms (Strinati 1992: 54).[3] Americanization has no single motor force; the input of such forces (politics is a third major factor) will vary from one historical-geographical situation to another. Thus, the question regarding the relative importance of driving forces can only be answered empirically in specific cases of dissemination and reception of American ideas, goods, services and practices overseas. Furthermore, Americanization has many strands and interrelated developments. Closer examination of specific processes as reported in the research literature has made clear that generalizations about

Americanization need to be tempered and specified. What may be true about some aspects of Americanization is not necessarily true of other aspects.

In this book, Americanization overseas — by which I invariably mean "USAmericanization" (Robertson 2003: 257) — is deliberately defined very broadly, that is, as a process in which economic, technological, political, social, cultural and/or sociopsychological influences emanating from America or Americans impinge on values, norms, belief systems, mentalities, habits, rules, technologies, practices, institutions and behaviors of non–Americans. These diverse influences are conveyed by the importation into foreign contexts of products, models or exemplars, images, ideas, values, ideals, technologies, practices and behavior originating from, or at least closely associated with, America or Americans. We should be aware that the division between economic, technological, political, social, cultural and sociopsychological dimensions concerns analytical, as opposed to empirical, distinctions. In reality, the various dimensions interpenetrate each other (*ibid.*: 260), demonstrating all kinds of interrelations and interplays.

This approach deviates from the prevailing tendency in the past few decades to narrow the meaning of the term to *cultural* Americanization, emphasizing the role of popular culture and entertainment, the mass media and cultural industries, as well as transnational consumerism. Much less attention is paid to other cultural aspects. It is also rarely connected with other forms of American influence overseas: economic, financial, social, political and military. This proclivity hinders a deeper understanding of the processes at issue, as will be outlined later.

BECOMING AMERICAN

Let us now focus on domestic Americanization and first consider the Americanization of foreign influences on American territory. This includes the processes by which ideas, artifacts, goods and cultural practices emanating from elsewhere become indigenized in the United States over the course of time, appropriated and incorporated into the American cultural repertoire to become an integral part of the national culture. John Blair Jr., for example, has shown how "modular" structures and cultural practices evolved as part of the emergence of distinctive organizational tendencies in the United States in the nineteenth century. He mentions diverse examples such as the American college curriculum, industrial assembly (i.e., musket manufacture by the "American System of Manufacture"), the structure of skyscraper architecture, Whitman's poetry, the musical structure of blues and jazz, American football, the rules for land tenure in property law, religious disestablishment. "Modularity results from conceiving a whole in such a way that its parts are open to replacement by or recombination with other parts that are compatible and systematically equivalent to each other" (Blair 1988: 3). This took place vis-à-vis earlier modes of organization in Europe of the *anciens régimes*, which dominated before the end of the eighteenth century and independent cultural development in the United States, and tended to treat structures and cultural practices as historically grown, organic wholes. "The modular, wherever it occurred, broke down earlier structures into relatively small units, which were functionally equivalent and implicitly rearrangable and substitutable. The American emphasis shifted from ... a predictable whole sanctioned by tradition to an assemblage of parts" (*ibid.*: 2).

Blair also stresses, however, that in various other fields, nineteenth-century Americans held on to recognizable European models, "dressed up in New Word trimmings," for instance, in classical music, theater, fashion (*ibid.*: 6). But, as noted earlier, there have also been attempts in the latter areas to develop American forms deliberately *not* built on foreign importations or models. This concerns a form of domestic Americanization not mentioned in Webster's definitions, which aims to go beyond indigenization of foreign imports and entails conscious efforts of "self-Americanization" driven by a nationalist longing for an authentic indigenous culture (Gienow-Hecht 2004: 50).

Today in America one can still see a modularizing, fragmentating attitude of mind at work in virtually all domains — in business and management, education, in the mass media, sports and games, in architecture, literature, politics, advertising, and so forth (Blair 1988). In this regard the United States has been (and still is) the site of both the Americanization of *modernity*— the condition that resulted/results from processes of modernization implied in a combination of rationalization, urbanization, industrialization, bureaucratization, secularization and so on — and the Americanization of *modernism*— the iconoclastic, anti-traditional movement in the arts that took off in late nineteenth-century Europe. In his exposé on literary exchanges between Europe and America, Malcolm Bradbury has outlined what he calls "transatlantic refractions" and associated mutual fantasies during the past three or so centuries (Bradbury 1995: 463, 2).[4] He argues that these two forms of Americanization (of modernity and modernism respectively) have now merged into one, within the crucible of postmodern culture in the United States:

> Modernity has passed beyond itself into a spirit of excess; meanwhile modernism is no longer an *avant-garde* adventure, but the daily site of the experiment of modern life, an habitual style for an age of general bohemianization. Into the random, eclectic energies of American change, into the melting-pot of avid American style-hunger, everything, old and new, nostalgic and futuristic, European and Asian, African and Latin, male and female, straight and gay, religious or criminal, has been incorporated [*ibid.*: 463].

But Bradbury hastens to add that the current postmodern condition is not restricted to the United States. All across the world we now see similar tendencies. Therefore to the contemporary observer from abroad, "the late modern way ... no longer appears distant, strange, exceptional, or simply the product of only one continent. Such is the power of the modernizing and Americanizing progress that it simply reflects the world as the world, in its form as a global equivalence of all cultures" (*ibid.*). Elsewhere I have indicated the drawbacks of such a totalizing approach in which, culturally, the United States is more or less seen as being both representative of, and exemplary for, the whole world (van Elteren 2006).

The second meaning in *Merriam-Webster*'s two-fold definition of Americanization, which is still the common usage of the term in the United States today, refers to the ways in which people of different classes and ethnic backgrounds — immigrants generally — became (or become) Americans in the USA. This concerns in particular the assimilation of immigrants in the U.S. to the predominant culture, and intervention strategies of U.S. political or business leaders aimed at political and sociocultural modification of American citizens' behavior into a collective American identity that is considered normative and therefore imperative by these elites.

Offering a link with Americanization in the first sense, the British Americanist George McKay has suggested that nowadays "in some ways, we are all American immigrants (we just haven't all got there yet), or ... American borders are so wide now they include us within them (the idea of the global as the American popular)" (McKay 1997: 14). This position follows the track set out by William Stead in *The Americanization of the World* (1901), who saw in the homogenizing dynamic of assimilation of different social and ethnic origins into a shared collective identity a tendency that would not remain restricted to one society. Rather, he discerned a developmental process that would ultimately encompass the whole world.

A crucial aspect of the European condition is that Europeans "have acquired a set of cultural codes that allow [them] to understand American cultural products, to appreciate them, to consume them, as if [they] were Americans" (Kroes 1993: 312). This also applies, of course, to people in many other parts of the world who underwent the influence of America's cultural radiation over a longer period of time. It means, too, that nowadays many immigrants to the United States do not "start at some point near American cultural ground zero" but "are already 'Americanized' to varying degrees in the countries of origin, a reflection of the global reach and widespread diffusion of American consumption patterns, lifestyles, and popular culture." Here one can speak of "pre-migration Americanization" (Rumbaut 1997: 948).

However, this context of apparent familiarity with American popular culture can create serious problems for foreigners in understanding everyday life in the USA. (Of course, this will often not be their intention, when they just want to enjoy America's cultural outputs.) Arguably the influx of American popular culture in foreign settings does not provide full access to the diversity and complexity of American culture and society. As the French Americanist Marc Chénetier has stipulated: "the accumulation of pseudo-knowledge of the United States through its mass cultural exports is a hindrance rather than a bonus to such necessary knowledge..." (Chénetier 1993: 350). But these problems are not merely a function of familiarity with American popular culture. International news coverage of the United States tends to focus on the more sensational and colorful aspects of American public life — enhanced by the increasing influence of infotainment — that provide a distorted picture of the more mundane character of daily life in the United States. These images and stories can serve simply to confirm ingrained negative stereotypes and prejudices about America and Americans (Singh 2003: 2–3), as well as positive preconceptions among certain groups.

Yet newcomers may also have developed firsthand knowledge about the United States through past visits. They may have established social networks there (including family and friends) with whom they keep in regular contact, or may even have lived in the United States for years before they seek immigrant status, which is likely to facilitate their assimilation.

AMERICANIZING THE WORLD

The historical record shows that "Americanization" (in the sense of America's impact abroad) is a loaded term that designates much more than just acknowledging the influence of one country over another. It is a term burdened by its history, steering people's thinking in particular directions, while divorcing them from others. According to several critics in recent years, the existence of well-established genres in the study of (cultural) Americanization has tended to inhibit the development of new perspectives to facilitate our understanding of the larger cultural processes at issue. While they may be correct in certain respects, I will argue that the new approaches that emerged in the 1980s, are analytically bounded to the local, often micro-social, context in a way that tend to steer its proponents towards overlooking the bigger picture of Americanization.

Originating in Europe, "Americanization" became "an ever shifting global discourse whose boundaries have constantly been realigned and redefined throughout time" (O'Dell 1997: 19). Until today, discussing Americanization means taking issue with a variety of problems and open questions, including processes of modernization, the value of Western democracy, capitalism, national identity, cultural autonomy, and so forth. By the same token, "America" functions as an intertext, that is, a common denominator for a variety of discourses and textual references dealing with the New World, North America, and the United States. This intertext "America" should be understood as a complex signifier and contested textual construct that is subject to historical change (Gemünden 1998: 16, 20). As such it is an essential part of the theoretical framework to be developed here, but a comprehensive approach to Americanization should also include non-discursive aspects, which I will discuss later. First I turn to the "textual" level.

Most authors in this field insist that the term Americanization does not really have a dual feature as Americanism does, but traditionally functions in a European discourse of rejection to refer to the varieties of processes through which America exerts its malicious influence on European cultures (Kroes 1986: 40), and fulfills a similar role in other non-American contexts. In his discussion of the term, Richard Pells signals that "…sooner or later, any discussion of America's influence turned into a debate, or more often a complaint about the spread of American culture" (Pells 1997: 204). The term has indeed often figured prominently in discourses of anti–Americanism. Various terms have been employed to indicate the influences from the United States on other societies and specific groups therein, in "descending order of paranoia" (McKay 1997: 18),[5] ending in more neutral points of view: contamination, corruption and infection, bombardment, invasion, collision, cultural transformation, influence, transfer, borrowing, downloading, percolation, appropriation, interpretation, diffraction, filtering, modification, absorption, adaptation, translation, creolization, incorporation, indigenization, domestication — a list that is neither exactly rank-ordered nor exhaustive, of course. However, there have also been positive discourses on America's radiance overseas, which was considered inspiring, modernizing, rejuvenating, revitalizing/spiritually renewing or even liberating to the cultures and peoples concerned. Ambivalent discourses on Americanization have been quite common as well. As a matter of fact, a negative discourse always entails ambivalence and dissensus among members of the nation or group who share this discourse; a merely neutral view seems hard to find (Wilterdink 1991: 30).

Americanization is often a case of ascription as opposed to self-description, as David Forgacs has pointed out: "…one tends to attribute Americanisation to somewhere else, either another society or a part of one's society from which, in the act of naming, one implicitly separates oneself. On the whole, people who see others as Americanised do not see themselves as Americanised" (Forgacs 1993: 158). Yet there have been (and remain) quite a number of cases in which a self-identification of being Americanized can be found, seen as either a positive or negative tendency depending on the content and actors concerned. Like ascriptions, such self-descriptions can also imply impressions and misperceptions by contemporaries who simply assign ongoing changes experienced among themselves to American influence, whereas these have more complex origins.

Americanization has frequently been perceived and portrayed as a relatively rapid, if not speedy, process rather than "the trickling flow of a meandering stream" (O'Dell 1997: 21). Some have argued that nothing signified the presence of Americanization better than the aesthetics of streamlining (Hebdige 1988: 58). In popular debates around the globe, incidences of Americanization have often been described as fads or trends. They are superficial events that belong to the present and have no deeper history to speak of. They will presumably disappear as quickly as they came, thus having no real future. Strictly speaking, this naturally conflicts with the view of Americanization as a profound, massive, erosive cultural effect that persists for a longer time, but such contradictions are not uncommon in these discourses.

As Bigsby put it, "Americanisation frequently means little more than the incidence of change" (Bigsby 1975: 6). It is seen as transient and fluid, and in this sense one might associate it with the modern, an all-encompassing phenomenon that "pours us all into a maelstrom of perpetual disintegration and renewal" (Berman 1988: 15). Indeed, Americanization and modernity are often closely linked phenomena, an issue to which I shall return below.

Generally, "Americanization" also entails a view of a highly directional flow that is primarily running outward from the United States. In this sense its meaning differs from concepts such as diffusion, and the more contemporary terms, creolization and hybridization. Diffusion implies some degree of directionality to the extent that it refers to something radiating outward from a center of concentration. Processes of diffusion also work to some extent from both sides of borders, but it concerns a rather ubiquitous movement towards equilibrium. Similarly, creolization and hybridization both imply a cultural exchange between the parties involved, leading to a mingling of meanings and cultural forms from different historical sources, originally separated from one another in space. Yet this process of "straddling borders" does not necessarily produce a balanced result, whatever that may be. In its common usage, Americanization lacks such a meaning of cultural mingling but it does imply the idea of an increased proportion of things American (possibly taken together with things Americanized) in the cultural mix that emerges. It does not (or at least not sufficiently) account for the processes of signification — by human actors positioned at the juncture of the local and the transnational — through which the various cultural impulses are transformed into something new as they meet and meld together.

The latter would mean, in fact, a rethinking of the flow of Americanization in terms of glocalization. The neologism "glocalization" is a combination of the word globalization and localization; it emphasizes that the two may be involved in each other rather than forming a polarity (Robertson 1995: 28). Glocalization in business practices "is a process which can be understood as a market strategy built around the notion of *dochaku* ... a global strategy which does not seek to impose a standard product or image, but instead is tailored to the demands of the local market" (Featherstone 1995: 9). "Americanization" has, especially in discussions of cultural imperialism, a much more aggressive connotation than the other terms, with implications of expansion, power, domination, and cultural corruption, moving in a single direction from a cultural center to the peripheries (O'Dell 1997: 21–22, 43).

DEFINING IDENTITIES AND
DEMARCATING DIFFERENCES LOCALLY

By offering alternative modes of identification, American culture in its various manifestations has played an important, if not crucial role in the articulation (or re-articulation) of existing identities and the shaping of new national identities (Fehrenbach and Poiger 2000: xiv–xv). One of the most dramatic effects of local people's preoccupations with Americanization has been the reflexivity it spawned. America has been seen as an alternative model of how things could be, for better or worse. And as such, it has continuously stimulated people to reflect upon their life situation, and often driven them to action, thus functioning as a stimulus for cultural processes of change and stability (O'Dell 1997: 227). This dynamic has been at work since the nineteenth century, but became much more important with America's rise to global power after 1945, especially in those countries and regions directly within the American economic, military, social and political sphere of influence.

Discussions of Americanization have often been closely intertwined with those of national culture and a national sense of identity, or of some larger regional culture and identity. This collective entity (for example, France, Germany or Britain, often "Europe") then served as the standard for comparison, so that the outcome of an exploration of American distinctiveness was geared to a discussion of its potential, real or imagined impact on the collective entity in question. Thus a process was always involved that has been called "triangulation," referring to the fact that the reflection on America as a counterpoint to some other collective entity (again, this was frequently "Europe") functions within a larger reflection on the latter's history and destiny (Kroes 2000: 166). That is why an examination of indigenous responses to Americanization can also uncover how locals conceived of their uniqueness as a nation or some other collective identity at a particular time. In this context we should recall that the anti–Americanism associated with concerns about cultural Americanization by national elites usually had "a suppressed class content, which means that it also function[ed] as a defense of dominant class definitions of the national culture in question" (Morley 1992: 71).

Preoccupations with Americanization may be a symptom of strong anxieties about one's own national identity, experienced as weak, in crisis or in need of affirmation or defense. Americanization is then usually constructed as a process by which something of the national-popular — for example, customs, traditions, or values — is replaced by undesirable, if not morally deplorable foreign elements that lead to a weakening of national bonds and a waning national health. This discourse is dominated by a zero-sum logic of cultural exchange. Americanization in this sense implies a process of substitution in which something is assumed to have been (or is expected to be) subtracted from the repertoire of the national as something else was added. The question then arises whether debate about Americanization is anything more than talk about national identity.

Reactions to American culture and society abroad have not only been about defining differences in national identity between the United States and "receiving" nations, but also about demarcating differences within these nations along the lines of gender, generation, class, race, and ethnicity. However, we should remember that the issue of Americanization involves more than the politics of identity construction and the specific narratives they produce. Culturally, it is also very much an issue of consumption, in which America in a positive discourse can itself constitute a package of dreams, an arena of playfulness, that is not always reflexively approached in all of its details. "America" is then a site of exploration that may be experienced as exciting and offering fun and pleasure (O'Dell 1997: 227).

Furthermore, the blanket term "Americanization" is frequently no more than an assumption about the origins of a cultural influence that may or may not be accurate. It can be used to label an array of factors seen as threatening to a people's national identity, way of life or values. With such pejorative use of "Americanization," a given country is seen as adopting social practices and cultural values that allegedly originate in the United States and are considered alien and/or undesirable. Besides making a direct geographical connection with the United States (or a specific part thereof), this can also entail some synecdoche[6] or metonymic reference, that is, a figure of speech consisting of the substitution of the name of one thing for that of another that can be an attribute or an association ("New York"[7] for the whole of America, "Washington" for the U.S. government, "Wall Street" for America's vested financial-economic interests, "Hollywood" for the American film industry etc.), or the use of a particular metaphor, a figure of speech, more specifically, a trope based on a comparison (as "Cocacolanization," "McDonaldization," "Disneyfication," "Rambofication," a transformation to "McWorld" etc.) to refer to the process in question. The guiding idea here is that the offending items are not meaningful within the receiving context merely because they make cultural sense to some local groups, but because they are heavily laden with their alien American origins. The discourse on this issue then assumes a uniquely national cultural-political identity and consensus threatened by U.S. imports (Bell and Bell 1998: 5; 2004: 98).

In this context not so much real American influences can be at stake but rather indigenous trends or parallel developments that would have set through anyway, and are imputed to American influence. The labeling of particular things as American is then merely a way of attributing to, and displacing onto, an external agent changes that on closer inspection turn out to be endogenous, generated from within the given society itself (Forgacs 1993: 158–159). It may also be more widely exogenous, that is, externally driven by broader international developments including those in the United States. Thus, "Americanization" both in common and scientific usage often stood for modernization, industrialization, technological innovation, spread of capitalism, market liberalism, consumer society, mass culture, modern entertainment as well as democratization and Westernization, or more specifically economic and political incorporation into Western geopolitical regions and Western transnational associations.

MODERNITY AT THE HEART OF AMERICANIZATION

In their social representations of the American people, Europeans (and Europeanized foreigners elsewhere) have persistently used constructions of time as a means of implicitly creating distance from them in terms of the Other. This fits a pattern elucidated by Johannes Fabian regarding the use of time by Western anthropologists studying other peoples, in which they used constructions of time as a means of creating distance from, and power over, the peoples they had studied and portrayed in their ethnographic writings (Fabian 1983). Images of, and references to, temporality are indeed significant in the construction of the Other. Time is still one of the signifying borders between the Self and the Other that continue and maintain the subjective impression of cultural distinctiveness/separateness in today's world. Thus developments in America have often been seen as representing the future for the rest of the "advanced" world. It is in this de Tocquevillean vein that the German scholar of American cultural and literary history, Winfried Fluck, employs the term "Americanization" to refer to "developments that have either already taken place in the United States or are in a state of advanced development there, so that they can serve as models, or, where still contested, at least indicate some of the problems and consequences connected with them" (Fluck 1990: 9). In other words, the United States is seen as prefiguring the future of other advancing countries, as one of the paradigmatic countries or sites of modernity, in both its positive and negative aspects (Fluck 2000: 151).[8]

Indeed, modernity in its many manifestations is at the heart of Americanization. The term "modernity" is preferable to "modernization" in this context, because it allows us to capture the ambiguities that are involved in modern phenomena, such as urbanization or industrialization, or the rise of commercial culture and mass consumption. Contrary to modernization theorists (most influential in the sociology of development in the 1950s and 1960s), who tended to attach merely positive values of progress to such processes, classical theorists of modernity recognized that the modern world was ambiguous in its capacity to deliver human happiness and fulfillment. Modernity, in particular the scientific rationality and the liberal-democratic political projects associated with the Enlightenment, delivered emancipation from many forms of domination. But modernity also entailed costs, new forms of cultural pathology that classical theorists have tried to capture through concepts like "alienation" (Marx), "anomie" (Durkheim), the "iron cage" of instrumental reason (Weber). In each of these views there was a recognition that one form of domination had been replaced by another — they differed in their precise analysis of the source of this domination (Tomlinson 1991: 142–144). To the degree that this heritage of classical sociology acknowledges the discontents at the core of modernity, it still has great merits as a living tradition for analyses of modern life today (Turner 1999), including those of cultural Americanization. By recognizing the ambiguity of modernity in exploring the links between Americanization and modernity, we also remain aware that Americanization is neither a uniform nor a unifying process by definition (Fehrenbach and Poiger 2000: xiv).

Historically, the perspective in which one saw America's and Europe's relation to history depended to a great extent on whether or not one espoused liberal political reforms or was more conservatively inclined and preferred the stability that came with a monarchy, or more generally a traditional, "organic" society. While those advocating the former line of thought held the American system up as a model for the future, the latter regarded it as an immature, unstable, young, and temporary experiment, more or less doomed to failure — a dystopian view of what the future would bring. There was almost unanimous consensus, however, about the understanding that America was young; it was a New World. Yet, while both liberals and conservatives perceived America in terms of youthfulness, the manner in which they interpreted this youth remained an issue of debate. For conservatives, America was often seen as lacking the depth of history, and the development and refinement that such a history brings with it. The United States was superficial, ridiculous, and infantile at best, representing something that Europe, France, Germany or Britain (or some other country that America was contrasted with) had surpassed.

Importantly, there is often an act of "forgetting" involved in social constructions of "Europe" versus "America." The tendency is to overlook or downplay the cultural diversity that is inherent to all nations and collectivities, as well as the transnational, in this case, transatlantic, cultural exchanges that have taken place in the past. Like personal memories, collective memories of groups of people are selective in remembering and forgetting things of relevance. Historical discontinuity tends to be forgotten through the incorporation of "invented" traditions (Hobsbawm and Ranger 1983) that provide continuity and closure in the narratives about America. The significance of invented traditions in this context lies in their ability to provide the illusion that they are bound to the "eternal" flow of time, with roots deeply anchored in the distant historical past. Thus, America is defined through the repetitive assertion of what it is, and implicitly (and sometimes also explicitly), what it is not. To the extent that new images of the American symbolic landscape have been established, they have been quickly "naturalized" (reified) as part of the old past as well. For example, an America portrayed as an urban landscape of violence could, and still can, be easily juxtaposed with the image of the Wild West with its origins seemingly buried in a distant historical past. America as Other was thus repeatedly constructed in a ritualized way, with many characteristics more or less taken for granted as "natural truths." This intricate process of remembering and forgetting has led to a repertoire of morally and/or politically charged symbolic landscapes from which repeated borrowings are made in discussions of America (O'Dell 1997: 77–80).

So on closer inspection of the narratives associated with the social constructions in question, we may discover biased views of developments both within Europe and America, as well as of the cultural exchanges between the two. Thus, in the European context, labels such as Americanization and Americanism have frequently been used to indicate more general phenomena and ideas such as democracy and Enlightenment, a rationalized economy or management practice, capitalism and mass consumption that all have deep roots in Europe but were (and are still today) symbolically attached to "America," where they developed at a very early stage and/or in a most distinctive way. This often occurred as part of a discourse of cultural critique whereby the commonly used terms refer to "non-European," "deviating from one's own national culture and being inferior to it," "massification," "soullessness," "lack of depth" and "superficiality," "cold materialism" and "pure profit thinking" (Jarausch and Siegrist 1997: 22–23). A basic truth, however, is that America has transferred ideas, values, forms and practices to Europe that it had previously received from the old continent and subjected to all kinds of reworkings and transformations in their new context (in other words, these things European had first become Americanized at home). As the German sociologist Ralf Dahrendorf pointed out in 1963, Europe thus got back the Enlightenment "in applied form" that it had sent over the Atlantic two centuries before. This, he noted, went against a form of conspiracy thinking implied in a notion of Americanization as a penetration of Europe by "alien values" prevalent in the 1960s. On the other hand, many of the culture critics involved seemed not to realize (or did not want to realize) that in Europe itself "the society of the applied Enlightenment" set through against inner resistances and survivals of traditionalism and irrationalism (Dahrendorf 1963: 224).[9] This was, of course, a clear reference to indigenous processes of modernization in Europe by this pioneer of transatlantic "modern sociology" — a discipline that was itself heavily involved in the making of modern societies as part of the movement of "applied Enlightenment," leaving little room for what were considered "far-reaching utopian designs of a radically different world" (*ibid.*: 225, my translations).

To date, discourses of Americanization often have as subtexts polarized views of modernization, elations or jeremiads about the local society as "a future America" that emphasize either the shiny promise of modernity or the barbarism of an economically-driven consumerism. Therefore the United States has been seen as the locus of progressive idealizations and threatening nightmares alike; as the positive promise and as the negative fate of the society under its influence. And metaphors of unidirectional power and influence inform both the utopian and dystopian ways of seeing the implications of the United States for the local scene. Between the discourses of Americanization, consumption, and modernization, tension-filled relations exist. It is in principle possible to analytically distinguish Americanization from modernization, and one should be wary of conflating the two concepts (Webster 1988: 179). However, they may also involve partially overlapping and/or complementary processes. In this sense Americanization can be conceived as a modern flow, and mass consumption as one of its primary avenues of influence.

But there are other discourses and corresponding real-life trajectories of modernity besides the U.S. variant. There is, for example, a post-World War II Swedish-inflected version of modernity. This entailed an institutionalization of modernity as a private consumption project in which Swedes became modern by making their homes modern as part of a forward movement towards a better future corresponding with the vision of Swedish modernity that prescribed a positivist, goal-oriented rationalism. It was dominated by a conception of the good life of Swedish citizens — whereby Swedish Social Democrats and other political parties set the tone — that placed much emphasis on the consumption sphere of the family and home, and an aesthetics of modernity that articulated the utilitarian, the simple, the practical, the restrained in its ideal of the beautiful.

This contrasted with the more individualistic conception of the good life as embedded in the American middle-class way of life, and the modernist vision of functional aesthetics (prominently displayed at "Futurama," the General Motors exhibit at the 1939–40 World's Fair in New York) directed toward the individual bent on "self-assertion," and laced with gadgetry and images of speed that appealed to many middle-class Americans eager to display their success in life through "conspicuous consumption." Their Swedish counterparts were more likely to be drawn to rational collective processes of social change and the development of statist welfare arrangements, and preferred a more subdued display of their socioeconomic success in a society whose public life favored the maintenance of a reserved disposition. They did so by purchasing cars such as those made by Mercedes that were not inexpensive–and thus still marked their socioeconomic status, but did not draw attention like the big, flashy American cars[10] — by opting for home interiors with less cluttered forms, open spaces, and modern Scandinavian furniture with the aesthetic style mentioned above (O'Dell 1997: 27, 132–142, 159, 201–205). Processes of modernity may be globally alike to the extent that they all entail the demolishing of the old order to make room for the new, poignantly expressed by Karl Marx as "All that is solid melts into air" (Berman 1988: 15). But the values, norms, and cultural forms and practices that result from these processes, the way in which they are interpreted, and even the driving forces behind them, may differ from one cultural context to the other (Therborn 1995).

Of course, we must always remember that Americanization is but one strand, albeit a very significant one, of the large political-cultural constellations that together constrain and construct notions of national power, sovereignty, community, culture, and identity. The United States gave a particular inflection to more global developments to which that nation itself was also subject. Since "Americanization is only one facet of modernity and America only one of its centers," it is necessary to find out "what roles Americanization plays in relation to other sites of constructing nations," as Fehrenbach and Poiger (2000: xxv) have argued. They mention imperialism and decolonization as other important processes of modernity.

Processes of decolonization and its impact on the colonizers (e.g., France, Britain, as well as nations such as Japan, Germany, Italy, the Netherlands who no longer had formal colonies) are very important when looking at developments in the post-World War II era. In the first postwar decades, U.S. cultural producers and commentators have frequently presented American culture as explicitly anti-colonial (for example, in the biblical epics of the 1950s and early 1960s made by Hollywood). But at the same time they, like U.S. politicians, have imposed a "benevolent supremacy" of the United States on both the formerly colonized and the former colonizers (McAlister 2001). In this context, Americanization and decolonization were often in tension with one another. For example, the story of French modernization and Americanization is inextricably intertwined with the story of France's reluctant decolonization. Postwar France exploited colonial populations and ex-colonial immigrants (particularly in and from Algeria) on the one hand and increased its cooperation with American capitalism on the other. In this connection Kristin Ross has described a Janus-faced engagement with two international relationships, simultaneously acting and being acted upon, and all the while renegotiating its own political position: "The peculiar contradictions of France in that period can be seized only if they are seen as those of an exploiter/exploited country, dominator/dominated, exploiting colonial populations at the same time that it is dominated by, or more precisely entering more and more into collaboration or fusion, with American capitalism" (Ross 1995: 7).[11] As Etienne Balibar has argued, "the economic and cultural Americanization of France could not have been felt as metaphorical colonization if it did not intervene on the persistent base of French's own constitutive identity as a colonizer" (Balibar 1992: 57–65, as paraphrased in Ross 1995: 196). In other words, the post-colonial French thus transposed the distinction between dominators and victims from the colonial to the domestic situation, in which they came to perceive themselves as the latter.

From this perspective, French resistance to U.S. culture then originated in the interplay between their self-image as a culturally specific people and their own colonial experience as economic and cultural imperialists. (This interpretation can be contested, however, and there is still room for other approaches that may work just as well, or even better as explanatory frameworks.) Thus, broadening the context in which bilateral relations between the United States and each of the countries involved are studied, allows for a more comprehensive understanding of the efforts and social costs involved in forging national industrial productivity and consumer societies in postwar Western Europe and Japan (Fehrenbach and Poiger 2000: xxiv-xxv).

In addition, we should recall that around the world many periphery-to-periphery relations have existed (and still exist today) and that America was not necessarily always relevant to the periphery (or rather peripheries). America's cultural significance, for example, was not very important in many parts of the world until the early twentieth century, after the arrival of modern, transnational mediascapes. And within the various world regions, some countries were more peripheral in this regard than others. For example, in the early 1900s the United States was for Sweden geographically, militarily, politically, and with regard to popular culture as far as the middle and upper classes were concerned, probably more peripheral than other European countries such as Germany, Britain, France, and even Russia with its revolution. Denmark, for its part, has in many ways defined itself as a nation in relation to Sweden. In that sense, Sweden has served as the cultural center of Scandinavia, an idea that is not uncontested, however (O'Dell 1997: 109). Similar center-periphery relations at the regional level existed — and still exist — in other parts of the world.

Depending on the transnational processes and phenomena that we choose to focus on, America can be seen as a center or a periphery. In the current era, even within a particular domain such as culture, different globalizing tendencies with regard to various forms can be recognized that neither all run parallel nor all show the same tempo, structuring the world in different center-periphery relationships. As Ulf Hannerz pointed out in the early 1990s:

American influence is at present very diverse, but perhaps most conspicuous in science, technology and popular culture. French influence on world culture is rather of the high culture variety, and in related fields such as sophisticated food and fashion; there is widespread interest in the organization and internal cultural engineering of Japanese corporations. In such more specialized ways, places like the Vatican or the Shia holy city of Qom also organize parts of the world into center/periphery relationships of culture, for certain purposes [Hannerz 1992b: 221].

Finally, the center-periphery metaphor can also be misleading in suggesting that there is necessarily a relationship between the center and the periphery, which need not be true. It is not by definition the case that the two or more involved partners actually relate to one another, at least not all of the time. Historically, as we saw in the first two chapters, specific local groups in countries in the periphery have often interpreted and manipulated images of, and ideas from, the United States in attempts to further their own ends and to relate not so much to America but to groups of fellow-countrymen. They did so in light of the power relationships in the specific local context concerned (O'Dell 1997: 110–111). Once again we are reminded that the interplay between the processes of the center and the periphery, between the American flows as part of the transnational and the involvement of the local, should always be taken into account.

The previous discussion also suggests that it is important to be wary of a linear teleological view of Americanization as defined by a progressive evolution of local practices through increased American influence or American engagements over the course of time — a view evident in the notion of Americanization as progressive modernization. In many cases the people involved deal with a "plurality of temporalities" (Zeitlin 2000: 21), that is, processes that evolve differently in time. In everyday reality we find multiple, overlapping, and cross-cutting engagements with Americanization. Historical actors do not always follow a consistent, "evolutionary" course; they may initially "catch up" with Americanization but then take a distance from and revert back to earlier practices. They may even completely reject adoption of American imports and develop deliberate counter-strategies against Americanization. At a given time various groups of actors can also act differently, and oppose or even contest each other in this regard.

Finally, I want to consider Americanization in relation to McDonaldization here. Since the 1960s, Americanization also includes McDonaldization, next to others forms of American economic, cultural, political and military imperialism.[12] Ritzer defines this as "the process by which the principles of the fast-food restaurant [as paradigmatic exemplar] are coming to dominate more and more sectors of American society and an increasing number of other societies throughout the world" (Ritzer 2000: 1). The process of McDonaldization is a direct consequence of the emergence of four related tendencies: a push for greater efficiency, predictability, calculability, and control particularly through the replacement of human with non-human technology.[13] McDonaldized businesses emphasize standardized products and quantity over quality. Their practices give McDonaldization a competitive advantage over other models of organization; they make it possible to manage large numbers of people (both employees and customers) in an efficient way. The diffusion of such rationalized models in service and production leads to increasing control and dehumanization of workers and consumers. Beginning in the United States, especially consumer culture, but also areas such as education, justice, health care, politics and religion, have increasingly become subject to such standardization.

However, McDonaldization may only temporarily remain a subset of Americanization, until it becomes so ubiquitous and codified[14] that it will exist as a process independent of the United States or any other nation (Ritzer and Stillman 2003: 34–36, 43). The latter fits with Raymond Williams's observation that specific products, goods or practices such as Ford, Kelloggs and Hollywood "are only as it were accidentally American in origin." He further suggested that, likewise, broader changes caught under labels like "massification," "standardization," "privatization," commodification," "commercialization" or whatever other processes of change that are relevant in this context (including those mentioned earlier) are "not innately American" but the results of the Second Industrial Revolution (Williams, qtd. in White 1983: 110)—and the newer forms of the Third Industrial Revolution and late capitalism, I would add. In other words, these processes are not inherent but contingent to American society and culture, and occur in all advanced societies to a lesser or greater extent. From a conceptual standpoint it is therefore very misleading to equate them simply with Americanization. Americanization refers to something less and more definite than the totality of such changes. In my view, Richard White hits the mark when he suggests that the study of Americanization necessitates "some sort of analysis of American economic power in relation to the process of ideology, cultural production, class and technology." He continues:

> Americanization most usefully refers to the fundamental reference points of a culture, and the extent to which they can be located in the United States rather than in the culture itself; not just cultural change, but what it has transmitted; not just the measure of American content, but its impact (if any) on behaviour and ways of thinking [White 1983: 110].

This view will also serve as the guideline for the remainder of this book. But in order to cover the full complexity of its object, our conceptualization needs to be expanded with other forms of Americanization besides the cultural.

DISMISSING AMERICAN IMPERIAL
INFLUENCE PREMATURELY

A number of international Americanists and other scholars studying America's impact and resonance overseas have revisited the issue of Americanization in recent years. Their focus tends to concentrate on cultural Americanization with few if any connections to other forms and aspects of Americanization, thereby employing insights borrowed from cultural and media studies and "postmodern" cultural anthropology. The general trend in research of Americanization in the past twenty or so years has been to conceptualize this process less as a force of imposition of homogenization abroad. Prevailing tendencies now focus on local assimilation, or diversity and transculturalization. The notion of "national culture" has been contested to the point that the very existence of a national cultural identity is put into serious doubt. Increasingly, globalization has become the focus at the expense of Americanization. The overall effect of these deconstructions of the concept is that it undermines its earlier meanings of imperial, hegemonic or dominant influence. For our purpose it is necessary to salvage "Americanization" as a useful notion to approach the processes that we are talking about here.[15]

The starting point for recent scholarship has been to reject the thesis of cultural imperialism. Although the term "cultural imperialism" had occasionally been used before, it was only in the 1960s, however, that this critique came to be formulated as a coherent argument. A revisionist, mostly New Left, historiography of U.S. economic and political imperialism formed its breeding ground. International mass communication research of U.S. media imperialism gave another strong impetus to it, as did UNESCO's increasing concern since the 1970s with the protection of national cultures and national cultural heritages (Gienow-Hecht 2000: 472–475). The 1977 edition of *The Harper Dictionary of Modern Thought* defines cultural imperialism as "the use of political and economic power to exalt and spread the values and habits of a foreign culture at the expense of a native culture" (qtd. in Arnove 1980: 2). Applied to U.S. influence, the term in its then prevalent, crude version suggested that Americanization should be understood as a process in which an hegemonic America manipulated and ultimately imposed its ways on passive recipients, reducing them to "colonized" people. This process would bring about a kind of global cultural synchronization or homogenization that served American interests. Those who followed this approach rebuked the U.S. government and the U.S. business community for imposing American culture on foreign countries.

Critics rightly argued that the process of Americanization was much more complicated and much less unilateral than the proponents of this notion of cultural imperialism assumed. The new critical approaches that have been developed have improved our apprehension of Americanization in many ways. But they have a tendency that can lead to its own form of bias or distortion, a proclivity to deflate the whole phenomenon. If exaggerated, each of these approaches minimizes the significance of Americanization and the constraining, disruptive and homogenizing effects that may be involved. Let us take a closer look at the various perspectives and the problematic issues that arise.

AMERICANIZATION AS LOCAL ASSIMILATION

One perspective that has become virtually dominant in the current literature about the subject, revolves around the leading idea of assimilation, that is, the receivers of American imports assimilate or domesticate what they receive. It focuses on how things American (or things Americanized) as part of the transnational flows of culture, are identified in local settings and attributed significance. The cultural exchanges involved are seen as closer to negotiation among equals than to transmission or transformation according to some American model or exemplar. Non-Americans pick and choose what they want from the American cultural repertoire and then turn these borrowings into something of their own. A good example of this approach is Richard Pells's book about Euro-American cultural exchanges after 1945 (Pells 1997), while my earlier work on the conceptualization of transnational flows of U.S. popular culture also reflects this view (van Elteren 1996b).

A variation of the assimilationist perspective is the semiotic approach to cultural transmission (see especially Kroes 1996a, 1996b, 1999b). John Fiske's work on creative appropriations of a wide diversity of American popular culture forms has led the way here (Fiske 1989). Apparently inspired by the notion of "traveling cultures" as put forward by postmodernist anthropologists like James Clifford (1997), Kroes has suggested that "Americanization" ultimately "should be the story of an American cultural language travelling, and of other people acquiring that language. What they actually say in it, is a different story altogether" (Kroes 1996b: 147). According to these experts, Americanization is essentially the reception of a cultural language, a set of symbols that Europeans (and other foreigners) within the U.S. cultural orbit have gradually mastered. Europeans can now playfully, and sometimes ironically, employ these symbols and meanings because other Europeans who are also acquainted with this cultural repertoire readily interpret them.

This approach celebrates the capacity of non-Americans to modify what they receive and has dropped the whole idea of U.S. cultural imperialism, which assumes that foreign countries under American influence are vulnerable to cultural imposition by the American invaders. Its exponents tend to see (cultural) Americanization as usually benign and unobtrusive, thereby downplaying or even completely ignoring cases in which Americanization has been disruptive and intrusive. These scholars have in fact adopted the broader view of consumption (in the era of consumer culture) as a self-conscious critique of the pessimistic view of mass consumption that was influential at an earlier stage among students of popular culture (Gorman 1996).

In the earlier type of investigations of mass-popular culture, consumption as a social practice was hardly covered. The analyses tended to focus on the institutions, mechanisms, and cultural significance of the marketplace. Such studies were less concerned with how people actually consume the commodities they have purchased than with the fact that the commodities are purchased. By focusing on the process of buying commodities (or commodified services) in the market, these analyses of consumption in fact restricted themselves to the moment of exchange in the "circuit of capital"—recognized in the general Marxist approach of the capitalist mode of production—that entails different moments: production, distribution, exchange and consumption. But they hardly paid attention to what the consumers do with those commodities after they have been purchased and removed for private use from the marketplace. Thus two very different analytical moments (exchange and consumption) were lumped together and treated as if they were identical. By implication the cultural meaning of consumption was thought to be always predetermined by its location within exchange relations, and "inscribed" in the character of the commodities being purchased.

Such analyses of mass consumption tended to assume a homology between the economic and cultural power of capital. A commodity was seen to have a stable and fixed single meaning that is "built into" that commodity during its production, and passed on to the consumer through the exchange process. According to this view, by purchasing the commodities concerned, consumers both in and outside the United States, also "buy into" the dominant ideology of American capitalism. This would occur through specific systems of representations built into consumption: the dominant meanings implicated in the imagery of advertising, the rhetoric of corporate capitalist production, and the significance attached to particular commodities associated with American society (Clarke 1991: 76–79, 81).

In contrast, the newer, revisionist view sees the social practice of consumption as the site of resistance to incorporation into dominant or preferred meanings. It emphasizes creativity and polysemy—that is, the plurality of meanings that can be attached to objects and texts—and links these to concepts derived from textual analysis, especially those of pleasure and the ways in which "texts" (understood here in the broadest possible sense) offer different subject positions to consumers/receivers. This results in approaches to consumption that stress the active role of the consumer in creating the meaning of the object or text being consumed. Individuals are conceived as cultural *bricoleurs*, assembling their own distinctive combinations of meanings and style from the rich cultural repertoire of available signifiers. At the heart of this view of consumption is the process of differentiation, both theoretically and practically. It sees meaning being generated through signification as the construction of differences, and the social process of consumption as the production and display of differences in lifestyle, taste, and politics. This argument emphasizes that everyone is experienced and adapt in using and manipulating the symbols of everyday culture.

There can be little doubt that analyses of consumption as cultural creativity has brought theoretical gains over the pessimistic views of mass consumption. Representatives of this approach contend that consumption as a social practice cannot be read directly from the processes of exchange and that consciousness is determined neither directly nor monolithically by the commodities that are consumed. They rightly insist on the necessity of seeing social subjects as active agents in the creation of their own life-worlds, rather than the passive victims of capitalism (*ibid.*: 81–85). However, by restricting the analysis and discussion almost exclusively to the reception side of cultural influence, this approach suffers from what I call "receptionitis," an overemphasis on the selective borrowing and active appropriation of cultural forms at the expense of interest in the political economy and cultural constraints set by power inequalities. Whereas the mass consumption analyses tend to focus on the moment of exchange in the "circuit of capital," the cultural assimilation view highlights consumption as an active social practice at the expense of an interest in exchange and commodity relations. The latter approach may come to border on what has been called "a near fetishization of agency and diversity," which is one pole of the continuum in the debates about Americanization that have swung back and forth between two sharply contrasting genres, in terms of global homogenization and increasing cultural heterogeneity in the "global ecumene" respectively (O'Dell 1997: 37–38, 46).

As the British cultural studies scholar John Clarke has pointed out in his discussion of this problem area:

> What we see is the excess of signs, not the conditions for production, distribution and exchange which make them available. The effect, ironically, is to replicate that view of capitalism which capitalism would most like us to see: the richness of the marketplace and the freely choosing consumer. The other side — the structures of production and the inequalities of access to the marketplace — are missing, and these absences emphasize the "free-floating" quality of the sign, making it available for any use of meaning that may be attached to it [Clarke 1991: 85].

He also sees a tendency of romanticizing the creative, freewheeling consumer-*bricoleur* that leaves the less glamorous experience of consuming in the contemporary world out of the picture, that is, the more mundane practices of subsistence consumption by people trying very hard to make ends meet. Subsistence consumption has of course also been affected by changes in the culture of consumption, including geographical, economic, and cultural restructurings of the retail sector. But quite another matter is whether all consumers have the same access to the possibilities of creativity, or experience the same pleasures of consuming, alluded to by the radical culturalists. All the things people purchase involve decisions and the exercise of their own judgment, choice, taste and so forth. Yet people do not single out what is available for them to choose from in the first place. Consuming offers a certain scope for creativity, but on closer inspection agency in the process may be more limited than seems to be the case at first glance. It may rather be like a toy, where the combinations are multiple but all the parts are still preselected (Williamson 1986: 230–231). Moreover, this view of consumption is geared to the spirit that gained much influence in the Western world with the rise of neoliberal policies during the past few decades:

> It both reflects and adds to the shift towards consuming individualism and away from the realm of collective, public and political agency ... it accepts the shift of cultural and political terrain towards consumption as the new ground for analysis rather than keeping open the tensions between consumption and other modes of power, control and creativity [Clarke 1991: 85–86].

Philip Schlesinger has described this as "a hermeneutic model of consumption" that "forces a breach between politico-economic arguments about the production of culture and the ways in which it is consumed and interpreted" (Schlesinger 1991b: 148–149). This emphasis on reception/consumption has been a predominant tendency within cultural studies since the 1980s, labeled as "new revisionism" (Curran 1990) in mass communication, "uncritical cultural populism" (McGuigan 1992) or "pointless populism" (Seamann 1992). It has evoked a significant counter-stream of "bringing sociology back in," or, rather, of reconnecting with the social sciences within the field from the mid–1990s onwards (Ferguson and Golding 1997; van Elteren 2001: 119–123) — in order to recover "the social" in culture and link up with politico-economic and other structural dimensions.

The primary, if not single, focus on consumption tends to reinforce the idea that consumption is the only site or form of control that should be addressed, rather than examining its intersection with other sites (for example, those of production or distribution) where struggles for control have been marginalized or delegitimized. Neither the exchange/commodity-based view nor the view of consumption-as-social practice and limitless creative appropriation is, by itself, a satisfactory way of analyzing consumption and more generally the reception of cultural products: "The structural pessimism of the former finds its mirror image in the cultural optimism of the latter, leaving us to choose between a view of people as broken spirits or free spirits" (Clarke 1991: 86). Neither offers a satisfactory conceptualization of the contradictory ways in which people deal with their daily living in capitalist society. The obvious solution is to try to steer skillfully between the pessimistic mass culture, exchange/commodity-based view of consumerism and the optimistic view of consumption-as-social practice and creative appropriation. A more adequate approach deals with the "dialectics of cultural consumption" in terms of the links between the production, dissemination, exchange and reception of any kind of commodities or commodified services that are at the heart of processes of cultural Americanization. Which means that "Americanization," to the extent that it is connected to the dissemination of cultures of consumption, can be a site for both the construction of hegemony and for popular resistance (Clarke 1990, 1991: 73–74, 97–110).

As yet these insights have not made much impact upon Americanists who study the transnational influence of American culture. The assimilation approach, undeniably valuable as it is in addressing a significant part of the complexities of Americanization — that is, the active involvements of the importing society — tends to deflate the American momentum. Although selective borrowing and creative appropriation do happen, and remain part of a broader integrative perspective, assimilation should not be exaggerated. Otherwise we run the risk of losing sight of the bigger picture or, rather, of missing it altogether.[16] We must realize that not everything that is imported from the United States is assimilated. The part that is *not* assimilated may be relatively large as, for example, in the French case in the 1970s and 1980s, according to historian Richard Kuisel. Moreover, assimilation is not by definition a way of sustaining diversity. Adopting U.S. formats and models may very well lead to U.S.-inflected changes in local practices and even national identities: "Adaptation, in the form of imitation, runs the risk of advancing rather than resisting Americanization. Mimicking the Americans has made the French more like their New World cousins" (Kuisel 2003: 102).

AMERICANIZATION AS TRANSCULTURIZATION

Some exponents of assimilation have come close to, or even switched over to an approach that deconstructs national cultural identities and sees an all-pervasive transculturalization at work. Strongly influenced by poststructuralism, this second approach rejects what it considers "essentialist" thinking about culture, in this case the notion that there is such a thing as "American culture" or some other national culture that has a relatively stable identity. Instead, the emphasis is on the contested character, variety, permeability and fluidity of culture. Central in this approach are processes of transculturation[17] that are always bi- or multidirectional and do not take place between stable, unified national cultures. So cultures are always seen as hybridized and hybridizing, multi- and intercultural, working through debates, controversies and negotiations. One deals with complex and often contested cultural flows from different locations and in different (postcolonial) discourses. This entails a focus on cultural encounters, "contact zones," or "zones of interaction" in which difference and inequality in terms of power are examined (Lenz 2002). Analyses of this kind link up to the anthropological literature on transnational cultural processes that became influential in the 1990s. Flows, border crossings, contact zones, hybrids et cetera are tropes that reflect the ways in which these authors visualize and frame rather abstract cultural processes that transcend national borders and affect people's lives across the world (O'Dell 1997: 18).

A prevailing tendency in such culturalist analyses is to use a linguistic metaphor to articulate that cultural identity is "a fabric of textual strands with no fixed boundaries" and to visualize the fluidity and complex dynamics of cross-cultural influences that do not by definition run parallel with international political relationships. In this perspective, the receiving culture and society are envisioned as "structured like a language, always in flux, but relatively homogeneous in the semantic distinctions that it expresses" (Bell and Bell 2004: 98) and Americanization is equated with "linguistic infiltration" that "does not so much replace or displace the local lexicon as supplement it and change its elements … change is effected throughout the whole structure even though no obliteration of a previous lexicon may occur" (Bell and Bell 1993: 202–206).

Günter H. Lenz argues that, when studying Americanization in this way as processes of cultural exchanges, transculturation, and "recodification," the "international/postnational" debate among Americanists will have to focus on the changing social roles of media, modes, and forms of popular or mass culture in transnational perspective. He suggests that the following questions need to be addressed, which are worth quoting at length here:

> In which ways are the products of American popular/mass culture transcultured in the different national or continental contexts? How has the specific quality of American culture as process and performance been negotiated with the cultural dynamics of other cultures? How have these encounters of cultures transformed the traditional hierarchical distinctions between high (elite), popular, or mass culture, and the prevailing notions of gender and race? How have alternative cultural practices and modes of cultural representation of other parts of the world affected and transformed culture(s) in the United States? How can the increasing awareness of the omnipresence of the hybridity, openness, and transformation of cultures contribute to a less stereotypical understanding of American culture that has usually be seen as a threatening as well as seductive unified, powerful, and imperializing "Other"? What are the political repercussions and the political potential of the products and processes of transnational hybrid or creolized and creolizing cultures in different national or local contexts? How have they changed the traditional self-definitions of national cultures and the "identity" of nation-states? [Lenz 2002: 98].

This critical approach to studying "national" culture stresses that American culture is not monolithic and that America has never transmitted a single, coherent message; "America" has a wide variety of meanings for non-Americans. Also what was once perceived as American may have changed over time. Similarly, the receiving culture is diverse and in constant motion. The idea of an "authentic" American (or other national) culture is untenable, because it has always been diffuse, in flux, without clear boundaries, and constantly remade through influences such as immigration, urbanization and industrialization, and, in recent times, also increasingly through transnational media and globalizing networks of all kinds.[18]

However, this approach, too, can be taken to such an extreme that Americanization disappears from sight. Despite all the mentioned relativizations and deconstructions, there is still a hard core in this cultural exchange. There are images and products, technologies and practices, that have historically been (and sometimes still are) closely identified with America. Some products have for a long time been endowed with "Americanness." Many products are not only perceived as American but are prized, valued, and consumed because of their associations with "America." There has been and continues to be something identifiably "American" about some American exports abroad, and these are not hard to find. Assignments of national labels have not disappeared altogether, even in an era of increased cultural flux. One should also not overdo the idea of diversity within receiving national societies, pointing to highly variable exposure to, and receptivity towards, America across classes, generations, genders, ethnic groups, and locations. In given cases, there may be more uniformity or homogeneity caused by Americanization than suggested by the transculturalization approach with its idea of culture continuously-in-motion. In recent times, even if Americanization continues to implicate various segments of a local population differently, America's local resonance may become so pervasive under the impact of television, Hollywood films, Internet, and the use of American English as *lingua franca*, that it affects almost all members of that population, thus adding a significant degree of cultural uniformity.

Furthermore, this approach tends to remain in the sphere of border *discourses*, due to the fact that it stems from literary studies and textual-inflected cultural studies or a kindred strain within cultural anthropology called "postmodern anthropology" (Clifford and Marcus 1986; Marcus and Fischer 1986; Lenz 1991). Although these intercultural contact zones are "inherently dialogical"(Lenz 2002), this does not mean that the "dialogues" or "negotiations" always take place on a level playing field; often they do not. The dialogue or negotiation has frequently been conducted within the language and culture of the greater power, and within a global economic structure in which the other party commanded only little power (Bell and Bell 1993: 201). Moreover, the focus on the media and popular/mass culture in Lenz's proposal, though worthwhile in itself— not least because of its recognition of two-way influences between the United States' and other cultures — is too restrictive. Not only does it overlook the political economy of global mass media (Herman and McChesney 1997; McChesney 2000) and insufficiently account for the role of the cultural industries in the production and distribution of culture (Hesmondhalgh 2002), it also leaves out other important components of America's cultural influence overseas — especially those processes which are not as visible and less obvious than the global U.S. impact through mass media and popular culture.

Surprisingly, in light of the self-proclaimed "postcolonial" character of this approach of Americanization as transculturalization, there seems to be a striking resemblance, if not relative continuity here with the more general lack of interest in power relations within area studies as these expanded to an unprecedented degree in the United States during the first two decades after World War II.[19] As Mark T. Berger writes in his historiography of Latin American studies with regard to the earlier postwar period:

> The language and area-studies programs emphasized language and culture as the key to under-
> standing the various areas of the world with which they were concerned. They did this within the
> context of the view that they were according the various cultures the same degree of respect. They
> studiously avoided power relations and the dynamics of subordination and domination which were
> characteristic of the cultures they subjected to scrutiny [Berger 1995: 74].

This applied not only to the study of U.S. influences on other societies and cultures
but also to economic and social relations within the United States itself in the predominant approach followed in American studies (as one such area studies), both at home and
abroad. Here the emphasis was on language and culture, while the economy, the military, politics, labor and ordinary social life in America were likely to be underexposed or,
in some instances, even ignored.

Yet another way to approach Americanization is to take the alternative route of globalization, which has become the dominant approach of transnational flows and influences.
(Several leading theorists about cultural globalization, however, have adopted the approach
of transculturalization mentioned earlier.) In fact, globalization here replaces Americanization as the more inclusive, if not all-encompassing, perspective. Thus Americanization is subsumed under, or surrenders to, globalization. Followers of this third approach
(see further Chapter 9) suggest that it is more appropriate to speak of global flows of ideas,
products and techniques rather than focusing on American influence. Those who prefer
globalization to Americanization call attention to the transnational rather than the "American" character of many of the locally imported ideas, products, practices and behaviors.
They suggest that it is also better to conceptualize the transmissions concerned as globalization. Anticipating the later discussion, I leave off with the following brief remarks at
this point. Globalization in the twentieth century has had (and to a significant degree still
has) an American imprint (see also Ellwood 1996–1997; Ritzer and Stillman 2003: 43–44;
Kuisel 2003: 105). At least for the time being, it has not pushed America aside as the
major driving force of capitalist globalization and prime producer and marketer of a large
part of globally disseminated mass culture and consumerism. For most of the twentieth
century, as well as for the early twenty-first century, the phenomenon may best be called
"American-style" or "American-inflected globalization."

AMERICANIZATION IN SOCIOPSYCHOLOGICAL TERMS

A fourth way to approach Americanization is to do so in behavioral terms. This line
of inquiry, which has hitherto rarely been followed, attempts to find out to what extent
Americanization has brought about changes in behavior, outlook, and identity among its
"recipients" at some point. For example, has it changed their self-images and diminished
their identification with the national cultural identity in question? Or, probing into some
other important aspects of human life, has it modified their basic values and ideas about
what constitutes "success" or "the good life"? A more robust assessment of Americanization of this kind is not easy to arrive at, at least for the time being — although approxi-
mations of it can be found in several in-depth studies of the reception side of
Americanization in Western Europe, Japan, Australia and elsewhere.[20]

A basic issue here concerns the kind of evidence that is actually necessary to trace
not only the actors' attributions of meaning to American imports and models but also to
measure the alleged changes in values and beliefs. And how should such evidence be collected? Consumption of American imports is not automatically proof of an attendant

psychological change. From a skeptical standpoint it can be argued that even if local people eat, dress, speak or entertain themselves like their American counterparts, this does not necessarily make them also think, feel and otherwise act like Americans (Kuisel 2003: 108). The latter has to be demonstrated through methods that tap more directly into the values, beliefs, and attitudes of the recipients of American influence.

It becomes clear that these sociopsychological dimensions cannot be simply deduced or derived from discourses as reconstructed through analyses of the contents of manufactured artifacts such as magazines, films and television programs, books and other "texts" or cultural outputs. The wider tendency in cultural studies (or American studies of a similar kind) to "read off" psychology from cultural products instead of locating psychological feelings and thoughts with individuals, entails discourse determinism.[21] As social psychologist Michael Billig poignantly put it: "Texts are psychologized, as the analyst's reading postulates the psychological characteristics of (other) readers" (Billig 1997: 213). This is well exemplified by the way in which one researcher, having studied the content of MTV videos, presented a psychologized portrait of the viewer in terms of a "decentred, a-historical model spectator that mimics the cultural formation of contemporary teenagers appearing to live in a timeless but implicitly 'futurized' present" (Kaplan 1987: 27, qtd. in Billig 1997: 213), without any actual spectator appearing in the text and without any empirical evidence about actual spectators views, experiences or actions. As a result, these psychological parts of reality are not empirically disclosed either. Culture does not appear as lived experience, and the analyses themselves tend to remain remote from everyday real life, thus revealing the French structuralist/poststructuralist heritage of cultural studies as represented in particular by Althusser and Lévi-Strauss/Foucault and Lacan.

A typical illustration of such "de-psychologized psychologizing" can be found in the work of Fredric Jameson, who writes about a "waning of affect" and the "decentering" of the subject in the postmodern world merely on the basis of analyses of contemporary cultural products, such as films, art and architecture (Jameson 1991, 1992). "The inference is made without analysing whether the citizens of the postmodern world are to be characterized by decentred egos or shallow emotions. It is *as if the psychology inheres in the textual products themselves*," comments Billig (1997: 213, my italics). In my view, this is methodologically not unlike the way the consensual symbol-myth-image school of explanation within U.S. American studies of the 1950s and early 1960s tended to "read" the (mentality of the) entire culture from inside American literary texts (Pells 1997: 105). A turn to highly reflexive ethnography in cultural studies as we have seen recently — which is partly a return to, and recuperation of, older anthropological approaches — can make a major contribution here, especially if accompanied by a psychological awareness. The leading idea thereby is that "'decentered egos' and 'waned affect,' if they exist anywhere, will exist in the actions and utterances of those who inhabit this world" (Billig 1997: 213–214).

With regard to people's thoughts, emotions, and behaviors in the present one could take resort to methodologies as developed within so-called rhetorical psychology which insists that psychological states, including both thoughts and emotions, are socially created (without adopting a social determinist position, however). This strain of psychology puts special emphasis upon the role of language in constructing psychological phenomena, and its approach examines the operations of language in practice,[22] rather than speculating about them and studying language as an abstract system, based upon hypothesized "rules of grammar." The general idea is that through the study of utterances made in particular rhetorical contexts, one can directly study the social constitution of psychological states. This approach offers ways of investigating in detail how ideological consciousness is constituted within, and reproduced by, the ordinary language of life (Billig 1997; Potter and Wetherell 1987; Wetherell and Potter 1992), and might thus also provide insights into everyday views and experiences of Americanization related to various relevant discourses. Needless to say, we are severely handicapped in studying historical cases of Americanization in this regard (including the *modi operandi* of actors' ideological consciousness) if we lack historical materials that contain extensive literal transcriptions of historical actors' utterances (or "speech-acts"), detailed information about the rhetorical contexts in which these were expressed, and meticulously registered observations of these people's non-verbal behaviors that would enable us to retrieve the "voices of people" in the past. But qualified investigators, inspired by the tradition of history of mentalities (*histoire de mentalités*), may try to immerse themselves in the life-worlds of historical actors as best as they can through combined cultural-historical and historical-anthropological approaches that enable them to carefully offer tentative interpretations of these people's attitudes, emotions and actions of relevance — "readings" of past behavior that seem most adequate within the hermeneutic circle of this interpretative research.

There is furthermore the issue of the possible discrepancy between a lack of subjective experience and awareness of Americanization among local recipients and an assessment that they have become Americanized in specific ways by external observers. David Forgacs has formulated the crucial questions:

> If people could be shown to have retained some local or national culture identifications, would this prove that they had not become Americanised or were less Americanised than had been claimed? If these people did not describe themselves as Americanised or recognise themselves in that term, would that mean that they were not Americanised or simply that they were not conscious of it? In other words, if a subjectivity of Americanisation cannot be empirically demonstrated, does it still make sense to talk about Americanisation? [Forgacs 1993: 158].

I am inclined to think that the latter may still be possible, if the cultural changes concerned can indeed be "proven" (in some empirical way) to have been induced by American influences. Importantly, recipients of such influence need not always be aware of cultural imposition or prestructuring of their options in everyday life if that happens to be the case. This is the very essence of the alienation that "colonization" of people's life-world by "imperial" system influence may bring about among locals.

6

Toward a More Balanced Approach to Studying Americanization Abroad

This chapter considers the negative implications of the social constructionism that has become influential in recent approaches to the study of Americanization (resulting from the textual turn in cultural studies and a kindred approach in cultural anthropology). It leads to a recognition of the need to focus more on material realities of Americanization, including structural inequalities and power differences in the exchange processes concerned. This entails a major shift away from the overemphasis on the creative appropriation of things American to a more balanced approach whereby the complex dynamics of Americanization are done full justice. The latter means that military, economic, technological, political and social forces, as well as structural constraints are included in the conceptualization.

THE PITFALLS OF EXTREME SOCIAL CONSTRUCTIONISM

The distinction between discourse and "reality" mentioned earlier must always be kept in mind when looking at Americanization abroad. America has to some extent always been a social imagination, a construct in the minds of both Americans and non-Americans, as many observers have asserted. And perhaps this is even more the case than with similar acts of social definition of other countries. It seems that no other nation has attained to such a high degree the status of a pure abstraction, in which an idea or symbol called "America" has taken over (Ceaser 1997: 2).[1] But one should not exaggerate this, and fall into the trap of an extreme social constructionism, which amounts to a form of neo-idealism in the epistemological sense. There is a stubborn historical-societal reality, a "real" America, out there, with economic, technological, military, social, political, cultural and other features that lie outside the realm of social imagination and may in themselves bring about material, structural and symbolic changes elsewhere, be it in the economy, politics, society or culture.

I am aware that this goes against the philosophy of anti-essentialism that by the 1980s had gained much influence in part of the humanities—especially modern philosophy and literary and cultural studies (including American cultural studies) in the United States itself—which considers the use of the term "real" as almost a provocation. This tendency of excessive social constructionism (and deconstructionism) is foremost due to the influence of radical poststructuralism as exemplified by French thinkers such as Michel Foucault (regardless of how he saw himself in relation to poststructuralism),

Jacques Derrida, Jacques Lacan, Jean-François Lyotard, Ernesto Laclau and Chantal Mouffe. I share Barbara Epstein's critique that this is a dead end for progressive thought: "...the rejection of metanarratives, the insistence that everything must be understood as socially constructed, the rejection of any claims of truth or value, are exaggerated versions of one-sided, partial insights" (Epstein 1995: 84). American literary and cultural criticism, dominated by this poststructuralist strain, dismiss "history" as an old-fashioned and dangerously "totalizing" myth, thereby also ignoring radical traditions or alternative critical approaches at home (Lenz 1990: 94). If taken seriously, this would also mean the death of sociology or political science as intellectual means to disclose basic structures and processes of social reality. Within the textual-inflected cultural studies strain, influenced by poststructuralism, a society (or a specific aspect of it) is simply "read" as a cultural "text" that is deconstructed in multifarious ways. In the extreme case, "the social" may even be completely nullified by proclaiming that the entire concept is historically restricted and obsolete in these postmodern times. Yet culture is still undeniably a *social* phenomenon that can very well be (and should *also* be) the object of empirical investigations from the perspective of anthropology, sociology, political science or social history.

　　In a critical discussion of cultural studies, the British sociologist Bryan S. Turner has pointed out that practitioners of textual analyses within the dominant strain of cultural studies lack a clear sense of the necessity to trace empirically the social effects of texts, signs or images. There is also little awareness of what he calls the "phenomenological concreteness" of people's experiences of cultural objects in specific times and places. The overriding tendency is "to subsume the social under the cultural" (Turner 1999: 281). As Turner rightly notes, the "reading" of all social relationships as cultural relations drives out the area of interest of what he calls "the tensions between scarcity and solidarity," the terrain *par excellence* that the social sciences should focus upon (*ibid.*: 282; Turner and Rojek 2001). The politico-economic dimensions of both the Marxist and the Weberian tradition of sociology run the risk of getting lost in a form of cultural studies that entails an "apolitical culturalism" because of the way in which multiculturalism tends to be approached:

> Because postmodern cultural studies assumes moral relativism, it cannot produce, let alone accept, a unified moral criticism of modern societies. It is intellectually unlikely that cultural studies could develop an equivalent to Weber's notion of rationalization or Marx's concept of alienation. Postmodern cultural studies finds it difficult to promote a political vision of the modern world apart from an implicit injunction to enjoy diversity. This lack of politico-moral direction exists in a context of increasing alienation of intellectuals from McUniversity and increasing rationalization of educational systems. Cultural studies, despite claims to a connection with critical theory, are not adequate as a contemporary response to politics and ethics [Turner 1999: 283].

　　Foucault's early works have been especially influential here. A closer examination (mostly "genealogical analysis") of the micro-politics of power relations in different localities, contexts, and social situations led him to posit an intimate relationship between the systems of knowledge ("discourses") that define techniques and practices for the exercise of social control and domination within particular localized contexts. The prison, the asylum, the hospital, the university, the school, the psychiatric institute are all examples of sites where a dispersed and piecemeal organization of power is built up independently of any systematic strategy of class domination. What happens at each site cannot be understood by appeal to some overarching general theory. The only irreducible entity in Foucault's conception is the human body, for that is the "site" at which all forms of repression are ultimately registered. While in Foucault's view all relations of power have built-in resistances, he also insists that no utopian scheme will ever be able to offer a way out of the power/knowledge relationship in non-repressive ways. The only viable option is to explore and build upon the open qualities of human discourse, and thereby intervene in the way knowledge is produced and constituted at the particular sites where a localized power-discourse prevails.

Foucault insisted that only through a multifaceted and pluralistic attack upon localized practices of repression might capitalism be challenged globally without replicating the repressions of capitalism in a new form. His ideas appealed to the various new social movements (feminists, gays, ethnic and religious groups, regional autonomists, etc.) that arose during the 1960s as well as to former Marxists (especially in France) disillusioned with the practices of communism and the politics of communist parties. However, Foucault's work does not make clear — especially in its deliberate rejection of any holistic theory of capitalism — how such localized struggles might add up to a progressive attack upon the central forms of capitalist exploitation and repression (Harvey 1989: 45–46). A more conservative reading of the sweeping notion of power in Foucault's work even ignores the political field of human agency and resistance altogether, which leads to political acquiescence. Sociologists John R. Hall and Mary Jo Neitz touched the sore spot of this strain: "What is disarming, even frightening, about Foucault is his depiction of a cultural domination that operates without conspirators yet reduces the agency of acting subjects to mere reflections of the cultural categories that frame social life…. We are all trapped within culturally constructed standpoints that imprison our reasoning" (Hall and Neitz 1993: 149–150). Thus, the power of culture is beyond the control of any group or social stratum.[2]

As David Harvey has pointed out, Foucault's thinking fits perfectly with the way in which postmodernism immerses itself, even indulges, in the fragmentary and chaotic currents of late-modernist change as if that is all there is. It makes no attempt to try to transcend or counteract it, or even define the structural developments that are taking place beneath the surface (Harvey 1989: 44). Foucault advises his readers, for example, to "develop action, thought, and desires by proliferation, juxtaposition, and disjunction," and "to prefer what is positive and multiple, difference over uniformity, flows over unities, mobile arrangements over systems. Believe that what is productive is not sedentary but nomadic" (Foucault 1984: xiii, qtd. in Harvey 1989: 44). Thus this Foucauldean-inflected postmodernism entails a Nietzschean current of thinking that emphasizes the deep chaos of modern life and its obstinacy to rational thought.

Due to poststructuralism's influence, relativism has become absolute, and consists of a set of "relativistic certainties," to borrow David Morley's oxymoron (Morley 1997). The development of a relativist, self-reflexive stance (bordering on an orthodoxy in some circles) is partly the result of a proper concern with the politics of knowledge, and with taking into account the power relations between subject and object of knowledge as manifested, for example, in the case of "postmodern" or "self-reflective" ethnography (Clifford and Marcus 1986). However, I agree with Morley, among others, who have come to the conclusion that the overall effect of deconstructionism in literary studies and cultural studies as influenced by this tendency, "has been a disabling one, as a result of which it becomes pretty hard for anyone to say anything about anyone (or anything) else, for fear of accusation of ontological imperialism" (*ibid.*: 122).

After the demise of the "grand narratives," there is no consensual basis for evaluating interpretative truth-claims anymore, according to this form of antifoundationalism.

Theoretical or methodological claims for interpretive adequateness — let alone for empirical validity and reliability, as in the mainstream social and behavioral sciences — are being unmasked as hidden power games: "The only consensus remaining seems to be that of a broadly defined antifoundationalism, which is strong in subverting arguments for general criteria on which claims for interpretive adequateness [or empirical validity] could be based, but weak in suggesting any criteria that would go beyond a mere performative voluntarism" (Fluck 1998: 52). The latter is manifested in professional practices within the humanities (especially literary and cultural studies) — and kindred (only marginal) strains within the social sciences — that stress daring and strength, not necessarily substance of argument, whereby the academic with the greatest persuasive power is likely to stand out the most. Thus, in judgeents and praises of "innovative works," the decisive criteria concern performative qualities expressed through major keywords such as "powerful," "on the cutting edge," "dazzling" and the like (Fluck 1990: 14).

Although poststructuralism is not driven by some conspiracy to destroy progressive movements, it nevertheless has negative effects on attempts toward a progressive analysis. Due to its implicit values, its celebration of difference and hostility to unity, poststructuralism is particularly inadequate as an intellectual framework for movements that need to come up with positive assertions about how society could be better organized and that also need to incorporate differences within a collective unity for social change (Epstein 1995: 84–85). The resulting emphasis on identity politics makes it very hard to develop and sustain a broader progressive movement aiming for commonalities regarding an envisioned good society and a community life that disparate groups might share with each other.[3]

The basic problem here is that poststructuralist theories are hypermodern as sociologist Alan Wolfe has indicated. Since they tend towards an extreme social constructionism and relativism, and are skeptical of supposed boundaries, these theories envision a world of almost perfect equality in which identities are more a question of choice than the result of a complex interaction between social determination and innate qualities: "If all differences are transient, then no firm basis for group life — short of some universal group that we share with all other species — is possible. Any effort by any group of people to protect and assign privilege to the particularities of their group will be understood as a futile and self-defeating strategy of protecting difference" (Wolfe 1992: 310–311).[4]

Importantly, poststructuralism also rejects the concept of alienation, of estrangement of one's environment, from others, from oneself and from oneself's work and output. The whole idea of alienation, argues Epstein, is "incompatible with poststructuralism," because it presupposes the existence of "human needs prior to the way in which they are constructed in particular societies, needs that are in some way innate and that are frustrated or met to one degree or another in particular social contexts" (Epstein 1995: 113). This has a crucial consequence: By rejecting the notion of a human nature outside social construction, and ignoring the existence of needs or capacities other than those constructed by a particular discourse, there is no solid basis for social criticism and no worthwhile cause for protest or rebellion. Poststructuralism actually naturalizes alienation, continues Epstein, in that it universalizes the estrangement that is a major (although not the only) current of contemporary social relations and culture. It sees all thought, language, and culture through "the lens of alienation" (= its own intellectual framework), taking this to be transparent. Poststructuralism regards alienation as inherent in culture rather than the dominant characteristic of a particular historical moment, illuminated by a particular perspective. In addition, poststructuralism legitimizes alienation, through its hostility to "totality" or unity, its celebration of difference, its rejection of common values, common goals, even a shared vocabulary that could possibly serve as a basis for community (*ibid.*: 113–115).[5] This convincing critique suggests that a poststructuralist approach will also be of little help when we deal with processes of Americanization that indicate a need for analyses in terms of cultural imposition, alienation and the like. I am aware, however, that, along with the rediscovery of ideological and historical critique and the call for a "rehistoricization" of criticism, the influence of poststructuralism has waned in more recent years, and that there are signs of a return to history and politics in literary and cultural studies.[6] Yet, for the time being, the residual effects of this intellectual strain can still be identified in conceptualizations of Americanization under scrutiny here.

On the other hand, in returning to the discussion on "discourse" versus "reality," we should realize that the concept of Americanization encompasses categories of perception and interpretation through which the people concerned filter "realities," identifying certain phenomena as distinctly American and others as distinctly non-American. This is, to be sure, not the same as identifying these perceptions and interpretations with the realities they refer to. The imagined reality in itself exercises a significant sociopsychological influence on the social actors involved, as W.I. Thomas's renowned adage expresses so well: "If men [humankind] define situations as real, they are real in their consequences" (Thomas and Thomas 1928: 572). The social behavior of people is indeed always mediated by their social definitions of the situations they are immersed in, and this also plays a significant role in social perceptions of America's influence by locals. The emphasis here is on the importance of what people observe and think and how this affects their emotions and actions. This microscopic, sociopsychological focus of the early Chicago School of sociology and the tradition of symbolic interactionism that emerged from it — as well as kindred strains in sociology, including phenomenological sociology and ethnomethodology — contrasts with the macroscopic, social-structural and cultural perspectives in sociology found in the traditions of Marx, Weber, and Durkheim (Ritzer 1992: 197). Both are relevant for the study of Americanization.

A NEED FOR RESTORING THE BALANCE

It is obvious that there is a need for a more balanced perspective that incorporates indigenization and transnational developments but does not lose sight of projections of power and possible imperial influences. A satisfactory approach, I believe, needs to account for the multi-dimensional interaction of production, dissemination and reception of things American at both structural and symbolic levels, giving due weight to all relevant components. Next to discourse analyses and other text-based approaches (and power inequities in this regard), a more complete transcultural perspective must also encompass non-discursive realities, including the economic, technological, political and social-structural constraints of cultural exchanges that tend to "force" them into certain forms and "steer" them towards certain results.[7]

It is true that political and economic subordination or being subjected to technological and institutional prestructuring do not inevitably lead to cultural disempowerment. The subordinate groups concerned are not a *tabula rasa* upon which the political and economic power-holders, deliberate or undeliberate imperialists, in question can culturally engrave anything they want. This did not occur even in an extreme situation when Africans and their descendents were kept in bondage by Euro-Americans during slavery in North America. On the contrary, a rich African-American folk culture evolved (Levine 1977; 1993: 78–85). Likewise, in modern society, the image of passive, helpless, unknowing, unreflective, all-absorbing consumers of culture is untenable. The same applies to the image of cultural industries peopled by powerful, prescient producers of culture, who know how to construct cultural products of such a character that these are immune to reinterpretation or modification by the consumers.

Basically, there is always some leeway for selective borrowing, creative appropriation and alteration of domineering cultural influences by subaltern groups, thus producing hybrids from their own heritage and ideas, ideals, values, and practices imposed upon them. Yet the cultural-mental space for doing this is more constrained than postmodern or poststructuralist analysts assume. We should incorporate such constraints — insofar as these can be traced — in any account of the cultural exchanges in question. The array of choices of cultural products or practices on offer sets limits on people's behavior. How people make meaning out of culture very much depends upon their own stocks of knowledge and on their own immediate situations. Especially relevant here are the types and volumes of cultural capital that people possess (not only regarding forms of "high culture" but also those of popular culture), as are class, ethnic, and gender differences. But the situated character of people's knowledge implies that the meaning of a "text" also depends upon the political and social circumstances in which it is "read" (Hall and Neitz 1993: 210–211).

This position takes a similar *theoretical* middle ground as historian Richard Kuisel has suggested (in a discussion of American influence on the French cinema) between the transmission model, that at one extreme is equated with a *crude version* of "cultural imperialism," and at the other extreme, the assimilationist view (espoused especially by "postmodernist" anthropologists as noted earlier) that can exaggerate the capacity of local recipients to indigenize imports. In order to strike a good balance, is it necessary to theorize (cultural) Americanization in a way that "America remains central to a process that is transforming the globe, but it must also be framed so that the exports of American images, sounds, and values are shown as blended and transformed by the indigenous society" (Kuisel 2000: 209). It should be apparent, however, that employing such a conceptualization does not imply that the actual process of cultural Americanization is by definition always a neat middle position between American projection of cultural power and domestication of American imports by local recipients. There may very well be cases in which this process gravitates towards either one of the two end points of the continuum of cultural exchange.

I agree that Americanization has all too often been discussed in "hyperbolic rhetoric and binary extremes" (Nolan 2003: 244), but this does not mean that we should then adopt a perspective of transnationalization or transculturization that leaves structural constraints and possible cultural imposition and U.S. hegemony out of the picture. Not all transcultural "dialogues" of this kind have taken (or take) place on an equal footing. It is still necessary to check in each and every case the extent to which the various types of power exercised by the United States have been able to shape the transnational context in which the cultural exchanges occur. Recent calls for a more transnational and less U.S.-centric approach to the American Century abroad seem reasonable indeed, provided that we do not overlook American projections of power. This means that the study of Americanization must include analyses of relevant developments at home and in U.S. foreign policy (understood in a broad sense, including nongovernmental interventions as well).[8]

Importantly, cross-cultural influences do not by definition run parallel with international political and economical relationships. For example, in discussing relevant developments in Australia, Philip and Roger Bell suggest that, at least since the end of the Cold War, the political and cultural spheres "have become increasingly independent of each other ... and Australia's military/political subservience to Washington offers little insight into the complex cultural relationships between the two nations" (Bell and Bell 2004: 87). These analysts contend more generally that "local cultures may become increasingly vernacular and confidently proclaim their distinctiveness to a globalised or American-dominated international community while, at the same time, the smaller nation-state (even an Anglophone, treaty-bound nation-state like Australia) aligns itself more intimately with American iniatives internationally" (Bell and Bell 1993: 199). Thus, Americanization does not take place evenly all across the board. A local society may demonstrate complex hybridizations in its indigenous production and reproduction of culture vis-à-vis a globalizing world, while as a nation it becomes voluntarily or involuntarily more implicated in U.S. projections of economic, military, social and political power.

Americanization is usually not solely a cultural, but a more comprehensive, multivariegated process. In its full-fledged forms, it takes place at several levels (including the economic-technological, political, and social realms) that are in certain ways connected with each other. This complex constellation of driving forces, intermediating and direct influences, borrowings, appropriations and modifications can only be comprehended through theoretically well-informed empirical studies of specific developments, past and present.[9] To study the degree and quality of U.S. influences on a local setting and people, the intertwinements between foreign policy, political economy and culture need to be assessed against the background of U.S. foreign relations and its internal history. In the final instance, Americanization "has to be grounded in an understanding of political economy and capitalist systems and the inequities in the power relations between peoples, institutions, nations and corporations," as historian Maureen E. Montgomery has forcefully argued more generally with regard to an internationalized American studies. This also means that we should retain a critical awareness of the major driving forces of transnational movements of people, capital and commodities across international borders and the conditions of inequity, disempowerment and exploitation (Montgomery 2002: 116; cf. Mitchell 1996: 219–220). As Chris Barker put it, "[w]hile we are all part of a global society whose consequences no one can escape, we remain unequal participants and globalization remains an uneven process" (Barker 2000: 119). That is because the complex dynamics that globalization entails are very unevenly distributed around the globe, between regions and between different strata of the population within regions. A significant factor is the unequal "power geometry" (Massey 1993) of the time-space compression involved in globalization. How individuals experience and respond to the forces of globalization is, to a great extent, a consequence of their economic, social and geographic positions in the world. Only if we incorporate a fundamental understanding of these realities will a perspective of transnationalization or transculturization be an appropriate addition to our conceptual framework of Americanization.

Most significant in this understanding is that the role of the nation-state, and the United States of America in particular, is more persistent than proponents of transculturation assume. The complete demise of nation-states across the world has not occurred, despite repeated predictions to the contrary. The increasing importance of transnational corporations and other non-state actors and agencies in this era of intensified globalization notwithstanding, many states have survived intact and a number of new ones have been founded. A different issue is the changing nature of the relationships between transnational and state actors and agencies about which more later (Chapter 9).

TOWARD AN ADEQUATE ANALYTICAL–EMPIRICAL APPROACH

Since discussions of American influence overseas often immediately raise the specter of "Americanization" as a notion fraught with political baggage, it comes as no surprise that a number of scholars have used it as an evaluative-descriptive term with similar meanings. Some have identified Americanization more specifically as a negative tool of U.S. imperialism. On the other hand, especially during the 1950s and 1960s (the heyday of modernization theories in the social sciences and associated development policies) but even more recently, scholars and policymakers employed a definition that equates Americanization with economic modernization and political and cultural democratization, assigning to it a positive meaning. Any of these tendencies may be involved in specific cases, but none of them can simply be equated with Americanization.

When referring to American influence abroad, Americanization can be retained as an analytical concept, in terms of the definition given in the previous chapter, without having an inherent evaluative connotation. But using this analytical tool should always imply contextualization and localization; Americanization must consistently be located in the specific context of the process in question. Context is to be understood here as a multidimensional, time- and place-bound phenomenon that includes: the geographic dimension, place or location of the process, the relational dimension, such as the social positioning of the actors involved, as well as the temporal dimension, such as historical memory (particularly of alleged or real American influences amidst other foreign influences in the past) and the juxtaposition of historical experience and interpretation among the recipients of American imports. This conceptualization is in line with most recent studies that understand Americanization overseas as the transfer of ideas, symbols, goods and practices from the United States to other countries and focus on how societies abroad have taken up and, in the process, transformed these influences. Their framework explicitly allows for the possibility of agency, choice, and modification in the conceptualization of Americanization (Fehrenbach and Poiger 2000: xiii-xiv, xxvi, xxix).

There is one crucial difference with the approach of this book, however. The framework to be developed here pays relatively more attention to projections of American power (or the imperial dimension) than the latter studies tend to do. It accounts for the fact that the view of selective borrowing of American imports and models that prevails in current approaches of Americanization may overstate the capacity of a receiving society to exempt itself from broad economic, social and cultural processes emanating from the United States that condition the very nature of selection, thus making "choice" a problematic issue in actual practice (Bell and Bell 1993: 203). Our framework aims to counterbalance a predominant inclination to put the most emphasis on the local appropriations of things American.

Especially in light of much scholarly emphasis in recent years on the localization of American influence, we should hold on to the idea that Americanization is "a powerful one-directional process that tends to overwhelm competing processes (e.g., Japanization) as well as the strength of local forces that might resist, modify and/or transform American models into hybrid forms" (Ritzer and Stillman 2003: 35). Otherwise this notion loses its basic meaning of an overpowering process, as it has consistently been used as part of a broader Marxian heritage with its conceptualization of economic imperialism and cultural hegemony (*ibid*.: 31). Americanization involves American powers bringing about a wide variety of changes abroad. It concerns transformations and modifications — in varying degrees of depth and reach — of foreign countries and peoples through cross-national transfers or local adoptions of the mentioned exports/imports. Such influences may occur at various levels of analysis: macro-, meso-, or mico-social, institutional or behavioral. And they may be limited to particular domains of life; particular groups of people in particular contexts; or extended to entire nations, broader transnational regions or virtually the entire globe.

While popular culture, mass media and the cultural industries have high visibility and receive much attention among students of Americanization, significant components of Americanization that concern economic policies and international politics and security are underexposed or ignored. As Jan Nederveen Pieterse has pointed out, the latter too are, to a degree, "cultural," but less overtly so, and not as visible in everyday life. They concern not only relations among advanced societies but also those with other levels of development. To give an idea of the structural tendencies that are involved in current "global Americanization," this sociologist distinguishes the following levels of analysis in the international scene: 1) structural dynamics, that include scientific and technological changes, pioneered by and exported from the United States, but which are ultimately part of an intercivilization heritage; 2) fundamental dynamics that are general to industrialized countries (trends such as mass production, mass consumption, mass media, car culture, suburbanization and information technology), but in which the United States was leading the way so that they carry an American gloss or imprint; 3) American corporations and cultural industries that seek to draw so-called monopoly rents from their contemporary lead by any means ("fair or foul"), a common business practice with many precedents in history; 4) international leverage (international financial institutions and the WTO) and regional arrangements through which the U.S. government tries to consolidate its lead and institutionalize the advantage of its multinational corporations. The core questions of global Americanization would then be the last two points: drawing monopoly rents and the institutionalization of the advantage of U.S. corporations and cultural industries through superpower leverage (Nederveen Pieterse 2003: 80–81).

Americanization has its own chronology, geography and dynamics. Historically, America's foreign outreach began modestly in the mid-nineteenth century in Europe, parts of East Asia (Japan and China), Central America and Oceania (especially Australia). In the 1890s American influences set through on a much larger scale in Western Europe and Latin America, penetrated further into China, and, after 1898, extended to the Philippines. Then "Americanization" expanded to other parts of the world, with major spurts in the 1920s and after 1945, and more specific temporal and geographical differences in breadth and depth of the phenomenon. By the end of the twentieth century virtually no place of the globe was left untouched by American influence in one way or the other.

The notion of Americanization derives from a state-centristic perspective, characteristic of mainstream Western sociology, and entails a methodological nationalism, which critics see as highly problematic in an increasingly globalized world (Beck 2003: 16–17). Yet, as will be argued later on, this nation-oriented concept is still tenable to some degree today and can also be used in other than strictly state-centrist ways. Even in the current era of accelerated globalization dominated by transnational corporations, there remain quite a number of instances where a nation-state perspective, or at least some form of institutional approach at the national level, is preferable in the study of Americanization processes. As has been concluded with regard to the Australian situation, "Even if one accepts that increasing globalisation of the economic or cultural spheres renders the nation only a theoretical or hypothetical agent, it is no less true that it is with an essentially American dialect of contemporary life that Australian society has had to negotiate during [its] history" (Bell and Bell 1993: 208). In my view, this also applies to any other modern society within the U.S. orbit. In fact, imperial-state theory and international-relations theory derived from Gramsci's hegemony theory prove still to be relevant here (Berger 1995: 1–8, 231).

Perhaps it is better to conceptualize the problem first of all as a form of "methodological populism" (Nederveen Pieterse 2003: 79), since the notion of Americanization does not specify which unit of analysis applies to which America or whose America. It does not, for example, distinguish between various institutional sectors — public institutions (state/government), private for-profit institutions (business), private non-profit institutions (civil society)— or more specific groups or subcultures of Americans. Today, the United States is the fourth largest country in the world in terms of population, quite heterogeneous in terms of class, ethnicity, subculture and lifestyle, and a place where regional and other local differences also play a significant part, all of which demands further specification in given cases of Americanization. Moreover, transnational flows run in multiple directions; there have also been trends of Europeanization, and more recently Asianization and Latinization of the U.S., economically and culturally. Transnational migrations have been changing the character of the nation all along, and their interminglings are part of America's make-up.

In order to get a good intellectual grip on Americanization overseas, one surely has to know "a considerable amount about the sociological characteristics of the USA itself" (Robertson 2003: 263). What then are the defining features of the unit of analysis at issue? Is it a set of "organizing principles" that remain more or less constant over time, as assumed by contemporary exponents of American exceptionalism in the social sciences like Seymour Lipset (1996) and others of a similar ilk? Or is it first of all a site of transnational synthesis and hybridization as, among others, advocates of a transnationalized American history/American studies approach suggest? One thing is certain: Because waves and layers of immigration, from the Irish to the Latino, have been shaping America, it is not possible to simply refer back to the Founding Fathers and the prevailing ideas and practices at the nation's inception in order to determine its basic characteristics once and for all (Nederveen Pieterse 2003: 79). The changing character of the nation's distinctiveness (*not* exceptionalism) in a global context has to be accounted for.

THE POWERS IN THE AMERICAN FLOWS

Let us finally focus more closely on the power issues that are at stake here. Americanization belongs to the broader category of processes of social change through which a more powerful group or collectivity comes to exercise control over less powerful/subordinate groups or collectivities as we find most markedly in the relationships between colonized people and their colonizers.[10] Take, for example, the context of the Anglicization of Britain's colonies, or the Frenchification of France's and other regions under their respective hegemonic influences in the era of European imperialism, or as manifested, in a different way, in the Sovietization of most Central and Eastern European countries in the post-Word War II era (Jarausch and Siegrist 1997). Just as "colonization" has its counterpart, "decolonization," which refers to "the process by which a territory sheds colonial status and becomes a legally sovereign independent state, recognized as such by other states" (Abernethy 2000: 22), "Americanization" also has its counterpart, "de-Americanization." Although uncommon, the term indicates the process by which a society, sector or group of people sheds American influences and becomes relatively autonomous vis-à-vis U.S. projection of power.[11] De-Americanization thus refers to the reversal of the flow of power (that marks periods of U.S. imperial expansion) towards a stronger articulation of local identity and powers. Although the term has been employed differently,[12] here de-Americanization refers simply to the decline of Americanism/American influence in a given foreign context.

Americanization involves the power to influence, that is, the ability to bring forth the results one wants, and, if necessary, to change the behavior of others to make this happen. Power has two components: the capacity to act and the will to act. Capacity is possession of the objective means to achieve a goal in a given setting. Such means include possession of relatively large amounts of population, territory, natural resources, economic strength, military force, political assets, cultural forms attractive to others and so forth. They also include resources that can be used to coerce, threaten, or induce others to comply with one's wishes. Will concerns the subjective component, referring to an actor's conscious desire to achieve a goal. Typically the goal is consistent with an actor's material interests, beliefs, values, and concerns over security and survival. Power is then conceptualized as the product of capacity multiplied by will. If either component is missing or stays below a minimal threshold, even an ample supply of the other will not sufficiently compensate for the weak overall basis to carry out a planned course of action. Thus, if actor X is able to act but has no inclination to do so, the result is inaction. If X wishes to act but lacks the means to realize its goals, this will not lead to successful actions. If other actors are able and willing to attain objectives they have in mind (that differ from X's objectives), X's inaction (or unsuccessful attempts to achieve a goal) indicates that X lacks power. From here it follows that explanations for why one party (X) gains power over another (Y) should take several things into account: X's capacity to influence Y, X's will to do so, and Y's capacity and will to resist, moderate, modify, deflect, or postpone's X's actions in question (Abernethy 2000: 29–31).

The application of power may not be limited to situations of observable or latent conflict. To the extent that a powerful actor is successful in promoting his/her ideas as universal and legitimate, others will "choose" to do what he/she prefers. This may even prevent conflict from arising at all. In such situations, there is no observable application of power. As Steven Lukes asked the rhetorical question in his seminal study of power: "Is it not the supreme exercise of power to get another or others to have the desires you want them to have — that is, to secure their compliance by controlling their thoughts and desires?" (Lukes 1974: 23). This anticipates our discussion of soft power in the final section.

Furthermore, as we shall see later (when discussing the concept of structural power), the Americanizing influence needs neither to be planned beforehand nor deliberately exerted by the "colonizer." It often takes place in informal ways and at a less conscious level, through various mechanisms of the market and public sphere, driven too by societal impulses and needs in the local context.

Power is always negotiated, even between apparently unequal parties; it may be resisted overtly or covertly, directly or indirectly. The term "implicated"[13] has been suggested to describe the relationship between the United States and the foreign nation or people concerned, so that one does not automatically see America *a priori* as the more powerful entity that directly dominates, colonizes, or imperially controls the other, allegedly always the weaker party. Although power is an essential concept in any analysis of this process, one should try to avoid pre-judging the issue and emphasize the various ways in which American influences may be differentially effective within the receiving context. It becomes necessary, then, to look at the ways in which the recipients seek to negotiate, resist, modify, and accommodate the various influences to which they are exposed. Moreover, the power and influence exerted by the "receiving" party on the greater power should also be examined (Bell and Bell 1993: xi, 201). The term "co-implicated" would be most appropriate for those cases in which the former has modified and put its own stamp on the relationship. However, according to current *Oxford Dictionary of English* definitions "implicated" also has the connotation of being involved or complicit in a criminal or harmful act.[14] As a matter of fact, there are cases of Americanization, involving specific forms of economic or military collaboration, in which local elites act as willing accomplices (or "compradors") of the United States, when the terms "implicated" and "co-implicated" in the latter sense may hit the mark. This can only be determined upon closer inspection by means of clear assessment criteria set in advance.

From this discussion it follows that analytical descriptions and explanations of American influence abroad in principle should always include both sides of the relationship. Next to the actions of Americans, it is necessary to look at the behaviors of the foreigners that are involved in the process. Indeed, non-Americans play a role (of varying importance) in the projections of American powers overseas, and affect the temporal and spatial pattern of American expansion and influence abroad, that is, when and where, and to what extent, Americanization occurs. Americans may be invited by the locals to participate in indigenous power struggles, for a variety of reasons, opportunistic or otherwise. It is possible that the locals are enticed by the United States (or specific aspects thereof) and eager to enter its orbit. Americanization may be consented to, and deliberately embraced by its recipients in the form of "self-colonization" (Wagnleiter 1993: 332) or "empire by invitation" (Lundestad 1986).[15] Such self-willed Americanization often takes place when locals (or particular groups among them) voluntarily base domestic practices on models and exemplars originating from the United States as perceived by them. America then fulfills the function of reference society — an analogue to the sociological notion of "reference group" (van Elteren 1992: 155). Consequently, features of non-American societies (or specific regions, sectors or groups thereof) that made such overtures and willful acceptance more likely — thus complementing American push factors with indigenous pull factors — should be included in our theoretical framework.

Further, Americanization involves both relational and structural power relations from the perspective of transnational empire theory (Strange 1989). The concept of relational power is clear and consists of the ability of X by coercion or persuasion to get Y to do what the latter would not otherwise do. It also comprises the ability of X to entice or seduce Y to emulate its beliefs, values, and practices. At least as important is the concept of structural power, however, especially in relation to politico-economic aspects. This type of power is not immediately transparent and requires further clarification here. Structural power consists in the ability of X to determine the way in which certain basic social needs are provided. The first form of power is the lever; the second is the framework. If the target of relational power, Y, decides not to do what is required by X, then Y has to suffer the consequences determined by X. In the case of structural power, the price of resistance is determined more by the system than by any other political authority. Structural power comes closest to the broadest definition of "regimes" in the relevant literature on international relations (Krasner 1983). It encompasses customs, usages, and modes of operation rather than the more narrow definition that remains closer to state-state agreements and state-centered institutions. Like relational power, structural power is ultimately also predicated on human actions. It concerns the aggregated results of human actions in the past that have solidified into an "objective" system with a momentum of its own (a process called "objectification"). These are the given historical circumstances under which human beings make their own history.

Applied to the global political economy, the relational aspect of the power of transnational capital concerns deliberate strategies and interventions by human actors and agencies. This dimension of the power of capital "operates at both domestic and international levels, and can be overt or covert in nature" (Gill 1990: 113). The Trilateral Commission (formed in 1972) with members of the political, military, international business, and academic elites from the USA, Canada, Europe, and Japan (the major centers of economic power in advanced capitalism), is an example par excellence of a forum within which, and from which this type of political pressure has been exerted. It was involved in the generation and promotion of patterns of thought compatible with a shift in the focus and organization of state actions towards what Gill has called the "transnationalization" of the state. The Commission, a "network of networks," and kindred private international relations organizations such as the Bilderberg meetings, a Euro-American formation in the Atlantic context during the 1950s and 1960s, and similar councils in the Pacific context after 1945, and the Euro-Pacific context after 1973, are forums through which a transnationally shared consciousness about necessary strategies have been developed, and in which power resources have been mobilized.

The second dimension pertains to "forms of international structural power which, under certain conditions, create constraints on national fractions of capital, certain states, and labour, as opposed to transnational fractions of capital, for whom they can be viewed as a positive power resource" (*ibid.*). The major form of structural power is the movement of large amounts of capital between countries, in the form of direct foreign investment, short-term capital flows and long-term portfolio investment, which constrains and "conditions" the behavior of governments, firms, trade unions and other groups. This power is based upon the vastness and greater mobility of transnational capital relative to the size of trade flows, the foreign exchange reserves of central banks, and the potentially countervailing resources of "national" capital and labor organizations. The growth of such mobility and scale, pressures governments, competing to attract foreign capital, to provide an appropriate business climate for foreign investors. This means that the government policies towards the market, towards labor-capital relations, and the provision of an appropriate social and economic infrastructure are transformed into an international framework that is geared to the ongoing process of economic globalization (*ibid.*: 113–114, 209).

Structural power is more important to an understanding of the global politico-economic system than relational power. Susan Strange analytically distinguishes four basic structures of the international political economy that are relevant here — each is interrelated with, and inseparable from, the other three. The assumption is that power in one tends to reinforce the others, even though they do not always exactly coincide. These structures relate to four basic societal needs of a modern world economy: security, knowledge, production, and credit. Who or what provides for these basic needs in a society or at the transnational level enjoys structural power via the capacity to determine the terms on which those needs are satisfied and to whom they are made available. From this perspective, the interrelations between the four structures are conceptualized as follows:

> Production is the basis of life and therefore the fundamental essential. But production (or wealth) cannot be enjoyed, or even produced, without order; and order requires the provision of security. Credit supplied by the financial structure is a necessary condition for all but the most basic production structures. In the highly developed, highly capitalized production structure of any industrialized economy, a decisive role is played by the provision of credit through the financial structure. But the choice of social goals and the means of reaching them is determined by the knowledge structure. The power exercised over the nature of the knowledge to be acquired, and over the means used for its storage and communication, is a necessary complement to power exercised through the other three structures. Only by considering all four can the study of economic and political power be treated together; and only by considering all four can power exercised by the primarily economic entities be seen in the context of power exercised by the primarily political authorities [Strange 1989: 166].

Of course, our interest in issues of power should not remain restricted to politico-economic and social formations, but also include the cultural realm in the broadest sense. We must thereby try to avoid the excesses of poststructuralism, outlined earlier, that is, subsuming the social under the cultural, and adopting a Foucauldean power/knowledge stance. The contributors to the seminal volume *Close Encounters of Empire* —a collaborative attempt to write a new cultural history of U.S.–Latin American relations — recognize the need to practice cultural studies in relation to political economy and other structural approaches of their subject; in other words, their purpose is to integrate material and cultural/discursive analyses (Joseph et al. 1998). By doing so they represent a current of critical approaches within "postcolonial studies" that deliberately tries to include the larger historical context of socioeconomic and political relations between the imperial power and colonized societies/subaltern groups. Therefore this exemplary work deserves our attention here.

The authors see their project as the exploration of "a series of power-laden 'encounters' — typically, close encounters — through which foreign people, ideas, commodities, and institutions have been received, contested, and appropriated in nineteenth- and twentieth-century Latin America." But they also insist that their "use of the term *encounter* in conceptualizing the range of networks, exchanges, borrowings, behaviors, discourse, and meanings whereby the external became internalized in Latin America should not be constructed as a euphemizing device, to defang historical analysis of imperialism." On the other hand, they take a distance from tendencies by certain students of imperialism to reify this phenomenon, "validating Leninist identifications of it as the 'highest stage of capitalism,' or imposing other teleological conditions for its study" (Joseph 1998: 5).

According to the introduction, the contributors aim for "a materially grounded, processual analysis of U.S. interaction with [indigenous] polities, societies, and cultures" (*ibid.*: 7). They focus on the deployment and contestation of U.S. powers, in scrutinizing the "contact zones" (Pratt 1992: 6–7) of the American empire. Here the use of terms such as *encounter* or *engagement* is not meant to suggest a "neutral notion of social gathering" as is common in many recent publications on postcolonialism. Rather, they designate a complex pattern of connections between "specific material and discursive interactions in the contact zones of empire" that are also "multivalent." There are also dualities and conflicting tendencies at work here. On the one hand, these terms refer to "attempts by people of different 'cultures' to enter into relationships that need not deny or obliterate the subjectivity of the other party: efforts to understand, empathize with, approach the other; gestures to establish some type of bond, commitment or contact." On the other hand, however, "encounter and engagement also connote contestation and conflict, even military confrontation...." Thus, these concepts point to processes and practices through which the other is approached as proximate or distant, friend or adversary, or assigned a more ambiguous, ambivalent status. Furthermore, these practices entail mutual social constructions, including misunderstandings and misrepresentations, in which "othering" (including "orientalizing"[16] or the reverse: "occidentalizing"), inherent to such power-laden contexts, takes place. The lead editor insists, however, that the interactions in Latin American contact zones "are usually fraught with inequality and conflict, if not coercion ... but *also* with interactive, improvisational possibilities" (*ibid.*: 7–8).

The focus throughout the book is on "multistranded encounters," which means, first, that the encounter is not singular, but entails a wide variety of meetings involving individuals, institutions, and agencies, such as government agents, merchants, plantation owners, mining corporations, skilled workers and technicians, managers, missionaries, tourists, and retirees. It means second, that these encounters involve more than one dimension (the economic, the social, the political or "the imperial" et cetera). While "older theoretical models" were embedded in political economy and supposedly overemphasized the shaping influences of foreign powers on local societies, the cultural studies approach adopted by the authors accentuates "multiplicity, indeterminateness, and the ambiguities of power" (Roseberry 1998: 516).

Undoubtedly, the present notion of cultural encounters in contact zones is valuable as such, in that it points to a transnational sphere that goes beyond a state-centrist perspective. This domain is often underexposed in traditional cultural histories of foreign relations and is becoming increasingly more important with the ongoing, enhanced globalization. Regrettably, however, the broader intellectual strategy which it is part of is burdened with all the drawbacks of poststructuralism, including a Foucauldean power/knowledge approach, as becomes apparent from reading Emily S. Rosenberg's explication of the approach in a "final reflection":

> Histories of foreign relations ... are being reshaped by the new emphasis in historical studies on postcoloniality, postmodernity, and cultural analysis. Modernist assumptions (both liberal and Marxist) about the centralizing and rationalizing momentum in international life are challenged by reversals: a decentering of organized capital, states made uneasy by transnational flows of people and capital, and cultures that variously accept, reshape, differentiate, and redeploy. Such assumptions are also "muddied up" by the proliferation of meanings and floating signifiers churned up by the communications revolution. Within these investigations, power remains the central concern. But power systems are now assumed to be multiple and complex, arranged simultaneously through nation-states and regional relationships; through networks of capital, communications, and technology; through constructions of sex, gender, ethnicity, race, and nationality.... [H]istories that capture these reversals and complexities avoid the universalist, objectivist master narratives of modernism and often tend self-consciously toward more modest goals: to illuminate partial glimpses, to attend to localized context, to deal sensitively with multiple stories and protean symbolic systems [Rosenberg 1998: 510].

The approach that I propose to adopt does recognize the problems of modernist approaches implied in existing theories of imperialism, and dependency and world-systems models, if these are taken to their extreme. This is certainly the case when an inexorable progressive development towards some higher stage (or other kind of teleology) is assumed and contestations and indigenizations of imperial influences in the receiving contexts are overlooked or ignored. The intellectual trajectory to be followed in the approach suggested here involves an awareness of the complex interplays of domineering and liberating forces that may be at stake in the encounters within the "border zones" of U.S. relations with foreign societies and peoples, even more so with the further development of thick globalization in the current era. And, indeed, this sometimes leads to unexpected results when deliberate U.S. attempts to alter local institutions or policies in America's own image — experienced as foreign impositions at the receiving end — are channeled and reworked by locals in such ways that they manage to use the foreign interventions mostly to their own benefit, occasionally even as a weapon against the colonizing power in some strategy of reversal. It also means that the conceptualization to be developed here must be geared to these complexities in the localization processes concerned. However, the intended approach should not lose track of centralizing, homogenizing and rationalizing tendencies (including those carried by corporate globalization and transnational communication systems) that are at issue as well. It also rejects postmodernist attacks on the critical Enlightenment project of social emancipation with its emphasis on the value of self-determination by human beings in a societal context, and its progressive engagement with political liberty, social justice, and cosmopolitanism (Bronner 2004).

The renewal of historical materialism in the past few decades has helped us to understand the seemingly free-floating phenomenon of postmodernist culture as an historical-geographical configuration with a particular social and economic basis. As David Harvey has explained in his seminal work on the "postmodern condition," important developments in theorizing made it possible to grasp the significance of the transformations occurring in the nature of state functions, in cultural practices, and in the time-space dimension across which social relations evolve. This historical-geographical materialism is an open-ended "mode of enquiry" rather than a closed and fixed stock of knowledge. It attempts to come to terms with the historical and geographical features that characterize capitalism both in general as well as in its current phase. This includes the recognition that the production of images and of discourses is an important component of human activity that has to be analyzed as an integral part of the reproduction and transformation of any symbolic order. Which means that aesthetic and cultural practices and the conditions of their production receive due attention. It also recognizes that the dimensions of space and time matter, and that there are real geographies of social actions, as well as metaphorical territories and spaces of power that play a vital role as organizing forces in the geopolitics of capitalism. At the same time, however, they are also the sites of numerous differences and forms of "otherness" that should be understood both in their own right and within the overall context of capitalist development. In this renewed conception, the scrutiny of difference and "otherness" is principally something to be practiced from the very beginning in any attempt to capture the complexities of social change (Harvey 1989: 355).

This critical basis has made it possible to launch a well-considered counter-attack against the excesses of postmodernism, "of narrative against the image, of ethics against aesthetics, of a project of Becoming rather than Being, and to search for unity within difference, albeit in a context where the power of the image and of aesthetics, the problems of time-space compression, and the significance of geopolitics and otherness are clearly understood" (*ibid.*: 359). This conception has been a major contribution to the development of a new version of the Enlightenment project that also informs the approach followed here. Which means that, because of its postmodernist/poststructuralist tenor, even the interpretive framework of a self-consciously critical postcolonial approach like the exemplary one outlined above should *not* be incorporated into the analytical perspective of this book.

Instead, our framework will be extended with concepts borrowed from contemporary cultural sociology and anthropology for analyses of power dimensions at the level of cultural encounters in contact zones. Next to the economic-technological bases and diverse social forces that condition the power arrangements of societies, and thus influence their cultures, there are the workings of culture in and of itself. A major issue here is the established cultural order as a medium of power, that is, the ways in which the institutionalized patterns of culture inform people's actions. Influential thinkers such as Durkheim, Freud, Marx, Weber, Gramsci, Adorno and Horkheimer, Habermas, and Foucault have each formulated a general view on this issue. A Gramscian approach in terms of cultural hegemony seems most appropriate here as a heuristic device that sensitizes us to social processes involved in the creation and maintenance of dominant power at the societal level. However, we should be vigilant to avoid falling into the trap of a new consensus interpretation, this time of "cultural hegemony," in which the American past and present are homogenized. In historical studies of American society during the nineteenth and twentieth centuries that emphasize culture rather than political ideology, the hegemony argument has often ended up being circular, as Eric Foner has noted. In such cases the interest is focused on the creation of an hegemonic culture and of various "counter-cultures" within the larger American society against the backdrop of the rise of mass culture, the mass media, and mass consumption. Rather than being demonstrated, the hegemony of mass culture and liberal values is then inferred from the absence of protest, and this absence is attributed to that same "hegemony" (Foner 1984: 64).

Paradoxically, this misappropriation[17] of the Gramscian approach led in fact to a revival of consensus historiography, albeit from a point of view critical of the liberal consensus framework. It is far removed from a nuanced neo-Gramscian mode of exploring the ways in which popular beliefs, values, and cultural practices are shaped, reshaped, and contested.[18] The approach suggested here looks at how social movements are organized among both the dominant and subordinate groups, and how hegemonic formations and "historic blocs" and "counter-blocs" are built and led. It takes into account that the building of hegemonic formations is not only a matter of ideological influencing, winning hearts and minds, but also an issue of participation, "in the sense of involving people both in cultural institutions — schools, churches, sporting events — and in long term historical projects — waging wars, establishing colonies, gentrifying a city, developing a regional economy" (Denning 1990: 14). A sophisticated analysis of this kind allows for the fact that diverse cultural practices can survive even in the face of apparent "hegemony" (Williams 1977). Lee Artz and Bren Ortega Murphy have made such an attempt with regard to contemporary American society in terms of race, gender, and class from a long-term perspective that may stimulate similar studies, past and present (Artz and Ortega Murphy 2000).

Yet cultural power can be approached much more directly than Gramsci or any other of these thinkers does. "If power is defined as the ability to make people do things whether they want it or not, then power to shape culture can be traced to those people and organizations that produce culture" (Hall and Neitz 1993: 151). Areas of interest that are relevant here are, among other things: the power to define reality (embodied in classification systems or ideologies that are instrumental in this); cultural hierarchies and the power to exclude; culture and knowledge as resources of power; power relations in, and power exercised by, cultural industries (Lamont 1989), as well as the global "power-geometry" (Massey 1993) concerning various transnational flows of culture, including those of mass-mediated popular culture. In this connection, five areas of interest and associated analytical frameworks can be distinguished, based on existing practices of research of culture,

which offer a rich reservoir of concepts and insights for our purpose: institutional structures of culture; cultural history and the persistence of cultural patterns; production and
social distribution of culture; societal effects and reception of culture; meaning systems
and social actions in relation to the reproduction and change of institutionalized culture
(Hall and Neitz 1993: 17–19; van Elteren 2005: 214–216). In taking note of the power
aspects in the various areas of interest we must consistently keep the various intersocietal
contexts of U.S. international relations in mind.

SOFT POWER UNRAVELED

Finally, we need to address the distinction between "hard power" and "soft power"
that has come into vogue in the area of international relations, and was coined by political scientist Joseph S. Nye Jr., former Assistant Secretary of Defense for International
Security Affairs in the Clinton Administration (Nye 1990: 32–33; 2002: 9–10). In Nye's
conceptualization, military and economic power are both forms of hard command power
that can be used to make others change their position. Hard power relies either on induce-
ments/rewards (carrots) or threats (sticks). But there is also an indirect way to exercise
power. A country (or to be more precise, its national power-holders, governmental or
nongovernmental)[19] may obtain the outcomes it wants because other countries or peoples
want to follow it, admiring its values, emulating its example, aspiring to specific practices or its general way of life. Of course, the modeling country and site of attraction, in
our case the United States, can be proactive in this regard, by trying to set the agenda in
world politics and appealing to others in various ways. It has frequently shown this tendency in the past, next to the use of military and economic force to change others, and
continues to do so today. Nye calls this form of power — "getting others to want what you
want"— "soft power." In contrast to the hard command power resting on tangible resources
like military and economic strength, soft power "co-opts people rather than coerces them,"
and rests on "intangible power resources such as an attractive culture, ideology, and institutions" (Nye 2002: 9).

Soft power is more than persuasion or the ability to move people by argument. It
rests on the ability to entice and attract, which often leads to acquiescence or imitation.
Nye recognizes a connection here with existing insights among political leaders and
thinkers such as Antonio Gramsci who "have long understood the power that comes from
setting the agenda and determining the framework of a debate" (*ibid.*). In Gramsci's case
this refers to the self-willed adoption of the hegemonic power among subaltern groups —
for the time being and to a certain extent (never completely)— thus allowing for contestations of the cultural hegemony (Gramsci 1971: 321–343). The notion of hegemony
entails more than dominance in the strictly military or politico-economic sense. It has a
connotation of leadership, which means that there is likely to be much consensus inter-
mingled with the usual coercion. As well as being feared for its power, the hegemon is
also admired for its achievements to the extent that others come to emulate the hegemon
(Taylor 1999: 5).

Needless to say, this is all in the eye of the beholder. Soft power varies with the targeted audience; what works well with some groups of people may not do so among other
audiences or may even repel them. A government can also gain and lose soft power depending on its performance at home, as perceived by foreign audiences (Nye 2002: 188n78).
Importantly, under certain circumstances soft power can become a "mere cover for 'tough

power' — that is, the tough creation of important new classes, and the tough politics of transnational-government relations" as Walter LaFeber signaled in the late 1990s with regard to the operations of U.S.-based media empires Murdoch and Turner and transnationals such as Nike acting in tandem with the U.S. government of the Clinton years (LaFeber 1999: 159). This made observers like him wonder if such soft power was merely "a new information-age disguise for age-old imperialism" (*ibid.*: 156). Not in his view, as it turned out: the reality was more complex. I tend to agree, although we should still allow for an element of imperialism, as I will argue later.

Nye tends to use his two concepts first of all with regard to relational power, and to underexpose structural power relations connected with transnational "regimes," although he does recognize the state powers attached to possession of military and economic resources. In order to convert America's potential power resources into realized power "well-designed policy and skillful leadership" are required (Nye 2002: 5). True as this may be from an international relations standpoint in terms of realpolitik, for Americanization to occur these requirements are not necessary per se as indicated earlier. Here the concept of structural power cannot be missed. In order to assess the effects of the powers as they are actually deployed, it is moreover necessary to look more closely at the encounters between the imperial power and subaltern groups in the "contact zones" concerned, something Nye does not sufficiently account for.

Nye states that, in general, "the universalism of a country's culture and its ability to establish a set of favorable rules and institutions that govern areas of international activity are critical sources of power" (Nye 1990: 33), and these sources of power have become much more important in world politics. From this perspective, America's soft power is based on the fact that the United States represents values and embodies practices that others want to follow. But it should be emphasized that this is a time-bound matter, and dependent on the nature of the dominant political and cultural strains in a given period. The values and practices that prevail in the United States at a certain time may also be less attractive to other parts of the world or even be rejected by some other cultures.

Historian Walter Russell Mead distinguishes four different contributions to America's soft power, each associated with a different strain of American foreign policy. These include what he calls the Jeffersonian commitment to liberty and equality; the Wilsonian approach in terms of benevolence, anticolonialism (or today's "liberal imperialism" and humanitarian interventionism), and support for democracy; and the commercial success that results from Hamiltonian politics regarding manufacturing, trade, and finance. But beyond all these there is the appeal to ordinary people abroad of what Mead terms Jacksonian America: "the spectacle of a country that is good for average people to live in, a place where ordinary people can and do express themselves culturally, economically, and spiritually without any inhibition." Since at least the 1920s, this concerns, the dominant consumer lifestyle of Americans — as perceived from afar, including diverse versions of an imaginary America — which wins the country many fans among ordinary people overseas. Its dissemination worldwide has made millions of foreigners feel somehow connected to, or even vicariously part of, the United States. Mead goes further, asserting, rather provocatively, that "[t]he cultural, social, and religious vibrance and unorthodoxy of Jacksonian America — not excluding its fondness for such pastimes as professional wrestling — is one of the country's most important assets" (Mead 2001: 261). Closely associated with this idea is the attractiveness of American popular culture as a significant source of America's soft power. In this domain, the United States possessed a great advantage over all other nation-states in the last century, and in this century it is likely to be "the single greatest force in global culture at least to the extent it was in the twentieth century and probably more so" (Rosendorf 2000: 117).

Hard and soft power are related — both are aspects of the ability to achieve one's purposes by affecting the behavior of others — and may reinforce each other. Sometimes the same power resources can evoke the entire spectrum of influence patterns from coercion to attraction. Some countries or peoples may be attracted to countries with hard power by the myth of invincibility or inevitability that surrounds them. Both the Hitler and Stalin régimes cultivated such myths. Sometimes command power may be used in trying to establish institutions that later come to be regarded as legitimate — consider the idea (or wishful thinking) behind "regime change" as a major aim of specific military interventions in recent history. Soft power is also relatively autonomous from, and not simply the reflection of, hard power. "The Vatican did not lose its soft power when it lost the Papal States in Italy in the nineteenth century. Conversely, the Soviet Union lost much of its soft power after it invaded Hungary and Czechoslovakia, even though its economic and military resources continued to grow" (Nye 2002: 10).

Countries with lesser military and economic weight may still have significant political clout because of their adoption of causes that are attractive to a larger part of the world community; compare, for instance, countries such as Canada, the Netherlands, and the Scandinavian states with their emphases on economic development aid and peacekeeping (*ibid.*). In this context the kind of power embodied by a strong civil society is highly relevant. What Germans call *Zivilmacht* (civil power) concerns a more muscular form of power, harder than Nye's "soft power" (Reid 2004). We must also account for these sources of power of other countries and peoples when trying to assess America's influence abroad. Moreover, U.S. soft power may also be experienced not as harmless entertainment and consumerism or well-intended developmental or humanitarian aid by foreign publics but as "the devil in disguise," that is, "hard power in sheep's clothing" in cases where it is combined (in an uncomfortable way) with the use of hard power. This occurred on several occasions when the United States aggressively pushed its military and/or economic agenda, and was seen as "an overbearing, even dangerous, imperialist power that ... does what it can and forces others to do what it must" (Rosendorf 2000: 127). Its image then turned into that of an evil rather than a relatively benign hegemon of global power. Therefore we should not exaggerate the mesmerizing or transformative effects of U.S. culture to the benefit of American interests; its impact may also be exactly the opposite under certain circumstances. It is obvious that the implications of projections of U.S. powers at a given time and place can only be adequately understood by considering the historical context of America's relations with the other countries or specific social entities involved.

7

An Interpretive Framework for Further Analysis

After having laid the theoretical foundations in the previous two chapters, it is time to construct a theoretical framework that will enable one to systematically approach the full range of foreign encounters with things American around the globe. It includes both the export side and the receiving end of processes of Americanization, as well as the intermediary level of cultural encounters in the contact zones concerned, and identifies the major institutions, agencies, avenues and processes through which American beliefs, values, goods and practices are carried abroad, introduced into foreign contexts, and acted upon by local recipients. This chapter concentrates on the exporters and disseminators of American influence at various levels of analysis in relation to U.S. foreign policy. It likewise gives a brief periodization of U.S. influence abroad and concludes by introducing the receiving side of the foreign encounters concerned. The next chapter provides analytical details about the social mechanisms and mediating processes involved in the borrowings from the American repertoire and appropriations by various cultures, subcultures, publics and audiences in the receiving contexts.

THE EXPORT SIDE OF AMERICANIZATION

Americanization abroad entails a complex constellation of relationships that involves many types of actors, on both sides of the exchange process, whose encounters take place in a multilayered setting. The following scheme gives an overview of the various levels of analysis and power resources, starting with the most comprehensive at the top and moving towards the smallest at the bottom, that should be taken into account. However, this schematic representation does not depict the specific transfer and transmission processes that are at stake.

It begins with the distinctive features of America's nationhood and political system (Smith 1993, 1997; Singh 2003; Kaufmann 2004; King 2005). Basic characteristics and continuing patterns of American culture and society are relevant with regard to the "Americanness" of the influences coming from the United States. These features are linked at a second level to America's position in the global system. At a third level one looks at the relevant sectors within the United States. Three sectors, that is, segments of a society's life in which people specialize in a certain kind of activity, have had a critical influence: public, private profit, and private non-profit. The public institutional sector, or the state level, concerns a nation's central government — leaders and institutions charged with formulating and implementing policies affecting the nation as a whole — which takes place through laws and the legally sanctioned threat and use of force. In the private profit sec-

Americanization abroad: A model

Units of Analysis	Components of Power
	— structural and relational power regarding politico-economical and social domains
	— cultural power in various areas of interest

Americans	Capacity to influence	Will to influence
America's distinctiveness in terms of nationhood and political system		
America's position in the global system (plus connection with U.S. foreign policy)		
Various sectors		
Public institutions (nation-state/government)		
Private profit institutions (business)		
Private non-profit institutions (civil society)		
Key individuals		

Transnational domain: multi-stranded encounters in contact zones transnational networks and practices

People Subject to Americanization	Capacity to accept/resist	Will to accept/resist
Distinctive features of foreign society involved		
Foreign society's position vis-à-vis existing constellation of economic-political power blocs		
Sectors within receiving society		
Public institutions (nation-state/government)		
Private profit institutions (business)		
Private non-profit institutions (civil society)		
Key individuals		

tor, people not directly and fully employed by government agencies seek to enhance their income, health, and material well-being over and above basic subsistence needs. They do so by pursuing economic-financial gains primarily out of self-interest.

In the private non-profit sector, often indicated in the literature as "civil society," one finds people who are involved in religious, philanthropic, social welfare, developmental, educational or cultural activities. Civil society is not merely a private domain but has public dimensions to it as well. Standing somewhere between the market and the state, civil society is a third form of regulation of modern society, next to market mechanisms and mechanisms of political allocation by the state. Modern capitalism contained the potential to destroy the very civil society that it helped create. In the eighteenth century, liberalism and the market were allies against the old order symbolized by the state. Civil society appeared as such by the middle of the nineteenth century as a result of the market's further penetration into the private sphere and the growing influence of the cash nexus that placed a monetary value on all things, which increasingly came to be seen as undermining the ability of people to find and protect a societal sphere that was uniquely their own. Then the meaning of civil society changed from a dualistic conception (private sector versus state) to a tripartite conception: civil society between market and state. It embodies neither the self-interest of the one nor the coercive authority and regulatory qualities (regarding equality and more generally "the good life") of the other, but, at least in the ideal situation, the autonomy and responsibility of citizens as moral agents aware of their obligations to others (Wolfe 1989: 14–19).

Of course, people's activities in a given sector may overlap and compete with what people in other sectors do. Nevertheless, each sector can be considered functionally distinct from others by virtue of its primary stated purpose and the institutions performing its work. The activities and interactions of sectoral institutions constitute vital factors behind American influence abroad. This means that only by looking at the composite whole of interacting sectors are we able to fully understand their impact in given cases.

American foreign policy can be seen as the deliberate policy part of the export side of Americanization abroad. Historically there are differences here with other nation-states. European states have tended to control or monopolize many domains of their interactions with other societies. In early modern Europe even international business was closely connected with states. Government and commerce were very tightly linked in commercial republics like Venice and Genoa. In Holland and Britain much international commerce was carried out by governmentally chartered enterprises like the Dutch and British East India Companies, which combined foreign ventures of both government and business. In building their empire on the North American continent, English monarchs chartered the London Company (that founded the Virginia colony), the Massachusetts Bay Company, and the Hudson Bay Company for this purpose. The missionary activities of many imperial states in Europe were also closely intertwined with their national imperial policies — thus simultaneously Christianizing and "civilizing" other peoples along the lines of the imperial powers involved. Indeed, the role of Catholic missionaries in Spanish, Portuguese, and French colonial ventures is characteristic of the way in which many activities we would now consider as those of civil society and nongovernmental actors were once directed by the state, or at least coordinated with its imperial policy abroad (Abernethy 2000: 31–40). American merchants and missionaries have acted more independently from the state, although both groups never hesitated to call for state support when they needed it and thought they could get it. On the other hand, the U.S. federal state *has* at times intervened in the civil societies of foreign countries, either directly or through "nongovernmental" agencies under its control.

The United States is the only major country in the world where big business developed before big government. Unlike most countries, where a large centralized state developed for military reasons, the absence of military danger throughout most of its history meant that there was no powerful federal government in place when large-scale national enterprises were being developed in America between 1880 and 1930 (Bracken 1997). Along with a more general reluctance among the ruling elites to control corporate business, this led to a more distinctive place of business in U.S. history and relatively more room to maneuver for corporations in the United States than in any other country. Yet American "free enterprise capitalism" has been embedded in, and moderated by party machines, Fordism, and government interventions such as regulatory measures during the Progressive Era and the New Deal period, postwar "military Keynesianism," GI Bill of Rights, export credits, research & development subsidies, local investment incentives, the "war on poverty" and affirmative action (Nederveen Pieterse 2003: 70–71). There is a long history of "corporate welfare" in which corporate business interests closely allied with kindred members of the federal government and politicians in Congress have benefited greatly from government investments and subsidies, as well as, pending on the historical context, from protectionist and "regulatory" measures or, instead, deregulatory measures taken at their instigations (Derber 1998: 66, 153–171; Nader 2004).

Throughout American history the distinction between state and private activities (business and civil society) has generally been less clear than in Europe, and fewer of the key activities have been led or carried out by the government. This is as true in foreign affairs as in many other areas of national life. Therefore U.S. foreign policy studies that focus merely on state activities tend to underexpose, and in some instances misjudge, the direction and effect of the broad engagement of the United States with the rest of the world from an early stage onwards. This is further enhanced by the fact that "nongovernmental" activities abroad that were steered or even led by U.S. governmental agencies have not always been conceived in these terms.

Moreover, sectoral institutions that could be considered the equivalent of those in other societies did not always exist in America. One may think of certain governmental agencies in Western societies that did or do not have their counterparts in the United States. The obvious example is "culture," which, as a specific area of systematic policy-making by a separate department of the U.S. government, has long been virtually nonexistent. The United States was the last among the major nations to establish an official program of cultural cooperation with other nations designed to foster closer relations and to win friends.[1] It was not until 1938, with the creation of the Division of Cultural Relations within the State Department by the Roosevelt Administration, that cultural diplomacy became a policy domain. Incited by the propaganda successes of the Axis powers (Germany, Italy, and Japan), especially in Latin America, and the pressures of the war, the United States moved within a period of only five years from a position of near indifference toward international cultural relations to a determined and focused worldwide cultural diplomacy policy consisting of a wide variety of activities (Gienow-Hecht 2000: 480–481).

There are many factors that may explain the development of U.S. foreign policy. These can be divided analytically into domestic and international factors, that is, those internal and external to the United States. There is, however, a substantial degree of interaction between relevant developments on the domestic and external planes. Domestic sources of U.S. foreign policy can be found at the level of society and/or the nation-state. An important societal factor concerns the power and preferences of special interest groups, which include corporate interests of various kind (e.g., in manufacturing, agriculture, financial services and, more recently, high technology), but also labor interests and, over the past few decades, environmental interests as well. Ethnic groups have been particularly influential in the security area (Foot et al. 2003a: 8). Political scientists have found that interest groups enjoy significant access to, and influence over, central government (Krasner 1978; Milner 1997).[2] Especially in foreign economic policy, where business interests are "conspicuously salient," interest group influence manifests itself. More recently, various foreign policy think tanks, many funded by business, have also helped shape the climate of foreign policy opinion to the benefit of U.S. corporate interests (Dumbrell 2003: 280).

A second explanatory factor concerns the structure of the U.S. political system. The U.S. federal system is characterized by division of political power within the national decision-making institutions. Yet power regarding foreign affairs is concentrated in the executive branch, although decision-making authority is shared with Congress. The U.S. constitutional separation of powers between the executive and the legislative branches is unique among major democracies and supposedly enables the executive in America to counter the usurpation of its power by other branches better than its counterparts in parliamentary democracies in Europe and elsewhere. But the other side of the coin is that it tends to obstruct accountability for governmental policies and leads to indecision and stalemate, whereas the parliamentary system, which combines the legislative and executive functions, is, at least in the ideal case, a more transparent and effective form of democracy.[3]

Due to the institutional fragmentation within Congress, individual members have a much larger degree of power than in any other democratic system in the world. The U.S. Congress chose to protect its institutional prerogatives through the creation of an elaborate committee system that delegated political authority for particular policy decisions to individual committees and subcommittees — what has been called "committee government." At the beginning of every Congress, each chamber creates permanent standing committees that are empowered to receive, write, and report legislation and conduct investigations. Thus all major legislation originates in the detailed investigative and legislative work undertaken by congressional committees (Sexton 1991: 162–168).

The Congress' committee system has traditionally represented the strongest countervailing forces to party rule and centralizing power, especially in the House. But the organizational structure has changed over the past few decades. As a consequence of the strengthening of party rule since the mid–1980s, fewer legislative measures are subjected to the committee-based process in question. Especially when policy issues are highly salient and important to the majority party, congressional parties play crucial roles in coordinating action within the legislature to the extent of modifying and even overruling and bypassing committees. The most important effects of the new procedures are to undermine and circumscribe the power of committees and strengthen the hands of party conferences and their leaders so that members of the House reach decisions that reflect major party preference. Contemporary House majority leadership is activist, strong, and highly interventionist at all stages of the legislative process. Members of Congress assert their representative and lawmaking roles and, at the same time, are increasingly held accountable for what their party achieves collectively, although in recent years congressional Republicans appear to act more in this fashion than previous Democratic majorities. On the other hand, however, since the Senate is fundamentally non-majoritarian, this acts as a partial counterweight to party-reinforcement in the Congress (Owens 2003: 205–212).

The president has more constitutional power in foreign policy, and in the associated domain of military affairs, than in any other area. The need for secrecy and dispatch, connected with particular constitutional arrangements, make foreign policy the preeminent domain of the executive branch and its presidential head. The need for rapid decision-making and steady direction — especially in the eras of international terrorism and weapons of mass destruction — bolster presidential authority even more. The Senate can give advice to the president, and his treaties and ambassadorial appointments require its stamp of approval. The House of Representatives's power is restricted in this domain to voting appropriations and declarations of war ("power of the purse" strings). However, the fact that only Congress can declare war has not prevented a number of presidents from using their power as commander-in-chief to commit American troops to fight overseas without congressional consent (e.g. the Korean War and the Vietnam War). Likewise, the power of judicial review over foreign policy is also severely limited. For example, treaties are explicitly declared "the supreme law of the land." So while courts interpret them, only the Supreme Court can alter them or declare a properly ratified treaty unconstitutional — a rare avenue indeed.

Moreover, no powers have been accorded to the states regarding foreign policy; yet some state and local governments have become active in foreign economic policymaking (notably in the area of foreign trade promotion) since the end of the Cold War. From their perspective they are better situated than nation-states to exploit the opportunities offered by economic globalization (Mead 2001: 51–53; Hart 2003: 174–175; Dumbrell 2003: 268, 274).

Key decisions in foreign policy are rarely made by presidents on their own though; they have to share power with Congress. Only Congress can declare war and only Congress has the constitutional authority to raise money for war and diplomacy. On the other hand, however, Congress often finds it difficult to challenge the president for structural, procedural, and political reasons. This is even more the case during a presidentially defined crisis. Furthermore, various interest groups can also be involved in the foreign policymaking process, especially those representing corporate business and specific ethnic groups (notably the Jewish, Irish and Cuban American lobbies in the past four or so decades), "advocacy" groups and nongovernmental organizations (that have proliferated since the end of the Cold War) as well as various foreign policy think tanks (many also funded by business).

Presidents even have to share power with the rest of the executive branch, although presidential advisers and operatives rarely if ever offer a real and sustained challenge to their boss. The U.S. foreign policy process is generally hierarchical, with the president assumed to have overriding discretion. Yet in recent history, political advisers — who track public opinion and foreign policy's connection with important domestic political battles — have played an increasingly prominent role, and in several cases have had a major influence on foreign policymaking.[4] This is not to suggest, however, that democratic "public opinion" ultimately determines U.S. policies; it is rather the other way around. Only in exceptional circumstances does foreign policy assume a high degree of salience for the American public. Presidents are generally able to lead and shape public opinion, at least in the short to medium term. The degree of attention paid to public opinion tends to vary according to the perceived intensity of views held by the public on different issues, as well as the degree to which particular presidents regard themselves primarily as servants or leaders of the public. Public opinion is communicated to presidents through various channels, notably friends and associates of policymakers, interest groups, the news media, the Congress and local elected bodies, and polls. Several of these intermediaries themselves serve to shape as much as to communicate opinion, however (Dumbrell 2003: 274, 279–281).

A third internal factor that may explain the development of U.S. foreign policy concerns divisions within the executive branch. As is more generally the case with bureaucratic politics, even though different executive departments share foreign policy responsibilities, they may yet have particular institutional interests and commitments. Traditionally, policymaking in the executive branch tends to be dominated by a rivalry between the Secretary of State and the National Security Advisor and staff. Tensions between the State Department and the Department of Defense are also common. In addition, coordination of foreign policy processes is also often less effective because of the existence of what has been called the "economic complex" and "security complex." (Nathan and Oliver 1987). These two clusters of executive agencies tend to work along separate lines with little coordination, even though an increasing number of issues are located at the intersection of these two issue areas.

A fourth factor centers on the political culture of the United States, which can best be seen as resulting from the interactions between multiple political traditions, including liberalism, republicanism/civic humanism, and ascriptive forms of Americanism that together constitute the culture. Illiberal ideologies and institutions of ascriptive hierarchy that assigned a lower political status to women, and racial, ethnic and religious minorities have been part of the national culture from the very outset. Naturally, these ascriptive hierarchies have been contested at certain points in U.S. history, which led to their erosion. One the other hand, they were sometimes reaffirmed by new legitimating ideologies, which carries on until the present age (Smith 1993; 1997).

A crucial enduring component of U.S. political culture with foreign policy relevance is the widely shared belief that American political and economic institutions are models that others should emulate. To many Americans, a world in which other countries come to resemble the United States and its people is likely to be safer and more prosperous (Foot et al. 2003a: 9–10).

U.S. foreign policy is also shaped by the external environment, that is, by the international context within which the United States operates. Four sets of resources/constraints warrant special attention: the global distribution of power resources, the international normative context, the foreign policies of other governments, and the performance of multilateral organizations in which the U.S. is involved.

The position of a nation-state in the global distribution of military, economic, political and ideological-cultural power will likely influence its approach to foreign policy. Therefore it is necessary to try to determine America's world power as it changed over the course of time, and precisely how this shaped its foreign policy, particularly with regard to unilateralism/multilateralism and internationalism/isolationism in which historically various forms and combinations can be found.

The international normative context is a second external source of U.S. policymaking. International norms help to establish what constitutes legitimate and acceptable behavior in relations among sovereign states. As states have become more interdependent after World War II, they have increasingly come to consider themselves as members of an international community. A strong expectation has developed that members of this community decide and act collectively rather than individually. Multilateral organizations such as the UN, NATO, GATT/WTO, NAFTA, APEC and so forth are the institutional expression of this contemporary norm, and they create incentives for all states, even the most powerful, to join and participate actively in them.

Thirdly, the diplomatic efforts of other governments, in particular close allies of the United States, may also influence U.S. foreign policymaking. Due to its size and power, U.S. unilateralism has been a major concern of other states since the mid-twentieth century. Consequently they share an interest in a more consistent and predictable U.S. foreign policy, preferably one that also reflects (at least to some degree) their own preferences. An important way in which these objectives can be achieved is to ensure that U.S. foreign policy initiatives are channeled through collective decision-making mechanisms. This applies especially in cases of aggressive forms of unilateralism in U.S. trade and defense policies, when America's major allies may lobby hard to ensure U.S. compliance with multilateral procedures.[5]

Fourthly, the performance of multilateral organizations — or rather how that performance is perceived by leading figures in the United States (which makes this also a domestic factor)— may also have a significant impact on the U.S. approach to these organizations, which form an important part of the institutional context of U.S. foreign policy. For example, the widespread belief— rightly or wrongly — that the UN failed in peacemaking efforts during the early 1990s, affected the level of enthusiasm and support that U.S. officials offered to UN operations in the latter half of the decade. This, in turn, altered the UN-related institutional context of America's foreign policy (*ibid.*: 11–14).

Finally, the United States has often exerted strong influence abroad, not so much as a result of its deliberate pursuit of foreign policy objectives but as unintended consequences of decisions taken for reasons unrelated to them. This concerns the inadvertent consequences for foreign peoples of policies adopted or actions taken by the United States for other reasons (which is similar to what can happen in the case of other powerful states, of course). For example, due to the sheer size of the U.S. economy, domestic policy decisions regarding economic or environmental issues — occasionally even measures taken by individual U.S. states or localities — may have large international effects (*ibid.*: 18–19; Foot et al. 2003b: 272).

HISTORICIZING THE FRAMEWORK

Next this framework of Americanization needs to be connected to the history of American engagements with other regions, states, and peoples in its broadest sense. Even though this encompasses more than the history of U.S. foreign policy and international relations, the latter is nevertheless an important part of it. A few basic insights are relevant here. First, because of the country's geographical location, the commercial and enterprising nature of American society, as well as its various forms of missionary universalism (both secular and religious) "globalization" has been part and parcel of American strategic thinking and policymaking throughout most of U.S. history. Foreign policy regarding the relationship of the American economy to the international economic system has historically been a central concern of national politics. U.S. foreign policy is inextricably linked to domestic concerns; its primary purpose was always to advance American commercial interests. Second, during most of American history the global economic order was centered on Great Britain, and therefore America's key national dependency on, and concern about, this order implied a close if sometimes conflictual relationship with Great Britain. Third, from the very beginning, the role of private citizens and agencies in spreading America's beliefs, values, goods, and practices abroad has been crucial, although the federal government gave clear support to private institutions, especially commercial interests. Since the birth of the new nation, American foreign diplomacy has consistently been operating to help open markets. Fourth, from the 1890s onwards, with the increase of U.S. expansionist/imperialist policies, American influences became much more strongly felt abroad, reaching a larger number of foreign countries than ever before. And lastly, returning to the first point mentioned above, U.S. foreign policy at any given time should be seen in relation to *both* the domestic constraints on the exercise of American power in the international system *and* the various challenges to this power that the United States faces abroad (Mosler and Catley 2000: 61–81, 153–179).

Importantly, American foreign policy has not proceeded from a single, unified worldview. Even at its heart, there are always differing viewpoints that revolve around the definition of national interests. American foreign policy rests on a time-bound balance of contrasting, competing beliefs and values. The framework for the foreign affairs that preoccupy U.S. foreign policy elites has traditionally been provided by the dialectical opposition between isolationism and internationalism. This opposition relates, albeit in a complex way, to wider conflicts, between traditionalism and progressivism.

"Isolationism" and "internationalism" are terms that bring to mind identifiable positions within historical and contemporary debates about U.S. foreign policy and its purposes. Advocates of the two positions also have clear perceptions of themselves:

"isolationists" as upholders of traditional, "America First" values and a corresponding unilateral foreign policy; "internationalists" as liberals and progressives, advocates of a multilateral foreign policy.

Internationalists have set the tone of U.S. foreign policymaking since World War II. They seek to intervene in foreign conflicts, to make treaties and alliances, and to advance the global, dominant reach and power of the United States — all as a way of promoting its democratic values as well as defending its material interests and security. Material interests are dominated by considerations regarding security for the country itself and for American assets abroad. Promoting democratic ideals and practices is often connected directly to a particular notion of American exceptionalism; that is, the belief that the United States has a particular historical destiny to export American-style liberal democracy, set in its capitalist, "free market" economic context.[6] These two strands are not mutually exclusive, of course. Most U.S. foreign policy leaders would argue that they are mutually reinforcing; U.S. security can only be strengthened if the world turns to liberal (in the classical European sense),[7] capitalist democracy, while the spread of democratic capitalism will benefit American prosperity.

This problematic reasoning (expressed in much public rhetoric) is enhanced by the fact that democracy is often defined in relatively narrow and procedural terms by its American promoters: free elections, competing political parties, a free marketplace and so forth, rather than in terms of human rights (including women's and minority rights), public space and access to common goods and social provisions, let alone economic democracy. For example, perceived security and economic interests at times have caused the United States to support dictatorial regimes in the developing world, and to ignore human rights abuses in other countries. As a British expert on U.S. foreign relations bluntly put it: "Excessive optimism has allowed the US to claim democratic success when various countries have simply opened up to world trade and made cosmetic improvements to electoral procedure" (Dumbrell 2003: 271). Moreover, postwar U.S. internationalism has not always been multilateralist. In the early twenty-first century U.S. foreign policy even veered towards a kind of unilateralist, "America First" *internationalism* through the efforts of neoconservative policymakers (*ibid.*: 283).

U.S. hegemony allows for broad discretion to use unilateral, bilateral, or multilateral means to achieve its goals that is not available to weaker nation-states. The United States can afford to carefully weigh the costs and benefits of multilateral cooperation and to be selective about the conditions of its engagement with international institutions. Perhaps the term "instrumental multilateralism" is more accurate in describing U.S. foreign policy since the mid-twentieth century when it became a hegemonic state. This means that

> America's decisions to cooperate in multilateral forums will be determined predominantly by the extent to which any specific organization is perceived by important US domestic actors to be an effective and congenial vehicle for the promotion of America's objectives [Foot et al. 2003b: 272].

From a different angle, foreign policy historians and political scientists have distinguished four strains of foreign policy, "realist," "idealist," "libertarian," and "populist." The historian Walter Russell Mead has named the schools that became deeply rooted in American culture and society and kept influencing U.S. policymaking over the years after four major political figures in American history: Alexander Hamilton, Woodrow Wilson, Thomas Jefferson, and Andrew Jackson (Mead 2001). Although his ideal-typical approach is certainly not without its problems (as are others), it nonetheless offers a sensible way to grasp the basic features of the major currents.

The Hamiltonian approach has been dominant throughout most of U.S. history. Hamiltonians see the first task of the American government as promoting the interests of American enterprise at home and abroad. They have historically attempted to ensure that the U.S. government supported the commercial endeavors of American merchants and investors abroad and have been quick to understand the importance of British world order for American interests. When the British Empire fell, Hamiltonians were the first to advocate the idea that the United States should succeed Britain as the leading nation of the world. The commerce- and finance-based Hamiltonians long pushed for protectionism (tariff policy) at home. Industrial protection was originally intended to make sure that the United States built a manufacturing economy rather than remaining mired in the colonial pattern of providing raw materials for British industry.

But the importance of protectionism diminished as American industry came first on an equal footing and then exceeded its competitors, in many cases achieving a substantial technological lead. By the end of World War II, when many of the world's industrial plants had been destroyed and American companies obtained unchallenged access to the only functioning financial market, the old system of industrial protectionism no longer served general interests. Indeed protectionism even undermined American interests then, since other countries needed to run trade surpluses with the United States in order to acquire the dollars they needed for food and reconstruction. At that time Hamiltonians felt obligated to give up one of their oldest and most cherished instruments of policy. Since then they have been in favor of "free trade" as an expedient economic policy for a hegemonic power, even though this doctrine was applied selectively in practice (*ibid.*: 86–89, 131).

The second school is dominated by those advocating American missionary universalism, who think that the United States has a moral and practical duty to spread its ideological beliefs and values across the world. Mead calls this the Wilsonian school, even though it also includes individuals who actively shaped American foreign policy long before Woodrow Wilson was born. (Mead justifies their inclusion because these Americans thought and acted along similar lines.) Emphasizing the legal and moral aspects of world order rather than the economic agenda of Hamiltonians, Wilsonians typically believe that it is in the country's best interest that others accept basic American values, therefore their foreign and domestic policies are geared to this end. They espouse the view that the United States can and should engage itself not only with the way other countries conduct their international affairs, but also with their internal, domestic policies. A major example of the Wilsonian tradition is the American missionary movement (both in its religious and secular variants), which through its many activities and lobbying has put a heavy stamp on U.S. foreign policy in many parts of the world. Moreover, the contemporary Wilsonian view insists that world order must also be based on principles of democratic government and protection of human rights.

In this regard a distinction must be made between right and radical Wilsonians. Right-wing Wilsonians are content with the status quo in the United States, believing that the nation has generally realized the dreams of the Founding Fathers, and therefore can, and should be, held up as beacon to the rest of the world. Their basic philosophy is that no further domestic reforms are necessary and that the primary aim of foreign policy should be to spread the values and practices of American society as they currently exist across the world. They may disagree with Hamiltonians over priorities and policies in specific cases, but as a rule these Wilsonians endorse the existing financial and corporate structure of the United States and believe that the value pattern to be exported abroad includes the dominant American way of doing business. In contrast, radical Wilsonians see great discrepancies between the true values and ideals of the nation and the everyday reality of American life. Americans must simultaneously act to reform the state of affairs at home as well as those of other nations within its political orbit. These Wilsonians likewise believe that American and transnational corporations (and everything they represent) form major obstacles to the spread of true American beliefs and values both at home and abroad (*ibid.*: 87–88, 92–93, 134, 138–139).

A third approach has typically been most concerned with the preservation of American democracy in a dangerous world, considering this the most urgent and vital interest of the American people. Its protagonists always tended to look for the least costly and risky way to defend U.S. independence against foreign encroachments, at the same time opposing attempts to impose American values and practices on other countries. Mead calls this the Jeffersonian school, while acknowledging the fact that Jefferson's own policy sometimes deviated from orthodox Jeffersonian principles. On balance, however, Jefferson's ideas about liberty and America's destiny correspond more closely with this approach than others. Jeffersonians believe that the specific political, social, and cultural heritage of the United States is a precious treasure to be conserved, defended, and passed on to future generations. They celebrate the unique (or "exceptional"), and extremely valuable, characteristics of American life and argue that the object of foreign policy should be to defend those values at home rather than to extend them abroad.

Like Hamiltonians, Jeffersonians think that the United States is, and ought to be, a democratic and capitalist republic. But Jeffersonians put relatively more emphasis on democracy, contending that capitalism cannot flourish unless society itself is healthy and democratic. Jeffersonians have also repeatedly warned that unbridled capitalism hampers democracy. They tend to be anxious about the development of great fortunes and private concentration of wealth, since it undermines the political process, in their view. Therefore democracy cannot be taken for granted and citizens must constantly remain alert in the defense of civil liberties. Jeffersonians have traditionally been wary of centralized federal government, and from the outset have also worried about the infringement on popular liberty by large economic concentrations (first manifested in Jefferson's resistance against the First Bank of the United States). Nevertheless, in their resistance to the wave of corporate powers in the late nineteenth century, Jeffersonians set aside their traditional worries about federal power to support anti-trust legislation.

Within the Jeffersonian school today there are right-wing libertarians who oppose what they see as big government (part of an oppressive world order) and who defend a way of life characterized by excessive civil privatism on the basis of civil liberties guaranteed by U.S. citizens' constitutional rights. But there are also leftist Jeffersonians who attack the country's involvement in capitalist globalization and big business's intertwinement with the American government through corporate welfarism (*ibid.*: 88–89, 92–95, 174–179).

The fourth approach represents a deeply embedded, widely spread populist culture of honor, independence, courage, martial patriotism and military pride. Mead has named this school after Andrew Jackson, not so much because of the latter's personal beliefs or foreign policy, but in recognition of his enormous popular appeal that helped to energize and transform American politics. With the help of Albany political boss Martin Van Buren, Andrew Jackson used the spoils system (the use of patronage for party principles), that had already been introduced into the federal service, on a scale unmatched until then. (Jefferson was the first president to use the system but did so with restraint.) He enabled the large mass of adult white males to enter the political arena by abolishing the high property qualifications many states had set for voters. Across the country, the Democratic Party was organized as the first modern political machine, with an elaborate hierarchy of party committees and well-funded propaganda directed at a mass audience. Since Jackson's presidency (1829–1837) every political party has in one way or another borrowed from the symbolism, the institutions, and the instruments of power (including the expansion of presidential power) that Jackson introduced (*ibid.*: 88–89, 223–224). Jackson's politics also entailed virulent racist policies towards African Americans and Native Americans. While the Jacksonians' producerist ideology denounced "parasitic" elites (including lawyers, bankers, brokers, and a few other privileged groups labeled as such) and celebrated independent artisans, skilled workers, small business owners and other "producers" (encompassing all employees and employers involved in "useful" pursuits), it espoused the enslavement, forced removal, and even extermination of people of color (Berlet and Lyons 2000: 33, 40–43).

Jacksonians are suspicious of elites and what they see as unbridled federal power (in which they resemble the Jeffersonians); they are also skeptical about the prospects of what they consider as domestic and foreign "do-goodism," that is, welfare provisions at home and foreign aid. Although they tend to oppose federal taxes and espouse self-reliance through honest work as the first principle of their code of honor, they very much appreciate those federal programs in the post–World War II period that primarily benefit the Jacksonian middle class, such as Social Security, Medicare, and mortgage interest subsidies. For the same reason they also welcome spending federal money on the military. Like Jeffersonians, Jacksonians can accept the exercise of federal power in the interest of regulating big business or economic protectionism against foreign (or more recently, transnational) powers. But for the rest they disagree sharply on the issues that justify federal intervention. Jacksonians are, like Jeffersonians, civil libertarians, deeply committed to preserving the liberties of ordinary Americans. However, there are important differences too. Whereas Jeffersonians emphasize above all the First Amendment, protections of free speech and separation of church and state (through its prohibition of a federal establishment of religion), Jacksonians point to the Second Amendment right to bear arms as the primary guarantee of liberty. Throughout American history, Jacksonians have played an active and substantial role in one war after another, often pushing for war when Washington politicians hesitated to go down that road. Jacksonian America sees military service as a patriotic, if not sacred, duty. This "folk community" has been the most consistently hawkish among the American people during the Cold War and after (Mead 2001: 223–224).

According to Mead, the interest groups, regions and to some degree, the economic interests represented by each school, have remained more or less constant in American history. But the policy proposals and priorities of the four schools have developed over time in response to social and economic changes both at home and abroad (*ibid.*: 89). Apparently, the relative influence over time of the various schools generally reflects the shifting relative importance of the specific interests — regional, economic, social, cultural — that each school represents, in conjunction with changes in the multiple traditions of American political culture. And what determines the specific course of U.S. foreign policy at a given time is the outcome of the competition for political influence between the four approaches (and of the various strains within each).

Be that as it may, we should recognize that, in the final analysis, the differences between the various schools were (and are) secondary in comparison with the strong continuities of America's foreign policy over time. The Hamiltonian school has basically been in charge most of the time, while one (or a mixture) of the other three schools was superimposed at one time or another. Since 1899, with few exceptions, leading policymakers in successive administrations shared much the same imperial vision of constructing an open and integrated world led by the United States. This vision reflected particular American interests and values, including the firm belief that an open economic order was requisite for prosperity at home and would ultimately reinforce democracy, economic growth, and the free flow of ideas in the world at large. According to this worldview, it was freedom rather than equality, social justice or the common good, that was the quintessential American value. The basic conviction was that greater economic openness — yoked to American power — would naturally lead to the ultimate triumph of "democratic capitalism," with the United States as the primary guarantor of order and enforcer of norms. The essential aim of this doctrine of liberal internationalism was to open the world to American enterprise. Only an "open world," governed by American "leadership," would enable the U.S. political economy to function effectively while simultaneously insuring U.S. national security. As the military historian and international relations expert Andrew J. Bacevich so eloquently phrased it a few years back:

> Though garnished with neologistic flourishes intended to convey a sense of freshness or originality, the politicoeconomic concept to which the United States adheres today has not changed in a century: the familiar quest for an "open world," the overriding imperative of commercial integration, confidence that technology endows the United States with a privileged position in that order, and the expectation that American military might will preserve order and enforce the rules. Those policies reflect a single-minded determination to extend and perpetuate political, economic, and cultural hegemony — usually referred to as "leadership" — on a global scale [Bacevich 2002: 6].

PERIODIZATION OF AMERICAN INFLUENCE ABROAD

It is further useful to distinguish various periods of U.S. foreign influence for our purpose here. American presence abroad was experienced early in the nineteenth century. American businessmen and missionaries were active in China since the 1830s (preceded by the so-called tribute system since 1785),[8] and after the Opium War (1839–42) as part of the "treaty port system" of western imperialism in China. In the 1850s, Commodore Perry's arrival in Edo Bay initiated "gunboat diplomacy" in Japan. In Central America, the United States intervened diplomatically since the 1820s, and annexed thirty percent of Mexico by 1848. Moreover, in the 1850s North-American adventurers sought to reintroduce slavery, acquire private fortunes and practice their own version of Manifest Destiny in Central America and the Caribbean (Berger 1995: 26–27). Western Europe was not immune from American economic and cultural influences either, and increasingly since the late nineteenth century.

However, America's presence (emerging from a complex mixture of motivations) by the turn of the twentieth century was most strongly felt in the Philippines and the Caribbean (Cuba, Panama Canal Zone, Puerto Rico, Haiti and Dominican Republic), as well as in China, the result of America's "Open Door" policy there (Ninkovich 2001). American foreign involvements subsequently expanded to the rest of Latin America and Western Europe, and after 1945 rippled outwards on a global scale. Yet in many parts of the world, and even in several European countries (mostly in the East), various phenomena of Americanization were hardly visible by the Second World War.

The following provides a more precise periodization that focuses on the times when forms of Americanization flourished and fanned out more widely from the 1890s onwards. It builds on, and expands, Emily S. Rosenberg's (1982) division in three stages of the development of the relationship between the U.S. government and U.S. private citizens and agencies operating abroad from 1890 till the mid-twentieth century, what she has termed "the promotional state," "the cooperative state," and "the regulatory state" respectively. It also incorporates more recent insights from various historical overviews.

1890–1912: the arrival and triumph of the "promotional state": economic, political, and cultural expansionism, national interest and international mission, U.S. colonialism; the Spanish-American war (1898); traders, investors, missionaries and philanthropists — and their intertwinements; the first wave of U.S. popular culture overseas.

1912–1932: significant increase of international communications: cables, radio, news services, motion pictures, aviation; World War I and foreign assistance and cultural expansion; U.S.-dominated internationalist associations and international relief; further economic expansion and the rise of the "cooperative state," assisting commerce and guiding investment abroad in the 1920s, along with a much broader and more intensive second wave of U.S. popular culture.

1932–1945: Great Depression and World War II; increased rationalization in business and industry; liberal internationalism; the New Deal and the rise of the "regulatory state"; beginning in 1939 in Latin America, first major cultural offensive of U.S. government with the creation of new culture and information agencies; relief, technical assistance, and training.

1945–1960: postwar reconstruction in Western Europe and Japan and U.S. military, economic, political, and sociocultural interventions within the framework of the Marshall Plan and the Cold War, also various political interventions in Africa, Asia, and Latin America; another major wave of U.S. popular culture overseas.

1960–1975: continuation of the Cold War; deeper penetration of U.S. corporate capitalism in many parts of the world but especially in Western Europe; much broader dissemination of U.S. popular cultural forms; worldwide radiation of political and new social movements of "the sixties" (civil rights movement; New Left; feminist and environmentalist movements etc.); oil crisis of 1973 marks breaking-point of period of economic prosperity.

1975–1989: last bursts and gradual termination of the Cold War; increased significance of transnational communications systems and information technologies; enhanced "time-space compression" and accelerated capitalist globalization, fostered by a strong influence of neoliberalism in the economy and politics since the Reagan years (1981–1988). Postwar U.S. superiority in decline in the aftermath of the Vietnam War, with a slowing economy, growing industrial competition of Japan and other Asian "economic tigers." Except for finances, diminishing U.S. economic power, particularly in manufacturing. Yet U.S. leadership in the global information revolution remained crucial.

1990–2000: post–Cold War era. The U.S. obtained dominant position globally in most areas within a new geoeconomic and geopolitical constellation. U.S. well endowed with regard to military, financial, political and cultural power. Clinton Administration deployed a centralized multilateralism (embodied by the "Washington Consensus" since the mid–1990s), increasingly organized around a triadic structure consisting of North America (NAFTA), Europe (the EU), and a looser network of interests build around trading relations in East and South-East Asia. U.S. economic imperialist policies carried out within the ideological framework of an allegedly "inexorable" globalization. Significantly increased importance of transnational corporations. Third Industrial Revolution driven by the global information revolution led by the United States. Hi-tech/dot.com stock-market bubble that burst by 2000, leading to major financial crisis, strongest in the U.S., enhanced by fraudulent accounting practices by some of its major corporations. World-wide dissemination of U.S.-inflected Internet and media cultures.

After 9/11, 2001 to present: A world dominated by the U.S.-led "war on terror" and increased neoliberalization. Renewed U.S. imperialist project of the George W. Bush administration characterized by unilateralist, "America First" internationalism through the efforts of neoconservative policymakers concentrated around the Project for the New American Century, joined by more liberal politicians who espouse humanitarian inter-ventionism through an "enlightened" U.S. imperialism. U.S.-led attempts at "regime change" through military interventions in Iraq and Afghanistan. Further corporate transna-tionalization and declining importance of U.S.-based or –owned TNCs. Enduring power of the Wall Street — U.S. Treasury — IMF complex to impose an international financial system carried by the Washington Consensus. Great instability built into the global eco-nomic system due to the rapidly increasing deficits of the United States. Sustained preva-lence of U.S.-accented Internet, media and popular culture forms around the globe.

ENCOUNTERS IN CONTACT ZONES

Next we focus on the multivariegated encounters in the contact zones and intersti-tial spaces of American empire. Local meanings and practices interact with the intrud-ing beliefs and practices of a globalizing power to create worlds of "hybrid Americas," defined by Slater and Taylor as "multiple ensembles of meanings and practices which intertwine the inside and the outside" (Slater and Taylor 1999: xi). They distinguish two general forms of this "geographical dialogue" from the perspective of world-system the-ory. Especially in the metropolitan countries of the capitalist world-system, the projec-tion of American power has been predominantly conceived as the diffusion and adoption of the "American way of life" of mass consumption and material prosperity. The appeal of the American Dream and the perpetual drive to affluence form crucial components of the processes of "Americanization" of these societies. But beyond these privileged metro-politan centers American power has been deployed in much more coercive forms, as man-ifested in tendencies to discipline, to restore order and to counter subversion, often combined with the will and capacity to wage war, and frequently coupled with the impo-sition of economic practices attuned to U.S. corporate interests. These two forms are by no means mutually exclusive, however, as the enticing images of affluence, freedom and progress also permeate countries in the Third World, which is partly reflected in the con-tinuing migration streams to the metropolitan centers of the world-system, especially the United States. This means that Americanization cannot be seen as separate from Ameri-can imperialism — which still tends to be the case in the usually separate literatures of these two projections of power — but as "two interwoven strands" of U.S. pursuits of power (*ibid.*: xi-xii).

On the receiving end, there has been an enormous diversity among local societies and peoples — they were certainly not identical when encountering American ideas, val-ues, products and practices. Therefore it is necessary, first, to identify the distinctive features of the particular society and people undergoing American influence. To what extent are local situations such that the people's actions facilitate or hinder willing acceptance of, or acquiescence to, economic, military, political, social or cultural American influence?

Next we must determine the local people's position and role vis-à-vis the existing constellation of economic-political power blocs in the global capitalist system. How do the people locate themselves in this regard, and conceive their political-cultural identity? What are the key characteristics of their political-cultural identity compared to those of the United States and those of other major powers or power blocs at a given time (Preston 1997): Great Britain and continental European powers such as France, Germany, and Russia, later also Japan, in the nineteenth and first half of the twentieth centuries, the Soviet Union during the Cold War, and the European Union and the Asian-Pacific region (admittedly not a political entity but rather a transnational economic grouping) in the late twentieth and early twenty-first centuries. What are the political affiliations, economic interests, and cultural affinities of the people in question? Needless to say, because of America's worldwide resonance since the mid-twentieth century, many foreigners have increasingly tended to articulate their local, national, and transnational cultural identities vis-à-vis those associated with the United States.

A more specific interest concerns responses of local people to various manifestations of U.S. imperialism (geopolitical, military, economic, cultural). At least one thing is clear: To the degree that non-western societies do not possess or value what Abernethy calls "the explore-control-utilize syndrome" to indicate the activist stance toward the natural world of western imperialism more generally, they are at a distinct disadvantage powerwise when encountering forms of American imperialism. Abernethy defines this syndrome in the historical context of western imperialism as a "combination of restless curiosity and self-aggrandizing manipulation, ... a worldview which assumed that what was unknown could and should become known. Closely associated with the drive to uncover what had previously been hidden was the drive to classify, possess, and put to practical use whatever was found" (Abernethy 2000: 34). Undoubtedly, this syndrome has been pronouncedly present in U.S. imperial encroachments in foreign contexts.

Local responses can of course take various forms. For example, in Latin America local elites facing difficult choices developed a range of responses over time to the realities of U.S. power. One expedient "solution" was mere capitulation; that is, people aligned themselves with U.S. power and/or succumbed to U.S. pressure, thereby hoping to salvage as much domestic control as possible. Locals also tried to join forces (e.g., the Bolivarian Dream of Latin American unity), thus creating a continental counterweight to the United States. Another option was to attempt to strengthen ties with, and seek protection from, European powers.[9] People attempted to establish subregional hegemony (e.g., Argentina's own variant of "manifest destiny" or Brazil's attempt to emulate the U.S.), thus challenging the United States or sharing power with it. They also tried to formulate doctrines of international law (in combination with the use of diplomacy) that would impose constraints on the United States. People in Latin America also developed nationalistic cultures of resistance (manifested, among others by Mexico, Cuba, Nicaragua) or continental solidarity movements, that have tended to be more of an expression of feeling than a strategy, however. These options were not all mutually exclusive, and they appeared in a variety of combinations and settings in successive periods (Smith 2000: 88–112).

More generally, acceptance of American influence can be a matter of "empire by invitation" (Lundestad 1986). For geopolitical or geoeconomic reasons, local elites may encourage Americans to take an active interest in their economic, military or political affairs. Economic motives may lead local economic elites to affiliate with U.S. financial and corporate interest groups. Similarly, political affiliations of foreigners with America or Americans can emerge. Local political elites have sometimes requested Americans to unite with them against one or more rival countries. Of course, foreign people for various reasons can also feel attracted to American culture and society, or specific aspects thereof, and voluntarily affiliate with American lifestyles and cultural models (Kroes 2000: 137, 181).

Finally we arrive at the level of societal sectors. Sectoral institutions equivalent to those in America do not always exist in other societies (and vice versa, as noted earlier). This was especially the case in non-western countries before being drawn into the orbit of western colonialism or imperialism. But if these exist, how and to what extent are the actors of these institutions able and willing to accept American influences emanating from the various sources? Or, to approach this from the negative side, how and to that extent are they able and willing to block agents of the U.S. government, American companies, and non-profit agencies from penetrating their societies?

Within any given country there are often variations in terms of engagement with American imports between different societal sectors, within and between single sectors, and even within individual institutions, public and business enterprises, and social categories (Zeitlin 2000: 24–35). Local subcultures — occupational, religious, recreational and what have you — are in various ways oriented toward their American counterparts (if they exist), which colors their reception of American imports. And certain local conditions may increase the likelihood of organized opposition to cross-national transfers of U.S. practices. Some groups are more susceptible to Americanization (or specific forms thereof) than others. The variety of responses to Americanization is due to: differences in travel experiences in America; in actual encounters with American people, institutions and everyday practices at home and in the U.S. itself; differences in exposure to the media, the press, radio, television, the Internet; or differences in levels and kinds of education. As a result, some locals are more knowledgeable, proactive, and self-reflective in this regard than others.[10] They differ with regard to political, economic, technological, and financial autonomy from the U.S., and in terms of cultural self-confidence and resilience. These factors also determine how gatekeepers and key decision-makers relate to American influence in the various domains concerned.

Within the receiving nation conflicts between sectors or groups at a given time are relevant insofar as they impinge on the country's external relations with America. For example, some parts of the local business world may want to affiliate with U.S. corporate capitalism while others do not, aiming instead for economic protectionism or even delinking. Forms of Americanization fostered by certain political-economical elites from above can conflict at some points with forms of Americanization carried by specific subordinate groupings from below. Cultural clashes may erupt over American popular culture entering the country. A specific group or coalition may team up against other locals, asking Americans to take sides in the dispute. A local pull factor thus reinforces external push factors mentioned earlier. Indeed, invitations to intervene in local peoples' affairs have enabled Americans at times to establish beachheads of influence and power at little expense to themselves.

Degrees of willingness in accepting, or success in resisting, things American has varied greatly from one society and time period to another. Throughout, local peoples watched each other's actions towards American influence as well. Within the context of political, military, economic or other alliances, observation and demonstration effects from one country's responses to American projections of power induced others to follow the same path.

8

Conceptualizing the Reception of Things American

This chapter completes our interpretive framework by adding analytical concepts for studying the various ways in which locals appropriate the American influences that reach them. It concludes with a brief discussion of the functions and effects of Americanization, and how these should preferably be conceptualized in the assessments one might want to make.

AMONG THE RECEIVERS

The first set of relevant dimensions of the actual reception process involves the scope and spatial limits of Americanization. This entails the volume ("size" and scale) of ideas, goods, services and practices imported or adopted from the United States, and the extent of their reach. The latter concerns the degree to which parts of the local political economy have come under American influence. But it also pertains to particular geographic areas and localities that are politically and economically influenced (or in specific cases even governed) by the United States, and the domains of society and culture it entered. What specific groups are reached, and to what degree? These points of interest suggest that one should look for national and regional differences and also for differences in urban density (city, town or village), standard of living and mass consumption that matter here.[1] It is also necessary to distinguish between the various areas that have come under American influence (recognizing that they all tend to be mutually related), which may include, among others: technology; production methods and organization of work; principles, methods, and patterns of political action and decision-making; goods and design, including architecture; patterns of individual and group behavior; high culture and mass-popular culture and entertainment (Sywottek 1993: 133). Moreover, from the outset, distinctions in terms of class, ideology, age (generation), gender, "race" and ethnicity deserve the attention of students of Americanization.

At this point it becomes necessary to identify more precisely what constitutes the things American that are on offer locally. This refers to the issue of availability: what is being imported as "American"? What is the actual content of the U.S. supply abroad? For example, what does the economic form of Americanization in a particular case entail as regards business and management practices, investments, marketing, advertising, distribution, exchange and selling of goods, accounting and consultancy practices, profits, tax payments et cetera? Similar questions about content can be asked with regard to all other forms of Americanization. Here we also hit upon the question as to whether the U.S. model or practice concerned should be considered a unitary or heterogeneous entity for adopters/

emulators abroad. A related question involves the extent to which the constituent elements of the American practice in question form a coherent whole of tightly coupled components — with the character of "all or nothing" to be accepted in a "take-it-or-leave it-way" by potential foreign adopters — *or* a loose array of relatively independent elements from which one can freely borrow piecemeal (Zeitlin 2000: 12).

It also makes a significant difference, of course, whether one deals with a direct American transplant, an American export filtered through an intermediating context (that is, has gone over some foreign "conveyer belt") or an indirect local imitation modeled after, or inspired by, an American exemplar. To the extent that American influences are present in the latter two cases, they have already been mediated by other agencies before they reach broader groups of locals, having become further detached from their original U.S. home base.

Specifically with regard to American commercial culture, the question arises about how the products in question are positioned (via marketing strategies, for example) and how they are perceived within the cultural economies of importing nations — possibly with regional variations within national boundaries. This also involves consumer behavior and choice: Which products (among those available) are consumed and by which sectors of the public? How are the goods treated and in what ways are they consumed? (Fehrenbach and Poiger 2000: xxviii).

If we consider the choices that local actors have at their disposal on the "international market of cultures," the borrowing from elsewhere often entails certain rigidities; in economic-sociological terms these include high transaction costs, time-consuming operations, twin products and the like. Locals are sometimes then faced with dilemmas in which there are no easy ways out. As Kovács has illustrated with regard to post-communist Hungary, "Could Hungary just import the culture of solidarity from Sweden without copying Swedish-style state interventionism? Could it follow the example of France in supporting elite culture without prompting French-style nationalism among its citizens? Or could it take over both the culture of self-reliance from the United States and the culture of nepotism from Japan?" (Kovács 2002: 173). Indeed such choices are not arbitrary, as if we were dealing with a cafeteria system whereby people can pick and choose as they like. Certain values are embedded in the existing local practices that constrain the borrowings and appropriations in question.

Political, institutional, and legal frameworks control the import and export of culture, and are dependent on government policies. Conscious efforts may have been made to restrict American influence in the receiving context. Calls to protect or promote local culture can intensify as a result of a stronger preoccupation with national or regional identity. Sometimes political opponents even join hands and form a "monstrous alliance." This can lead to cultural protectionism in the form of quota systems and other regulations, which several governments (including France, Britain, Canada) have tried to impose (with varying degrees of success) upon imports of Hollywood films or other cultural products such as TV programs or popular music from the United States. At the same time these countries sought to stimulate the production, distribution and showing, playing or performing of local cultural alternatives (Tunstall 1977: 62; Strinati 1992: 60–61; Petterson 2000).[2] If taken to extreme, cultural protectionism may culminate in forms of censorship as in the case of Nazi Germany, the Soviet bloc, communist China, some Islamic states and various other authoritarian regimes, past and present.

When considering the American influx, we must also take into account that the "receiving" countries may be influential in their own right. For example, at the same time that things American enter a country through "self-colonization" (or otherwise) it may itself be involved in colonial or imperial projects abroad (e.g. post-World War II France). In the past few decades, Britain has been a sort of "media imperialist" through its popular culture exports (particularly music and to a lesser extent, TV programs and films), having made some impact upon the American market[3] and elsewhere. Some other countries have also exerted counter-influence in this regard. Since the 1980s, for example, Australia increasingly became an exporter as well as an importer of commercial Anglophone culture, especially TV soap operas (Bell and Bell 1998: 7).

We should also locate and "weigh" America's influence appropriately amidst other foreign influences on the domestic situation. The incoming culture is not simply American but usually encompasses other cultural flows and borrowings as well. For pragmatic reasons, empirical studies of Americanization often block other cross-national transfers.[4] This may, if not cautiously done, lead to myopia in that important influences from other countries or regional subglobalizations are downplayed or even completely ignored. A good example is the ideology and associated practice of the modern housewife and the modern family, living in a new apartment or single-family house, filled with new household technology that emerged in the United States during the interwar years and in Western Europe from the late 1950s onwards. Modernizing influences in Europe did not only come from the United States, but also from within Europe itself, where similar ideologies of domesticity and the consumption of similar consumer durables evolved (e.g. the Frankfurt kitchen and Bauhaus projects or the functionalist furniture and homes displayed at the 1930 Stockholm Exhibition). The combination of consumption with rationalization and efficiency was seen as the hallmark of modernity in the home. Modernity — that is, efficient female housekeeping — was to be produced through the housewife's rational purchase and use of consumer durables. This vision of the modern home and housewife also held the promise of a transformation of masculinity, femininity, and family life — a redrawing of lines between public and private spheres — and the continuity of history and memory among those concerned. Whereas in the United States this vision was seen as quintessentially American,[5] in Europe it was simultaneously and confusingly labeled as international, American, and Swedish, or British or German (Nolan 2003).

Moreover, "Americanization" may at some time cease to be the exclusive or prime target of local actors preoccupied with menaces to their own national identity. In Europe more recently, for example, the U.S. shares space in the dock with other, real or purported, threats connected to immigration and European integration (Kuisel 1993: 226). In other parts of the world we find similar tendencies. It is possible that today's "global imperative" in economics, culture and politics will become the main focus of attention, with little more than a side glance at America's impact on globalization. Last but not least, we must realize that the domestic culture is not exclusively "national" (when it concerns a nation-state) but consists of a cultural mix in itself; that is, all cultures are hybrids, although some more than others. Indeed, cultural hybridity takes varying forms; the actual mix and meanings of the various components differ from nation to nation. In the ideal case the proportions of the ingredients of the cultural mix and the speed and quality of the mixing are specified in the studies of Americanization concerned (Fehrenbach and Poiger 2000: xxviii; Kovács 2002: 169).

American cultural forms and practices can play a significant role in the articulation of alternative models developed by states undergoing American influence. Fascinating examples are authoritarian states like national-socialistic Germany, fascist Italy, and imperial Japan in the interwar years. The authoritarian governments of these states were heavily preoccupied with developing cultural means for the ideological mobilization of their populations to the political goals of their regimes — one of the "lessons" learned during the Russo-Japanese War and World War I. As the German historians Fehrenbach and Poiger have pointed out, these mobilization strategies were consistently put up against what the leaders of these regimes saw as the successful American variant. But American cultural products and practices came to serve both as contrast and stimulus. On the one hand, American culture was studied in order to unravel the underlying mechanisms of its mass appeal (its ability to transcend class, gender, and nationality). On the other hand, however, meticulous attempts were made to separate form from function. These regimes sought to emulate the production methods, technical and aesthetic forms, as well as packaging, but also tried to foster national consensus over consumer individualism by employing a rhetoric of national defense and difference. They were faced with the problem of how to develop a mass-appealing ideological alternative to Hollywood (and the U.S. popular music industry) that would summon the "centralizing" powers of cultural consumption (whereby commercial culture functioned as a "social glue" to make audiences think and respond like "Germans," "Italians," or "Japanese"), but that would at the same time defuse centrifugal tendencies that encouraged identification on the basis of subnational groupings such as class, generation, gender, ethnicity.

These same regimes and cultural producers and distributors also spent a lot of energy trying to find out (by examining American popular culture) how to construct a popular mass-cultural alternative that would both serve its political nationalistic purposes and have an attractive export quality that would facilitate circulation within the expanding boundaries of their respective empires. Although the alternative cultural products of these authoritarian states were created in competition with, and opposition to, the United States, they were characterized by a certain fluidity, even a relative openness, through cultural borrowing, emulations, and reworkings of U.S. films, musical styles (e.g., some forms of jazz and swing) and so forth. Thus, intense engagement with American popular culture helped shape to a great extent the nature of its Nazi and fascist counterparts. These examples clearly demonstrate how American cultural forms can be adopted and employed for non-democratic ends, which is contrary to the discourse of Americanization in terms of democratic modernization (Fehrenbach and Poiger 2000: xxii-xxiii).

Trying to articulate national identities by means of locally appropriated and modified American cultural forms and practices has worked out differently in other contexts. A self-confident national identity that leads to flexing that people's cultural muscles in public through nationalist expressions can produce paradoxical results in this regard. Take for example Australia. Locally much-heralded expressions of Australian nationalism in films such as *Gallipoli* and *Breaker Morant*, and public displays of patriotism in the early 1980s, were conscious or unconscious borrowings from American models. Whereas the surface may have been Australian, the substance was clearly American-derived, as Richard White explained with regard to *Gallipoli*: "It is ... an attempt to define an Australian identity in terms of a chauvinist and increasingly conservative American-style republicanism, a search for Australia's own Boston Tea Party.... [This] opposition of Australian and British identities reflects a deeper Americanisation in the same way that earlier nationalist images of Australia were reflections of a colonial status" (White 1983: 120).

A second example that White presents is again Australian (at least in theory), but it too is patterned after U.S. patriotism, seeking to stimulate an Australian version of American-style patriotic fervor. In 1979 the Australian government launched Project Australia, a three-year national promotion campaign — with large corporations like Mobil,

Mitsubishi and Mount Isa Mines represented in the organizing committee — meant to rally national pride around the slogan "Advance Australia." It aimed at associating large corporations and an aggressive free enterprise ethic with Australian sentiment. Multinational corporate advertising in Australia has been working as well along the same lines for a number of years. The latter tendency is evident in the late 1970s General Motors ad campaign to sell their Holden cars in Australia by referring to their essential "Australianness": "Football, meat pies, kangaroos and Holden cars. They go together under southern stars," which was a direct transposition of the advertising text for GM in the United States: "Baseball, hot dogs, apple pie and Chevrolet. They go together in the good old USA" (qtd. in Sinclair 1987: 116).

But an influential analyst (and deconstructionist) of cultural imperialism like John Tomlinson has interpreted this differently, stating that it does not entail global cultural homogenization (let alone Americanization). In their transnational advertising, these multinational corporations consider the "cultural defenses" of their target markets and adapt their strategies accordingly. This leads to other outcomes than homogenization in the crudest form. Even the most aggressively global brands like Coca-Cola, Marlboro and McDonald's made a serious effort to take the salient cultural features of their target markets into account. The major results of such transnational marketing strategies may be to insert the messages of advertisements into the connotations of the (intrinsically problematic) stocks of knowledge that constitute particular national cultural identities. The mentioned slogan to sell Holden cars in Australia would then be merely an "expedient translation" of one for General Motors in the United States (Tomlinson 1991: 114).

This interpretation runs into difficulties, however, at least regarding the given Australian examples. From a perspective that wishes to sustain something like a national cultural identity, the Americanization process becomes far-reaching when, as White maintained, even "the fundamental concepts of a national identity are remodelled in the American image" (White 1983: 120–121). As Sinclair comments on the General Motors car advertisement: "This example illustrates how audiences have no way of knowing when an appeal which seems to address them in their own national vernacular is in fact just a version of a global campaign, and makes it clear that there are more *insidious strategies* in global marketing than the world brand" (Sinclair 1987: 167, my italics).[6]

Even if overstated, one cannot deny a clear U.S.-inflected influence on the formats that were used. The forms of advertising, their recurrent repositioning of widely held, nationalist-populist "Aussie" values next to local and imported brand-names, and their addresses to "real Australian" consumers, were after all modeled on basic elements of American consumer culture. Whereas the message of these forms remained tied to typical "Aussie" myths, they masked the economic networks carried by U.S. corporations like Coca-Cola, Ford, General Motors, and Johnson and Johson that Australian consumerism was partially entwined with. In addition, there was a confluence of "American" and "Australian" images, products and genres of television advertising through the linkage of both local and imported commodities to borrowings from, or imitations of. the iconography of American movies and television fiction (Bell and Bell 1993: 175–176).

On the other hand, though, the assumption regarding the existence of a unified, authentic local culture under attack by American goods, images, and values, may in itself be problematic, and not only in Australia. For example, much of what was deemed "authentically British" in post-World War II Britain was in fact of upper-class and high-cultural character. No unified, authentic British culture existed prior to the American "invasion," which manifested itself in a differentiated reception of U.S. popular culture as we saw earlier (Chapter 2). Moreover, earlier American imports may have been incorporated into the indigenous culture to such an extent that they have become "naturalized" and at some point are no longer recognized as of American origin. In Japan, more than elsewhere, encounters with foreign imports have implied a thorough domestication of the foreign (Tomlinson 1991: 92–93).[7] This indigenization has occurred so rapidly and been so successful that it has been suggested that the Japanese therefore have been less concerned with the social and moral implications of American cultural influence than, for example, their counterparts in postwar Western Europe (Fehrenbach and Poiger 2000: xxvi–xxviii).[8]

Insights such as these can be derived from the work of anthropologists and historians who are interpreting the concept of an "authentic" national culture as a construction of modern nationalism. They emphasize that in the modern world, a "national culture" is never purely locally produced, but always contains the traces of previous cultural borrowings or influences that have been part of a thorough assimilation process. What the people of a given nation consider to be their own culture at any time is the result of a process of "totalization" of cultural memory up to that point. This is a particular and selective process, whereby political and cultural institutions such as the state, mass education and the mass media play a significant role (Anderson 1983; Hobsbawm and Ranger 1983). Admittedly, this knowledge makes "Americanization" more complicated but not so problematic that we should therefore reject the whole concept out of hand.

LOCAL REWORKINGS OF AMERICAN
EXAMPLES AND IMPORTS

This section focuses more closely on the ways in which domestic actors actually rework and modify the incoming American products and practices. One might label this (as far as cultural Americanization is concerned) "American culture as a resource for locals," borrowing Hannerz's suggestion with regard to the Swedish situation (Hannerz 1992a: 15–16). It refers to the fact that American culture consists of a great many aspects that can have different levels of appeal (or unattractiveness) to different people.

At this point it is appropriate to scrutinize predominant assumptions and mentalities in the receiving culture, because they are likely to act as filters in processing the incoming U.S. influences. These filters "test" so to speak the extent to which the U.S. imports are compatible with indigenous practices (Berghahn 1995: 75). Local people's perceptions, structures of feeling, and mentalities play a significant role in responding to possible changes in existing values, beliefs and practices under U.S. influence (Jarausch and Siegrist 1997: 32). Here we find differences in responses to American influences between countries based on the intensity and continuity of previous interactions with the U.S. (and experience with earlier forms of Americanization) as compared to other foreign points of reference. Indeed, historical memory, and the juxtaposition of experience and interpretation within specific historical contexts are crucial elements of the "national" reception process. This also includes the indigenous cultural debate about Americanization, which is in itself one of the most important components of the process.[9] There may be cases, however, in which there has been little local debate about Americanization (White 1983: 110–111).

While America made its appearance abroad at an early stage in the form of expanding business interests and missionary work, cultural importation and interaction intensified

in the late nineteenth century and became the object of persistent governmental, business, and public concern by the 1920s in Western Europe, Australia, Japan, Latin America, and other places being pulled more closely into the U.S. orbit. Thus, most of cultural
Americanization cannot be understood outside the context of the rise of modern nation-
states, consumer capitalism, and mass culture, and the particular constellation that existed
at the national level at a given time (Fehrenbach and Poiger 2000: xviii-xix). And nations
cultivated different relationships with the United States, which had a specific impact on
their dealings with American imports after World War II, as indicated by the authors of
the NIAS statement on the European reception of American mass culture:

> The most obvious case historically is Britain, America's most significant political and economic
> competitor until World War II. With a common language, greater United States investment and a
> choice of dependence, Britain not only absorbed more American culture but became more adept
> than any other country in Europe at transposing it and re-transmitting it to more culturally
> embattled societies. Germany's experience of long-term occupation gave it a particularly complex
> and intense relationship with American mass culture. Italy's need for a new development model in
> the wake of the "economic miracle" of the 1950s brought another kind of Americanisation to that
> country. France was for a long time the site of the most intense debates for and against American
> influence [Ellwood et al. 1993: 330].

Furthermore, American ideas, goods, services and practices reached individual countries often through other ones (or specific regions or cities within these), whose citizens
or institutions, in turn, gave their own particular interpretations and reinterpretations,
and might even add creative flourishes of their own. The further detachment of forms of
U.S. popular culture from their roots in American society, culminating in what Bigsby
(1975) termed a "superculture" (see below), was strongly enhanced by this process. These
dynamics of cultural transmission and recontextualization apply especially to smaller cultures exposed to the radiation of larger cultures before the arrival of global mass media,
large-scale international educational exchange, tourism and so forth, which brought the
former more directly and instantaneously within the U.S. orbit. For instance, in Denmark, the Netherlands and Belgium, the reception of "roaring twenties" culture (films,
modern body cult, dances, and so on) took place partly through second-hand borrowings from Paris, London and Berlin, the "New York" of Europe at the time (van Elteren
1991). For Finland during the early decades of the twentieth century, Sweden and Germany (even during the 1930s) played the role of "middleman" for American popular culture, particularly with regard to records, films, and "light literature" (Kivikuru 1988: 17).

Great Britain likewise functioned as a significant intermediating context in the reception of American teenage culture on the European continent during the 1950s and early
1960s. Appropriations of American pop and rock music (or other forms of popular music)
were often mediated through British interpretations (Zimmermann 1984; Minganti 1993;
van Elteren 1989, 1997). In the case of borrowings from British beat music of the 1960s
this concerned a distillation of the original musical and cultural forms with sometimes
very creative additions on the British side.[10] In all of these cases, a process took place of
what I more generally prefer to call *secondary appropriation* of things American.

Yet the role of intermediary regarding American popular culture in postwar Europe
was not restricted to cultural industries and news media based in England. By the 1960s,
German television was equally functioning as an important "conveyer belt" in this regard
through "filtering and reinterpreting America's popular culture for East Germany, Austria, Czechoslovakia, Hungary" (Pells 1997: 383 n 4). This occurred in other parts of the
world as well. Since the late 1960s, Mexico and Brazil, for instance, have mediated U.S.

popular culture through their television systems to other nations in Latin America (although Brazil also exported its own versions of soap operas), while Japan and Australia did the same for parts of Asia. In New Zealand much of the experience of things American has been channeled to its citizens via Sydney or Melbourne. In the 1950s, for example, radio soap operas, first devised by American radio companies, were broadcast in New Zealand after having been recorded in Australian studies. And since the 1980s Australian adaptations of American-style television soap operas were broadcast in New Zealand as well. Regarding structure and style, these and various other Australian TV programs borrowed heavily from U.S. formats (three or four-part "mini-series" and medical hospital soap operas), which has been called a process of "Americanization once-removed" (Lealand 1988: 27–28).

Naturally, the United States was not dependent on foreign intermediaries to break through to other audiences. Even before the arrival of international satellites and cable television networks — which made it possible to broadcast directly and immediately overseas — the American mass media and other cultural industries managed to reach audiences all across the world (Hesmondhalgh 2002: 181–185; Pells 1997: 207). At the same time, the United States itself has operated as an intermediary and converter of other countries' cultural forms abroad. Compare, for instance, the ways in which Americans have interpreted European fashions (e.g., Italian clothing fashion) and exported their versions to other countries. In the current era of globalization initially non-American goods have sometimes become "American" (and from thereon also global) cultural prototypes, for example, Porsche as a yuppie symbol (Kovács 2002: 178 n 2).

From here we may proceed and attempt to determine what social meanings the locals involved attribute to the ideas, artifacts, goods and practices emanating from America, and how they respond to them. As noted earlier, the idea that the circulation of things American abroad has a single and stable set of meanings is highly questionable. So much also depends on the local circumstances in which they circulate (Forgacs 1993: 160). The consumption of American products, whether as material entities or as mediated images, is often an occasion for cultural elaboration as well as accommodation, for syncretism and creolization as well as homogenization, for resistance as well as enthusiasm. Although these goods and practices tend to have "preferred readings" (Hall 1980) — fostered by encodings that prestructure, "lead" or "steer" the recipients' responses to some extent and in particular ways[11] — the actual appropriation may still differ radically from the intention with which they were originally produced or developed. "Thus, although goods, technologies, and symbols created within the United States clearly 'carry' a great deal of cultural baggage as they cross borders," Hunter and Yates suggest, "they are often, upon reception, subject to the forces of indigenization and hybridization" (Hunter and Yates 2002: 325).

One other element is important here: Since at least the mid-twentieth century, for people looking for signs and symbols of a lifestyle American popular culture has presented itself as one big "self service store" — everywhere present and with almost unlimited choice and opportunities. American popular culture has become a superculture. According to the British Americanist Christopher Bigsby "Beyond the confines of America, [this culture] changed both meaning and structure, becoming plastic, a superculture, detached from its roots, and widely available for adaptation, absorption and mediation" (Bigsby 1975: xiii). Its infinite variety of components, both real and imagined, could be assembled and re-assembled abroad by different groups in an unlimited number of combinations. Hollywood films, advertisements, design, body aesthetics, music and dance — all offered a rich reservoir of images, sounds, and "texts," an iconography that was (and remains) open to all kinds of readings. This "superculture" constitutes a reservoir of cultural elements from which one may borrow as much and in as many ways as one wishes. "And the meaning of each selection is transformed as individual objects ... are taken out of their original historical and cultural contexts and juxtaposed against other signs from other sources" (Hebdige 1988: 74). Yet the selections thus made often hold the aura of Americanness — "Américanicité," as Roland Barthes (1977) called it — in common: fundamental connotations of freedom, casualness, liberality, vitality, modernity and youthfulness.

One important caveat should be made, however. Exaggeration of assimilation or domestication by local recipients may culminate into "mistaking the subplot for the main narrative" (Kuisel 2003: 100), as discussed in Chapter 5. There is a crucial difference between "having power over a text" (i.e., the goods and practices on offer), exercised through selective borrowing and creative appropriation, and having "power over the agenda within which the text is constructed and presented" to local recipients (Morley 1997: 125). The latter refers to the structural power that producers and distributors of culture have over their offerings, which sets limits on the room to maneuver for creative appropriation. In other words, one should not ignore Michel de Certeau's important distinction between "the strategies of the powerful" and "the tactics of the weak" (de Certeau 1984) when analyzing the recipients' actions.

Because of their participation in specific social life-worlds, the responses of receivers, adopters, or emulators of American influence are not merely individual endeavors, but bounded to "interpretive communities" (Fish 1980).[12] Thus, a specific American import may evoke a variety of responses or negotiated meanings but one can expect certain segments of the local population to respond in similar ways. These different responses are related to dissimilarities in nationality, class, status, profession, political stance, religion, cultural milieu, ethnicity, gender, generation and other relevant dimensions.

Reactions to American culture have tended to revolve around constructing and reconstructing differences within receiving nations, and have therefore played a significant role in the process and politics of communal self-definition. For example, in the post-World War II era, as Fehrenbach and Poiger have pointed out, authorities in Western Europe and Japan employed normative notions of gender difference to reject American imports and contain the consumer behavior of teenagers, who were specifically targeted by American and indigenous advertising and marketing agencies. In this domestication campaign, U.S. culture was associated with a sexualized femininity and hypermasculinity — in short, a lack of decency. The consumption of American popular culture was denounced as a threat to social, sexual, and familial relations and, by extension, to national health and integrity, precisely because it was seen as encouraging alternative individual and group identities that challenged normative national models of femininity and masculinity (Fehrenbach and Poiger 2000: xv-xvi; van Elteren 1989; Maase 1993).

Similar contestations about identities happened in relation to the adoption of American popular musics — ragtime, jazz, rhythm & blues, rock 'n' roll — borrowed or derived from the African-American cultural repertoire. These cultural imports have been employed to confront and reformulate notions of racial difference in receiving nations. White audiences within the United States and abroad have often felt strongly attracted to the expressive styles, bodily rhythms and more generally, the sensual-aesthetic qualities of black or black-derived musics. Perhaps they even felt titillated by straddling existing color lines (compare the phenomenon of slumming[13] among white Beats, blues or jazz aficionados), whereas other audiences merely were repelled by what they perceived as racial transgression implied in these varieties of American culture. In the interwar years, for example, German opponents of jazz associated it with black musicians, Jewish promotors, "primitiveness" and sexual lasciviousness, and combined anti-black and anti–Semitic sentiments to reject jazz as "un-German." But even after ideas about biological racial hierarchies (that since the nineteenth century were at the heart of the development of modern national identities in Europe, the United States, and Japan) became unpopular, efforts to articulate notions of national identity based on cultural and racial differences have continued, albeit in more subdued ways.

Up until now subcultures within receiving nations have at times been able to use cultural forms of racial and ethnic minorities in the United States to question existing indigenous visions of racial purity or monocultural national identity. Yet specific American popular culture forms (e.g., black minstrel shows, Wild West shows, portrayals of tribal cultures at World Exhibitions at the turn of the twentieth century, "fetishized blackness" in some forms of hip-hop today) have also been adopted abroad to disseminate intensely racist ideas. Thus, American culture abroad has taken complex and varying meanings in constructions of racial (and other) hierarchies within receiving nations (Fehrenbach and Poiger 2000: xvi).

Time and circumstances are both critical to the meanings and effects of American imports. The impact may be restricted to a specific period or be stronger at some times than others. U.S. (would-be) exporters of a given model or practice may shift their priorities in response both to changing economic and political situations at home and to external challenges. It is also possible that the acceptance of, or resistance against, U.S. influence among locals varies markedly over time. Americanization through popular culture holds potentialities which may be different in various periods — for instance, serving as source of resistance in one case and target of opposition in another: "For a young black European in the 1990s it may offer a model of resistance through rap music, while for a young white European in the late 1970s it may be part of the system you construct your identity in opposition to, through punk rock" (McKay 1997: 163).

On several occasions, American influences have revitalized European culture; a seminal period was that of the late forties. The United States that Europeans then came to know and long for, particularly through Hollywood films, was a glorified and/or romanticized replica. American public life and entertainment at the time were still deeply influenced by the cultural-political heritage of the New Deal period. The United States was represented through very convincing, artistically persuasive images and its popular culture had likewise been greatly enriched by the contributions of a considerable number of creative European emigrés who had escaped Nazism. Many of them had found work in the entertainment industry. Moreover, longer-settled American Jews and black artists helped shape US entertainment in decisive ways then too.

In many ways, American popular culture of the forties — or rather the parts of it that Europeans became acquainted with — think of John Ford, Frank Capra, Billy Wilder, John Houston, Howard Hawks, Fred Astaire, Duke Ellington, Coleman Hawkins, Charlie Parker, Billie Holiday, Benny Goodman — may be compared to the most vital periods of European culture (Schou 1992: 146–149). Even in the turbulent 1960s, during the heyday of political anti–Americanism in postwar Europe, leading critics of America's official politics were positively oriented toward cultural achievements that were linked or could at least be associated with countertendencies in American culture itself — ranging from political essays to blues and rock music. For many leftist critics America then was at the core of a repressive, capitalist and imperialist system while simultaneously serving as the main source of revitalization — cultural innovation, creative deviance and radical alternatives.

Clearly the meanings associated with a specific product or practice may change over the years. For instance, something that initially is surrounded by an aura of Americanness with strong appeal to locals, may over time become commonplace. More generally, sociologist Peter Berger calls this the transition of "sacramental" to "non-sacramental" consumption. The notion of sacramental is taken from Anglican (and by implication, Roman Catholic) theology, which defines a sacrament as the visible sign of an invisible grace. By the same token, some consumption of the globalizing popular culture, such as eating a hamburger — especially when it takes place under the golden icon of a McDonald's restaurant — is a visible sign of the real or imagined participation in global modernity with an American face (Berger 2002: 7). The McDonald corporation actively seeks to stimulate this process by employing advertising campaigns and promotional stunts to create not only an experience of fun, of family togetherness, but also of Americanization itself that is associated with the McDonald's experience (Kellner 1999: 188).[14] Many other companies (U.S.-owned or not) follow similar strategies with regard to the consumption of "American" sign values associated with their products and services. The meanings, even of the same product or practice, are likely to become different, however, as America's economic and geopolitical position in the world changes.

AMERICAN CULTURE AS A POTENTIAL
RESOURCE FOR LOCAL EMPOWERMENT

A possible strategy among foreign receivers of American culture is to resort to what Meaghan Morris, a leading cultural studies scholar in Australia, has identified and assigned the label of "positive unoriginality."[15] It combines "cultural assertiveness" and "economic pragmatism," attaining "survival and specificity" through the revision of American formats and codes by indigenous texts allowing for different readings by different audiences or individual recipients of American culture (Morris 1988: 246–247).[16] Examples of this strategy in popular music include the appropriation of rock 'n' roll and country music by Eurasians and Amboinese (repatriates from the former Dutch colonies of Indonesia) during the 1950s and early 1960s in the Netherlands (Mutsaers 1990); blues by white British or Dutch musicians in the 1960s; and African-American rap by people of color from the West Indies in Britain, from the Netherlands Antilles and Surinam in Holland, as well as those from former French Africa in France since the late 1980s (Wermuth 1993; Prévos 1997; van Elteren 1996b: 74–76). This strategy may produce creative cultural expressions according to the "truth-to-convention" principle (Frith 1989), which holds that authenticity is first of all a matter of being true to the stylistic conventions concerned. But it can also lead to mere epigonism and highly derivative versions of the American models in question as, for instance, in the case of most Dutch country music (van Elteren 1998).

An interesting example of a mixture of "positive unoriginality" and idiosyncratic local additions and alterations is the practice in Italy of covering American pop songs (and its attendant emulation of other American cultural artifacts) from the mid–1950s to mid-1960s, out of which came a wide variety of syncretisms between Italian and American cultural products. As Franco Minganti has argued, the Italian lyrics and adaptations of imported musical styles (and associated cultural hybrids in the form of locally produced teenage films) turned a controversial influence into acceptable content to a wider audience. In the Italian context, these local translations often dealt facetiously with the rules and effects of the transformation of the American imports. "Covering" American songs usually implied changing the content of lyrics dramatically through both deliberate and accidental misunderstandings. The Italian covers tended to celebrate images of 'good' boys and girls, thus eliminating the against-the-grain character of American originals, erasing African-American traces, and making American music and behaviors respectable. At the same time, however, some Italian musicians anticipated the serious, explicitly political vein of the *cantautori*, the singer-songwriters who would flourish in the 1970s. They were inspired by American vernacular musical traditions (jazz, with its particular bebop attitude, and folk) and the bohemian subculture of the Beats, as well as European existentialism (Minganti 2000).

Paradoxically, non-American groups may articulate their own regional or ethnic identities through specific reinterpretations and modifications of American popular cultural forms. A good example of the use of American popular music in this kind of local "identity politics" is the strain of Dutch pop/rock groups since the mid–1980s who sing in a regional dialect or the Frisian language, and borrow from older musical traditions in the Netherlands, such as old sailors' ballads, accordion music, street-band (carnival-like) music, brass band music and polka dancing. Although these Dutch musicians try to distance themselves from the hegemonic Anglo-American pop music and emphasize their regional cultural roots within the Netherlands, they still borrow from the U.S. musical cultural repertoire. By taking American "local authenticity" styles (e.g., Cajun music, Tex-Mex music, "Midwestern" or "Southern" rock) that deviate from mainstream U.S. pop music, as their sources of inspiration, these groups may succeed in presenting a particular identity of their own in their homeland. Thus they carve out a cultural niche that seems to offer the participants in this particular music scene some sense of place. In a heavily globalizing "postmodern" world there is no space that people authentically occupy, and so popular culture fills the gap by manufacturing images of home and rootedness (van Elteren 1997: 135–139; Chase and Shaw 1989: 1, 15).

As noted earlier, there is also the case of the creative appropriation of African-American rap music by certain groups outside the United States. Identification with, and emulation of the hip-hop subculture in the U.S. may help young blacks and other people of color as well as certain immigrant groups abroad (e.g. Moroccans, Turks, Algerians and other North Africans in Europe) in boosting their self-esteem, thereby empowering them in their struggle to obtain a better quality of life. It is not unheard of, however, for rappers from the ethnically dominant middle-class to borrow freely from the African-American rap idiom to articulate their dissatisfaction with, and to set themselves apart from, what they see as the homogeneous mainstream — Japan is a notable example (Condry 2000). Nevertheless, in all of these cases rap is deployed as a kind of generational protest. But at times adopting this musical style has also become attractive to some of these rappers to explicitly criticize social injustice at home. Through this culture of "secondary orality" disseminated by transnational mass media and other networks, kindred groups of youngsters all over the world may very well simultaneously develop common cultural identities within a global hip-hop culture and express their own particular identities in the local contexts where they live (van Elteren 1997: 139–141).

Ultimately, this positive discourse of popular culture and Americanization entails a search by many publics outside the U.S. for a cultural space of their own. Paradoxically, however, they often seek to do this within the wiggle room afforded by dominant American frameworks and products exported and disseminated by the cultural industries concerned (McKay 1997: 46). This problem even arises in situations where one would least expect it, as in the case of the European variant of the 1960s counterculture — oriented on an "alternative" America — which led to the adoption of a new kind of consumerism rather than a truly nonconformist lifestyle. In her study of the British underground's rock festival culture of the late 1960s and early 1970s, Elizabeth Nelson argued that these festivals manifested a new kind of consumerism. A large number of the people involved were consumers and spectators rather than participants. Ironically, though the British counterculture may have aimed to reject "straight" society's acceptance of the American way of life — including American consumerism — "it became imbued itself to a large extent with what might be termed the 'American way of the alternative future'" (Nelson 1989: 99). This assessment dovetails neatly with the way in which the sixties counterculture was commodified and incorporated into mainstream American culture itself (and its critical content defused) through the strategic interventions of the cultural industries, as Thomas Frank has persuasively demonstrated (Frank 1997).

Yet American culture as consumed by subordinate groups in repressive sociopolitical climates has a potential critical charge. Cultural forms emanating from the U.S. most in tune with dominant, conservative values, can, oddly enough, act in a different social and political climate as a frame of reference through which the hegemonic local order is ridiculed or otherwise criticized (Webster 1988: 179). Such things have happened, for instance, in Eastern-Central Europe where communist regimes were in power after World War II. According to some observers, Americanization even seems to have promoted cultural autonomy; the *glasnost*-inspired Americanization of Soviet TV (Barnathan 1989) and subsequent developments in post-communist Europe would have elements of this (Sklair 2002: 169). This raises the question concerning the extent to which the people involved were really able to make choices between various options, or had no other choice but to embrace Western capitalism in the transition towards Western societal forms. As Hunter and Yates conclude, "At the end of the day … we are still faced with the present reality of America's powerful if not dominant role in processes of globalization" (Hunter and Yates 2002: 325). Moreover, Western imports need not always be a real political-ideological threat to oppressive non-Western regimes but may be "harmlessly" incorporated into the existing social, political and cultural conditions through national gatekeeping policies (especially restrictive legislation). One can observe this phenomenon, for instance, in the case of a Western media corporation, Rupert Murdoch's News Corporation, which managed to penetrate the Chinese market in the mid–1990s by taking the communist regime's political restrictions into account and selectively attuning its supply of programs to the government's preferences (Hesmondhalgh 2002: 187).[17] Similar opportunistic strategies were recently introduced by Internet service providers Google, Yahoo!, and Microsoft, and network company Cisco Systems in making certain websites that are not agreeable to the Chinese regime inaccessible to ordinary Chinese people who use the search engines of these companies when surfing on the Internet.

In very different settings than those mentioned above similar recontextualizations and appropriations for the purpose of creating a mental space of one's own may occur. A striking example is the popular reading among working-class people in Britain, as Ken Worpole has analyzed in his book *Dockers and Detectives* (1983). He interviewed retired trade unionists and political activists about the books they read in the 1930s, when they were young. Many mentioned American writers, the naturalists such as Theodore Dreiser and Upton Sinclair but also more experimentalist, socially engaged novelists such as John

Dos Passos (in his early years). However, American detective fiction had also been very popular among them. It provided a model of an urban vernacular "masculine style." The readers were happy to find the absence of snobbery, gentlemen, or middle-class adulteries in this American fiction. One should also remember that several of the writers they admired were active in the Popular Front culture in the United States at the time (Denning 1996), which was part of an international leftist culture that these British workers and activists shared.

DOES AMERICAN PRESENCE BY DEFINITION MEAN AMERICAN INFLUENCE?

When considering the complexities of the reception process, we should note that the presence of American goods and artifacts in a local setting abroad does not automatically equate with American influence, as the Swedish Americanist Rolf Lundén has emphasized. He also suggested that "[i]t is only when the presence of foreign phenomena leads to changes in attitudes and values that an influence may be said to take place" (Lundén 1991: 141). This is certainly true when we focus on cultural change in the receiving context, and sociopsychological changes among locals in particular. Yet we must likewise recognize that the mere presence of American goods and practices has a momentum of its own when, as a whole, they go beyond a certain threshold of "minimal volume" and crowd out other options (foreign and domestic), which involves a distinctive prestructuring of the choices people have in carrying our their daily lives. In other words, such a situation makes it harder for locals to choose for other ways of life than tend to be associated with the American products and practices that are on offer. In my opinion, this argument does *not* entail falling into the trap of making "unwarranted leaps of inference from the simple presence of cultural goods to the attribution of deeper cultural or ideological effects" that Tomlinson considers to be "one of the fundamental conceptual mistakes of the cultural imperialism argument" (Tomlison 1997: 180), or what John B. Thompson calls "the fallacy of internalism" (Thompson 1995: 171). My reasoning avoids this trap because it locates the critical situation that is at issue here at the level of *structural constraints* that lie beyond, and set limits on, the actual reception process. It does not reduce culture to its material goods, and still acknowledges that culture should be seen as consisting of "existentially meaningful symbolization and experience" (Tomlinson 1999: 83), although the latter do build partly on the goods and practices that are present in a local people's life-world.

It is useful to pause here to distinguish between visible and invisible influence, as Lundén does. Borrowing from linguistics and literary criticism, he calls the first kind of American presence "foregrounded" or "defamiliarized" in the sense that it is experienced as being alien to the indigenous culture. After a period of time, the alien (visible) element is either rejected or incorporated into the indigenous culture. In the case of invisible influence the American presence is not immediately apparent, but the phenomena in question still may have been inspired by, or immediately taken from the American cultural repertoire. These phenomena can then by analogy be labeled "backgrounded" or "familiarized," and are likely to have a comparatively much stronger impact on another's country culture. Indeed, American influence is not restricted to the dissemination of highly visible consumer goods and material artifacts, nor is its diffusion always the result of deliberate policies by governmental or private American institutes. We may think of less visible American influences as, for instance, conveyed by cultural practices in business and management, psychotherapy, education and pedagogy, as well as the associated theories and models in the behavioral and social sciences.[18] These hidden streams of influence may ultimately be more powerful than visible ones in changing the recipients' attitudes and behavior geared towards an Americanized local practice in a specific domain. Or, as Lundén boldly states: "real power in society is silent," whereas "apparent power is loud, sometimes shrill" (Lundén 1991: 142). He even draws the following general conclusion: "the more visible a foreign element is the less influential it is, and, vice versa, the more an element is part of the 'shadow' of the national psyche, to use Jung's terms, the more profound the impact" *(ibid.)*. I have no problems with this statement, except for the mystifying Jungian reference, which in my view ought to be replaced by one that connotes the change of an originally American element into a taken-for-granted component of the receiving country's national identity.

The question arises, however, whether a thorough invisible incorporation of, in our case, an American good or practice into the receiving culture — whereby it becomes naturalized as an integral part of that culture — cannot just as well be called a very successful form of (unconscious?) local appropriation. In other words, to what extent is there a difference between a profoundly silent change (Americanization) along these lines and an optimal form of local modification in which the receiving culture has fully "digested" the incoming influence? For instance, in reference to popular British TV programs, Strinati wonders how far these represented "Americanisation of a more pervasive and subtle kind in that they were often domesticated and anglicized versions of American programmes" (Strinati 1992: 59). Ritzer considers indigenous clones of McDonaldized enterprises to reflect an underlying basic transformation — the McDonaldization of those societies — and thus as silent, "insidious" forms of Americanization that bring about worldwide homogenization (Ritzer 2001: 6–7, 171–174). Watson and his associates (1997), among others, reject such an interpretation and think in terms of highly successful localizations that do not represent any real change in the fundamental realities of these same societies. In my view, Ritzer is correct as far as the adoption of standardized principles (or fundamental operating procedures) regarding the new means of consumption and associated business practices hailing from America is concerned. At least at this juncture, they all seem to be part of a worldwide movement in the direction of American-style patterns of consumption (see also final chapter).

FUNCTIONS, EFFECTS, AND ASSESSMENTS

Last, but certainly not least, one should try to inform oneself about the functions that a particular form of Americanization fulfills in the local setting concerned — however difficult this may be. Of course, then one always needs to ask: functional for whom or what, and as seen from which perspective? One might focus, for example, on the export of American cultural products through U.S. media and cultural industries as a possible means to secure the interests of U.S. foreign policy and/or those of its financial-economical and political elites. Methodologically, it is important to disentangle the policy aims and intervention practices of the U.S. government from those of U.S. businesses operating in foreign markets, which have not always coincided historically. It may also be interesting to analyze in depth by whose interventions and for what purposes policies transferred from the U.S. are emulated and deployed in the receiving countries (Dolowitz 1998).

Further questions need to be asked regarding effects. How does American influence in various domains impinge on the locals' quality of life? Recipients of the projection of U.S. power may either be beneficiaries or victims (Slater and Taylor 1999: xi) or, as I would hasten to add, individuals may simultaneously benefit in certain respects while suffering in others. Does the American impact foster cultural subjugation and political acquiescence as the "classic" thesis of media imperialism, or broader, cultural imperialism[19] would suggest? Or does it bring about the very opposite, and, for instance, stimulate (further) democratization of the receiving society, or more specific empowerment or revitalization of certain groups? Does it reinforce the status quo, strengthen opposition and/or feed resistance to oppressive regimes, or does it have more mixed effects? How pronounced are the changes due to American influence and how long do they endure?

When trying to answer these and other questions of this kind, one must remain cautious not to lapse into a functionalist-mechanicistic way of reasoning, whereby the observer merely projects her/his interpretation of what s/he supposes goes on among locals onto the given situation, and the active involvement of recipients in the process of borrowing and appropriating of the American imports is not, or at least not sufficiently, taken into account. This "fallacy of internalism" is a major conceptual mistake in the conventional cultural imperialism argument in that "it ignores the hermeneutic appropriation which is an essential part of the circulation of symbolic forms" (Thompson 1995: 171).[20] After all, there *is* the possibility of deliberate "self-colonization" by local people as Wagnleiter has indicated with regard to the rapid development of "an American-European consumption-oriented society" in post–World War II Europe (1993: 78),[21] but which has a much broader reach, both past and present.

Furthermore, in making assessments it is necessary to distinguish between various areas of American influence, some of which may be more susceptible to creative local appropriation than others. With regard to the current era of American globalism, for example, one cannot transpose the argument about the hegemony of America being open to contestation and reinterpretation by local audiences in the area of consumption (and the "texts" of popular culture in particular) indiscriminately and without qualification to the areas of production and finance where the dominance of American corporate and global capital seems much less open to opposition, "appropriation," "subversion," and "resistance" (Strinati 1992: 53). Moreover, the role of the United States, or of specific U.S. agencies or practices, in influencing local developments in both public and private spheres refers to a wide range of formal and informal effects, varying from official policy and documented efforts and results to more tacit attitudes, daily practices, and ways of life. Needless to say, merely defining the possible scope of each of these matters is a complex enterprise, let alone assessing their actual magnitude, duration, and long-term significance (Ermarth 1993a: 1).

Finally, it is less fruitful to think of cultural imperialism as an attack on "pure" subordinate cultures *at the individual level* (McGuigan 1992: 230). A more productive way of formulating the domination involved in cultural imperialism might be in terms of the culture as a whole, as Tomlinson has suggested: "…whatever the divergence in individual responses to cultural imports, domination is occurring where the "autonomy" of a culture — roughly speaking, its right to develop along its own lines — is threatened by external forces" (Tomlinson 1991: 95). McGuigan applied this suggestion to the fall of communist states in Eastern Europe in the late 1980s, about which Tomlinson remarked: "[w]hat is interesting about the changes in the planned socialist economies is that the desire for more consumer goods is linked with the desire for the political freedom of liberal democracies (*ibid.*: 131).

But, as McGuigan rightly commented, we may wonder what real choices the people involved actually had. To what extent were they able to develop "autonomous solutions ... or, contrary to their aims in many cases, were merely swapping one form of domination for another, the dictate of communism for the dictate of global capitalism, a cruel irony indeed"? (McGuigan 1992: 230). Put so bluntly, the answer was obvious: for the former subjects of communist oppression, the drawbacks of massive economic and cultural upheaval were preferable to acquiescing with the (then) status quo. With the benefit of hindsight one might try to formulate an adequate in-depth explanation of the cultural dimensions of the collapse of communism. Here we hit upon a substantial difference (in analytical terms) between an approach that emphasizes cultural-political factors versus one that puts the weight of explanation on cultural-economic determinants of the fall of communism. Authors like Stuart Hall have stressed the democratic aspirations and appeal of Western consumerism. Others such as Fredric Jameson, in line with his thesis of postmodernity as the cultural reflection of the latest stage of capitalism (Jameson 1991), focused on the incorporation of post-communist countries into global capitalism,[22] something that even reform communists aimed for (Hall and Jameson 1990).

Admittedly, on this issue neither position is, strictly speaking, right or wrong. But the difference in focus does matter, since it raises important questions about power and self-determination (McGuigan 1992: 232–233). These two positions highlight different aspects of social reality and look for corresponding remedies to peoples' lack of self-determination. The first position does not depart significantly from the liberal-democratic viewpoint espoused by Timothy Garton Ash in Britain and Francis Fukuyama in the United States.[23] In the 1990s, proponents of this view did little more than endorse the idea that a transition to Western European-style consumer capitalism, with West Germany as the shining exemplar, would set through rapidly once the magic of "the market" was allowed to perform its expected role. The second position focuses on the effects of globalizing capitalism and Western cultural imperialism in post-communist societies. In the early 1990s, exponents of this view foresaw that as a result of a Western-imposed political-economical "shock therapy" (with Poland and the former Soviet Union as primary examples), some post-communist societies would turn into countries with a kind of Third World status and widening disparities of wealth and opportunity. This is not the place to discuss the developments that actually took place thus far. Hopefully, however, the gist of my argument is clear about the different views regarding the constraints to self-determination by people involved in these sweeping societal changes, which also leads to different assessments of the "Americanizing" tendencies involved.

The question of real choice — which is not always easy to answer — can and should of course be raised in all situations in which American influence prestructures the range of alternatives in significant ways over the influences from other sources (local and foreign). The next chapter focuses on the domain that is most relevant here — the contemporary world of corporate globalization.

9

Americanization as
U.S.-Style Corporate Globalization

This final chapter first examines current theorizing on globalization in relation to a persistent tendency among leading theorists to discard the whole idea of Americanization, a rejection that turns out to be premature. Today the United States continues to exert much influence abroad as a superpower (many observers label it even the "only superpower"), while its supporters and detractors agree that it is the world's first truly globe-straddling empire. Yet it is crucial to move beyond a state-centrist approach in order to also grasp the full extent of the significantly increased influence wielded by transnational corporations. Therefore, secondly, this chapter addresses the ways in which transnational corporations — in relation to U.S.-dominated, international governance — spread capitalist modernity worldwide. Here we are faced with a paradox. While the U.S. economy remains the major engine of global growth, the country's economic power has lost ground over the past thirty years or so. Yet, at least for the time being, U.S. corporate norms and practices keep having a domineering influence in the world of transnationals. In what follows an attempt will be made to explain how U.S. business leaders and affiliated political power-holders still manage to set the agenda of much of the global economy and why many of their foreign counterparts have adopted similar neoliberal policies. The chapter concludes with a discussion about the historical contingency of the intertwinement of Americanization and globalization. This is necessary to oppose the idea that the former is essential to the latter. Countervailing powers that might bring about transformations of the prevailing form of economic globalization are considered as well.

It should be clear that the perspective offered here focuses on only part of a broader process, that is "a regime of capitalism in motion" rather than globalization as a whole. In other words, this is not an attempt to reduce globalization to a socioeconomic complex (Antonio and Bonanno 2000: 52). Globalization is a broader, complexly intertwined, and indeterminate process (or rather a combination of various processes at several levels) that includes many other factors whose relative weights are difficult to determine beforehand.

A CLOSER LOOK AT GLOBALIZATION THEORIES

The term "globalization" became popular in the 1980s in the context of fundamental changes in the world economy and the arrival of technological networks for real-time data transmission. It stems from the notion of "financial globalization," which refers to those structural changes in the international financial world that decoupled capital markets from the boundaries of nation-states and increased dependency of national systems of production on the world market. It should also be noted that the globalization concept gained currency just as communication networks began to be deregulated and privatized. This process took off in the U.S. banking sector during the 1970s, but attained a much stronger momentum from 1984 onwards, with the dismantling of the American Telegraph and Telephone Company which had until then enjoyed a virtual private monopoly in telecommunications. Management and marketing experts also extended the notion of globalization to include networks of economic and cultural flows (Mattelart and Mattelart 1998: 139).

Globalization theory, which seeks to develop adequate theoretical frameworks to address these realities, emerged as a major concern in the social sciences in the 1990s. It evolved both from the social changes it seeks to explain and internal developments in social theory, most notably as a response to earlier perspectives such as modernization theory and its Western, evolutionist bias (although vestiges remain in some variants of globalization theory).[1]

Setting aside the differences on a number of issues, globalization theorists all share a primary interest in the world as a whole. They focus most of their attention on processes that transcend individual societies or nations and operate on a global scale, more or less detached from these separate local settings. These processes cut across various types of geographical boundaries, integrating and connecting communities and organizations in new space-time combinations, making the world objectively and subjectively (that is, in the experience of people) more connected. Thus, globalization implies a movement away from the classical sociological concept of a "society" as a well-bounded system — geographically identified with the territory of a nation-state or region — in favor of a perspective that concentrates on "how social life is ordered across time and space" (Giddens 1990: 64). Most theorists likewise recognize that globalization implies uneven processes both in time and space. Accelerating more recently, globalization is not experienced uniformly across the world. Globalization theorists all share the idea of time-space compression — one of the main features of the latest phase of globalization — that is, the speeding up of global processes, so that events in one place increasingly have immediate impact on people and places far away, and the world feels smaller and distances shorter (Harvey 1989: 201–323). Finally, most theorists hold that globalization entails a greater "consciousness of the world as a whole" (Robertson 1992: 8).

The existing theories are usually classified firstly on the basis of their primary focus on economic, political/institutional or cultural factors, and secondly, whether they emphasize homogeneity or heterogeneity (Steger 2002). Sometimes social globalization is treated as a separate category (encompassing the spread of peoples, cultures, images and ideas) that includes political globalization; that is, the dissemination of constitutional arrangements and democratic state structures, and the development of international rules and institutions (Nye 2002: 83–84). Although a good case can be made for this option, it is rather "the social" that is often subsumed under the headings of political/institutional and (socio)cultural globalization as I do too below.

Economic accounts of globalization are premised on the idea that the phenomenon in essence involves "the increasing linkage of national economies through trade, financial flows, and foreign direct investment (FDI) by multinational firms" (Gilpin 2000: 299). Expanding economic activity is seen as both the primary feature of globalization and the driving force of its fast development. Scholars who share this perspective consider today's economic globalization as an unparalleled transformation in the world economy. The central task of their research agenda is the close examination of the evolving structure of global economic markets and their principal institutions. According to many analysts the emergence of a transnational financial system is the most crucial feature of the current era. In the late 1980s the process of financial globalization shifted into higher gear as capital and securities markets in the United States and Europe were deregulated, which allowed for increased mobility among different segments of the financial sector with fewer restrictions and a global view of investment opportunities. The explosive growth of financial trading was significantly enhanced by advances in data processing and information technology.

Thus, over the past three decades transnational corporations have operated in an increasingly deregulated global market. The increased access to cheap labor, resources, and favorable production conditions in Third World countries foster both the mobility and the profitability of TNCs. Transnational production systems enable these companies to circumvent the nationally-based political influence of trade unions and other workers' organizations in negotiations about wages and other labor conditions (Steger 2002: 24–28).

Theorists who emphasize economic factors tend to focus on homogeneity, and generally see globalization as the spread of neoliberalism and the market economy throughout the world. Yet these authors acknowledge some forms of heterogeneity as well; for example, the existence of flexible specialization that entails niche marketing and the tailoring of products to the specific needs of various groups of local customers (Harvey 1989; Piore and Sabel 1984; Sklair 2002).

The discussion of political globalization concentrates mostly on assessing the fate of the modern nation-state. A first group of scholars views political globalization as a process intrinsically connected to the expansion of economic markets, driven especially by steady advances in computer technology and global communication systems such as the World Wide Web. In their view, politics is severely eroded by an unstoppable and irreversible techno-economic development that will crush all governmental attempts to implement restrictive policies and regulations. This combination of self-propelled economic development and technological innovation has ushered in a new stage in world history in which the role of government will ultimately be reduced to a mere conveyor belt for free-market forces. A highly influential exponent of this view, the Japanese business strategist Kenichi Ohmae, envisions the rise of a "borderless world" brought about by the irresistible forces of capitalism, resulting in the nation-state becoming irrelevant in the global economy (Ohmae 1990, 1995).

One should notice that a number of neo-Marxist scholars have given a similar techno-economistic interpretation of political globalization. They tend to consider politics merely as an epiphenomenon of global processes driven by a reinvigorated capitalism that has now reached a stage wherein accumulation is taking place on a global rather than a national or otherwise more restricted territorial scale. Power is seen as being located in global social formations and exercised through global networks rather than through territorially-based states (Thomas 1997: 6; Burbach et al. 1997).

A second group of scholars contests that view and emphasizes the central role of politics in unleashing the forces of globalization. Since economic globalization is politically determined, shifting political preferences should be capable of creating different social conditions. Representatives of this perspective basically argue that the rapid expansion of global economic activity since the 1980s is first and foremost a result of political decisions made by governments to lift the international restrictions on capital. Once these decisions were implemented, the technology came into its own, accelerating the speed of communication and calculations that helped bring the movement of financial capital to a fevered pitch. The implication is that nation and territory still make a difference — even in a globalized context (Sassen 1996a; 1996b; 1998). Most representatives of this view also recognize that the development of the past few decades has significantly set limits on the political options open to states, especially in developing countries. Yet they continue to think that in principle it is always possible to counter or even reverse seemingly irreversible globalizing tendencies by state efforts (Scholte 2000).

A third group of scholars has concluded that globalization is propelled by a mixture of political and technological factors. Some among them are more pessimistic about the developments in question than others. An example of the former is the British political theorist John Gray, who portrays globalization as a long-term, technology-driven process (firmly embedded in the rational-instrumental Enlightenment tradition as rather one-sidedly depicted by him), whose contemporary character is politically determined by the world's most powerful nations. The ultimate aim of what he sees as a neoliberal Anglo-American project is to create a global free market (see later in this chapter). But Gray also contends that no nation has the hegemonic power to make this happen. In his dooms-day scenario, he expects the world economy to collapse as its imbalances become insup-portable, which in turn will spur increasing international anarchy (Gray 1998)

A much less pessimistic perspective that integrates technology and politics to explain globalization is offered by sociologist Manuel Castells in his three-volume study on the information age (Castells 1996; 1997; 1998). In this seminal work, he distinguishes three independent processes that drive globalization: the information technology revolution; the economic crisis of both capitalism and states and their subsequent restructuring; and the flourishing of cultural social movements. These developments have brought about elab-orate networks of capital, labor, information, and markets that have jointly created con-ditions favorable to the further expansion of the global economy. Castells notes the rise of a new "informational capitalism" based on information technology as the crucial instru-ment for the effective restructuring of socioeconomic processes central to enhanced cap-italist globalization. He also signals the erosion of the nation-state as a sovereign entity and the devolution of power to regional and local governments and to various suprana-tional institutions. However, Castells also articulates the continued relevance of nation-states as important bargaining agencies that set their stamp on the changing world of power relationships. As new political actors (especially the new social and cultural movements) emerge and new public policies are implemented, the role of culture increases. Culture as a source of power and informational power as the source of capital carry the new social hierarchy of the Information Age.

Finally a fourth group of scholars should be mentioned here whose primary focus is on political globalization from the perspective of global governance. They analyze the var-ious national and multilateral responses to the fragmentation of economic and political systems and the transnational flows that permeate through national borders. Political sci-entists such as David Held and Richard Falk emphasize the need for effective global gov-ernance in response to various forces of globalization that diminish the sovereignty of national governance. They have also suggested that political globalization "naturally" fos-ters a development toward cosmopolitan democracy (Falk 1995; Held 1995a; 1995b). Their view has elicited severe criticism of a number of academics who contend that it entails an abstract idealism that fails to account for current political developments at the policy level. "Globalization skeptics" have argued that even though globalization increas-ingly interlinks cultural patterns, this does not automatically lead to mutual accommodation and tolerance of differences but may just as well incite resistance and opposition (Holton 1998: 202–203; Steger 2002: 30–34).

Another way to distinguish among globalization theorists whose primary focus is on political factors, concerns their relative emphasis on homogeneity or heterogeneity. On the one hand, globalization tends to bring about a certain "sameness" to the surface appearance and institutions of modern social life across the world. Authors like Meyer et al. (1997) focus on the existence of worldwide models of the state and the emergence of corresponding ("isomorphic") forms of governance. Globalization also "universalizes" other aspects of modern social life such as the multiplicity of institutions, among others, identified by Keohane and Nye (1989). On the other hand, globalization involves the assimilation and re-articulation of the global in relation to local circumstances, such as very different interpretations of human rights; and different versions of Islamic practice in various countries—that also depend on the specific strain that dominates locally, of course (McGrew 1992: 74). In response to globalizing forces we also find ethnic, fundamentalist, and reactionary political movements at the local level that involve an intensification of ethnic, religious and nationalist identities (Barber 1995; Appadurai 1996), leading to a greater heterogeneity. This encompasses not only political/institutional dimensions, but also cultural aspects, of course.

At the extremes, the globalization of culture can either involve a trend toward common codes and practices or a situation in which many cultural influences interact to create a cultural pastiche of hybridized forms. Several influential theorists have come up with assessments that link globalization to new forms of cultural diversity. They usually employ a dialectical perspective on the interplay between homogenizing and heterogenizing forces. Roland Robertson, for example, asserts that global cultural flows often elicit a rearticulation of local cultural niches. Instead of increasing cultural homogenization, he expects a further pluralization of the world as localities produce a variety of cultural responses to global influences. He uses the term "glocalization,"[2] a complex interaction of the global and the local characterized on the one hand by cultural penetrations and encroachments of global forces in the local sphere, and cultural borrowings and active appropriations by local recipients on the other (Robertson 1992; 2001). Similarly, Ulf Hannerz outlines the complexity of an emerging "global culture" consisting of new zones of hybridization. In these regions, meanings from different historical sources that were originally separated in space, have coalesced to mix extensively in multifarious ways. Instead of simply being overrun by Western consumerist forces of homogenization, local difference and particularity transform into new cultural mélanges and discourses (Hannerz 1992b: 96). Many other authors echo a similar theme (e.g. Appadurai 1990; 1996; García Canclini 1995; Nederveen Pieterse 1995; Abu-Lughod 1997). However, a minority of theorists, including authors such as Benjamin Barber and George Ritzer (see below), see clear tendencies of Western-led (or more specifically U.S.-led) cultural homogenization.

Given the voluminous writing on globalization theory (which has developed into a flourishing cottage industry) and the rate at which the literature is still growing, it is of course impossible to cover the full range of perspectives (for compilations, see Beynon and Dunkerly 2000; Lechner and Boli 2000). But for our purpose, an examination of the relationship between processes of globalization and Americanization and the ways in which current globalization theory deals with relevant matters in this regard, will suffice.

On balance, the concern with America's global reach is at right angles to the prevailing tendency especially among cultural globalization theorists to reject a focus on the United States or the West in general, as well as on the processes of Americanization or

Westernization (Featherstone 1991: 27, 142; Giddens 1990; Robertson 1992; Friedman 1994: 99; Nederveen Pieterse 1994: 163). This proclivity can be traced partly to the fact that much thinking about international processes in the past tended to be positively biased towards the U.S. and the West. This was especially true with regard to modernization theory, a dominant framework in the sociology of development current in the 1950s and 1960s. However, subsequently it increasingly came under attack because of its Western-centrism (if not U.S.-centrism), its premise that modernization was normative, and for obscuring the embeddedness of individual societies in wider social systems.

Importantly, Talcott Parsons, a leading representative of U.S. sociology at the time, asserted that postwar America's affluence and democratization were realizing the promise of liberty and equality, while drawing the genuine support of the populace, rather than mere formal or ideological legitimacy imposed from above. Depicting the United States as the "lead society," Parsons was convinced that "Americanization" would extend the advantages of progressive modernization's latest evolutionary breakthroughs to the rest of the world. In the same breath he criticized the New Left's "ideological pessimism" and what he considered to be premature claims about the rise of a "postmodern society" as expressed by such analysts and social critics as the radical sociologist C. Wright Mills and the neo-Marxist philosopher Herbert Marcuse (Mills 1959: 165–176; Marcuse 1964). In Parsons's view, progressive modernization still had more than a century to go before it would begin to exhaust its energy (Parsons 1971).

Today most cultural globalization theorists argue that the "classic" modernization and westernization perspectives are too narrow and that the world has dramatically changed in the meantime, pointing to enhanced "time-space compression" and the multiplicity of interplays between processes at the global and the local levels. The contemporary world has indeed become subject to multi-dimensional processes that go in many different directions. So from their perspective a focus on the U.S. and the West, or Americanization and Westernization, would be too restrictive and inadequate to study current global realities. Regardless of their objectives, it seems to me these globalization theorists have prematurely rejected other substantive perspectives and alternative theoretical orientations (including those that focus on diverse forms of imperialism and the persistent influence of the nation-state) that still have considerable merit — if brought up to date with contemporary developments both in theory and society.

From our perspective, they have in fact thrown the proverbial baby out with the bath water, namely an interest in America's multivariegated impact globally. Even historian Richard Kuisel, who is highly critical of the "crude notion of cultural imperialism," suggesting that it is inadequate to deal with the complicated historical process of Americanization, maintains that the notion of Americanization "is more helpful in conceptualizing contemporary trends than some forms of globalization theory, which tend to underestimate the central role of America in this history of cultural exchange. The thesis of Americanization, if properly nuanced, is a useful way to approach the cultural history of the twentieth century" (Kuisel 2000: 222). Proper usage means that transmission, appropriation, and transnationalization are all seen as integral components of Americanization today.

Since the mid–1990s broader theoretical debates over neoliberal restructuring of the global economy were carried out largely under the rubric of "globalization." After the 1989 collapse of Eastern European communism and the U.S.-led multinational military intervention in Iraq in 1991 a new (post–Cold War) era began. The new geopolitical realities opened large new areas of the world to capitalist investment, labor regimes, and prod-

ucts, aptly expressed by President George H. Bush's reference to the "new world order."
For the first time, a truly globally-integrated capitalism was possible. At the time of his
writing working as a deputy director of the U.S. State Department's Policy Planning Staff,
political scientist Francis Fukuyama proclaimed "the end of history" and the worldwide
triumph of neoliberalism and "democratic capitalism" as the sole remaining alternative
(Fukuyama 1989). Widely discussed in the popular media and debated by social theorists, his essay became a prime text marking the victory of the U.S.-led "West" over all
alternative sociopolitical systems. It also heralded the end of the postwar era dominated
by U.S. "military Keynesianism" that had substantially increased state expenditures, state
regulation of the economy, and social welfare and public goods, but lacked comprehensive income distribution, social welfare programs, and governmental planning as were
common in Western European mixed economies (Antonio and Bonanno 2000: 36–37;
Harvey 2003: 51, 56–57).

Fukuyama believed that, in the wake of collapsed communism and failed postwar
liberalism (in the American sense), "liberal democracy" (i.e., free-market capitalism) was
the only option for any nation aspiring to be modern (Fukuyama 1992: 51). Taking a distance from the idea of American hegemony, he also suggested that "in the last few centuries something like a true global culture" had emerged, "centering around technologically
driven economic growth and the capitalist social relations necessary to produce and sustain it" (*ibid.*: 126). By the end of the 1990s, however, even Fukuyama had to admit that
America's position as the sole remaining superpower made it "inevitable" that Americanization would accompany globalization (Fukuyama 1999; Steger 2002: 4).

By the turn of the new millennium, Thomas L. Friedman's best-selling book *The
Lexus and the Olive Tree* (2000) was perhaps the most comprehensive expression of the
optimistic view of economic globalization aimed at a wider audience, and celebrated by
the American mass media as the preeminent guide book to globalization. Many commentators at the time stated that Friedman's book should be seen as the "official narrative of
globalization" in the United States and it received a ringing endorsement from the Oval
Office (Clinton Administration) as well as declarations of strong approval by leading
figures of both major parties (Bacevich 2002: 38–39).

In referring to "Americanization-globalization," the award-winning foreign affairs
columnist of the *New York Times* revived the postwar theme of the United States as the
world's lead society. In *The Lexus and the Olive Tree* Friedman argues that the country is
perfectly equipped for global competition and for its role as the "ultimate benign hegemon and reluctant enforcer" in the current globalizing world. Espousing the virtues of
neoliberal globalization and embracing cosmopolitan modernity, Friedman believes that
modernization is driven by global "free markets" and consumer-investor choices — which
he equates with democracy. He claims that the "electronic herd" made up of millions of
stock, bond, and currency investors all across the world and executive officers of large
transnational corporations who move their production sites to the most efficient, low-
cost producers, make the economy grow so effectively that all nations aspiring to be modern must converge towards the American model. Refusal to put on this "golden
straitjacket"— the defining political-economic garment of this globalization era — can be
disruptive and occasionally elicit a dangerous "backlash" (Friedman 2000: 104–111, 152,
367, 383).

Overall the tenor of his book is positive and fully in line with the so-called "Washington Consensus,"[3] which, like other proponents of this consensus paradigm, Friedman
sees as a natural product of diffuse, rational choices rather than as a consequence of Amer-

ica's economic and military power. However, Friedman distances himself from the right in supporting a social safety-net in the United States and its multicultural character. He enthuses about the stock-market boom at the time, an enriched professional middle class, and a revised neoliberalism (paying lip service to social provisions) in line with the politics of the Clinton and Blair Administrations (Friedman 2000: 367–388, 438–439, 463–467, 475).

Recently Friedman changed his position regarding U.S.-led globalization, however. In his new bestseller *The World Is Flat* (2005) the core message is that due to a significant increase of outsourcing work (including a wide variety of highly-skilled tasks) to South-East Asian countries and the inadequate response by leading politicians and policymakers, economic globalization threatens America's position as world power, while Europe faces the prospect of a larger impending decline.[4] The future lies with India and China, which will be the West's major competitors.

Friedman thinks that in this fastly changing world, survival is only possible by adopting a Blairite political approach (= New Labour's Third Way). This includes innovating the economy (transformation into a "knowledge economy") and the creation of a more flexible labor market that emphasizes education and the development of adequate skills and "employability" to insure workers are well-adapted to the new global economic reality. In Friedman's utopian view on capitalist progress, globalization will ultimately result in one economic system, that will make wars, tyrannies and poverty obsolete (Friedman 2005). Ironically, as he himself acknowledges, it resembles orthodox Marxism in its way of reasoning about the future development of capitalism.

But there are other approaches that draw a very different picture. Since the mid-1990s a number of thinkers have argued that globalization entails an increasingly homogenized global culture premised on American ideological beliefs and values. In *Jihad vs McWorld*, the political theorist Benjamin R. Barber warned against the cultural imperialism of what he calls "McWorld," a soulless consumer capitalism that is rapidly transforming the world's cultural diversity into a blandly uniform market. In his view, McWorld is a product of a superficial American popular culture, pushed by expansionist commercial interests. It has a U.S. "template" (or "speaks American") and is driven by free market deregulation and innovation in information and communication technologies. Barber acknowledges that McWorld is not monolithic, but is received differently throughout the world, producing local fusions, hybrid forms and resistance from local cultures. The colonizing tendencies of McWorld evoke "Jihad," local tendencies to reject and fight Western homogenization forces wherever they can be found. These responses are fueled by all kinds of ethnonationalism and religious fundamentalism and represent the dark side of cultural particularism.[5]

Barber does not oppose global markets and consumption *per se*, and admits that they have virtues, favoring them over the closed, insular traditional forces that arise in reaction. But he is highly critical of U.S. neoliberalism's equation of free trade, free markets, and consumer-investor choice with democracy. He contends that genuine democratization requires much wider participation than consumers and investors and a much broader concern than the individual interests that rule in market choices (Barber 1995: 58–72, 78–79, 293–300).

More recently Barber proposed a U.S. national security strategy to implement "preventive democracy" across the world in order to fight terrorism at its roots. Put forward as a peaceful and progressive alternative to the "pre-emptive war" strategy of the George W. Bush Administration, it constitutes a progressive version of U.S.-style humanitarian interventionism. Legitimated by a new "declaration of interdependence" to be signed by the people of the world ("citizens of one CivWorld"), it is predicated on the central belief that America's democracy, tied to its cultural diversity, should be held up as an exemplary model to the rest of the world (Barber 2003: 213–214).[6]

In presenting his view on a U.S.-led homogenization of organizational structures, sociologist George Ritzer has coined the term "McDonaldization" to describe the process by which the principles of the fast-food restaurant have come to dominate more and more sectors of American society as well as the rest of the world. He suggests that, in the long run, McDonaldization worldwide will lead to a dramatic reduction of cultural diversity and the dehumanization of social relations (Ritzer 1993; 1998; 2001). From the perspective of globalization theory, McDonaldization is subject to the forces of pluralism. When McDonaldized models are imported they are always undergoing indigenous adaptation (Watson 1997). These models can develop locally in a process of emulation and a McDonaldized model can be employed for a variety of purposes.

According to Ritzer, however, the net result is most likely increasing structural homogeneity because the emulation in question leans towards "organizational isomorphism" leading to a similarity of form between initially competing organizational structures. So "while structural diversity in means is increasingly limited, both real and cosmetic diversity [= spurious variety] of ends persists" (Ritzer and Stillman 2003: 39).[7]

At the turn of the new century, thinkers across the political spectrum concurred that neoliberal policy had become a globally hegemonic idea, but they disagreed over its origins and how it is sustained. Proponents of the Washington Consensus, such as Friedman and a number of influential economists and policymakers, tended to see it as a natural outcome of diffuse, individual, rational choices. Critics however argued that it is forged by U.S. economic and military power, achieved as a consequence of America's "enormous structural power" that is "deeply inscribed into the nature and functioning of the present world order" (Held et al. 1999: 425).

A well-informed analyst of globalization theories, Manfred Steger, concluded that the neoliberal "globalization" discourse amounts to "a gigantic repackaging enterprise — the pouring of old philosophical wine into new ideological bottles" (Steger 2002: 12). In the 1990s, two centuries of classical liberalism were relabeled "the new economy" by ideologists of globalization, who thus wanted to emphasize the novelty of the dominant ideological-economic framework of their time. Steger also pointed out that "globalization's claims and political maneuvers remain conceptually tied to a Spencerian nineteenth-century narrative of 'modernization' and 'civilization' that presents Western countries — particularly the United States and the United Kingdom — as the privileged vanguard of an evolutionary process that applies to all nations" (*ibid.*: 12–13). Moreover, Steger suggested that in this regard "globalism" is similar to Marxism, which has the same intellectual roots, and shares a belief in "irresistible," "inevitable," and "irreversible" progress to describe the projected path of future development

On the basis of a critical analysis of trends in the global political economy, development studies scholar Ankie Hoogvelt signaled the resurgence of the United States after two decades of supposed economic decline and its growing geopolitical dominance that safeguards the stability of neoliberal regimes. Referring to Peter Gowans's analysis in *The Global Gamble: Washington's Faustian Bid for Global Dominance* (1999), she even boldly posited that the "globalism" discourse ... also serves to obscure the fact that global capitalism is an American political project serving the interests primarily of American capital and the US domestic economy" (Hoogvelt 2001: xvi-vii, 155). Similarly, in his book

False Dawn, John Gray, Professor of European Thought at the London School of Economics, declared that neoliberal globalization is an "American project" fashioned with much support from the U.S. state (Gray 1998: 78–79). He also argued that neoliberalism reflects an Enlightenment rationalism and universalism adapted to distinctly American conditions and then exported worldwide, without regard for local cultures or contexts and ignoring the diversity of capitalisms that as yet exist. In this view, which lambasts the fantasies of economic globalizers and ideals of liberal universalists alike, the former Soviet Union epitomized a rival Enlightenment utopia: that of "a universal civilization in which markets were replaced by central planning" (*ibid.*: 3). Both universalizing Enlightenment ways share the idea that one economic model works in every setting. One aims for a single global market as its version of a universal civilization and its communist counterpart envisions a centrally planned, universal, classless "world society." However, Gray contended that neoliberal globalization generates such uneven development, severe inequalities, and intense political instability that it undermines the very sociocultural foundations of its markets.

This view contrasts sharply with the unbounded optimism of those who believe that neoliberal globalization is the result of universal rationality. Friedman has even suggested that if a "visionary geoarchitect" was asked a century ago to design the model society for a globalized world, s/he could hardly have done better than the U.S. system in 2000 (Friedman 2000: 368). But his enthusiasm about the wonders of neoliberalism paled next to the "revolutionary" rhetoric found in the manifestos of several dot-com entrepreneurs in the late 1990s (e.g., Schwartz et al. 1999). By contrast, Gray asserted that the magical rationality attributed to global markets is a fiction that renders an air of inevitability to neoliberal globalization and deflects contestations or thoughts about alternatives. Combined with American ethnocentrism, this state of affairs foreclosed discussion of the crucial policy question: "how to reconcile the imperatives of deregulated markets with enduring human needs" (Gray 1998: 132).

The results of a late 1990s study by sociologists James Davidson Hunter and Joshua Yates among senior managers and chief executives of U.S.-based transnational firms and nongovernmental organizations — all global leaders in their respective fields — revealed strong American ethnocentrism. The researchers found that these leaders shared a "market idiom" that equates neoliberal deregulation with "human progress and enlightenment" and resistance to the process as thick-skinned irrationality. The executives claimed to be totally objective and neutral about their views on globalization, and seemed oblivious to the fact that their American background might limit their vision. The most striking feature was the sense of "moral innocence" that these CEOs maintained about the world they were helping to create, which became apparent when they appeared to be baffled by the hostile responses to their endeavors.

Hunter and Yates call these American globalizers "parochial cosmopolitans," whose attitudes germinate from a pattern of large-scale physical (and virtual) mobility and a strong tendency of remaining in a protective "sociocultural bubble" through similar physical localities, means of traveling, lodging and leisure and entertainment all across the world, which precludes them from serious engagements with the indigenous cultures that they influence. When they visit other countries, they stay in U.S.-style hotels, health clubs, restaurants, office buildings and so forth, and associate almost exclusively with like-minded Western-educated professionals who are conversant in English, thereby sidestepping the necessity of learning foreign languages. Their way of working also shields them from serious doubts about their activities because of insufficient feedback from locals and others. There are notable exceptions to some degree among people employed by international nongovernmental organizations that focus on environmental protection, human rights, religious evangelizing, emergency humanitarian relief, and the like. These individuals tend to have more face-to-face interaction with local populations and organizations at the grassroots. However, even the less insulated among the globalizers operate according to the dictates of their organizational and professional agendas rather than in the terms set by local customs, traditions or practices (Hunter and Yates 2002: 332–336).

Of course, opting to live in a particular sociocultural bubble is not an exclusively American practice. Similar tendencies are found among other nationalities or language groups, as well as among members of international professional organizations and organizations such as the European Union, the Association of Southeast Asian Nations, the Arab League, the United Nations. Nonetheless, because Americans predominate among the movers and shakers of current globalization (and the associated U.S.-style infrastructures and life-worlds are prominently present worldwide), they continue to play a central role in setting the agenda and general tone of today's globalization.

CULTURAL HYBRIDITY WITH AMERICAN OVERTONES

More generally, leading cultural theorists on globalization emphasize "deterritorialization" as one of the major driving forces in the modern world (e.g., Appadurai 1990: 301). It is not a new process, of course; local cultures have long been influenced — and even shaped — by outside forces, and, historically, have become "disembedded," detached from their local anchorings under capitalism (Harvey 1989: 199–352; Giddens 1990: 21–29). The current phase of globalization differs from the past because of the dramatically increased transnational movement of material foods, images, and people, which leads to new mixtures of culture or hybridization. Transnational capitalism's division of labor and free trade produce multivariegated fusions, blurred borders, cultural "homelessness" as well as cosmopolitanism. Its worldwide infrastructure of airports, malls, computer terminals, chain restaurants, and other "nonplaces" erase distinct space and history, whereas its basic means of communication, the Internet, is even more radically deterritorialized (Tomlinson 1999: 108–120).

Cultural goods with indefinite origins abound; what appears to be traditional, on closer inspection is invented, and what seems to be homogeneous, is hybrid. "American made" products often entail design and engineering ideas, parts, and labor from many nations, which makes it hard to specify a country of origin. Yet globalization's "nonplaces" and many of its hybridized cultural forms bear a clear American imprint. American tourists and expatriates often feel at home in these spaces, while locals may undergo at least a tinge of unease or displacement, even while simultaneously enjoying the consumption of things American. (However, some locals are so thoroughly acquainted with American culture through vicariously taking part in it and regular visits to the country that they do not have any trouble adjusting.) The implications of what Antonio and Bonanno aptly call "U.S.-accented cultural hybridity" are apparent in the tendency of both advocates and critics of capitalist globalization (e.g., Friedman and Barber) to treat McDonald's as the quintessential symbol of "Americanization-globalization" (Antonio and Bonanno 2000: 55–56)

Let us take a closer look here at the issue of cultural hybridization. What we do know from the anthropological and historical records is that all cultures are hybrid. Therefore the concept of hybridity is problematic in so far as it suggests the mixing of completely separate and homogeneous cultural spheres or identities. In fact, "contemporary accelerated globalization means the hybridization of hybrid cultures" (Nederveen Pieterse 1995: 64). The concept is acceptable, though, "as a device to capture cultural change by way of a strategic cut or temporary stabilization of cultural categories" (Barker 2000: 203). But hybridization has another side that makes it even more complex. Referring to a general tendency, Nederveen Pieterse mentions examples like the following (of which many more could be given): "Mexican schoolgirls dressed in Greek togas dancing in the style of Isidora Duncan" that reflect "transnational bourgeois class affinities, mirroring themselves in classical European culture." "Chinese tacos and Irish bagels" that manifest "ethnic crossover in employment patterns in the American fast food sector." "Asian rap" that "refers to cross-cultural convergence in popular youth culture" (Nederveen Pieterse 1995: 50). Paradoxically, what appears from one perspective as hybridization, can from another angle be interpreted in terms of transnational affinities in sensibility or attitude. In other words, the reverse of cultural hybridity is transcultural convergence in cases such as these.

The emerging global culture brings along transnationally shared discourses encompassing sets of common structures and categories that organize differences. This means that the various cultures of the world are becoming different in uniform ways. The anthropologist Richard Wilk calls this phenomenon "structures of common difference" (Wilk 1995; cf. du Gay 1997: 42–43) The term refers to a new global hegemony that is a hegemony of structure, not of content. The new global cultural system promotes difference, but selects the dimensions of difference. As Wilk explains:

> The local systems of difference that developed in dialogue with Western modernism are becoming globalized and systematized into structural equivalents of each other. This globalized system exercises hegemony not through content, but through form. In other words, we are not all becoming the same, but we are portraying, dramatizing and communicating our differences to each other in ways that are more widely intelligible. The globalizing hegemony is to be found in what I call structures of common difference, which celebrate particular kinds of diversity while submerging, deflating or suppressing others [Wilk 1995: 124].

An excellent example of such structures of common difference can be found in the way in which popular music today is categorized in distinct genres by transnationally operating music businesses. In distinguishing genres, the big record companies (only four remain after several mergers) have created categories like "folk music," "world music" or "indigenous music," into which the immense variety of globally available music styles is forced. The local producers and musicians concerned — many living and working in developing countries — have had little control over the categorization of their music. Moreover, Western consumers largely determine the criteria for "authenticity" and quality. In order to gain recognition and compete on the world market, these musicians are obliged to adapt their products to the established categories and expectations (Breidenbach and Zukrigl 2001: 116). Consequently, structural molds such as these tend to be biased towards a Western, predominantly Anglo-American staple that expresses the global hegemonic position of the metropolitan centers concerned.

Other examples that fit even better with our interest in America's global influence, are Hollywood film awards for "foreign films" and the production of "European films" for a global market. The definitions of the film genres and the films that tend to be selected and win at least a modicum of popularity often are geared to American audiences, attuned to U.S.-dominated aesthetic standards and stereotypical views of "Europeanness," "Europe" and the national characters of individual European countries. This tendency has also been fostered by American production companies heavily involved in filmmaking in Britain, Italy and France during the 1960s, for instance (Pells 1997: 226–227). Other cultural locations likewise show "the grammars of national cinemas" being transformed for American, respectively "world," distribution. In recent years Chinese films, for example, have been tailored to American sensibilities and outlooks in order to gain prestige and sales, among other things, by exoticizing Chinese culture and history for American/Western audiences (Ritzer and Stillman 2003: 37).

Finally, as Nederveen Pieterse points out, we must recognize that power inequities are involved in hybridization itself:

> Relations of power and hegemony are inscribed and reproduced within hybridity for wherever we look closely enough we find the traces of asymmetry in culture, place, descent. Hence hybridity raises the question of the terms of the mixture, the conditions of mixing and mélange. At the same time it's important to note the ways in which hegemony is not merely reproduced but *refigured* in the process of hybridization [Nederveen Pieterse 1995: 57].

If one is interested in U.S. cultural power, as we are in this book, a perspective on relations of power and hegemony should preferably be used when examining the degrees of freedom that recipients of American and other external cultural influences have at their disposal in specific cases. The basic issue here is the existence, in varying degrees, of a "U.S.-accented cultural hybridity." This gives rise to a series of important questions such as: What are the conditions of the cultural mélange in question? To what extent are the terms of the borrowing and mixing that go on at the local level set by U.S.-based or U.S.-related emitters and distributors? What is the actual substance of the American influence? And if there is a cultural hegemony on the part of the U.S., how exactly is this reproduced at the receiving end? Moreover, if this hegemony is also being refigured, what kind of transformation is taking place? Is the American stake becoming stronger or weaker in comparison with other foreign influences at the local level? Have the carriers of American influence, deliberately or not, aligned themselves with conveyers of other foreign influences in order to form a new power bloc, and are there any tensions or conflicts between these forces?

But one should not leave it at this; one must preferably try to get behind or underneath the cultural sphere. Underlying cultural globalization are "structural inequalities" and "systems of exploitation that sustain them," which "in the new conceptual world order of cultural globalization ... slide quietly out of sight" (Murdock 1997: 101) or, as I would add, may never come to light at all. The following is an attempt to chart the structural dimensions that are below the cultural surface of today's Americanization-globalization.

RECONFIGURATION OF THE NATION-STATE GEARED TO NEOLIBERAL GLOBALIZATION

"Hyperglobalist" thinkers of globalization, across the political spectrum, contend that transnational capitalism, international governance, and hybrid global culture have effectively put a halt to the modern nation-state (Held et al. 1999: 3–5). However, their concept of globalization tends to underestimate the persistence of the nation-state as a political form and economic entity (Golding and Harris 1997: 8). The existing evidence points to the sustained importance of the nation-state as a political and economic entity, and this certainly applies to the United States. On balance, nation-states are not withering, but rather are undergoing a transformation in their structures and processes, which implies the modification of their institutional forms and their policies by transnational forces (Shaw 1997; Cohen and Kennedy 2000: 89–93). These changes are a pre-condition for further globalization *and* a consequence of it. But this reconfiguration is also to some extent a question of deliberate choice, in which the state participates in "legitimating a new doctrine about its role in the economy," central to which is "a growing consensus among states to further the growth and strength of the global economy" (Sassen 1996b: 22). As Robinson emphasizes, "we are not witnessing 'the death of the nation-states' but their transformation into *neoliberal states*" (Robinson 1996: 36, italics in original). This has also led to a significant shift in power between capital and labor, because the transnationalization of markets — and the expansion of their spatial scope — leaves labor with declining resources, weakened organization, and as yet only meager opportunities for adequate counter-strategies (Ross 2000: 79).

Since economic globalization is politically determined, shifting political preferences should be capable of creating different social conditions. The rapid expansion of global economic activity since the 1980s is first of all a result of political decisions made by governments to lift the international restrictions on capital. Once these decisions were implemented, the technology came into its own, and accelerated the speed of communication and calculations that helped bring the movement of money to an extraordinary level. The implication is that nation and territory do still make a difference — even in a globalized context. As yet these conventional political units remain important, operating either in the form of modern nation-states or "global cities" where global processes carried by corporate complexes and supporting specialized services (financing, accounting, information processing etc.) actually take place. The latter strategic places are embedded in national territories and therefore stay, at least partly, within the juridical orbit of various state-centered regulatory systems (Sassen 1996a, 1996b: 1–30).

In the ongoing process of capitalist transnationalization, corporate geography has been reconfigured into a new system of worldwide time-space connections, but they are hardly decentered nor fully integrated, retaining a hierarchical structure and uneven distribution. Like other business organizations, TNCs are certainly not "placeless" or "deterritorialized entities" (Dicken 1998: 193–200; 1999: 43–44). Most are based in the richest "developed countries," that usually provide the best overall socioeconomic, political, and legal bases for their operations, and where their owners and managers reside. It comes as no surprise, then, that by the late 1990s the United States was the number one host- and home economy to transnational corporations, and that New York, as a major global city, was the world's largest center of fiber-optic cable services (Sassen 1998: 184–194; Antonio and Bonanno 2000: 57).

Secretary of Labor in the first Clinton Administration, economist Robert Reich, argued in *The Work of Nations* that wealth is accumulated at the site where managers design corporate plans and make strategic decisions, and technicians carry out research and development, not where the corporations or manufactured goods originate (Reich 1991). For the time being, in the case of American TNCs that site is usually still some "location" within the United States — even though higher-skilled jobs in research and development, for example, are also increasingly moved abroad. But rather than outsourcing to a local company or a foreign affiliate of another TNC, off shoring usually takes place internally through the establishment of foreign affiliates (called intra-firm "captive offshoring"), especially in cases where strict control of an activity is crucial, information is sensitive, and internal interaction is important, or when a company seeks to capture savings and other advantages (UNCTAD 2004b: 25–26).[8] This does not mean that TNCs do not pose problems for national policymaking, but instead that the withering of the nation-state in the face of these corporations has been exaggerated.

One should bear in mind that the "territory" from which today a disproportionate amount of goods, services, information and cultural practices emanate, the United States, remains crucial. Ritzer has made this argument specifically with regard to fast-food restaurants and credit cards, and other, what he calls "new means of consumption" (including superstores, cybermalls, televised home shopping networks, theme restaurant chains, and so on), which he considers "very distinctive products of the United States, that is of a single nation-state" (Ritzer 1998: 82–83). In my view, this "American territory" also encompasses U.S. enclaves and transnational corporations outside the country that are within its military, political-economic, and cultural orbits. Furthermore, I want to broaden this to include other goods and practices from the U.S. that have been exported abroad.

Ultimately, it is the transnational corporations that lie at the base of McDonaldization and the new means of consumption, and who benefit most from their success. More generally "Americanization — globalization" is to a great extent driven by such corporations. They operate largely free of state control and follow their profit-oriented interests, which means that U.S.-based corporations may leave their country of origin if that suits their bottom lines better (Misyoshi 1993: 737; Ritzer 2001: 180). For this reason TNC-led "Americanization — globalization" needs to be set within the framework of a restructuring of capitalism that is aimed at increasing production, trading areas, and profit through further rationalization of both production and consumption on a transnational scale.

Sklair's "global system theory" entails a conception that focuses on transnational corporations and transnational practices, which offers fruitful insights here. These practices are analytically distinguished on three levels: economic, political, and the realm of what Sklair calls "culture-ideology." While acknowledging that not all culture is ideology, even in capitalist societies, he combines the two terms because in his view consumerism in the global system can only be fully understood as a culture-ideology practice.

Although consumer cultures have existed for centuries, today we are dealing with "the systematic blurring of the lines between information, entertainment, and promotion of products," which has led to "the reformulation of consumerism that transforms all the mass media and their contents into opportunities to sell ideas, values, products, in short, a consumerist world-view" (Sklair 2002: 108). This consumer culture is foremost exemplified — both symbolically and substantively — by the shopping mall, not only in North America, but increasingly across the world. In a world that is largely structured by global capitalism, each of the levels is typically characterized by a major institutional form. The transnational corporation is the major locus of transnational economic practices and the transnational capitalist class[9] of transnational political practices, while the major site of transnational cultural practices can be found in the culture-ideology of consumerism.

TRANSNATIONAL CORPORATIONS AND THE U.S. IN THE GLOBAL ECONOMIC SYSTEM

Several analysts have depicted the transnational economy at the turn of the new century as an "empire" ruled by the United States, with strong support from its G7 partners,[10] and assistance from local members of the transnational capitalist class in other parts of the world (Gowan 1999; 2001; Harvey 2000: 53–72; Panitch 2000; Balakrishnan 2003). Even if one does not accept this concept of U.S. imperialism, it is hard to deny that the transnational capitalist system is, at least partly, the result of the United States' neoliberal policies, its use of economic, military, and sociocultural might, and the support given by U.S. allies. After having summarized the state of affairs in the late 1990s, in *Globalization Unmasked*, the international developmental sociologists Petras and Veltmeyer came to the unreserved conclusion: "To the degree that the TNCs control the world economy, it is largely the U.S. that has re-emerged as the overwhelmingly dominant power. Insofar as the very largest companies are the leading forces in eliminating smaller companies through mergers and acquisitions, we can expect the U.S.-based TNCs to play a major role in the process of concentration and centralization of capital" (Petras and Veltmeyer 2001: 62–63).

In 2000, the United States was home to fifty-nine of the hundred largest companies in the world by market value — compared to thirty-one for Europe and seven for Japan. Of the 500 largest global companies listed in the *Financial Times*, 219 were American, 158 European, and 77 Japanese. In foreign direct investment (a significant indicator of global economic influence), America invested and received nearly twice as much as the next ranking country (Britain) and accounted for half of the top ten investment banks. American e-commerce was three times that of Europe and seven of the top ten software companies were located in the U.S. Forty-two of the top seventy-five brands were American, as well as nine of the top ten business schools (Nye 2002: 36).

Yet in recent years there have been major shifts in the relative importance of the TNCs' home countries and the number of TNCs that are not or hardly U.S.-owned or -managed has increased. According to an UNCTAD report on foreign direct investment and transnational corporations, in 2002, almost 90 percent of the top 100 TNCs were headquartered in the Triad (European Union, Japan, the United States), and the EU was leading with more than half of the top 100. The United States accounted for somewhat more than a quarter, while Japan's share had decreased to less than ten percent. In 2004, of the 140 largest *Fortune*-500 firms 61 were headquartered in Europe and only 50 in the United States. And of the 500 largest firms, only 185 then had their home base in the United States, while non-American TNCs grew much faster, especially those in Japan, Mexico, and Brazil (UNCTAD 2004a: 11; Drucker 2005).

Economic power today is multipolar, with the United States, Europe, and Japan representing two-thirds of world product, and China rapidly becoming a major player as well. Although the United States is strictly speaking not an economic hegemon and often must bargain on an equal footing with Europe, it is economically still very dominant because it constitutes such a large part of the global market in trade and finance. In some parts of the world it even has regained economic supremacy. This applies especially to what the United States traditionally sees as its own "backyard," Latin America (Smith 2000: 236). In the last few years, however, there has been a revival of leftist populism and socialism in several countries of this continent that aim to counter U.S. economic dominance.

To date, the U.S. economy remains the major driving force of global growth, but this is more due to the massive consumption of its citizens than to leadership in productive industries. The United States has a slight advance in high-tech communications and biotechnology but not in manufacturing technology as a whole — it lost its dominance in global production during the 1970s. And in its overall volume of production and trade the United States is roughly on a par with two other economic blocs, about level with the European Union, somewhat ahead of Japan/East Asia. Notwithstanding its strong position in these organizations, the United States can also not act unilaterally in bodies like the World Trade Organization (WTO), the G8, OECD and other global organizations of economic coordination. Moreover, rival regional blocs benefited more from the end of the Cold War than the United States. Although the United States is still the world leader in finance, its power in global finance began to erode in the 1990s. As yet the dollar is the world's reserve currency, but the world's bankers are showing a tendency to hold more of their balances in euros. The value of Wall Street trading is almost two-thirds that of the whole world's stock markets. Foreigners invest through Wall Street in the U.S. economy, offering leeway to American consumers to amass large debts and American government to finance their massive trade and budget deficits (Mann 2003: 49–50; Harvey 2005: 193, 197).

Neither the United States nor the global economy has been in good shape recently. For decades there has been the marked tendency of capitalist overaccumulation in the global economy (Brenner 2002). During the 1990s this was covered up by the financial dealings that culminated in the hi-tech/dot.com stock-market bubble and the ensuing bubble burst, leading to a major financial crisis that was strongest in the United States, enhanced by fraudulent accounting practices by some of its major corporations, like Enron and WorldCom, assisted by well-established accountancy firms like Arthur Anderson. The severe decline in U.S. equity values also reverberated on U.S. bond markets. This is a structural problem, resulting from the dominance of finance over productive capitalism in the United States that is basically a problem for the entire global economy and demands multilateral cooperation, involving coordination among the United States, Europe, Japan and more recently China. American unilateral militarism, especially when it leads to severe budget deficits, only exacerbates the problem (Mann 2003: 50–51).

Crucial in current globalization is that the American market serves as "buyer of last resort" for the global economy, because it is the only major economy that year after year absorbs the large surpluses of production from other nations (Greider 2004).[11] Since 1994 the annual outflow of financial returns paid to foreign investors on the assets they held in America exceeded all of the profits, dividends and interest payments that American firms and investors collected from their investments abroad (Greider 1997: 201–202). In 2005 the balance-of-payments deficit was 5.8 percent of the Gross Domestic Product (725.8 billion dollars), 17.5 percent higher than the deficit of the year before and close to 70 percent of the sum of all deficits globally. It was the fourth year in a row that the negative balance between exports and imports increased. In 2005 the budget deficit was almost 3 percent, not uncommon in the advanced capitalist world, but in Europe and Japan citizens continued saving (Henwood 2005; Schinkel 2005b).[12] Ironically, the United States is thus behaving in a Keynesian way — accumulating large federal deficits and consumer debts — while insisting that everyone else must follow neoliberal rules. Contrary to traditional Keynesianism, however, the redistributions in this case go to the big corporations, their CEOs, and their financial and legal advisors at the expense of the poor, the working and middle classes, even ordinary shareholders (including the pension funds) — not to forget future generations (Harvey 2005: 142; Duménil and Lévy 2004; Giroux 2004; Jacobs and Skocpol 2005).

Basically, this enormous foreign lending keeps the U.S. economy going so that American consumers can keep buying ever more imports, thus increasing the already high trade deficits. This makes the U.S. economy extremely vulnerable to the flight of capital and a collapse of the dollar, but this vulnerability is two-sided — it also applies to those foreign economies that use the U.S. market as the major repository for their excess productive capacity. If the United States crashes economically, they will go down with it. The fact that central bankers of countries like China, Japan, and Taiwan lend large amounts of money to cover U.S. deficits has a strong element of self-interest. It is predicated on a basic economic logic: thus they fund U.S. consumerism that constitutes a major market for their own products. In the end, this heavy, unbalanced reliance on finance capital that the United States employs to assert its dominance, has a self-destructive element in it. There is a limit to the degree in which other countries are capable and willing to fund the U.S. deficits (Harvey 2003: 68–74; Johnson 2004: 265–267).

Despite America's economic vulnerability and diminished economic world power especially in manufacturing, it still puts a heavy stamp on today's corporate globalization, however.

INSTITUTIONAL ARRANGEMENTS POSITIVELY SKEWED TOWARD U.S. FINANCIAL–ECONOMIC INTERESTS

U.S. power over the IMF, World Bank and other international development banks has significantly increased after the end of the Cold War. Importantly, both the IMF and the World Bank were during the 1980s progressively invaded and influenced by neoliberal thinkers and their dogmatic belief in market liberalization as economic remedy in each and every case. The Keynesian interventionist principles upon which the World Bank had been founded, were now considered to be disruptive for "private sector growth" (Hutton 2003: 242–251). International economic cooperation and economic development were moved from being the primary domain of the United Nations to that of the World Bank, the IMF and the WTO. The UN Economic and Social Council was degraded to a mere discussion platform at which countries receiving aid could only ventilate their hopes and longings. Formally, foreign countries are sovereign states, free to reject neoliberal programs for economic development. But this becomes a problem when they fall into debt, for they are highly dependent on U.S.-dominated loan conditions and interest rates. In fact, the U.S. Treasury controls the IMF and World Bank, and if they do not honor a loan request, all the other international lending organizations will refuse a loan. This means that the U.S. Treasury is effectively the world's creditor bank and insists on neoliberal terms for debt repayment in the form of "structural adjustment programs" (Mann 2003: 62–65).

Many members of the transnationalist capitalist class (TNC executives, investors, bankers, globalizing politicians, state officials and other governmental actors, professionals, consumerist elites — categories that partly overlap, of course) are U.S. citizens and take the lead in the further global dissemination of neoliberal beliefs and practices that help transnational capitalism. American policymakers (both governmental and nongovernmental) are influential in circuits of the World Bank, the IMF, WTO, private international relations councils and think tanks that are active in this domain and more generally "Davos culture" (named after the Swiss ski resort where globalizing businessmen and politicians meet at the annual World Economic Forum summits). These institutions, as well as commodity exchanges, the G8 countries, the U.S. treasury, and so on are mostly controlled by those who share the interests of the major TNCs and the other way around.

But it is difficult to assess the precise significance of U.S. influence, as other countries (particularly America's G7 partners) generally tend to support the policies advocated by these American actors and agencies. There is a growing critique of the Washington Consensus from within the capitalist system, however, particularly with regard to development programs imposed on countries in the Third World by the World Bank and IMF (Makinson 2000).

The Organization for Economic Cooperation and Development (OECD) is one of the other major bodies promoting neoliberal globalization. This became especially clear in the OECD series of proposals (negotiated from 1995 onwards) for a Multilateral Agreement on Investment (MAI). If this would have materialized, it would have seriously diminished the already limited autonomy of local and state authorities to regulate foreign investments and the operations of TNCs in the realms of economic, environmental, and social affairs. However, the abandonment of the MAI was due as much to opposition from a wide variety of transnational and local campaigning groups as to a diminished appetite for further financial-market liberalization among some governments after the Asian crisis of 1997–98 and disagreements among G7 countries. In the end it was France's withdrawal from the process that led to MAI's demise in December 1998. The international campaign coordinated by "Friends of the Earth," "50 Years Is Enough," and other international and local groups succeeded in amplifying and leveraging government disagreements up to the point of defeating the MAI.[13]

But this defeat was a temporary — some observers would say, a Pyrrhic — victory for "global civil society." The issues to be covered under the MAI are back on the public global agenda again due to the inclusion of the General Agreement on Trade in Services (GATS) in the framework of the WTO. GATS encompasses a much wider area of activities than financial investment alone, and has become a major target of intense opposition from anti-capitalist globalization activists worldwide (Desai and Said 2001: 60–61).

One may safely conclude that "The international financial system has been shaped to extend US financial and political power, not to promote the world public good.... In the process it has opened up a bridgehead that has created opportunities for many more US corporate interests beside those of finance" (Hutton 2003: 251). This means that the United States does not have to rely on the kind of formal imperial institutions used by earlier leading powers such as Spain, France or Britain, as the British political scientist Alex Callinicos contends, since "the operation of the existing global order is structurally biased in its favour" (Callinicos 2001: 78–79). The latter has been strongly enhanced by America's soft power (that often turned out to be a tough power as well), which entails the ability "to structure a situation so that other nations develop preferences or define their interests in ways consistent with one's own nation" (Nye 1990: 191). In other words, the international financial system that is positively skewed toward U.S. interests includes voluntary affiliations with U.S. financial-economic and political power, and "self-colonization" (Wagnleiter 1993: 332) or "empire by invitation" (Lundestad 1986) among foreign elites and their constituencies. There is a link here with the Gramscian concept of hegemony and the associated idea of a deliberate creation of political consent across a sufficiently large spectrum of the population to acquire and retain power, in this case not only nationally but also internationally (Chapter 6).

When neoliberalization has to be accomplished by democratic means, it requires the active construction of political-ideological consent, as has happened since the early 1970s, beginning in the United States and Britain as epicenters, where neoliberalism became dominant during the Reagan (1981–1988) and Thatcher (1979–1990) years. From there it spread to many other parts of the world, varying from place to place. This forging of consent occurred through a wide variety of avenues: the corporations, the media and the many institutions that constitute civil society, such as the universities, schools, churches, voluntary and professional associations. The circulation of neoliberal ideas through the organization of think tanks (with corporate backing and funding), the capture of segments of certain media, and the turn of many intellectuals towards neoliberal ways of thinking, created a climate of opinion in support of neoliberalism as the sole guarantor of freedom and prosperity. These movements later took hold of political parties and, ultimately, state power.

Appeals to traditions and cultural values played a major part in gaining popular support for all of this. A programmatic approach employing rhetorics in terms of advancing the cause of "individual freedom" and the like could attract a mass base and conceal the drive to restore class power or install new class power. Furthermore, once the state apparatus made the neoliberal turn the government could take resort to persuasion, cooptation, bribery, and threat to maintain the climate of consent necessary to sustain its power. Reagan and Thatcher were particularly adapt as political leaders in this regard. In some cases neoliberalization occurred largely through coercion, either military as in Chile, where an early experiment with neoliberal state formation took place after Pinochet's coup in 1973 — followed by a similar restructuring in Argentina after a military takeover three years later — or financial via the operations of the IMF in the Philippines or Mozambique in the 1990s, for example. However, coercion can produce an acquiescent, even servile acceptance of the idea that there was and is no alternative but some neoliberal approach. Furthermore, as many oppositional movements attest, consent has often weakened or failed in various places. But, as David Harvey rightly emphasizes, we must look beyond this wide variety of ideological and cultural mechanisms to the qualities of everyday experience in order to identify the material foundations for the production of consent. It is at this level that neoliberalism permeated "common sense"[14] understandings of people and in many parts of the world increasingly came to be seen as a necessary, if not "natural" way of regulating the social order (Harvey 2005: 39–41).[15]

CONTINUING DOMINANCE OF U.S.-STYLE CORPORATE BUSINESS PRACTICES

Notwithstanding the ongoing further transnationalization, many of the corporations concerned have, at least for the time being, distinctive "American" features both with regard to corporate values and practices and the production and circulation of a wide variety of cultural goods. The ways in which transnational corporations and the transnational capitalist class have developed may have further loosened the connections between the U.S. and transnational flows of goods and practices carried by corporate globalization, yet beliefs and practices tied to American consumerism are still saliently being mediated to other parts of the world.

Even though in specific cases most of the capital comes from European, Japanese, Canadian, Australian or other foreign investors (more recently especially from India and China), the American-style "sameness" of many transnational corporate cultures and of the values, beliefs, and practices they disseminate across the world is apparent. For this to happen, these companies need not be U.S.-based or -owned nor even be governed by

American top managers or other staff. This is partly due to the fact that in most fields U.S. firms have led the way and set the standards with regard to corporate management practices and production techniques—though their origins are not always exclusively American[16] and to some extent local reworkings have taken place, thereby diminishing the American component. While capitalism developed in different ways in the leading industrial countries from the late nineteenth century through to the 1950s (Chandler 1990), the postwar reconstruction in Western Europe and Japan arguably laid the seeds for the later U.S.-led economic globalization and dominance of corporate capitalism along American lines. During the postwar boom there was some imposition from the U.S. side and considerable copying and local adaptation of the American (then predominantly Fordist) corporate model, but also some counter-reaction (Zeitlin and Herrigel 2000).

In the 1970s and 1980s, corporate models generally changed under the pressure of recession and competition. The resurgence of U.S. industrial competitiveness in the 1990s took very different forms across sectors such as automobiles, steel, electronics, telecommunications, and biotechnology. Some elements of the American "industrial revival" were rooted in domestic institutions and policies ranging from antitrust, health care, and defense procurement to the development of interorganizational networks between firms, universities, and government agencies. But others were heavily dependent on selective appropriation and modification of "Japanese" (remade in America) methods of flexible production, rapid product development, and collaborative supplier relations. Consequently, there was no single, coherent American model of production to emulate.

Meanwhile, the behavior of transnational firms is becoming much more responsive to multiple governments beyond the government of their country of origin. This inevitably sets a process of homogenization in motion, a process that is further enhanced by the growing practice of joint ventures and strategic alliances between two or more companies of different nationality (Strange 1997: 190). Today, however, several conditions apparently pressure TNC business organization and production across the world to converge on the U.S. model of "free market" capitalism characterized by relentless globalization of production, investment, and capital markets; the creation of new opportunities for detaching domestic firms from national systems of finance, innovation, skill formation and industrial relations; and celebration of "glamorous" fast-moving American commercial/managerial culture and its hero worship of CEOs (in contrast to more levelheaded forms of managerial culture tied to forms of social market capitalism) that appeals to members of the transnational capitalist class intent on quick moneymaking (Zeitlin 2000: 46–48). These conditions include the massive growth of international trade, the huge U.S. trade deficits since the mid–1990s (with the precarious intertwinement of American and foreign economic interests at the background), and the accelerated, more immediate influence of financial capitalism, in combination with the size of the U.S. market, the (selective) U.S. pressure at the WTO and elsewhere to attain level playing fields in antitrust and corporate governance, as well as U.S. pressures on international business standards after Enron.

Yet most important in this homogenization of TNC cultures has been the voluntary adoption of neoliberal beliefs and practices characteristic of the American form of capitalism by corporate managements of many stripes elsewhere in the world. In the 1990s, many countries in Latin America and Asia, Eastern Europe and Russia moved toward tough-minded forms of capitalism on their own. In this process the United States became "a role model for shaping *world* capitalism" with the resurgence of the U.S. economy and its "hard-edged form of capitalism that tends towards the Darwinian" compared to its

European counterparts (Bracken 1997: 11, 16). The management of some TNCs may deviate to a degree from the American exemplars (for instance, with regard to personnel management or social policy), but nevertheless feel compelled to conform by the need to become and remain competitive in the global marketplace.

The U.S.-style, relative homogeneity of corporate cultures can further be explained by a conducive combination of social mechanisms and institutional arrangements. First there is the education and socialization of newcomers into U.S. management styles. Most business education is dominated by American managerial ideologies and practices. Business schools started out in the United States, and were then introduced in Europe, and have shown an enormous growth since the 1960s, increasingly also in the rest of the world. Leading American business schools have formed strategic alliances with counterparts elsewhere in the world, which also led to the founding of international business schools, as yet positively biased toward U.S. business models. Other routes through which U.S. managerial thinking has reached other countries are the operations of foreign affiliates of successful and well-known American companies. Of special interest are the large American management consulting firms that have been operating all across the world. Quite a number of non-American executives have participated in management development programs abroad, especially in the United States or their affiliated counterparts in Europe (e.g. INSEAD and IMD in Switzerland) and elsewhere.

U.S. neoliberal think tanks (such as the Heritage Foundation, the Hoover Institute, the Center for the Study of American Business and the American Enterprise Institute), experts, and mentors have infiltrated important domains such as the media, education, professional organizations and politics. They have also been influential to economists, globalizing politicians and businessmen abroad, for example, in various countries in Latin America (Dominguez 1997). Since about 1990 neoliberalism has dominated most economics departments in the major U.S. research universities as well as the business schools (including those of prestigious universities such as Stanford and Harvard). The U.S. research universities were and are also training grounds for many foreigners who take what they learn back to their countries of origin (in education, research, the media and policymaking) as well as into international institutions such as the IMF, the World Bank, and the UN. Thus a transnational discourse of neoliberalism has been created that has a global reach by now (Harvey 2005: 44, 54).

Another source of inspiration have been the frequent speaking tours of American management gurus abroad and a widespread focus on American companies and management practices in media and business magazines. A significant influence in the diffusion of the American way of management[17] in many Western and Westernized parts of the world is also the large number of popular books on management originating in the United States, either in their original version, in translation, or as summarized in books written by local management thinkers.

Particularly in Europe there are some counter-strains in management thinking that recognize gaps between management theory as derived from North American business schools and local practices. They advocate a management style more based on local characteristics such as the political and cultural pluralism of Western Europe (Thurley and Wirdenius 1989). During the past few decades Japan has often been mentioned in this connection as a country especially apt in borrowing U.S. management practices and adapting them to the local environment. The question arises, however, to what extent current practices differ from the American-style corporate model. The *keiretsu* system of tight relationships with suppliers and financial institutions remains a distinctive feature of Japanese businesses' institutional framework, that constrains "Americanization" of Japanese corporate policies. The system's group ties with permanent suppliers hinder free competition to set price levels of their products. But since the 1990s there has been much pressure on Japan to give up the close relationships and cross-subsidies concerned, and to adopt the U.S. competitive model. We must also remember that U.S. corporate capitalism both at home and abroad does not always live up to its self-professed free-market doctrine either. While "embedded liberalism" as it developed during the postwar boom is in decay (Ruggie 1994), American "free enterprise capitalism" is still subjected to various government interventions, albeit hardly of a New Deal-type anymore.

Recently, within European business circles occasional calls have been made for completely abandoning the U.S. corporate model, referring to its overemphasis on narrow-minded shareholder interests and short-term thinking by mighty, self-interested CEOs obsessed by stock market results, and its associated highly competitive, individualistic culture within the firm. One example is the Dutch entrepreneur Donald Kalff, who argues that instead of continuing or adopting this "sharks model," which is detrimental to corporate achievements in a broader sense, one should build on the various valuable business models that can still be found in continental Europe and are closer to European norms and values — which models aim first of all for economic value addition rather than mere financial profit. Kalff suggests that this should entail more pluriformity in managerial thinking and a more team-oriented corporate culture based on trust and cooperation.

In this conception, the primary focus is on social innovation, since technology and financial investments are abundantly available in Europe. It means in particular that experienced and well-informed private financiers and bankers in Europe (including those of the European Investment Bank) maintain long-term relationships with entrepreneurs and managers of companies and are intensively involved in designing custom-made, and, according to expectation, strongly competitive solutions that can easily be adapted to the company's changing position in the global market (Kalff 2004). However, while the significance of middle managers' operations is duly recognized, there is little interest here in the contributions of the rank and file among employees to the company's achievements and the ways in which trade unions, or more generally labor representatives, could be involved. Dissenting voices like Kalff's, and kindred ones among senior managers of a few large European companies, are notable exceptions to the general rule. The overall trend towards U.S.-style managerial thinking remains a fact.

JUDICIAL AND OTHER REGULATORY MECHANISMS IN THE AMERICAN MOLD

The strong global impact of the Anglo-American[18] form of capitalism is also reflected in the juridical domain. From the early 1990s onwards, in business law the Anglo-American model of the business enterprise and competition began to replace the European-continental model of legal artisans' and corporatist control over the profession (Sinclair 1994). Globalization and governmental deregulation have not entailed an absence of regulatory regimes and institutions for the governance of international economic relations. Private regulatory systems such as international commercial arbitration and a variety of institutions including debt security and bond rating agencies that fulfill rating and advisory functions, are essential for the operation and expansion of transnational capitalism. Although they are functioning as mechanisms of what Rosenau has called "governance without government" (Rosenau 1992), these agencies still tend to have ties to specific nation-states, and Anglo-American agencies in these domains have significantly expanded their influence abroad.

Since the 1980s there has been an enormous growth of arbitration resulting from the globalization of economic activity which led to sharp competition for the arbitration business. Multinational legal firms further increased the competition, using their capacity to look for those institutions, sets of rules, laws, and arbitrators best suited to their interests. Thus, the large British and U.S. law firms have used their power in the international business world to impose their conception of arbitration and more largely of the practice of law. This was at the expense of among others France, which used to have an outstanding position in financial and insurance services, but French law and accountancy firms found themselves at an increasing disadvantage in legal and accounting services given the difference between the French legal system (the Napoleonic Code) and Anglo-American law that dominates international transactions (Carrez 1991; Sassen 1996b: 44).

Specialists in conflict and arbitration belong to the two major groups that have dominated legal practice in the United States: corporate lawyers, experienced as negotiators in the creation of contract, and trial lawyers, specialized in jury trials. As Dezalay and Garth have pointed out, the growing importance in the 1980s of such transactions as mergers and acquisitions, as well as antitrust and other litigation, contributed to a new specialization in which judicial attacks and behind-the-scene wheelings and dealings are strategically combined to reach the optimum outcome for the client. Under these conditions, judicial recourse becomes a weapon in a struggle that is most likely to end before trial (Dezalay and Garth 1995; Sassen 1996b: 20–21). "Notwithstanding its deep roots in the continental tradition, especially the French and Swiss traditions, this system of private justice is becoming increasingly 'Americanized,'" as Saskia Sassen astutely observes (Sassen 2000: 59).

As with business law, since the mid–1980s U.S. debt security and bond rating agencies have become much more influential abroad, particularly in Europe, Japan, and Australia (Salacuse 1991; Sinclair 1994: 150). Also other U.S. legal practices such as the legal device of franchising are being spread across the world as is the emerging field of conflict resolution in business matters. This growing Anglo-American impact can be seen as "both a function and a promoter of U.S. financial orthodoxy, particularly its short-term perspective" (Sassen 1996b: 58). More generally, it demonstrates the changed yet still important role of the state in implementing the new global economic systems and in producing and legitimating the new legal systems within which such systems operate. However, the growing importance of electronic space in the global economy, and the accompanying "virtualization" of economic activities does raise questions of control in the global economy that not only go beyond the state but also beyond current notions of non-state-centered systems of coordination (Sassen 2000: 59).

Americanization has also become manifest in accounting practices. On January 1, 2005 the European Union introduced new accounting standards for all companies registered on the stock exchange in its 25 member states that are expected to make some difference regarding corporate transparency and accountability. These concern the existing International Financial Reporting Standards (IFRS) that have been developed worldwide in the previous years, which countries such as Australia, China, Japan and a number of Latin American and African countries have already introduced or will do soon. Their purpose is to make the financial reporting of companies more transparent through a common set of accountancy rules, which, as expected consequence, will make them better comparable for investors from different countries. (The latter seems to be a rather optimistic view, because of the separate laws that are still in place in the various countries that have to be taken into account as well.) In light of the turn towards Anglo-American-inflected regulatory measures, it comes as no surprise, then, that this system had already moved in the direction of the other major worldwide system, the American US GAAP, while the latter had shifted somewhat towards the IFRS, albeit more slowly.

The core of IFRS is that each financial year the balance sheet figures must all represent their current "real market values." The idea behind this is: what is the company worth financially if it would be sold right now?, which easily leads to great fluctuations in the annual figures over time, due especially to vicarious values of the so-called derivatives, and to a lesser extent also of its estimated goodwill and financial obligations regarding pension rights. European CEOs and financers are inclined to consider this short-term focus as "very American." Traditionally, they tend to look more at a company's continuity over the years (de Graaf 2004), although in recent years one can notice a move towards the former perspective among European businessmen. This means that as yet the American accounting rules are apparently more influential in setting the overall tone.

SHORT-TERM COMPETITIVE ADVANTAGES OF
SHAREHOLDER OVER STAKEHOLDER CAPITALISM

There is another key factor, however, that explains the growing importance of U.S.-style capitalism globally. American corporations, or other firms that model themselves after these, have — at least in the short term — powerful competitive advantages compared to businesses firmly embedded in social market economies in Europe and Asia. The social costs that the latter firms carry, and which enable them to function as social institutions without undermining the social cohesion of the larger societies in which they operate, are at the same time burdens in any competition with enterprises operating in global free markets. Hitherto American corporations have only few obligations to deal with such "externalities." Hence the kind of stock-market based, corporate capitalism aimed at short-term interests of CEOs and shareholders that American companies epitomize — and is linked to a minimal welfare system and flexible labor markets — tends to crowd out social market capitalism and other forms of associative, stakeholder capitalism (Gray 1998: 78–79). Needless to say, this changeover is also deliberately assisted by those members of the business world and political elites at the local level who welcome U.S.-style corporate capitalism.

In the case of stakeholder capitalism, which still exists in various forms in Europe in particular, management of these companies retains the notion that shareholders should not become an overprivileged sectional interest group and try to take care of the interests of the corporation as a whole. This includes honoring the social contract conception regarding employment regulation and the character of the welfare state, and also meeting certain obligations to the society of which the company is part. Such an inclusive approach may be reinforced through a shareholder base being committed to the company whatever the share price (for example, family or employee ownership or cross-share holdings in which friendly companies hold shares in each other — especially relevant in attempts to counter hostile takeovers) or through a system of corporate governance that protects the company from free-market extravagances (Hutton 2003: 180–181).

Europe's stakeholder capitalism is under continuing pressures from both the capital markets and neoliberal ideologues, and part of Europe's business and financial elite is increasingly attracted to American capitalism with its high financial benefits for top exec-utives and glamorous deal-making. The European Union has also tried (although not con-sistently) to enforce the free-trade rules of the WTO, thereby, oddly enough, even challenging the United States in specific cases when individual U.S. states such as Mass-achusetts and Maryland (in 1997–1998) tried to uphold American laws to prevent con-tracting with European companies doing business with brutal dictatorships in Burma and Nigeria respectively (Nader 2004: 236–237). Yet, notwithstanding these pressures and temptations, the distinctive European approach to capitalism, which is deeply embedded in Europe's economic and social institutions and values, has been able to survive thus far. One may wonder how long this situation is going to last. Based on thorough field research of globalizing capitalism in Western Europe and interviews with leading experts on both sides of the Atlantic, Will Hutton, journalist and director of the Work Foundation (a British think tank), concluded a few years ago:

> The single currency and single market, if they are not organised as an economic and social space around European values, uniquely expose European capitalism to its de facto Americanisation — with all that implies in terms of asking Europe's employees to accept greater risk, an enfeebled social contract, wider inequality and a challenge to the stakeholder routes taken by European enterprise to raise productivity. Europe's increasingly lightly governed economic space has come into being just as globalisation has taken wing, endowing corporations and financial markets alike with yet more autonomous power at the expense of the traditional state. Each individual Euro-pean country finds itself trying to protect its own system, with the EU offering scant support. This Europe, with its democratic deficit, dedicated as it is to enlarging the four economic free-doms — free movement of goods, capital, people and services — while building a single currency and single market is, despite itself, developing as an engine of the conservative right and a friend of corporate Europe [Hutton 2003: 387].

This observer on the social-democratic left then still saw opportunities for sustain-ing Europe's various stakeholder capitalisms and their accompanying social contracts. He thought this would be significantly enhanced if Europeans acted "systematically and in concert," and in cooperation with liberal countervailing powers in the U.S (*ibid*.: 46). But it does not look like this is going to happen soon, if ever.

In the late 1990s, John Gray expected that "A global market framed to reflect Amer-ican business practice will undermine social markets built on the post-war German model; but it will not turn German capitalism into a variation of market individualism. Instead it will result in a transmutation of capitalism in both Germany and America" (Gray 1998: 58–59). Contrary to his view, it seems today that, due to global power differences and enticements to local corporate and political elites, this "transmutation" is likely to bring Germany closer to America's model than vice versa. A leading French businessman and intellectual Michel Albert in *Capitalism vs. Capitalism* (1993) predicted a future struggle between the preservation of a reformed German-style capitalism throughout Europe ver-sus the Americanization of Europe's continental economies. His view has proved to be correct for those Western European countries with a "Rhineland" form of organized cap-italism. Those with other models of organized capitalism show similar "Americanizing" tendencies. As political scientist Gregory Albo correctly foresaw in the mid–1990s, "it is not the Anglo-American countries who are converting to the Swedish or German mod-els but Germany and Sweden who are integrating the 'Anglo-American' model of income and work polarisation" (Albo 1994: 168). The French, relatively more state-led model of capitalism has not been immune to neoliberal influences either.

Perry Anderson, editor of the *New Left Review*, has stipulated that all existing tendencies of change in Europe point in one direction: "From labor market flexibility, shareholder value and defined contributions to media conglomerates, workfare and reality TV, the drift has been away from traditional patterns towards the American standard." And he also signaled that notwithstanding large European investments in the United States, there is hardly any evidence of reciprocal influence. "This unilateralism counts most, but features least in current complaints about U.S. international politics" (Anderson 2002: 26). However, this observation overlooks the massive involvement of European investors and corporate businesses in American capitalism. Part of the failure of a "social Europe" may be due to the mobilization of U.S. firms in Europe against Europe's social agenda from the early 1980s onwards (Lambert 1991). But it is also the spread of direct foreign investment, with mutual interpenetration among European, Asian (lately especially Chinese), and U.S. capitals, that reinforces this tendency of what political economist Robert Cox has called "emulative uniformity" (Cox 1987: 298–299).

DISSIMILAR GEOGRAPHICAL DEVELOPMENTS AND LIMITS TO AMERICA'S GLOBAL REACH

For the time being, there are still different national styles of capitalism, which are the results of the relations between big business and governments in question, the historical trajectories of each country and styles of regulation and corporate governance (Hampden-Turner and Trompenaars 1993; Berger and Dore 1996; Crouch and Streeck 1997; Hutton 2003: 298–322). But the crucial question is, how significant such differences ultimately are. In the current era of globalization most governments have less power over domestic and foreign TNCs than they once had, which makes it harder to take regulatory measures. A substantial number of governments also want to refrain from this and actively push neoliberal globalization further, which can be explained by the structure of the transnational capitalist class and the role of politicians and governmental officials therein, bent on capitalist globalization in this vein. It is in this regard that TNCs benefit from state power and public resources; the neoliberal "free market" does not exclude generous state business assistance (Antonio and Bonanno 2000: 58). Structural changes in the world market economy brought about by policy decisions and corporate strategies taken by those with structural power — as opposed to relational power (Strange 1989; Gill 1990) — are decisive here. It is particularly the combination of American structural power — military, financial and commercial — that has produced the asymmetry of regulatory power among the governments of capitalist countries outlined earlier (Strange 1997: 184–185, 189–190).

The governments of almost all states, from those that resurfaced after the collapse of the Soviet Union, post-apartheid South Africa to old-style social democracies and welfare states such as New Zealand and Sweden, have adopted, either voluntarily or in response to coercive pressures, some version of neoliberal theory and brought at least some policies and practices in line with it. This does not mean, however, that the rapid proliferation of neoliberal state forms throughout the world from the mid–1970s onwards is solely the result of U.S. imperial influence. As Harvey correctly points out, one should also take the domestic component of the neoliberal turn into account (which is not necessarily always the same as "empire by invitation" orientated on the U.S.). It was not the United States that forced Margaret Thatcher in 1979 to opt for a neoliberal approach or Deng Xiaoping in 1978 to embark on a course towards economic liberalization in communist

China. The same applies to Japan's move towards neoliberal reform under Prime Minister Junichiro Koizumi, leader of the ruling Liberal Democratic Party since 2001. Nor can the partial moves towards neoliberalization in India in the 1980s, Sweden in the early 1990s and the Netherlands since the mid–1990s easily be attributed to the imperial reach of U.S. power. On the other hand, however, there can be little doubt about the strong overall influence of U.S. economic power in this regard over the past thirty years (Harvey 2005: 9).

In order to understand the complicated and geographically uneven paths of neoliberalization it is necessary to examine more closely the class forces at work here. We may think of interventions on the part of business elites and financial interests in the production of ideas and ideologies through investment in think tanks, in the training of economical experts and technocrats, and in the command of the media. Other relevant phenomena are financial crises caused by capital strikes, capital flight, or financial speculation, or deliberately engineered to facilitate what Harvey calls "accumulation by dispossession"[19] and the latter-day enclosure of the commons (Harvey 2003: 137–182).

Attention should also be paid to local contextual conditions and institutional arrangements that vary greatly — the transition to neoliberalism has varied as a consequence. The changing internal balance of class forces within a particular state over time is an important factor. This refers to the relative powers of organized labor on the one hand and businesses and corporations on the other, and their respective capacities to put pressure on state power. Most interesting is the outcome of the complex interplay between external forces and internal dynamics. While in certain cases the former may reasonably be interpreted as dominant, in many instances the relationships are more intricate, whereby specific local groups adopt neoliberal restructuring as the way forward. In Chile, for example, it was the upper classes that sought U.S. help in mounting the coup of 1973, and it was they who opted for neoliberal reform with the help of a group of U.S.-trained local economists (known as "Los Chicago boys" because of their adoption of the neoliberal theories of Milton Friedman then teaching at the University of Chicago). In Sweden it was the employers who sought European integration as the means to "lock in" a neoliberal domestic agenda that was in jeopardy. IMF restructuring programs are unlikely to be implemented without a modicum of internal support from some influential locals. A number of countries that successfully rejected IMF advice regarding structural neoliberal reforms (including Malaysia and South Korea in the 1990s) suggest that there are limits to the U.S. Treasury — Wall Street — IMF complex's power.

Governmental attempts to create a "good business climate" to attract and retain geographically mobile capital also played a role in adopting neoliberal policy (or aspects thereof), particularly in the advanced capitalist societies (such as France). The degree of neoliberalization present in a society was increasingly taken by the IMF and the World Bank as an indicator of a good business climate, which led to significantly enhanced pressure on all states to adopt neoliberal reforms (World Bank 2004). Contingent geopolitical considerations have played their part as well. Compare, for example, South Korea's position as a frontline state in the Cold War that initially won it U.S. protectionism for its state-led developmentalism. On the other hand, U.S.- backed counter-revolutionary governments in Central America and elsewhere have frequently become the target of the IMF's penchant for neoliberal restructuring (Harvey 2005: 7–9, 115–118).

A HISTORICALLY CONTINGENT PROCESS
AND POSSIBLE TRANSFORMATIONS

A crucial issue remains the Americanness of much of today's globalization. "While it is wrong to characterise the US as monolithically and single-mindedly building a world order around a coherent strategic plan," contends Hutton, "it is equally wrong to characterise globalisation as some politically neutral force springing from ICT and the anonymous forces of trade and financial liberalisation…" (Hutton 2003: 230),[20] thus rejecting both the idea of a straightforward, undivided U.S. imperialist plot to rule the world and a depoliticized techno-economistic view of globalization. He bases his interpretation of current globalization as heavily U.S.-accented on the following argument, which deserves quoting at length:

> Globalisation has been politically shaped by the US deploying three simple guiding principles in an ad hoc but increasingly determined fashion. First, the US looks to exercise its power unilaterally rather than having its autonomy constrained by international alliances and treaty obligations. Second, it focuses aggressively and unilaterally on promoting the interests of those sectors and companies that plainly benefit, because of their ascendant market position or technological lead, from globalisation — notably financial services, ICT and, latterly, those with leadership in intellectual property. Third, it instinctively looks to market solutions and remedies, both as a matter of intellectual and ideological conviction, and because over a period these render it more likely that American interests will prevail. The bigger and more powerful tend to succeed in "free," unregulated markets. These three propositions have always been present in the United States as an autonomous continental great power, supported by its own conviction of its special destiny as an exceptional civilisation. But as conservatism has grown in influence and the various countervailing, international checks to the deployment of American power have fallen away, so each has become more marked [*ibid.*: 231].

As understood here, Americanization-globalization means the imposition and adoption of neoliberalism, a "free-market" orientation and the rule of the cash-nexus in virtually all domains in many places of the world through unilateral policies pursued by the U.S. as superpower, that do not meet strong countervailing checks internationally. The U.S. government thereby promotes and supports especially those sectors and corporations that clearly benefit from current globalization (notably financial services, high-tech information technology and intellectual property rights) because they are at the heart of it. This neoliberalization involves adherence to American-style programs of development, management and governance that entail specific forms of re-regulation and governance by new regulatory regimes structurally biased in favor of dominant interests in the USA, as well as those of the factions of the transnational capitalist class involved.

Thus the lion's share of the ongoing globalization of corporate capitalism amounts to the full-fledged "Americanization" of capitalism as a neoliberal project (Smith 2003: 455). To be sure, the current American face of a great deal of capitalist globalization is not essential or inherent to it, but a *contingent* form of a process that is necessary to the global diffusion of neoliberal ideas, values, and practices.[21] This means that if U.S. influence could be excluded, or in the as yet highly unlikely event that the United States ceased to foster corporate capitalism, this form of globalization need not end but could very well be continued by other states or agencies that are strong proponents of it. It has been suggested that this is likely to involve the handing over of the baton to a transnational, hegemonic capitalist constellation carried by major TNCs (Robinson 1996: 12).

To some extent economic globalization might obtain a different character, if American social liberalism would set the tone again in U.S. politics as it did with Roosevelt's

New Deal and Lyndon Johnson's Great Society programs in particular, and cooperate with political strains in Europe that value the public realm, equality and the importance of the social contract, and wish to promote fairness and equality of opportunity. In this regard Europe houses the major *potential* of countervailing power and values to U.S. neoliberalism today (Hutton 2003: 231–232), although Europe's actual condition is less rosy than some believers in the European Dream suggest (Rifkin 2004). On the other hand, however, the joint involvement of European and American political and economic elites in the further opening up of a "free market" in Europe concerns a form of subglobalization of the worldwide operations of corporate capitalism.

There are signs of growing resistance towards and resentment of the powers of the Wall Street–U.S. Treasury–IMF complex. Within the transnational capitalist class some divisions have become manifest in recent years. Rifts have emerged among the corporate elite (particularly over climate change and sweatshops) and among officials of the World Bank and other parts of the international financial establishment (specifically over the Asian financial crisis). Furthermore, some members of the OECD and G8 have expressed their skepticism on neoliberal globalization, and within the UN there have been some important struggles over closer links with corporate partners. Some of its earlier supporters (including the economists Jeffrey Sachs, Joseph E. Stiglitz, and Paul Krugman) and participants (such as the former international speculator George Soros) have come to criticize neoliberalism's major tenets, even to the point of suggesting some return to a modified Keynesianism or a more "institutional" approach — from better regulatory structures of global governance to closer supervision of the speculations of the financiers (Sklair 2002: 282; Sachs 2000; Stiglitz 2002; Krugman 2003; Soros 2002).

More radical challenges to neoliberalization come from the "anti-" or "alternative" globalization movement that includes many of the new social movements concentrated around environmental, feminist, minority liberation, labor or welfare issues, as well as movements for regional autonomy and specific religious movements. They all are joining hands in protest manifestations against the strategies of the principal globalizers of "Davos culture," trying to develop alternative forms of globalization on the basis of other, more humane social views. Some seek to de-link totally or partially from the process of neoliberal globalization. Others (such as the "Fifty Years Is Enough" movement) seek global social and environmental justice by reform or dissolution of the IMF, the WTO, and the World Bank (although, oddly enough, the core power of the U.S. Treasury is rarely targeted). Still others (particular environmentalists such as Greenpeace and Earth First!) emphasize the theme of "reclaiming the commons" (Gills 2001, Mertes 2004; Harvey 2005: 200–201).

The alternative globalization movement includes left-liberal strains (Held et al. 1999: 447–450) or those aimed at "reconstructing world order" along the lines of a "cosmopolitan social democracy" (Held and McGrew 2002: 118–136; Held 2004). Other counterstrains are an emerging anti-capitalist movement on a worldwide scale (Desai and Said 2001), partly explicitly aiming for "socialist globalization" (Sklair 2002: 298–321; Callinicos 2001: 110–120), and local alternatives to capitalist globalization like, for instance, certain counter-tendencies in China (Kang 1998). There is also a progressive-populist movement in the United States with aspirations to reign in corporate capitalism and make it much more accountable to all stakeholders both at home and globally. It builds on alternatives in the form of employee stock ownership companies (ESOPs) and a more far-reaching cooperativism as a community-based economic and social alternative to corporate America in which economic democracy in the form of workers' control of all kinds of cooperatives is envisioned and also practiced here and there. This also involves local experiments with new production and consumption systems (such as the local economy trading systems, LETS) embedded in other kinds of social relations and ecological practices than those of mainstream America (Derber 1998; Korten 2001). A more political variant is the leftist-egalitarian populism represented by one of the most relentless critics of corporate America, consumer advocate Ralph Nader, who ran for President as an independent candidate in 1996, as the Green Party's official nominee in 2000, and as the Reform Party's candidate (in some states as an independent candidate) in 2004. Global Trade Watch, one of the six major divisions of Nader's major nonprofit organization, Public Citizen, has emerged as a leading watchdog organization monitoring the activities of the IMF, the World Bank, and the WTO. It was founded in 1993 as a direct response to the passage of NAFTA in Congress (Steger 2002: 104–109; Nader 2004). Many of these diverse currents now meet at the World Social Forum with the purpose of defining their commonalities and building an organizational power capable of challenging neoliberalism in its various manifestations.

In several parts of the world (including South Korea and South Africa) energetic labor movements have emerged, while Indonesia is witnessing the rise of a labor movement of great potential importance. There are also countertendencies that concentrate on conventional political party structures (for example, the Workers Party in Brazil or the Congress Party in India in alliance with communists) with the aim of attaining state power as a first important move towards global reform of the economic order. In much of Latin America progressive-populist and socialist movements are flourishing, if not in power, and likely to transform grassroots resistance into state-led, sometimes strongly nationalist, oppositions to U.S. economic encroachments (Harvey 2005: 199–201). They all offer counterweights to today's predominance of U.S.-led neoliberalism.

Various observers have suggested that a possible, albeit temporary, solution within the bounds of any capitalist mode of production would be some kind of new "New Deal" that has a global reach (Brecher et al. 2000: 67–80; Steger 2002: 145–147; Harvey 2003: 76).[22] In their manifesto *Globalization from Below*, alternative globalization activists Jeremy Brecher, Tim Costello, and Brendan Smith offer a comprehensive blueprint for a global "New Deal," predicated on seven basic principles. The first principle demands an upward leveling of labor, environmental, social, and human-rights conditions by imposing on corporations minimum global standards for labor and environment. The second principle calls for the democratization of social institutions at all levels, from local to global. It explicitly includes involving all citizens of the world in the debate on the future of the global economy. The third principle holds that decision-making processes should occur as close as possible to those they affect. This implies that corporations should be held accountable for "externalities" of their policies to local, community-controlled institutions.

The fourth principle suggests a leveling of inequalities between the rich and poor globally. Next to global redistribution measures, this includes a plea for canceling the remaining debts of the poorest countries by international financial institutions such as the IMF and World Bank. The fifth and sixth principles call for a strict enforcement of international environmental agreements, and policies aimed at the fostering of prosperity in accordance with human and environmental needs. The seventh principle envisions a more effective system of protection against global recessions. One often-cited suggestion in this connection is the so-called "Tobin Tax" on international financial transactions, whose proceeds would be invested in poor countries' development efforts (Brecher et al. 2000: 67–80).

This bold prospect necessarily involves a significant redistribution of wealth and a redirection of capital flows towards the production and renewal of physical and social infrastructures within the United States. At the time of writing, however, this seems highly unlikely in the light of America's institutional-political fragmentation (that severely hinders implementation of radical social transformations and consistent policies), and political and economical developments that clearly point in a very different direction. There is also no global alliance of social agents really capable of translating the global New Deal vision into practice. Despite a growth of democratic-egalitarian alliances at the global level in recent years, they are no match for the hegemonic transnational networks. For possible global progressive reform, such as the provision of global public goods and the regulation of international finance and transnational corporate capitalism, America in its role of world power is likely to be a major bottleneck at the current juncture of globalization (Nederveen Pieterse 2003: 67–68).

Moreover, state-centered strategies of economic and social reform have run out of favor in a neoliberal context dominated by the curtailment of the power of nation-states to control the economic activities of the private sector — either as a result of their governments' deliberate choices or (as in the case of many "less advanced" countries) of structural adjustment programs forced upon them by the World Bank, the IMF or other "financial assistance" agencies. The grand vision of a global New Deal entails the need to construct a Keynesian system of controlled capitalism (or mixed economy) on a global scale. In an era that has witnessed many labor parties and unions in Europe and elsewhere embracing the neoliberal tenets of the "Third Way," the chances seem slim that progressive-liberal and social-democratic forces would endorse drastic reforms in the near future (Steger 2002: 147). More importantly, it is difficult to imagine a global New Deal since states would not agree to a single New Deal authority. But one could perhaps envision regional New Deals, for example in Europe, possibly after some global financial crisis put a devastating blow to the present international trading and financial system.

For the time being, the neoliberal "globalization from above" is likely to continue its course. And it is in this domain that U.S. economic might, though fragile given the nation's enormous external debt, still dominates the global economy. Yet, next to India's growing influence, there is China's rising economic power (due to massive growth of trade and foreign direct investments), that entails the further dissemination of a state-led economic neoliberalization characterized by ruthless "free market reforms" at home that have significantly increased class and regional inequalities, shrunk welfare arrangements and social provisions and made at least 20 million people unemployed (Harvey 2005: 120–151; Pocha 2005). It may not take long before regional alliances form and disrupt the Washington Consensus, thus undermining the global financial framework that has until now been much to the United States' benefit (or rather that of its economic-financial elites and their political allies). What this means for the future of neoliberalization in the international arena and the power balance regarding corporate globalization remains to be seen.

Notes

Introduction

1. Notable exceptions were studies of economic-technological and industrial Americanization in Western Europe and Japan after World War II (e.g. Zeitlin and Herrigel 2000).

2. For the intellectual background of a perspective in this vein, see political scientist Stephen Bronner's (2004) update of the critical-emancipatory tradition, in which he calls for reclaiming the Enlightenment in a movement toward "a politics of radical engagement" revolving around a defense of political liberty, social justice, and cosmopolitanism.

Chapter 1

1. In this book, de Tocqueville was the first author to refer to the United States as exceptional, that is, qualitatively distinctive from all other countries. He is therefore considered to be the initiator of the numerous writings on American exceptionalism that would follow. Although the book has almost no explicit references to France or any other country, in his personal notes de Tocqueville indicated that he never wrote about America without having France in mind (Lipset 1996: 17–18).

2. Between both reviews Mill's thought changed significantly: after the death of his father in 1836 he became more of a heterodox conservative than a utilitarian in the sense of the philosophical strain represented by James Mill and Jeremy Bentham (Johnson 1979: 40–41).

3. While in 1870 Britain still produced 32 percent and the United States 23 percent of world industrial output respectively, by 1914, the U.S. share of world industrial output had increased to 36 percent and Britain's share had dropped to 14 percent. Nevertheless, Britain continued to account for the largest share of world foreign direct investments until after 1945 (Dicken 1999: 36–37).

4. Russell Kirk adopted the position that American liberty is the heir of the British tradition rather than of natural rights theory and political science as practiced by the founders. Basically, conservatives like him wanted to turn the American founding into a "British" project. In recovering an American conservative tradition that laid such emphasis in its view of the American Revolution, Kirk's books *The Conservative Mind* (1953) and *The American Cause* (1957) revealed a usable American conservative past that contributed to strengthening this "Americanizing" impulse (Kirk 1953, 1957; 1983; Nash 1976: 69–76, 206–209).

5. This text appeared first in one of the articles of art criticism that Baudelaire contributed to the journal *Le Pays*, and subsequently republished in *Les Curiosités esthétiques* (Ory 1990: 53 n 11).

6. The classic example is Chateaubriand who traveled in America and glorified its nature in his stories *Atala* and *René*. Chateaubriand's admiration concerned an imaginary America of a particular kind; he had only bitter words for the reality of America. He dealt with this contradiction by means of paradoxes: "I love your country and your government but I do not love you at all," or: "a pitiable people in a splendid land." This became the general tendency of Romantic writing in the early nineteenth century: whereas nature was exalted, society was despised. However, when in the 1830s and '40s the great migration began, a special literature to stimulate and advise the emigrants emerged. These publications painted a much more positive view of the New World, asserting that America was a good land for the common people, a genuine democracy and so on, although usually they admitted some of the shortcomings as well. But generally the higher classes and intellectuals kept their negative stance towards the United States and brought up the same objections again (Schulte Nordholt 1986: 11–12).

7. We may wonder to what extent William Stead's book with the same title in English, published three years before (Stead 1901), influenced Dehns's writing.

8. According to *Merriam-Webster's Collegiate Dictionary* (2001: 267), covetous means "1: marked by inordinate desire for wealth or possessions or for another's possessions; 2: having a craving for possession < ~ of power>."

9. The term "iron cage" is actually a (poetic) mistranslation by the American sociologist Talcott Parsons of the German original *stahlhartes Gehäuse*, whose accurate translation is "steel encasement" (Ceaser 1997: 185–186).

10. Ritzer's work is strongly influenced by Weber's view of rationalization.

11. Weber, however, also wrote some excellent accounts of the workings of the real America, especially descriptions of the American political parties, after having visited the United States. And, generally, he held a quite positive view of the United States (Ceaser 1997: 184).

12. It should be clear that by "leftists," in this context, I do not mean those on the left of the French Revolution mentioned earlier in this chapter — whose political views mostly remained within the broader liberal framework — but those who were adherents of some form of socialism, anarchism, or Marxism, and held anti-capitalist views.

13. These were most famously highlighted in Werner Sombart's *Why Is There No Socialism in the United States?*, first published in his native language in 1906.

14. In this context, rationalization was used in a more specific sense than in Max Weber's sweeping and pessimistic approach of the "disenchantment of the world" that portrayed rationalized modernity as bleak and repressive. Weber used the term to depict the development of the modern economic and social order in terms of instrumental rationality, pre-

dictability, calculability, systematic organization, and the abolishment of tradition, arbritrariness, and magic. In the popular debates on economic-industrial reform of the 1920s, "rationalization" referred more specifically to twentieth-century visions of industrial restructuring and economic modernity, even though those visions were still permeated by the broader features and goals that Weber discerned as the essence of rationalization. At the factory level, rationalization meant increasing productivity by integration and consolidation, technological modernization and labor process reorganization, the assembly line, and the time-and-motion studies of Frederick W. Taylor. For some, rationalization also meant new consumer products, improved marketing, and possibilities for enhanced consumption. For others, it entailed an austere but scientifically regulated society from which conflict would have been eliminated (Nolan 1994: 6).

15. Heidegger's thinking on America as the symbol of the crisis of our age, which would also be the deepest crisis of all time, has left an imprint on thinking of the extreme right, but also on the left, in the form of existentialism; a strain of utopian Marxism embodied by his student Herbert Marcuse, among others; postmodernism (e.g. Jean Baudrillard's "America"); and a strand of anti-technological ecologism (Ceaser 1997: 187–213).

Chapter 2

1. It was also one of the intellectual roots of cultural studies in Britain. Stuart Hall, one of the founders of cultural studies in Britain, was under its influence in his early intellectual career. For a classic example of a left-Leavisite approach, see the work he wrote together with Paddy Hall on "the popular arts" (Hall and Whannel 1964).

2. This oedipal relationship was most pronounced among male artists of this generation. In the case of Wim Wenders and Peter Handke, these father figures included the American filmmakers John Ford, Sam Muller, and Nicholas Ray. Fassbinder turned to Douglas Sirk, and Rolf Dieter Brinkmann praised William Burroughs and Andy Warhol. Others, like Werner Herzog, called themselves fatherless and constructed the myth of starting out of a vacuum — but even then relied heavily on their "grandfathers," including an Ameri-

canized F.W. Murnau (Gemünden 1998: 32–33).

3. In the early 1990s, after half a century of studies and discussions about the more general political, economic, social and cultural developments in West Germany during the first post-World War II decade, scholars interpreted this period still in very different ways. Basically there were two antithetical positions here. One assumed that in this period a radical break was made with the German past, culminating in a fundamentally different social order and political culture — more open, liberal, egalitarian, and unreservedly modern in orientation. This "new beginning" position was yoked to a benign positive Americanization-as-modernization thesis, whereby American influence was seen as entailing a clean sweep of the past in favor of a "better" German (and West European) future, characterized by unprecedented levels of prosperity and stability. The opposing "restoration" thesis held that highly traditionalist, national conservative, and extreme-right (former Nazi) elements and attitudes — authoritarian, patriarchal, statist, and intolerant — persisted throughout this period, reinforced by America's Cold War mongering and West-Germany's material success. This thesis was accompanied by a negative argument about Americanization in terms of commercialization and bogus democratization. Since then a critical rethinking of these two deeply entrenched historiographical perspectives has taken place, precipitated by the "quiet" German revolution of 1989–91 and the ensuing reunification of both Germanies. Gradually, this gave rise to more sophisticated historical interpretations of American influence in Germany (Ermarth 1993a: 3–4; Jarausch and Siegrist 1997).

4. These included body politics such as the use of the clenched fist, shouted and sung words, picket signs, the expressive styles of the organized marches, sit-down demonstrations, and catchwords such as "civil disobedience," "Black Power," "youth revolt," "demonstration," "student protest," "one man-one vote," and "peace" that forced people to take a position and inspired their thinking (O'Dell 1997: 197).

5. Debray would turn towards a (left-wing) neo-Gaullist variant of anti-Americanism in the 1980s.

6. Lacorne and Rupnik see the predominant structure of feeling changing with Edgar Morin's book *Journal de Californie* (1970): "I feel an

enormous elation to find myself in California.... It is also an intense excitement to feel myself inside the homing device of spaceship earth, to be a living witness of this crucial *hic et nunc* of the anthropological adventure ... I am in my element here where new possible worlds are being forged..." (Morin 1970: 250, qtd. in Lacorne and Rupnik 1990: 8).

7. This includes right-wing nationalist and anti-democratic descriptions of the United States in France that were inspired either by Gaullist principles or by a conservative tradition that harked back to thinkers like Jacques-Bénigne Bossuet, Joseph de Maistre and Charles Maurras. This form of cultural nationalism entailed an updated critique of the influence of Lockean and Rousseauean principles in the United States — that is the "natural liberalism" (Hartz 1955) of American culture. The wartime writings of Céline, among others, and developments within the French New Right (*nouvelle droite*) from the 1980s onwards can be located in the rather mixed bag of this discourse (Mathy 1993: 12). A manifestation of the *nouvelle droite* that is especially relevant here — even when it concerned a small minority — was the extreme right-wing *Groupes de Recherches et Etudes pour la Civilisation Européenne* (GRECE) whose ideologues asserted a philosophy of *enracinement* or "rootedness" and the rather uncommon political concept of a "pagan" and neutralist Europe, that is, without any real or potential contact with the United States. The identity of the "New Europe" would derive from the right to be different that would be directly threatened by the "virus of non-differentiation" spreading from the American racial and cultural "melting-pot" to Europe and elsewhere. Therefore all measures necessary to end infiltration by American ideas should be taken (Lacorne and Rupnik 1990: 9, 20–21).

8. French intellectuals in particular have displayed extreme ambiguity as well as enormous variations in this regard; for instance, loathing a political leader like Reagan in the 1980s while being enthusiastic about American technology and indulging in jazz or rock; or condemning the invasion of Grenada while wearing their Levi's with pride. Exemplary cases are Baudelaire in the nineteenth, and Sartre in the twentieth century, who were both great fans of American literature while also being severe critics of "Americanism" in their time (Lacorne and Rupnik 1990: 3; Pells 1997: 184, 247–258).

9. In his exposé on Americanization Duncan Webster contends that "American culture represents not capitalist seduction but an expression of the desire for some form of social and cultural hegemony" (Webster 1988: 230), a position contested by McKay who suggests that it can be both (McKay 1997: 35), which I endorse.

10. But, as Richard Pells has pointed out, there was an element of condescension in the European intellectuals' praise of America's novelists too (Pells 1997: 252).

11. One must be careful, however, to distinguish between the use of "free psychological space" and "resistance," which is not necessarily the same. People may express themselves freely and articulate their wishes and desires *without* actually resisting oppressive social situations they are involved in, as happens, for example, during certain rituals at religious revival meetings (Schaefer 2004).

12. Unfortunately, Minganti's essay omits the source where P.J. Ravault's point of view can be found.

13. Contrary to a prevailing view among critics of Theodor Adorno's position in this regard, this leading representative of critical theory of the Frankfurt School was also well aware of this side of American "mass culture" — particularly the positive aspects of its material and sensuous satisfactions — as Adorno publicly expressed later in his life (when he became more pragmatic as a social science professor, being involved in concrete matters of cultural betterment). In the public lecture, entitled "Mehr Eiscreme, weniger Angst" ["More ice cream, less fear"], that Adorno repeatedly gave between 1956 and 1966 in the Federal Republic of Germany, he attempted "to shock the self-righteousness of his German contemporaries," as Kaspar Maase has pointed out. In a dialectical exposé on mass production and mass consumption Adorno treated "mass consumption as a materialization (although deeply perverted) of the pursuit of happiness," arguing that the affluence on which mass consumption is based entails an element of realized utopia (Maase 1996b: 201–202, 204, 208).

14. Webster refers to Reyner Banham, who has argued that the influence of American architecture cannot be gauged through normal influence studies. Instead one must look at the effect of certain American scenes and environments as they work through the popular media. The effects he is talking about cluster around suburban lawns, the Manhat-tan skyline, the Los Angeles freeways and Las Vegas. The point that is useful here, is his argument that the influence of American environments performs less *in* the media than *around* them. American architecture is seen as "the building blocks out of which are assembled the environments in which the action of Pop takes place, a kind of continuous back-projection" (Banham 1975: 73). Pop signifies here not just music but a whole culture of films, fashion, advertising, and television. This "back-projection" plays a significant role when listening to American music or attempting to describe it. American music is heard with visual images in mind — at least by people who have been immersed in this cultural repertoire — and not just when it is actually attached to visual images (film, advertising, videos). Then memories of films, television, photography are brought into play among people well acquainted with U.S. popular culture — mediating music through ideas and images of the American city or country. The back-projection image implies an identification of popular culture and America. Paradoxically, this may even give to foreigners in Europe and various other parts of the world within the U.S. cultural orbit some "sense of place" through experiencing an imaginary *American* landscape, as it refers to deep-rooted feelings linked to experiences when growing up in the post–World War II era under the impact of American popular culture. We find foreshadowings of these since the 1920s, particularly in Europe.

15. Paradoxically, the adoption of these forms of expressive individualism often occurred, and still occur today, in a communitarian way, in the context of what Bradley has called a "resistant communality" (Bradley 1992: 125). This communality does not always have a "resistant" character, however, so that a more neutral term might be more appropriate here.

16. A special variant of this Americanophile tendency emerged in France in the 1980s among the class of young executives who wanted to set themselves free from "little France" and link up with neoliberal trends and expressive individualism in the U.S. This coincided with the rising popularity of several intellectual gurus who rejected the traditional contempt of U.S. culture and society among large factions of the French intellectual elites. This orientation found a clear expression in the cultural pages of the *Nouvel Observateur* or issues of the review *Autrement* on California and New York. This review offered striking evidence of the then trendy French metropolitan left's abandonment of the revolutionary ideology of 1968, in favor of the style-conscious, media-dominated, Americanophile world as witnessed in the 1980s. However, one must also recognize that a review such as *Autrement* represented only one small instance of a widespread enthusiasm for American popular culture that was shared by French people at large, and particularly young people, and that was not only the preserve of a trendy Parisian in-group (Pinto, 1990; Rigby, 1991: 162–163).

17. The British mods' "Europeanism" entailed a visual "cool Continental" style drawn from Italy or France but filtered through American images in films and magazines. The influence of the Continent, including Italian zoots and scooters, was experienced by a subculture that took its music from black American culture: modern jazz, but especially rhythm & blues and soul music. In their style, the male mods displayed the elegant dandyism of specific categories of young blacks in America, in which they adopted the American hipster style. They put much emphasis on acting as cool as possible: one had to keep perfect control of oneself and outwardly one should not show what one felt or thought. "Cool" also implied a specific way of walking and especially of standing around. In this the mods identified with such remote "others" as urban cool blacks and their marginal position in the States (Chambers 1985: 38–39; Webster 1988: 211–212; Strinati 1995: 35–37).

18. Foreshadowings of this kind of U.S.-inflected subcultural activity by European youth can be found even in such unlikely places as Nazi Germany during World War II when anti-Nazi youth groups known as *Hottjungen* or *Swing Jugend* ("Swing Youth") positioned themselves as outsiders to majority culture. Their use of Western frontier imagery, adoption of African-American jazz club names and immersion in hot swing music culture implied a degree of resistance both to the war effort and to the dominant Nazi ideology of racial purity (Beck 1985) — although this never went beyond ritual gestures and therefore posed no serious threat to Nazism.

Chapter 3

1. Eventually all Native Americans were officially declared U.S. cit-

izen by the Indian Citizenship Act of 1924. But even after the introduction of this Act, at the state level, new Native American citizens were still victims of forms of disenfranchisement and other forms of discrimination similar to those imposed on African Americans (Ragsdale 1989: 400).

2. The Roosevelt administration then reshaped governmental policy to attempt to retain the cultural integrity of tribal life. The Indian Reorganization Act (IRA) of 1934 also empowered the tribes to use constitutionalism and incorporation as vehicles to carry tribalism forward to the ultimate goals of self-government and economic self-sufficiency. Still, the erosion of Indian religion and culture would continue in the years to follow, which the American Indian Movement (founded in 1970) tried to counter, winning some support for its efforts from Congress through the American Indian Religious Freedom Act of 1978 and the Indian Land Consolidation Act of 1983 (Ragsdale 1989: 427–430).

3. Most likely there was some discrepancy between Roosevelt's public and private attitudes, however. Howard Zinn gives the example of Roosevelt's differentiated response to a lynching of 11 Italian immigrants by a mob in New Orleans in 1891. Roosevelt publicly expressed his thought "that the United States should offer the Italian government some remuneration, but privately he wrote his sister that he thought the lynching was 'rather a good thing' and told her he had said as much at a dinner with 'various dago diplomats ... all wrought up by the lynching'" (Zinn 2003: 300; cf. Dickerson 2005: 78).

4. Of course, Kallen thereby failed to pay sufficient attention to the claims to indigenousness of such "primary" ethnic groups as "native" Indians and Inuits ("Eskimos"), blacks, New Mexican/Texan Latinos, and Louisiana Cajuns (Kaufmann 2004: 286, 292).

5. Bourne also went beyond Kallen in the intensity of his distaste for the *assimilado*, what was later to be called the "marginal man," the person living between different cultures and not fully assimilated into any one of them. Ironically, as F.H. Matthews has indicated, Bourne's denunciation of assimilados is in some way reminiscent of native outbursts. Bourne stated, for example: "Already we have far too much of this insipidity — masses of people who are cultural half-breeds, neither assimilated Anglo-Saxons nor nationals of another culture.... Our cities are filled with these half-breeds who retain their foreign names but have lost the foreign savor.... It is not the Jew who sticks proudly to the faith of his fathers ... who is dangerous to America, but the Jew who has lost the Jewish fire and becomes a mere elementary animal" (Bourne [1916] 1964: 118, qtd. in Matthews 1970: 13–14).

6. In a Gramscian interpretation of Americanism as a central element in the "common sense" of popular culture in the United States — as adopted by Rupert — it is understood that "[i]n a society which is fundamentally structured along contradictory lines, the world views of the masses of people — their 'folklore' or 'common sense' — will also be fragmented and contradictory, will be amenable to conflicting interpretations, and will therefore potentially support different modes of political action which grow out of those interpretations" (Rupert 1995: 4).

7. In those years the percentage of naturalized citizens rose, for example, from about 25 to 50 percent of all Poles, Yugoslavs, Italians, and Hungarians.

Chapter 4

1. The term "substitute socialism" was coined by Hermann Kriege, a former member of the League of the Just and a German immigrant to the United States who, like several other allies of Marx and Engels, had taken refuge in the New World after the upheavals of 1848 in Germany. Almost immediately upon arrival Kriege stated that Americanism was a surrogate for his former socialism; in his new homeland he had come to believe that free land and a homestead act would provide a permanent solution to any American social problem. Remarkably, almost all of Marx's coworkers in the German Workers Club who came to the United States after 1848 abandoned socialism upon settling there (Moore 1970: 4–5; cf. Wittke 1952).

2. More generally, and also outside the CIO context, by adding Americanism to workers' traditional cultural life, and emphasizing the constitutional rights and political opportunities of American citizens, both radicals and ethnics could present their socialist and communitarian ideals in the language favored by old-line Americans (Kammen 1993: 29–30). A good example is the working-class Americanism cultivated by the Independent Textile Union of Woonsocket, Rhode Island, the most powerful textile workers' union in New England at the time, with Franco-Belgian socialists and French-Canadian Catholics as its major actors. In the 1930s and early 1940s, leaders of both ethnic groups were able to bring up a critique of capitalism by using, each in their own way, the traditional political discourse that conservative Americanizers had developed at the turn of the century (Gerstle 1989).

3. At heart, Capra's and many other Hollywood's Depression films were about redemption. With the help of unspoiled individuals like Deeds, Smith, and Doe — of whom America presumably still had many — Americans who were caught up in a crazy competition for nothing and involved in corruption, could redeem themselves. Capra's concern was clearly not the politics of social restructuring or revolution but the politics of conversion and social regeneration (Quart 1977: 6). Whereas films of the early Depression had flirted with the need for social change and authority, Capra's films emphasized the need for a return to the basics of American tradition. But, as Lawrence Levine has pointed out, in these films something deeper was going on than the mere re-articulation of past virtues. Capra was searching for ways to make the traditional values and means of communication of small-town America work again in contemporary America, in which he was doomed to fail (Levine 1993: 249–253). Another reading of Capra's films is possible, however, which also hints at a more ambiguous ethos of this mainstream Americanism. As Stanley Aronowitz has suggested, "with the exception of the sentimental and immensely popular film *It's a Wonderful Life* [a postwar film, 1946], which is virtually a case study in Popular Front democratic and antimonopoly rhetoric, and is characteristically read differently today, all of Capra's protagonists are antiheroes.... [E]ven in Capra's small-town epic, there is little attempt to glorify ordinary life. For Capra, it is clear that the mundane tasks of a small-town banker, however fulfilling a life of service may be in abstract terms, is mostly suffused with frustration, routine, and crises that can only be made romantic with the assistance of an angel, a kind of deus ex machina who must constantly prod the ever-fading, semisuicidal hero. Viewing it today, we can see that, despite its conciliatory, sentimental ending, *It's a Wonderful Life*, remains,

for the most part, a searing critique of middle-class existence in an era when small-town life was giving way to the corporate/urban sprawl" (Aronowitz 1993: 162). He also adds that "...Frank Capra's unabashed advocacy, in a dozen films, of small-town values against the growing trustification of American life and especially the growing cynicism and manipulations that accompanied it, thematized the contraries of wilderness and the city, face-to-face interaction and mass society, and innocence and decadence into popular culture as well as political philosophy" (*ibid.*: 175–176).

4. This concerned an adaptation of Durkheim's anomie theory to the strain of structural-functionalist sociology of which Merton was to become a leading figure in the 1950s and 1960s.

5. Rupert is incorrect in using the term "neoliberalism" in this context.

6. The 1997 Commission on Immigrant Reform concluded that in order to succeed, Americanization should be a "two-way street." This notion was meant to break decisively with the coercive assimilationist and exclusionary tendencies of earlier Americanization endeavors, and to dissociate "Americanization" from its earlier, largely racialist, connotations. Desmond King has rightly questioned whether a genuine "two-way" process of Americanization can be reconciled with the political ends formulated by the same commission, that is, uniting persons from all over the world in a common civic culture, whereby immigrants must accept the obligations imposed by the federal government. The commission defined Americanization as the "process of integration by which immigrants become part of our communities and by which our communities and the nation learn from and adapt to their presence. Americanization means the civic incorporation of immigrants, that is the cultivation of a shared commitment to the American values of liberty, democracy and equal opportunity." According to King, this entailed "a fulsomely patriotic version of the process of 'becoming American,'" as illustrated by a workshop based on *Becoming American/America Becoming* (Pickus 1997) coinciding with the commission's deliberations, in which the subject of Americanization evoked persisting disagreement. Critics maintained that the United States' failure historically to realize the values of the U.S. Constitution was so severe that retaining a shared conception, attainable though Americanization, was untenable (King 2000: 4, 25–26).

7. ACLU Briefing Paper nr. 6, "English Only," 1996 (http://archive. aclu.org/library/pbp6.html, accessed on June 3, 2004); John Dougherty, "'English-only' group launches new push," World Net Daily, August 16, 2001 (http://www.worldnetdaily.com, accessed on June 3, 2004); U.S. English, Inc., "About U.S. English," 2004 (http://www.us-english.org/inc /about, accessed on June 9, 2004).

8. Proposition 63 (California's Offical English bill in 1998), for example, was supported by 72 percent of whites, 67 percent of blacks, and 58 percents of Asians, although a majority of those identifying as "liberal," whether Hispanic or white, were opposed. A year later a poll found that 67 percent of blacks, 67 percent of Asians and 64 percent of Hispanics favored the passage of Proposition 63 (Kaufmann 2004: 265–266).

9. Hanson's work is supported by the Claremont and Hoover Institutes, both receiving significant funding from the Olin Foundation, that has also supported *Bell Curve* author Charles Murray and the neoconservatives' "Project for the New American Century" (Lovato 2004: 17).

10. Huntington sees the purported erosion of U.S. national identity threatened especially by a tiny fraction of Americans in whom national pride, patriotic loyalty, religious faith, and regard for the work ethic are weaker than is necessary for the preservation of national identity. In his opinion, this fraction includes the heads of transnational corporations, members of the liberal elite, holders of dual citizenship, Mexican Americans, and what he refers to as "deconstructionists," an heterogenous group of people who preach dissent from the values of the American "core culture," among whom are Democrats Bill Clinton and Al Gore, the political theorist Michael Walzer, and the philosopher Martha Nussbaum. Huntington actually means by "deconstructionism" bilingualism, affirmative action, cosmopolitanism (associated with Nussbaum), pluralism (Walzer), and multiculturalism (Clinton and Gore). Huntington now considers multiculturalism as essentially "anti-European civilization" and as basically an "anti-Western ideology" (Huntington 2004; Menand 2004).

11. In August 2005, the Democratic governors in Arizona and New Mexico declared states of emergency in several counties. Their aim was to extract more money from the federal government for border policing, while taking a position to the right of

the White House on immigration issues. Joe Kay, "US House Passes Draconian Anti-Immigrant Bill," December 19, 2005 (http://www.wsws. org, accessed on December 21, 2005).

12. Alex Meneses Miyashita, "Advocates Press Congress for Immigration this Session," February 2, 2005 (http://www.hispaniclink.org/newsse rvice, accessed on December 21, 2005); National Immigration Law Center, "A Discussion of Immigration Reform Bills Introduced in 2005," Immigrants' Rights Update, vol. 19, issue 4, September 16, 2005 (http://www.nilc.org/immlawpol-icy/CIR, accessed on December 22, 2005); "Kennedy Discusses Comprehensive Immigration Reform With Mexican Foreign Minister Derbez," by Congressional Desk, October 26, 2005 (http://www.americanchroni-cle.com/articles, accessed on December 21, 2005); John Cloud, Mike Allen, "Playing Both Sides of the Fence," *Time Magazine*, December 5, 2005 (Time Archive, http://www. time.com/time/archive, accessed on December 12, 2005); Joe Kay, "US House passes draconian anti-immigrant bill," December 19, 2005 (http://www.wsws.org, accessed on December 21, 2005).

13. We should acknowledge that this standard is higher than in most other countries. For example, the Dutch law on domestic investigations and security services sets fewer restrictions on police wiretapping of Dutch citizens. To monitor communications by fixed and mobile phone, secret services in the Netherlands have to ask the Minister of Justice for permission, a request that is almost always honored as a matter of routine. No such permission is required for monitoring communications by satellite or individuals with suspected foreign contacts (Meeus 2005).

14. "ACLU Memo to Interested Persons Regarding Analysis of Senate Intelligence Committee Patriot Act Reauthorization Bill," May 18, 2005; ACLU, "Senate Intelligence Committee Considers Patriot Act Expansion Bill in Secret: ACLU Calls for Open and Public Debate," May 26, 2005 (http://www.aclu.org, both accessed on May 31, 2005).

15. Rather than investigating the legality of the NSA surveillance, the Justice Department's response was to seek out individuals who disclosed information on the program. However, a number of government officials doubted the legality of the thousands of warrantless wiretaps on American citizens engaged in international calls. Several people in the

NSA refused to participate in them, and a deputy attorney general even declined to give permission for some aspects of these wiretaps. The special FISA court has raised concerns as well, and a judge of this court has resigned, obviously in protest (Holtzman 2006: 13). "ACLU Memo to Interested Persons Regarding the Conference Report on the USA Patriot Improvement and Reauthorization Act of 2005," December 7, 2005; "ACLU Praises Senate For Standing For Freedom, Rejecting White House Pressures," December 16, 2005 (http://www.aclu.org, accessed on December 17, 2005); "In New Ad, ACLU Steps Up Call for Investigation of President's Spying Order," January 5, 2006; "ACLU Calls on Congress to Make Meaningful Changes to Patriot Act, Says Privacy and Civil Liberties Still Remain at Risk," February 2, 2006 (http://www.aclu.org, accessed on February 8, 2006).

16. Initially, in late December 2005, the Senate had voted for a term of six months that would have given Congress more time to make the meaningful changes called for by a bipartisan group from both the Senate and House, the ACLU and likeminded organizations aimed at protecting the privacy and constitutional rights of U.S. citizens. But the House decided differently, and the Senate went along with the much shorter term. "ACLU Welcomes New Senate Compromise on Patriot Act Reauthorization, Calls on Congress to Fully Address Concerns on Privacy and Freedom," December 21, 2005 (http://www.aclu.org, accessed on December 23, 2005); *NRC Handelsblad*, December 22, 2005: 5 and December 23, 2005:5.

17. "ACLU Says Cosmetic Changes to the Patriot Act Hollow," March 7, 2006 (http://www.aclu.org, accessed on May 31, 2006.

18. The Strasbourg-based Council of Europe is the guardian of the Human Rights Convention signed by 43 countries, including all 25 EU members.

19. Geoff Meade, "EU countries 'knew about CIA torture flights,'" January 24, 2006 (http://www.independent.co.uk); David Lindsay, "EU governments complicit in shady CIA activities," The Malta Independent Online, February 9, 2006 (http://217.145.4.56/ind/news.asp?newsitemid=27085); "CIA flights reports 'credible,'" The Guardian, December 13, 2005 (http://www.guardian.co.uk), all accessed on February 9, 2006.

20. Draft interim report by Temporary Commitee on the alleged use of European countries by the CIA for the transport and illegal detention of prisoners (Rapporteur: Giovanni Claudio Fava), April 24, 2006, p. 7 (http://www.europarl.europa.eu/comparl/tempcom/tdip/feault_en.htm, accessed on June 15, 2006); "Extraordinary Rendition in Depth," May 11, 2006 http://www.aclu.org/safetree/torture/25546res20060511.htlm, accessed on June 15, 2006).

21. "ACLU Applauds House Support for McCain Anti-Torture Amendment, But Denounces Proposed Secret Deal to Undermine Rule of Law," December 14, 2005 (http://www.aclu.org, accessed on December 17, 2005).

22. This verification program would be an expansion of the voluntary "Basic Pilot" program in current law (a program that is juridicially "faulty" according to the ACLU). "ACLU Opposes Faulty 'Border Security' Bill, Proposal Would Require Workers to Get Government 'Permission Slip,'" December 15, 2005 (http://www.aclu.org, accessed on December 18, 2005).

23. Joe Kay, "US House Passes Draconian Anti-Immigrant Bill," December 19, 2005 (http://www.wsws.org, accessed on December 21, 2005).

24. The Kennedy-McCain bill (S. 1033/HR 2330) bill collapsed into this bill (S. 2611). National Network for Immigrant and Refugee Rights, "Immigration Reform" (http://www.nnirr.org/projects/immigrationreform/index.htm, accessed on June 18, 2006).

25. "ACLU Urges Senate to Oppose Flawed Immigration Bill, Says Legislation Fails to Protect Due Process and Privacy," May 25, 2006 (http://www.aclu.org/immigrants/gen/25666prs20060525.htlm, accessed on June 16, 2006).

26. The Pentagon shared the information with other government agencies through the Threat and Local Observation Notice (TALON) database, which was initiated by former Deputy Secretary of Defense Paul Wolfowitz in 2003 to track groups and individuals with possible links to terrorism. "ACLU Sues Pentagon for Documents on Peace Groups," June 14, 2006 (http://.aclu.org/safetree/spyfiles/258880prs20060614.htlm, accessed on June 17, 2006).

27. Report of American Civil Liberties Union (ACLU), "Freedom Under Fire: Dissent in Post-9/11 America," May 2003 (http://www.aclu.org, accessed on June 3, 2004); ACLU Written Statement Submitted by Timothy H. Edgar, Legislative Counsel, at a Hearing on S. 2679, the "Tools To Fight Terrorism Act of 2004" before the Subcommittee on Technology, Terrorism and Homeland Security of the Senate Judiciary Committee, September 12, 2004, mentioned in Azulay 2004; "ACLU Praises Senate For Standing For Freedom, Rejecting White House Pressures," December 16, 2005 (http://www.aclu.org, accessed on December 17, 2005); "ACLU Seeks Pentagon Files on Peace Groups," January 2, 2006 (http://www.aclu.org, accessed on February 8, 2006).

28. Although a member of an old New England family, George Bush Sr.'s political base was Texas.

29. The major catalyst was the U.S. Internal Revenue Service's move in 1978 to revoke the tax-exempt status of all private schools started after 1953, on the basis of their presumed discriminatory status. The majority of these private schools in the South were Christian academies established to avoid the racial desegregation mandated by the U.S. Supreme Court decision, *Brown v. Board of Education of Topeka, Kansas* (1954) (Goldfield 2002: 59; Micklewaith and Wooldridge 2004: 83–84).

Chapter 5

1. The primary American interest in Americanization in terms of assimilation meant that as late as the 1980s the larger issue of Americanization abroad had hardly been conceptualized by Americans. Richard White, an astute observer of the Australian experience of Americanization, signaled in 1983 that a comprehensive bibliography of a major site of Americanization abroad, U.S. popular culture, contained no category for Americanization (Lewis 1978) and that standardized subject headings of the Library of Congress, increasingly used in libraries outside the United States, only allowed the citizenship or assimilation meaning of the word. White suggested that critical observers might see this as a classic case of cultural imperialism: a dominant culture that not only determined the structure of the debate, but could even refuse to admit, through its use of language, the existence of the phenomenon. It also came as no surprise that the debate about Americanization abroad was largely initiated and sustained from outside the United States (mostly by European scholars interested in U.S. cultural imperialism), with only a few notable exceptions (e.g., the work of the American

media expert Herbert I. Schiller). For this reason discussions of this form of Americanization remained rather one-sided, open to the charge of being "ineffectual anti-American rhetoric" (White 1983: 109–110). However, the *Dictionary of Americanisms* already gave the following two definitions of "to Americanize" in its 1951 and 1966 editions: "1. *tr.* To render American in character; to make similar to the people, customs, or institutions in the U.S.... 2. To become American in character"— the latter with references to 1875 Howell's *Foregone Conclusion* 77 "He was Americanizing in that good lady's hands as fast as she could transform him" and the October 19, 1905 *New York Evening Post* (p. 5): "I fancy Asia will not Americanize very fast." This dictionary also mentions a reference in *The Nation* of February 2, 1893 (75/1) to "The spread of American influence and domination abroad, known as 'Americanism' [which article apparently does not contain the term "Americanization"] (*A Dictionary of Americanisms* 1966: 27). Furthermore there is a long-standing interest in American imperialism (but not focused so much on the actual process of Americanization) among American scholars, including Charles A. Beard during the first half of the twentieth century, and, since the late 1950s, the "Wisconsin School" of revisionist history of U.S. foreign policy, founded and inspired by William Appleman Williams (Gardner 1986; Bacevich 2002: 11–31), and more recent historical work in a similar vein.

2. See also *Webster's Third New International Dictionary of the English Language*, vol. 1 (1981: 69). Another major dictionary, *The New Oxford Dictionary of English* (2001), does not distinguish between the two meanings as it gives the following overarching definition of the verb "to Americanize" from which the noun "Americanization" derives: "make American in character or nationality."

3. Sometimes we may find combinations of both, but these are hardly ever well integrated (e.g. Hebdige 1988).

Dominic Strinati has tried to combine both approaches with regard to Americanization in the domain of popular culture by using Thompson's (1988) conception of popular culture as a kind of circuit (bearing certain similarities to Marx's analysis of the circuit of capital), consisting of three distinct objects of inquiry, or stages, which are closely related and linked together by the ways they influence each other: 1) the social and histori-

cal conditions under which the production of popular culture takes place (or the political economy of Americanization); 2) the formal analysis of the discourses of popular culture as texts, as sets of images, words, and representations; and 3) the analysis of how these aspects of popular culture have been understood and "read" by those who consume, produce, and evaluate them (Strinati 1992: 54–55).

4. This has a much wider relevance than the domain of literature, of course, which becomes clear in reading Bradbury's historical account.

5. Interestingly enough, after World War II a standard image of Americanization in the negative sense seems itself to be borrowed from American horror films, with *The Invasion of the Body Snatchers* as its prototype: the invasion of the alien, the replacement or transformation of the local; the community (viewers, consumers) becoming mindless zombies (Morris 1988: 246–247; Webster 1989: 65–66).

6. A synecdoche is one form of metonymia — that is, a rhetorical figure of speech by which a word with a smaller content is substituted for one with a larger content or vice versa. In the case of Americanization, a part is put for the whole (*pars pro toto*). The term "America" in this book is used to refer only to the U.S. areas of the northern part of the Americas, a synecdoche in itself.

7. For Baudrillard, America is urban East Coast America, expressed by the term "New York" : "...the entire world continues to dream of New York, even as New York dominates and exploits it" (Baudrillard 1989: 23).

8. Fluck refers to the following juxtapositions and contradictions: "the doctrine of individual rights and a relentless individualism; democracy and capitalism; a promise of social independence and an oppressive cultural conformity; ... cultural dehierarchization and the culture industry," and emphasizes that "Nowhere are these contradictions of modern, democratic societies carried to greater extremes than in the U.S., which, as it appears from today's perspective, may very well prefigure the future for other countries and societies as well" (Fluck 2000: 151).

9. This was not new, however. Two decades earlier Hendrik de Man had already suggested that "the American civilization is basically nothing else but the modern European one in a chemically pure form" (qtd. in Haufler 1997: 408, in turn quoting from Franzen 1952: 147, my transla-

tion). Dahrendorf was later to become a major representative of transatlantic modern sociology, and settled in Britain where he became a naturalized citizen, dean of the London School of Economics, and a Member of the House of Parliament.

10. It was certain working-class youths in Sweden, called "raggare," who felt heavily attracted to the big, chromed American cars, which they associated with freedom, (consumer) democracy, and the promise of tomorrow and "the open road." Their appropriation of the streamlined American car of the late 1950s and early 1960s became a threat to the middle class, and the object of debate, in which concerns about morality, violence, and sexuality were central. This counterstrain continued among later generations of working-class youth and like-minded juvenile elders in Sweden at least until the late 1990s (O'Dell 1997: 142–159).

11. Ross mentions Richard Kuisel's well-known *Seducing the French: the Dilemma of Americanization* (1993) as "a good example of a political/economic history that focuses entirely on the 'French economic miracle' and Americanization without any consideration of the end of empire" (Ross 1995: note 9, 198).

12. According to Ritzer and Stillman, in recent history Americanization includes "the worldwide diffusion of the American industrial model in the post-Second World War era; the worldwide diffusion of the American consumption model in the 1990s; the marketing of American media, including Hollywood films, popular music and NBA basketball, abroad; the marketing of American commodities, including coca cola, blue jeans and computer operating systems, abroad; extensive diplomatic and military engagement with Europe, Asia and South America, including efforts to support democratization; the training of military, political and scientific elites in American universities; and the development and use of the international labor market and natural resources by American corporations" (Ritzer and Stillman 2003: 35–36).

13. Ritzer's theory is derived from Max Weber's work on formal rationality. Weber contended that the modern Western world was characterized by an increasing tendency towards the predominance of formally rational systems, leading to what he called a further "disenchantment of the world" (Weber 1981).

14. McDonaldized systems have already been imported back to the

United States (for example, The Body Shop, based in the UK).

15. For the following three sections I am indebted to Richard Kuisel's discussion of the various approaches to Americanization (Kuisel 2003: 98–110).

16. Richard Pells's book *Not Like US* (1997*)* is a good example of the drawbacks of an exaggerated form of the assimilationist approach. Despite its comprehensiveness and wealth of interesting details, politico-economic factors, the driving forces of U.S.-based corporate capitalism and the production side of cultural industries, get much less attention than they deserve. Power imbalances between the United States and Europe, or specific European countries, are underexposed (also due partly to the omission of most non-English language sources), fostered by Pells's tendency to locate "Americanization" mainly at the symbolic level. When dealing with America's cultural impact in Europe, the author explicitly links up with active reception theory, and its associated uncritical cultural populism and neoliberal ideology of "consumer sovereignty" and "freedom of choice" (Pells 1997: 279–283). In the end, Pells suggests that the postwar influence between both continents was in various respects a process of "cross-fertilization," a reciprocal exchange on a more equal footing than many European writers and political leaders claimed, a conclusion that is open to question. More recently, Pells has outlined his view on the globalization of American culture in the twentieth century along similar lines, thereby emphasizing the strong reciprocity of America's cultural connections with other countries and the "cosmopolitanism" of its mass culture (Pells 2004).

17. Transculturization here, in the context of the relationship between the United States and the rest of the world in the late twentieth century and beyond, is meant to be a general, abstract and neutral term referring to processes of cultural transformations across national borders (Hornung 2002: 110). But it has traditionally been employed to refer to cultural encounters between members of metropolitan centers and colonized subjects. Given its current connotations as a result of its use with reference to interactions between the U.S. and the rest of the world, possibly implying United States' cultural hegemony, we may need to historicize the term (Montgomery 2002: 117).

18. Kaspar Maase, who appears to share this view, therefore doubts whether the concept of (cultural) Americanization with its historical heritage of meanings in Europe (as described in the first two chapters) is a useful instrument to understand the transnational cultural exchanges concerned. At least for Germany, he contends, the diagnosis "Americanization" was not developed to apprehend what Breidenbach and Zukrigl have called the "dance of cultures," but to discredit and to contain such processes (Maase 1999: 88–89). He makes the ironic remark that Americanization is like other ghosts or specters. One has to take them seriously, because many people believe in them and react accordingly. But one should not assume that they actually exist (*ibid.*: 82). My position is different as will be come clear later, when I defend an analytical usage of the term with necessary specifications and qualifications with regard to the instances of Americanization at issue.

19. This was followed by increased interest in U.S. imperialism and a variety of domestic societal issues, as well as interrelations between foreign and domestic policies, within American studies in the late 1960s and 1970s, which appears to be an intermezzo with hindsight.

20. See, for example, some case studies on generational differences and appropriations of elements of American culture among youths in Germany in the 1950s and 1960s (Fehrenbach and Poiger 2000) and more generally for indications about sociopsychological changes involved in the Americanization (or American-led globalization) of French culture as "read from" changes in how the French speak, eat, dress and entertain themselves in the second half of the twentieth century: Kuisel (2003: 95–96, 109–110).

21. This touchy issue is usually downplayed or ignored in cultural studies that lean heavily on theorizing derived from Foucault or Lacan, as well as in cultural-historical work employing similar hermeneutic approaches and sources.

22. Billig (1997) points out that the intellectual roots of this approach have a strong affinity with a similar approach to language by Mikhail Bakhtin (1981, 1986) — see especially a book published under the name of Volosinov (1973) but thought by many to be the work of Bakhtin. Although this Russian thinker is often quoted in cultural studies texts, his theoretical insights are hardly taken as starting point for empirical work by practitioners of cultural studies.

Chapter 6

1. However, political scientist James W. Ceaser points out that "the real nation remains the object of the symbol, and 'America' always points back to the United States. In this respect America differs from other well-known geographical symbols where the object designated is not a political entity or society but a spiritual or intellectual activity, as is the case with 'Jerusalem' (the biblical region), 'Athens' (philosophy), and 'Rome' (the Catholic faith)" (Ceaser 1997: 2).

2. There have been some critical reworkings of Foucault's theory of power, though. Feminist scholars have formulated the most extensive critique of Foucault's political theories, developing "a sophisticated Foucault-feminist literature in the process," particularly with regard to body politics and gendered relations of power and resistance (Katz 2001: 125). However, these are less relevant for the purposes of this book.

3. For a similar view on excessive identity politics in the form of "culture wars" and the fragmentation of the left in America in the past decades, see Jacoby (1994); Gitlin (1995).

4. For this reason an overt hostility toward sociology can be found among many poststructuralist and postmodernist thinkers. On the other hand, sociology is an academic field that has been hardly susceptible to postmodern tendencies (Rosenau 1991).

5. However, the usage of the concept of alienation with regard to "the condition of postmodernity" (Harvey 1989) is not without its problems, because "it refers to problems of identity derived from production, whereas postmodernity is best understood with regard to consumption and consuming identities in a global marketplace, which may or may not be a problem depending on where you stand with respect to postmodern discourse" (McGuigan 1992: 208). In my view, labor and the workplace (or the lack thereof, in case of unemployment) still have a significant influence on people's identities and ways of life in this globalizing, late-modern world, and are not replaced by consumption and membership of a consumer society as the sole determinants of people's identities and stances in life. In this regard, the concept of alienation can still be used with some obvious modifications concerning the changed nature of much of work, and the greater im-

pact of consumerism in people's everyday lives.

6. Already announced at an earlier stage by Miller (1987), among others.

7. Masao Miyoshi's book *Off Center* (1991) is an interesting attempt at such an approach with regard to post–World War II cultural relations (particularly in the area of literature) between Japan and the USA, even though the author seems to be more inclined than I am to perceive what he calls "cultural convergences" along the lines of a transnational discourse that assumes "a world in which parts and margins are seen in their own terms, in their relations not to the center of power, but to a world that has no ordering center at all" (Miyoshi 1991: 5). But he does take the position that "The literary and the economical, the cultural and the industrial, are inseparable, of course. The usual formalized and abstracted arguments about literature and cultural problems must be reimmersed in the specific and concrete, in the everyday life of production and consumption, hegemony and acquiescence" (*ibid*.: 3–4).

8. My position corresponds with Walter LaFeber's criticism of a recent project to internationalize the study of American history developed by a group of distinguished international scholars, as summarized in Bender (2000): "This report ... tends to play down American exceptionalism [I would say, American distinctiveness] by insisting that the American experience be compared within, and placed inside of, transnational and other international developments over the past several centuries. It is possible to wonder, however, whether the emphasis on the transnational context and the need for multicultural approaches underestimates the various types of power employed by the United States in the early twenty-first century to shape that transnational context, and consequently makes the report less relevant to a meaningful national debate because the report neglects the importance of using history directly to shape political debate within the United States itself. The report is interesting for discussing cross-cultural influences, but it has little to say about the more important subject of how Americans used power to formulate and extend (or refuse to extend) their interests across cultures, including American cultural interests" (LaFeber 2003: 45, n. 4).

9. The more complex view on Americanization suggested here

means, *inter alia*, that in order to get a good grip on U.S. influences abroad and the multivariegated interactions between the U.S. and other nations or regions one should ideally use combinations of the methods of diplomatic, economic, social, cultural, and political history, as well as incorporate fields of research such as sociology, political science, anthropology, ethnography, psychology, linguistics, studies of literature and media, and so forth — as Reinhold Wagnleiter suggested more specifically with regard to American and European cultural developments and interchanges after World War II (Wagnleiter 1993: 306). It is obvious that there are limits to what an individual researcher can manage to do in a particular case, given his or her capacities and resources, and that team research only may offer a solution up to a degree here.

10. Needless to say, although similarities exist at an abstract level, there are major differences between colonization of, for example, a country like Nigeria that does not have a strong overarching national culture nor a nationally-owned production potential of any significance, and "colonization" of a modern Western European nation-state like France or Germany by the United States as seen through the eyes of opponents of U.S. cultural imperialism.

11. Ritzer and Stillman consider the increasing McDonaldization of the United States, including the disappearance of regional and ethnic difference in cuisine leading to greater homogenization across the country, as the "de-Americanization of America," meaning a diminishing of cultural and regional diversity; that is, replacing them by a single, homogeneous system (the fast-food restaurant as prototype of such rationalized systems in all kinds of domains). This only makes sense, of course, if one takes the melting-pot as metaphor for the "true America" and norm for the assessment. One might just as well call this process "Americanization" in the sense of a further assimilation to the hegemonic mainstream culture of regional and other subcultures across the continent. (Compare the term "Americanization of the South" in this connection). Ritzer and Stillman apparently have considered this possibility, but thought it "odd, to say the least, to think of the Americanization of America" (Ritzer and Stillman 2003: 41).

12. Recently the term "de-Americanization" has been used to refer specifically to the further "cosmopoli-

tanization" of the USA internally resulting from Latin-Americanization and Asian-Americanization, and more generally, to the intensified globalization of culture as it impinges on America (Robertson 2003: 262; Beck 2003).

13. The following definitions may all be applicable here: "*Implicate*: 1. To intertwine, twist or knit together; 2. to entangle, connect closely; 3. to involve in its nature or meaning, or as a consequence; 4. to involve or include in the operation of something; 5. to affect or cause to be affected; 6. to insinuate; to involve by signification. *Implicated*: Interwoven, involved, intertwisted, entwined. *Implication*: 1. The fact of being implied or involved without being plainly expressed; 2. the process of involving or fact or being involved in some condition" (*Oxford English Dictionary* definitions, as qtd. in Bell and Bell 1993: vii).

14. The first definition given in *The New Oxford Dictionary of English* (2001) has direct connotations of delinquency, criminality, or more generally of harmfulness or guiltiness: "*Implicate*: 1. show (someone) to be involved in a crime ... *be implicated in*: bear some of the responsibility for (an action or process, especially a criminal or harmful one)...."

15. During the Cold War one could find a certain analogue of this, in the form of "self-willed Sovietization" in West Germany in the case of part of the communist (Stalinist) left in the 1940s and 1950s and so-called "K-Gruppen" in the 1970s, whereas in East Germany, informal cultural Americanization was embraced by oppositional groupings and various subcultures of "rebellious" youth. These processes illustrate the radiation of the Soviet model and American model beyond the borders of the FRG and DRG, within the political and cultural orbit of the United States and the Soviet Union respectively (Jarausch and Siegrist 1997: 24).

16. There is a tendency in postcolonial studies to use the term "orientalism" more loosely to designate the process in which people in the periphery are perceived and depicted as exotic, strange, deviant etc. by people from the metropolitan centers in the West. Thus it is used differently from the original meaning of the term in Edward Said's analysis of Eurocentric (specifically British and French) attitudes towards the Middle East in *Orientalism* (Said 1978).

17. Another common misappropriation, particularly in the early re-

ception of Gramsci in the United States, has been to understand the concept of hegemony as a functional equivalent of commodification and reification; this tendency conceives of "hegemony" as "domination through managed consumption and manipulated desire" (Denning 1990: 13).

18. This is not identical to the way in which the concept of hegemony was framed in Jackson Lears's influential essay "The Concept of Cultural Hegemony" (Lears 1985); that is, in terms of the opposition between accommodation and resistance, thereby attempting to demonstrate how subordinate groups are complicit in their own victimization, confused by an opaque mixture of "true" and "false" consciousness. This approach, followed by a number of other American scholars, remains confined to the question about the degree to which the working classes are incorporated, and rests on a functionalist premise that leads to a focus on how ideas reinforce or undermine existing social structures. In practice, Gramsci's ideas have thus largely been used as a means to explain the futility of efforts to change capitalist societies (Denning 1990: 13–14), and "hegemony" is possibly even simply reduced to a form of resignation (Artz and Ortega Murphy 2000: 69).

19. As Nye explains, "...many soft power resources are separate from American government and only partly responsive to its purposes. In the Vietnam era, for example, American government policy and popular culture worked at cross-purposes. Today popular U.S. firms or nongovernmental groups develop soft power of their own that may coincide or be at odds with official foreign policy goals" (Nye 2002: 11).

Chapter 7

1. For many years, the U.S. government relied on philanthropic foundations, business firms, religious missions, private societies, and individuals to carry out intellectual, technical, and welfare activities deemed necessary for this purpose. Abroad, nongovernmental U.S. organizations, such as the Rockefeller Foundation, the American Library Association, and the press corps, were often the most active promotors of American culture (as understood here). Congress and the State Department frequently had to be pressured to pursue an active policy of cultural diplomacy, or were left out of the process altogether (Kraske 1985).

2. These authors use the term "weak state" in this context, which is misleading given the strongly interventionist character of the federal state since the mid-twentieth century.

3. In a parliamentary system, power is unified and responsibility is clearly fixed in that the legislative majority governs, and the cabinet, a committee of that majority, leads the legislature and directs the executive branch. Prime ministers and their cabinets can in principle act more quickly and decisively than in the American sytem, but are still held accountable by the requirement that, to remain in power, they must maintain the confidence of the parliamentary majority in question.

4. Since the Reagan years (with clear foreshadowings earlier in the post–World War II period) the use of opinion polls, and other means to assess public sentiments such as focus groups, has become a crucial component of presidential policymaking, and American politics more generally (Mead 2001: 53).

5. This occurred, for example, during the 1980s and again in 2002 over U.S. plans to construct a national missile defense, and in reponse to the Bush Administration's decision in February 2002 to impose tariffs on steel imports, in defiance of WTO rules.

6. Isolationists too have often expressed their position in terms of American exceptionalism, albeit with a different twist. Drawing upon Puritan doctrines of the "city on the hill," they sought to provide a model for the world by achieving perfection at home. International entanglements, treaties, commitments, alliances and obligations were all seen as obstacles to that goal.

7. Classical liberalism in the European sense means freedom from governmental interference, a strongly anti-statist doctrine emphasizing the virtues of laissez-faire. This concerns first of all "liberal" or more recently "neoliberal" economics: free-market economics asserting the primacy of individualism and the need of commercial entrepreneurs for room to maneuver. On the other hand, liberalism in the United States today means (since the New Deal era), in Hutton's nice phrasing, "the Creed that advocates a rational, universal infrastructure of justice built on complex trade-offs between liberty, solidarity and equality" (Hutton 2003: 5). This kind of liberalism recognizes from a social justice perspective the need for state intervention in the form of regulation of economic life

and governmental investments in public infrastructures and utilities, as well as social provisions provided by the government to those in need.

8. Westerners, perceived as inferiors to Confucian moral superiority by the Chinese, were permitted to trade with China only on terms that reflected the unequal status of the two civilizations. This system of trade was dictated by the Chinese and was designed to limit the impact of the foreign presence on their way of life (Ninkovich 2001: 154–155).

9. This could, for example, take the form of *hispanidad;* that is, glorification of things Spanish; or francophilia.

10. In this respect there are clear differences in the nature of the reception of American culture at various places and times. For example, Russian culture has historically been influenced by several Western cultures, particularly those of France, Germany and Italy, while American culture was unfamiliar to Russians until the twentieth century (Ostrovsky 1993: 71–72). Although Western Europeans have become more familiar with the United States at an earlier stage, their visions of America tended to be distorted and reliant on overgeneralizations until deep into the twentieth century. Nevertheless, after World War II there was a growing awareness of the heterogeneity of American society and culture in Western European countries. This meant, among other things, that concepts of an "other" or "alternative" America, unknown to the generation of the first postwar years, received much attention during the following decades. Eventually, the generalized atttitude toward American culture typical of the late 1940s — especially as derived from Hollywood films at the time — was transformed into a more differentiated view and appraisal of specific trends within that culture (Schou 1992).

Chapter 8

1. For interesting examples of such geographical differences in Italy during and just after World War II from the first arrival of Allied troops in 1943, see Forgacs (1993: 162–163).

2. Interestingly, the United States was the first country to introduce quotas, to break the dominant position of the French film industry at the turn of the twentieth century (Wagnleiter 1993: 322).

3. This has led to cultural exchanges of films and TV programs in

which Britain sold to Americans "Americanized" representations of itself, and bought back American produced and validated constructions of "Britishness" (Strinati 1992: 57–58).

4. For example, in the volume edited by Jarausch and Siegrist (1997) this is deliberately done with regard to French and British influences as well as the impact of European integration and its supra-national institutions and associated ideas and practices on post-World War II West Germany (*ibid.*: 14).

5. Modern American domestic architecture built on pre-World War II borrowings from Europe (Germany, France, and the Netherlands), while during the 1950s the American home and its furnishings continued to be influenced by ideas and products from Italy and Scandinavia (Nolan 2003: 249).

6. It is the U.S.-style cultural practices of consumerism rather than simply the commodification of national symbols that constitute a supposed threat here.

7. Modern Japan stands out in this regard, often turning foreign things into merely empty form or ritual. Examples in several domains (architecture, designs, customs and lifestyle, language, etc.) indicate that "the Japanese give preference to the forms and often the rituals of things borrowed from outside sources without being concerned with the significance of the 'orginal.' In the process of being influenced by (elements of) foreign cultures, they give new meaning(s) to the borrowed element — which meaning is often incompatible with that of the original — or else they manage to 'void' associable meanings, thereby turning the thing into empty form or ritual" (Bognar 2000: 63). Delanty signals an all-pervasive "subversion of Americanization" in Japan's encounters with America which would set severe limits to the Americanization of Japanese culture (Delanty 2003).

8. However, in the 1980s, when frictions arose between the USA and Japan over the substantial trade imbalance in the latter's favor, a multifarious America-bashing movement (including academics, writers, journalists, politicians, governmental officials) emerged in Japan that had two themes: Japan's superiority and America's inferiority in various respects. This was paralleled by an influential Japan-bashing movement of American and other western academics and journalists dominated by Eurocentric, exclusivist and essentialist interpretations of Japanese culture and society (Miyoshi 1991: 62–94).

9. In the case of former colonies of European nations such as Britain or France, this indigenous debate has been part of a derived high culture from the former motherland (or today's British or French Commonwealth). Australia and anglophone Canada offer good examples; until recently, Australian and English-speaking Canadian intellectuals have quite naturally engaged in the same discussions as in Britain, inheriting assumptions about the superiority of Oxbridge intellectual traditions, the virtues of empiricism and the validity of more recent English doubts about both. It is also as a provincial reflection on those debates about Americanization that part of the local intelligentsia set out to "discover" and legitimate a distinctive Australian and Canadian culture respectively; in recent years they have also been involved in broader discussions about "post-colonialism" (White 1983: 110; Davies 1995: 163–167). Intellectuals in former French colonies, for example in Africa, have acted similarly in relation to high-culture institutions and intellectual traditions in France and the indigenous culture they were (and remain) a part of.

10. Beat music was in itself a cultural mix that drew on American popular musics such as rhythm and blues, rock 'n' roll, early sixties black girls' singing groups, and country & western, along with elements from the British musical hall tradition in some instances (the likes of the Beatles or the Kinks).

11. Hall (1980) makes a rough heuristic distinction here between three different codes: the "dominant code" (representing the view of the *status quo*), the "negotiated code" (representing a limited challenge), and the "oppositional code," constituting a direct opposition to the established order. Because of unclarities about what exactly a code is, Billig suggests to replace it by the term "account" (Billig 1997: 224). With some obvious alterations, Hall's distinctions might be employed to categorize different local responses (and associated accounts) to the encodings or accounts tied to American imports. But I agree with Billig that this threefold division is less suited for advanced capitalism that is strengthening its position globally, and has not been characterized by a single mode of thinking but by "an expanding, market-driven [discursive] heteroglossia" (Billig 1997: 225).

12. The term "interpretive communities" originates in the literary versions of cultural studies, and calls attention to interpretation as a social act and readers as inhabitants of a social world. It refers to the fact that people reveal similar or common responses because they already share common "interpretative strategies" when faced with particular cultural texts (Fish 1980). However, when adopting this term, one has to take care that the "community" referred to does not remain sociologically thin as is usually the case in this kind of literary approach, when it points to a world of relations that is rarely examined in itself. There is a need for "thick descriptions" of the community backgrounds of receivers that will enable observers to understand their reactions. This means that recipients should be located through the social processes by which "texts" influence and engage them in actual circumstances (Jensen and Pauly 1997: 158).

13. This entails seeking pleasure by visiting slums or places considered slums (in this case black ghettos and jazz clubs, dance halls, juke joints and restaurants located there) especially out of curiosity.

14. In this regard we find differences in the local impact of McDonald's restaurants, for example in East Asia. In Beijing, as in other places, when McDonald's was a newcomer, people did not just visit the place to eat a hamburger meal but to participate vicariously in American-style modernity. In places like Tokyo or Tapei, however, where McDonald's has been active for a long time and has become an integral part of everyday life, eating a hamburger is just one consumer choice among many — and not "sacramental" (in whatever way) at all (Watson 1997; Srinivas 2002: 99). In other places the burger is invested with a different symbolism; young adults who eat at McDonald's in New Delhi are thus first of all demonstrating their status, wealth, and upward social mobility. Interestingly, consumption of McDonald's fast food in India does not carry with it the cultural freight of freedom, democracy, human rights as it did, for example, in the former Soviet Union.

15. Morris distinguishes two other positions opposed to "cultural imperialism" in her discusion of three type of responses (premised on "three theories of unoriginality and national cinema") among Austrialians to "global-yet-American" film: 1) "an ideal of native accent, positive authenticity," based on cultural nationalism and an associated "closed concept of culture it must at some level

assume" and 2) "positive unspecifity," that is, an acceptance that the local culture is so Americanized that questions of authenticity, independence or originality are not of relevance anymore: "The eye of the beholder, whenever it's placed, is always American anyway" (Morris 1988: 246–247; cf. Webster 1989: 65–66).

16. Morris gives the Australian example of the *Mad Max* series' appropriation of road movies.

17. In 1993, Murdoch's News Corporation purchased the struggling Asian satellite service, STAR TV, and within a few years it had made significant inroads into television markets in a number of countries, including China, India and Taiwan. In courting the Chinese communist government, Murdoch suspended the BBC's World Service from STAR TV in 1994, and made sure that his recently acquired publishing company, HarperCollins, did not publish the memoirs of former Hong Kong governor Chris Patten, one of China's main international political bogeymen. Although STAR TV transmits programs that offer a similar mix to that familiar in the West (including an emphasis on individualist and consumerist values), they also articulate other values that do not straightforwardly support capitalist accumulation, including stories emphasizing the virtues of family and community loyalty (Hesmondhalgh 2002: 187; cf. Ong 1999).

18. Lundén discusses the incorporation of Positive Thinking (originating from the U.S.) into management practices, where he signals a tendency of steering towards an individualist, competitive entrepreneurial system commonly associated with America; psychotherapy and education; and also in the religious sphere (particularly local variants of neo-Pentecostalism and charismatic Christianity) in Sweden, displacing to some degree the more skeptical and pessimistic world view of Lutheranism but not fully overtaking it (Lundén 1991: 143–150). Seen from a long-term perspective, however, here a two-way influence took place between Europe and America: the méthode Coué ("Day by day, in every way, I am getting better and better") as a method of auto-suggestion originated from France, not without its followers in Europe, and "American" perhaps only because of its enormous popularity in the U.S. (Kroes 1991: 6). But I would add that this method of "positive affirmations," as it came to be called in the New World, was also Americanized there in the course

of its transformation and incorporation into forms of mental healing such as Mary Baker Eddy's Christian Science variant before being re-imported to Europe.

19. Although I am aware of the problems involved in the term "cultural imperialism," I still find it useful to indicate the relatively one-sided cultural influence from one country, region or culture area on others. But the phenomena it refers to should preferably be approached in a different way than is common in much of the literature (van Elteren 2003).

20. This has, for instance, been the case in many studies of the influence of media in developing countries during the 1960s and 1970s (Tomlinson 1991: 34–67).

21. Although I agree with Wagnleiter's suggestion that this has much to do with the further development of capitalism (Wagnleiter 1993: 78), I would add "for the time being, as spearheaded by the United States," which is contrary to his viewpoint that this has less to do with Americanization.

22. This is not necessarily identical with U.S.-based capitalism, of course, although Jameson emphasizes the "Americanness" of global capitalism: "This whole global, yet American, postmodern culture is the internal and superstructural expression of a whole new wave of American military and economic domination throughout the world…" (Jameson 1991: 5).

23. Garton Ash's journalistic writings on the 1989 events were framed by the leading idea that liberal democracy and the benefits of market capitalism were the inspiration of revolt (Garton Ash 1990). The more hawkish Fukuyama interpreted the events as confirming his "end of history" thesis, put forward in advance of the fall of 1989 (Fukuyama 1989); see also next chapter.

Chapter 9

1. For example, Anthony Giddens's attempt to theorize globalization as late and reflexive modernity shows this tendency (Giddens 1990).

2. Robertson borrowed this term from Japanese management theorists who coined the verb "to glocalize," a neologism that has appeared in the *Oxford Dictionary of New Words* since 1991. In line with the new management and marketing schemes, it indicates that all strategies in a globalized market should be both local and international.

3. In this context, "Washington"

refers not only to the U.S. government, but to all those institutions and networks of opinion leaders centered in the world's de facto capital of the world economy — the IMF, World Bank, think tanks, investment bankers and finance ministers, all those members of the transnational capitalist class who meet each other in Washington and share the conventional wisdom of the moment that neoliberal economic policy is the key to economic development and prosperity (Makinson 2000; Sklair 2002: 85).

4. Friedman also mentions the existence of a class system in the United States, whereby through various social mechanisms talented people from the lower classes are prevented from becoming part of the elite.

5. Barber's usage of the notion of "Jihad" is problematic. He uses a word with specific connotations within Islam to categorize a wide variety of protests against global capitalism. For Barber, the word connotes "a generic form of fundamentalist opposition to modernity that can be found in most world religions" (Barber 1995: 205). Even though Barber demonstrates interest in detail and nuance at various points in his analysis, according to historian Nicholas Guyatt, he "collapses the diverse forms and causes of discontent into a single 'fundamentalist' movement, and then gives it a name which enshrines its inaccessibility and irrationality (especially when ranged against 'modernity')." Thus Barber gives his readers a sense "that the battle against global capitalism is based not on the economic injustice of free markets and the dismantling of government services but on anti-modern, fundamentalist tendencies which are culturally determined" (Guyatt 2000: 190). Another critique of Barber's view is that he ignores the ways in which U.S. fundamentalist religious movements are involved in the process of modernizing and globalizing themselves. Particularly in the case of new Christian fundamentalism the globalizing of the faith is closely intertwined with the homogenizing influences of consumerism, mass communication and production in ways that have a strong elective affinity with the creation of a transnational market culture by global capitalist institutions (Brouwer et al. 1996: 3).

6. Elsewhere I have commented on this form of U.S. "liberal imperialism" (van Elteren, 2006).

7. In this context, three related

processes make competing organizational structures look more and more alike. First, organizations are coerced by cultural expectations. Second, organizations tend to model themselves on other organizations in an environment of "symbolic uncertainty." Third, the process of professionalization develops formal credential systems that generate strong norms among managers (Di Maggio and Powell 1983). Ritzer and Stillman add a fourth component, which plays a significant role in McDonaldization, that is, the competitive advantage that rationalized systems have over competing models of organization (Ritzer and Stillman 2003: 37–38).

8. Sometimes offshoring occurs through a combination of outsourcing and captive models. The expansion of international offshoring has contributed to the emergence of a new kind of TNCs that provides services to other companies, thus imitating contract manufacturers. Most of such "contract service providers" hail from the United States, accounting for two-thirds of all export-oriented information and telecommunication service projects, 60 percent of call-center projects and 55 percent of shared-service projects during 2002–2003. Some of them have become global players by setting up their own international networks of foreign affiliates (UNCTAD 2004b: 26, 28).

9. Sklair distinguishes three fractions within the transnational capitalist class: "Those who own and control the TNCs organize the production of commodities and the services necessary to manufacture and sell them. The state fraction of the transnational capitalist class produces the political environment within which the products and services can be successfully marketed all over the world irrespective of their origins and qualities. Those responsible for the dissemination of the culture-ideology of consumerism produce the values and attitudes that create and sustain the need for the products" (Sklair 2002: 85). For further details, see Sklair (2001).

10. Founded in the mid-1970s, the G7 includes the United States, Canada, Japan, France, Germany, the United Kingdom and Italy (usually indicated as the world's most important industrial nations). Starting in 1994, the G7 met with Russia at each summit (referred to as the P8 or Political Eight). Since 1997 Russia participates in all but financial and certain economic discussions, with the group recast as G8. (However, the G7

continued to function alongside the formal summits.) At the Kananaskis Summit in Canada in 2002, it was announced that Russia would host the G8 summit in 2006, thus completing the process of becoming a full member. In addition, there are briefer "G8+5 meetings" for the finance ministers of the G8, as well as China, Mexico, India, Brazil, and South Africa (G8 Information Centre, University of Toronto, "What is the G8?," http://www.g7.utoronto.ca, accessed on January 5, 2006).

11. Ben Bernanke, the new chairman of the American Federal Reserve Board (since February 2006), has explained this situation in terms of the "global savings glut" thesis: the U.S. balance of payments deficit is not due to Americans saving too little and spending too much; rather, the rest of the world saves too much and invests this redundant money in the United States, hoping for a better return than at home (Schinkel 2005a). But top economist Stephen Roach of business bank Morgan Stanley (in the late 1990s one of the few economists who remained skeptical about the "New Economy" and the first to recognize the recession following the crash of the stock market and the oil price peak in the fall of 2000) has depicted this as a time bomb ticking underneath the world economy. *NRC Handelsblad,* March 19/20, 2005: 23.

12. Early in 2005, the dollar assets (mostly U.S. government bonds) of the central banks of Asia collectively surpassed $1 trillion. They were the ultimate source of the massive borrowings by American consumers against the rising value of their houses — then more than $2 trillion since 2000. At the end of 2005, Americans' savings were *minus* 1.5 percent compared to percentages fluctuating around 10 percent in the 1970s and 1980s. The decrease in savings was especially strong during the first five years of the new millennium (Schinkel 2005b).

13. It was the first major worldwide campaign against neoliberal globalization, bringing together a network of hundreds of organizations from all over the world, many mobilizing on a local basis, united (notably through the Internet) in their opposition to what would have amounted to a carte blanche given to TNCs, if realized. It must be emphasized that organizations from the USA (the "other America") and Canada had a substantial part in this countermovement; they provided over 200 of the 600 nongovernmental organi-

zations in sixty-seven countries that made the case against the MAI (Sklair 2001: 299–300; Sklair 2002: 287–291).

14. This is to be understood as what Gramsci calls "the sense held in common," which typically underlies consent. Common sense is constructed out of long-standing practices of cultural socialization often deeply embedded in regional or national traditions. It differs from the "good sense," that can be developed through critical engagement with daily issues. This means that common sense can be deeply misleading, obfuscating or concealing real problems under cultural prejudices (Gramsci 1971: 321–343).

15. For an analytical account of relevant developments in the U.S. and Britain, see Harvey 2005: 41–63; regarding the U.S. in the 1990s, see Frank 2000; and for the turn of the 21st century, see Giroux 2004.

16. This is, for instance, not the case with mass marketing (Sklair 2001: 289).

17. Admittedly, these American books on management do not constitute a homogeneous category. Both the most prominent proponents of various versions of what may be called the mainstream management approach and its most outspoken critics are represented among them. But the overall picture is that the mainstream American-style management approach predominates. The actual influence of the contents of these books is of course dependent on the way in which these have been appropriated locally, which necessitates more detailed empirical research.

18. After the Reagan and Thatcher years, governments on both sides of the Atlantic, including the Clinton Administration and the Blair Administration (pursuing New Labour's Third Way), have continued neoliberal policymaking to a great extent. Today it is customary to distinguish the "Anglo-Saxon" or Anglo-American (that is, British-American) variant of modern capitalism from the German (or "Rhineland"), Swedish, French and Japanese models. There are also significant continuities and similarities between British and American law. Therefore it is opportune to use the adjective "Anglo-American" in this context.

19. This is an updated and more fine-tuned version of what Marx called "primitive accumulation"— with privatization and commodification, and more extreme forms of financialization as key elements.

20. In this regard Hutton dis-

tances himself explicitly from globalization theorist Anthony Giddens's thinking on globalization, referring to the latter's Reith lecture series "Runaway World" (Hutton 2003: n 4, 474). In a public disussion between Wil Hutton and Anthony Giddens, also leading proponent of the Third Way in the New Labour project in Britain, Giddens made a distinction between "globalization from above" — the spheres of financial markets, trade, and technological innovation — in which the United States and the West "are easily the dominant powers," and fundamental processes of "globalization from below" — e.g., the role of nongovernmental organizations, interest groups, and pressure groups operating on a worldwide level — which would to some extent counterbalance the other forces. Hutton was much more negative about U.S. economic dominance than Giddens: "My point throughout this conversation is that the conservatives are in the ascendent; and that they have been ruthless in pursuit of their interests, compromising the Clinton presidency and shaping globalization in U.S. interests" (Hutton and Giddens 2000: 58–59, 61–62).

21. For a similar argument with regard to consumer culture, Sklair (2002: 169). However, I disagree with Sklair's rejection of the thesis of U.S.-driven cultural imperialism, which in my view still contains a granule of truth today (van Elteren 2003). I also find his definition of Americanization, "loosely understood as the method of the most successfully productive economy in human history" (Sklair 2002: 169), much too limited.

22. Here we may recall that Henry A. Wallace, when Vice-President during Roosevelt's third term (1941–44), advocated a global version of the early New Deal, based on large public-works projects modeled on the Tennessee Valley Authority, with concerted collective efforts to build international highways and airways (Rosenberg 1982: 191). It was his contribution to what Wallace was publicly calling "a messianic liberalism of abundance," to ensure peace and elementary rights for all of mankind. Wallace insisted that "the peace must mean a better standard of living for the common man, not merely in the United States and England, but also in India, Russia, China, and Latin America — not merely in the United Nations [as the Western alliance then called itself], but also in Germany and Italy and Japan." In an obvious attempt to take a distance from Henry A. Luce's imperialist conception of the "American Century" (Luce 1941), he emphasized that the century mankind was entering "can and must be the century of the common man" (Wallace 1942) in a speech, delivered in May 1942, that was repeatedly reprinted and widely distributed throughout the United States and the world during the war (see also Wallace 1943). The cornerstone of this Rooseveltian, globalizing America was laid by President Franklin Roosevelt in his Annual Message to the Congress in January 1941, when he identified the "four essential human freedoms" for which the United States would fight in the future: "freedom of speech and expression"; "the freedom of every person to worship God in his own way"; "freedom from want," and "freedom from fear" — all four freedoms to be realized "everywhere and anywhere in the world" (qtd. in Slater 1999: 18). But Wallace led a more specific coalition of Progressives and liberals that supported a set of ideals that envisioned extending New Deal-style reforms throughout the world, with "self-determination everywhere, an end to economic and political imperialism, and vast economic development programs to ensure freedom from want" (Hamby 1968: 154). Wallace was especially annoyed about some of the overtly self-interested and commercial elements in Luce's vision of the American century, including Luce's urgent pressure to use the "tremendous possibilities" for world trade. In proposing a "people's century" in contradistinction to Luce's vision of global Americanization, Wallace expressed his hope that the postwar order would be a resolute break with the status quo and his belief that only a more equitable global arrangement could peacefully harness the social and political forces of the developing world. According to Guyatt, this polemic between Luce and Wallace represented an important political and ideological distinction between "Americanization" and "internationalism," that was largely absent during the four decades of the Cold War (Guyatt 2000: xiv). (It was hardly represented in the political discourse of transatlantic policymakers, I would add — there was an awareness of this in other circles.) For Luce, the United States should use all available opportunities to exploit its power and predominant status in the winning of new markets abroad, and the expansion of American political and cultural influence. Wallace, on the other hand, argued for a U.S. responsibility towards the developing world *and* the right of poorer countries to determine their own path of development, with American assistance but without submitting to American empire. Wallace and his associates hoped that a strong United Nations, with some sort of police power, would preside over this revolutionary progress, which would be the effective realization of One World. They also opined that a world united in such a worldwide United Nations required at that time the maintenance of the wartime antifascist alliance and Soviet-American friendship (Brinkley 2003). With the obvious exception of the latter alliance, Wallace's proposal can be seen as some kind of precursor of the current proposals. However, like all other approaches of international socioeconomic isssues advocated by internationalist factions within the Roosevelt Administration, Wallace's intended approach still assumed a vigorous U.S. economic expansionism — albeit regulated by the U.S. government and to some extent policed by a United Nations as understood here — and "a vision of the future that included a central role for the United States in both inspiring and shaping a new age of democracy" (*ibid.*: 12). Evidently, this differs significantly from the much larger-scale and multi- or transnational character of recent proposals of this kind that do not presuppose an expansionist United States as lead society in economical and political world affairs.

Bibliography

Abernethy, David B. (2000) *The Dynamics of Global Dominance: European Overseas Empires, 1415–1980.* New Haven: Yale University Press.

Abu-Lughod, Janet (1997) "Going Beyond Global Babble," in Anthony D. King (ed.) *Culture, Globalization and the World-System: Contemporary Conditions for the Representations of Identity* (pp. 131–137). Minneapolis: University of Minneapolis Press.

Adams, James Truslow Adams (1931) *The Epic of America.* Boston: Little, Brown.

Albert, Michel (1993) *Capitalism Against Capitalism.* Trans. Paul Haviland. London: Whutt Publishers.

Albo, Gregory (1994) "'Competitive Austerity' and the Impasse of Capitalist Employment Policy," in Ralph Miliband and Leo Panitch (eds.) *Between Globalism and Nationalism: The Socialist Register 1994.* (pp. 144–170) London: Merlin Press.

Anderson, Benedict (1983) *Imagined Communities: Reflections on the Originis and Spread of Nationalism.* London: Verso Editions and New Left Books.

Anderson, Perry (2002) Editorial "Force and Consent," *New Left Review*, 17 (September–October): 5–30.

Ang, Ien (1985) *Watching Dallas.* London and New York: Methuen.

Antonio, Robert J., and Alessandro Bonanno (2000) "A New Global Capitalism? From 'Americanism and Fordism' to 'Americanization-Globalization,'" *American Studies* 41, 2/3 (Summer/Fall): 33–77.

Appadurai, Arjun (1990) "Disjuncture and Difference in the Global Cultural Economy," in Mike Featherstone (ed.) *Global Culture: Nationalism, Globalization and Modernity* (pp. 295–310). London: Sage.

_____. (1996) *Modernity at Large: Cultural Dimensions of Globalization.* Minneapolis: University of Minnesota Press.

Arnold, Matthew (1962) "Democracy," introduction to "The Popular Education of France," *The Complete Prose Works of Matthew Arnold*, II (pp. 3–29), R.H. Super, ed., Ann Arbor: University of Michigan Press.

Arnove, Robert F. (ed.) (1980) *Philanthropy and Cultural Imperialism: The Foundations at Home and Abroad.* Boston: G.K. Hall.

Aronowitz, Stanley (1993) *Roll Over, Beethoven: The Return of Cultural Strife.* New York: Westview Press.

Artz, Lee, and Bren Ortega Murphy (2000) *Cultural Hegemony in the United States.* Thousand Oaks, CA: Sage.

Bacevich, Andrew J. (2002) *American Empire: The Realities and Consequences of U.S. Diplomacy.* Cambridge, MA: Harvard University Press.

Bacon, David (2005) "Beyond Braceros," *The Nation*, 281, 22 (December 26): 5–6.

Bakhtin, Mikhail (1981) *The Dialogical Imagination.* Austin: University of Texas Press.

_____. (1986) *Speech Genres and Other Late Essays.* Austin: University of Texas Press.

Balakrishnan, Gopal (ed.) (2003) *Debating Empire.* London — New York: Verso.

Balibar, Etienne (1992) *Les frontières de la démocratie.* Paris: La Découverte.

Banham, Reyner (1975) "Mediated Environments *or: You Can't Build That Here*," in Christopher W.E. Bigsby (ed.) *Superculture: American Popular Culture and Europe* (pp. 69–82). Bowling Green, Ohio: Bowling Green University Popular Press.

Barber, Benjamin R. (1995) *Jihad vs McWorld: How Globalism and Tribalism Are Reshaping the World.* New York: Times Books.

_____. (2003). *Fear's Empire: War, Terrorism, and Democracy.* New York — London: Norton.

Barker, Chris (2000) *Cultural Studies: Theory and Practice.* London: Sage.

Barthes, Roland (1977) *Image-Music-Text.* London: Fontana.

Basler, Otto (1930) "Amerikanismus: Geschichte eines Schlagwortes," in *Deutsche Rundschau*, vol. 224. August: 142–147.

Baudrillard, Jean (1986) *Amérique.* Paris: Grasset.

_____. (1989) *America.* Trans. Chris Turner. London and New York: Verso.

Bauman, Zygmunt (1987) *Legislators and Interpreters: On Modernity, Post-modernity and Intellectuals.* Ithaca, NY: Cornell University Press.

Baym, Nina (1989) "Early Histories of American Literature: A Chapter in the Institution of New England," *American Literary History*, 1, 3: 459–488.

Beck, Earl R. (1985) "The Anti-Nazi 'Swing Youth' 1942–1945, *Journal of Popular Culture*, 19, 3: 45–53.

Beck, Ulrich (2003) "Rooted Cosmopolitanism: Emerging from a Rivalry of Distinctions," in Ulrich Beck, Natan Sznaider and Rainer Winter (eds.) *Global America? The Cultural Consequences of Globalization* (pp. 15–29). Liverpool: Liverpool University Press.

Bell, Philip, and Roger Bell (1993) *Implicated: The United States in Australia.* Oxford: Oxford University Press.

_____, and _____. (1998) "Introduction: The Dilemma's of 'Americanisation,'" in Philip Bell and Roger Bell (eds.) *Americanization and Australia* (pp. 1–14). Sydney: University of New South Wales Press.

_____, and _____. (2004) "American/Global: Australian/Local," in Rob Kroes (ed.) *Straddling Borders:*

225

The American Resonance in Transnational Identities (pp. 87–99). Amsterdam: VU University Press.

Bellah, Robert N., Richard Madsen, William M. Sullivan, Ann Swidler, and Steven M. Tipton (1985). *Habits of the Heart: Individualism and Commitment in American Life*. New York: Harper.

Bender, Thomas (1988) "New York in Theory," in Leslie Berlowitz, Denis Donoghue and Louis Menand (eds.) *America in Theory* (pp. 53–65). New York — London: Oxford University Press.

_____. (2000) *La Pietra Report: Project on Internationalizing the Study of American History, a Report to the Profession*. New York: Organization of American Historians, New York University.

Benjamin, Ross (2005) "Mother Nature's Son (review of *The Novices of Sais* by Novalis," *The Nation*, 281, 3 (July 18/25): 36, 38.

Berg, Peter (1963) *Deutschland und Amerika 1918–1929. Über das deutsche Amerikabild der zwanziger Jahre*. Lübeck: Matthiesen.

Berger, Mark T. (1995) *Under Northern Eyes: Latin American Studies and U.S. Hegemony in the Americas, 1890–1990*. Bloomington: Indiana University Press.

Berger, Peter L. (2002) "Introduction," in Peter L. Berger and Samuel P. Huntington (eds.) (2002) *Many Globalizations: Cultural Diversity in the Contemporary World* (pp. 1–16). Oxford: Oxford University Press.

Berger, Suzanne, and Ronald Dore (eds.) (1996) *National Diversity and Global Capitalism*. Ithaca, NY: Cornell University Press.

Berghahn, Volker R. (1995) "West German Reconstruction and American Industrial Culture, 1945–1960," in Reiner Pommerin (ed.) *The American Impact on Postwar Germany* (pp. 65–81) Providence — Oxford: Berghahn.

Berlet, Chip, and Matthew N. Lyons (2000) *Right-Wing Populism in America: Too Close for Comfort*. New York — London: The Guilford Press.

Berman, Marshall (1988) *All That is Solid Melts into Air: The Experience of Modernity*. Harmondsworth: Penguin.

Bérubé, Michael (1994) *Public Access: Literary Theory and American Cultural Politics*. London — New York: Verso.

Beynon, John, and David Dunkerley (eds.) (2000) *Globalization: The Reader*. London: The Athlone Press.

Bigsby, Christopher W.E. (1975) "Europe, America and the Cultural Debate," in Christopher W.E. Bigsby (ed.) *Superculture: American Popular Culture and Europe* (pp. 1–27) Bowling Green, Ohio: Bowling Green University Press.

Billig, Michael (1997) "From Codes to Utterances: Cultural Studies, Discourse and Psychology," in Marjorie Ferguson and Peter Golding (eds.) *Cultural Studies in Question* (pp. 205–226). London: Sage.

Blair, John G., Jr. (1988) *Modular America: Cross-Cultural Perspectives on the Emergence of an American Way*. Westport, Conn.: Greenwood Press.

Bognar, Botond (2000) "Surface above All? American Influence of Japanese Urban Space," in Heide Fehrenbach and Uta G. Poiger (eds.) *Transactions, Transgressions, Transformations* (pp. 45–78). New York — Oxford: Berghahn.

Bourne, Randolph S. (1916a) "Americanism," *New Republic*, 23 September: 197.

_____. (1916b) "Trans-National America," *The Atlantic Monthly*, 118, July: 86–97.

_____. (1916c) Editorial, *Seven Arts*, 1, November: 52–53.

_____. (1918) "Americans in the Making," *New Republic*, 2 February: 30–32.

_____. (1964) *War and the Intellectuals: Essays by Randolph S. Bourne, 1915–1919*. Carl Resek, ed. New York: Harper.

Bracken, Peter (1997) "The New American Challenge," *World Policy Journal*, 14, 2: 10–19.

Bradbury, Malcolm (1995) *Dangerous Pilgrimages: Trans-Atlantic Mythologies and the Novel*. Harmondsworth: Penguin.

Bradley, Dick (1992) *Understanding Rock 'n' Roll: Popular Music in Britain 1955–1964*. Buckingham and Philadelphia: Open University Press.

Brandt, Anthony (1981) "The American Dream," *American Heritage*, 4–5 (April-May): 24–25.

Brecher, Jeremy, Tim Costello, and Brendan Smith (2000) *Globalization from Below: The Power of Solidarity*. Cambridge, MA: South End Press.

Breidenbach, Joanna, and Ina Zukrigl (2002) "Up and Down the Music World: An Anthropology of Globalization," in Andreas Gebesmair and Alfred Smudits (eds.) *Global Repertoires: Popular Music Within and Beyond the Transnational Music Industry* (pp. 105–117). Aldershot: Ashgate.

Brenner, Robert (2002) *The Boom and the Bubble: The U.S. in the World Economy*. London: Verso.

Brinkley, Alan (1982) *Voices of Protest: Huey Long, Father Coughlin, and the Great Depression*. New York: Knopf.

_____. (2003) "The Concept of an American Century," in R. Laurence Moore and Maurizio Vaudagna (eds.) *The American Century in Europe* (pp. 7- 21). Ithaca, NY: Cornell University Press.

Bronner, Stephen E. (2004) *Reclaiming the Enlightenment: Toward a Politics of Radical Engagement*. New York: Columbia University Press.

Brouwer, Steve, Paul Gifford and Susan D. Rose (1996) *Exporting the American Gospel: Global Christian Fundamentalism*. New York — London: Routledge.

Burbach, Roger, Orlando Nunez, and Boris Kagarlitsky (1997) *Globalization and Its Discontents: The Rise of Postmodern Socialisms*. London: Pluto Press.

Callinicos, Alex (2001) *Against the Third Way: An Anti-Capitalist Critique*. Cambridge: Polity Press.

Carrez, Jean-François (1991) *Le developpement des fonctions tertiaires internationales à Paris et dans les métropoles regionales*. Report to the Prime Minister. Paris: La Documentation Française.

Castells, Manuel (1996) *The Rise of the Network Society*. Oxford: Blackwell.

_____. (1997) *The Power of Identity*. Oxford: Blackwell.

_____. (1998) *End of Millennium*. Oxford: Blackwell.

Ceaser, James W. (1997) *Reconstructing America: The Symbol of America in Modern Thought*. New Haven and London: Yale University Press.

Chambers, Iain (1985) *Urban Rhythms: Pop Music and Popular Culture*. Basingstoke: Macmillan.

Chandler, Alfred (1990) *Scale and Scope: The Dynamics of Industrial Capitalism*. Cambridge, MA: Harvard University Press.

Chase, Malcolm, M., and Christopher Shaw (1989) "The Dimensions of Nostalgia," in Christopher Shaw and Malcolm Chase, *The Imagined Past: History and*

Nostalgia (pp. 1–17). Manchester: Manchester University Press.

Chénetier, Marc (1993) "America Degrained," in Richard P. Horwitz (ed.) *Exporting America: Essays on American Studies Abroad* (pp. 347–362). New York and London: Garland Publishing Inc.

Clarke, John (1990) "Pessimism versus Populism: The Problematic Politics of Popular Culture," in Richard Butsch (ed.) *For Fun and Profit: The Commercialization of Leisure into Consumption* (pp. 28–44). Philadelphia: Temple University Press.

_____. (1991) "'Mine Eyes Dazzle:' Cultures of Consumption," in John Clarke, *New Times and Old Enemies: Essays on Cultural Studies and America* (pp. 73–112). London: HarperCollins.

Clifford, James (1997) *Travel and Translation in the Late Twentieth Century*. New Haven: Yale University Press.

_____, and George E. Marcus (eds.) (1986) *Writing Culture: The Poetics and Politics of Geography*. Berkeley: University of California Press.

Cobb, James C. (1982) *The Selling of the South: The Southern Crusade for Industrial Development, 1936–1980*. Baton Rouge: Louisiana State University Press.

_____. (1984) *Industrialization and Southern Society*. Lexington: University of Kentucky Press.

_____. (1993) *The Selling of the South: The Southern Crusade for Industrial Development, 1936–1990*. 2nd. ed. Urbana: University of Illinois Press.

Cohen, Lizabeth (1990) *Making a New Deal: Industrial Workers in Chicago, 1919–1939*. New York: Cambridge University Press.

Cohen, Robin, and Paul Kennedy (2000) *Global Sociology*. London: Macmillan.

Cole, David (2005) "The Missing Patriot Debate," *The Nation*, 280, 21 (May 30): 18, 20–21.

Condry, Ian (2000) "The Social Production of Difference. Imitation and Authenticity in Japanese Rap Music," in Heide Fehrenbach and Uta G. Poiger (eds.) *Transactions, Transgressions, Transformations* (pp. 166–184). New York — Oxford: Berghahn.

Cooper, Marc (2005) "High Noon on the Border," *The Nation*, 280, 22 (June 6): 20–24.

_____. (2006) "Showdown on Immigration." *The Nation*, 282, 13 (April 3): 18, 20–22.

Costigliola, Frank (1984) *Awkward Dominion: American Political, Economic, and Cultural Relations with Europe, 1919–1933*. Ithaca, NY: Cornell University Press.

Cox, Robert W. (1987) *Production, Power, and World Order: Social Forces in the Making of History*. New York: Columbia University Press.

Crouch, Colin, and Wolfgang Streeck (eds.) (1997) *Political Economy of Modern Capitalism: Mapping Convergence and Diversity*. London: Sage.

Cubberley, Ellwood P. (1909) *Changing Conceptions of Education*. New York: Riverside Educational Monographs.

Cummings, Stephen D. (1998) *The Dixification of America: The American Odyssey into the Conservative Economic Trap*. Westport, Connecticut — London: Praeger.

Cunliffe, Marcus (1961) "Europe and America, Transatlantic Images, I," *Encounter*, December: 19–29.

_____. (1963) "European Images of America," in Arthur M. Schlesinger, Jr., and Morton White (eds.) *Paths of American Thought* (pp. 492–514, 586–589). Boston: Houghton Mifflin.

_____. (1986) "The Anatomy of Anti-Americanism," in Rob Kroes and Maarten van Rossem (eds.) *Anti-Americanism in Europe* (pp. 20–36). Amsterdam: Free University Press.

Curran, James (1990) "The New Revisionism in Mass Communication Research — A Reappraisal," *European Journal of Communication*, 5, 2–3 (June): 135–164.

Dahrendorf, Ralf (1963) *Die angewandte Aufklärung: Gesellschaft und Soziologie in Amerika*. München: R. Piper & Co. Verlag.

Davies, Ioan (1995) *Cultural Studies and Beyond: Fragments of Empire*. New York: Routledge.

de Certeau, Michel (1984) *The Practice of Everyday Life*. Berkeley: University of California Press.

de Graaf, Heleen (2004) "IFRS: eindelijk eenheid in de boeken. Europa voert nieuwe regels voor financiële verslaglegging in," *NRC Handelsblad*, November 20/21: 21.

de Graaff, Bob (1986) "Bogey or Saviour? The Image of the United States in the Netherlands During the Interwar Period," in Rob Kroes and Maarten van Rossem (eds.) *Anti-Americanism in Europe* (pp. 51–71). Amsterdam: Free University Press.

Delanty, Gerard (2003) "Consumption, Modernity and Japanese Cultural Identity: The Limits of Americanization?," in Ulrich Beck, Natan Sznaider and Rainer Winter (eds.) *Global America? The Cultural Consequences of Globalization* (pp. 114–133). Liverpool: Liverpool University Press.

Denning, Michael (1990) "The End of Mass Culture," *International Labor and Working-Class History*, 37, Spring: 4–18.

_____. (1996) *The Cultural Front: The Left and American Culture in the Age of the CIO*. New York: Verso.

Derber, Charles (1998) *Corporation Nation: How Corporations Are Taking Over Our Lives and What We Can Do About It*. New York: St. Martin's Press.

Desai, Meghnad, and Yahia Said (2001) "The New Anti-Capitalist Movement: Money and Global Civil Society," in Helmut Anheier, Marlies Glasius, and Mary Kaldor (eds.) *Global Civil Society 2001* (pp. 51–78). Oxford: Oxford University Press.

Dezalay, Yves, and Bryant Garth (1995) "Merchants of Law as Moral Entrepreneurs: Constructing International Justice from the Competition for Transnational Business Disputes," *Law and Society Review* 29, 1: 27–64.

Dicken, Peter (1998) *Global Shift: Transforming the World Economy*. 3rd ed. London: Paul Chapman.

_____. (1999) "Global Shift — The Role of US Corporations," in David Slater and Peter J. Taylor (eds.) *The American Century: Consensus and Coercion in the Projection of American Power* (pp. 35–50). Oxford: Blackwell.

Dickerson, Debra J. (2005) "The Great White Way," *Mother Jones*, 30, 5 (September–October): 77–79.

A Dictionary of Americanisms: On Historical Principles (1966). Ed. Mitford M. Mathews. 4th impression. Chicago: The University of Chicago Press, 1951.

DiMaggio, Paul J., and Walter W. Powell (1983) "The Iron Cage Revisited: Institutional Isomorphism and Collective Rationality in Organizational Fields," *American Sociological Review*, 48 (April): 147–160.

Dolowitz, David P. (1998) *Learning from America: Policy Transfer and the Development of the British Workfare State*. Brighton: Sussex Academic Press.

Dominguez, Jorge I. (1997) *Technopols: Freeing Politics and Markets in Latin America in the 1990s*. University Park, Penn.: University of Pennsylvania Press.

Drucker, Peter F. (2005) "Trading Places," *The National Interest*, 79 (Spring): 101–107.

du Gay, Paul (ed.) (1997) *Production of Culture/Cultures of Production*. London: Sage.

Duhamel, Georges (1931) *America, the Menace: Scenes from the Life of the Future*. Trans. Charles M. Thompson. Orig. 1927. Boston: Houghton Mifflin.

Dumbrell, John (2003) "Foreign Policy," in Robert Singh (ed.) *Governing America: The Politics of a Divided Democracy* (pp. 267–285). Oxford: Oxford University Press.

Duménil, Gerard, and Dominique Lévy (2004) "Neoliberal Income Trends: Wealth, Class and Ownership in the USA," *New Left Review*, 30 (2004): 105–133.

Eco, Umberto (1986) *Travels in Hyperreality*. Trans. William Weaver. Orlando, FL: Harvest Books.

Editorial *The Nation* (2005) "Conspiracy to Torture," in special issue "The Torture Complex" of *The Nation*, 281, 2 (December 26): 3–5.

Editorial *The Nation* (2006) "Immigrants & US," *The Nation*, 282, 16 (April 24): 3–4.

Egerton, John (1974) *The Americanization of Dixie: The Southernization of America*. New York: Harper's.

Ellwood, David W. (1996–1997) "The American Challenge Renewed: U.S. Cultural Power and Europe's Identity Debates," *Brown Journal of World Affairs*, 4, 1 (Winter-Spring): 271–283.

_____. (2004) "A Bridge, A Beacon or the 51st State? The Specialness of Tony Blair's Relationship With America," in Ruud Janssens and Rob Kroes (eds.) *Post-Cold War Europe and Post-Cold War America* (pp. 19–29). Amsterdam: VU University Press.

_____, Mel van Elteren, Mick Gidley, Rob Kroes, David E. Nye, Robert W. Rydell (1993) "Questions of Cultural Exchange: The NIAS statement on the European Reception of American Mass Culture," in Rob Kroes, Robert W. Rydell and Doeko F. Bosscher (eds.) *Cultural Transmissions and Receptions: American Mass Culture in Europe* (pp. 321–333). Amsterdam: VU University Press.

Epstein, Barbara (1995) "Why Poststructuralism is a Dead End for Progressive Thought," *Socialist Review*, 25, 2: 83–119.

Ermarth, Michael (1993a) "Introduction," in Michael Ermarth (eds.) *America and the Shaping of German Society, 1945–1955* (pp. 1–19). Providence — Oxford: Berg.

_____. (1993b) "*The German Talks Back*: Heinrich Hauser and German Attitudes toward Americanization after World War II, in Michael Ermarth (eds.) *America and the Shaping of German Society, 1945–1955* (pp. 101–131). Providence — Oxford: Berg.

Ewen, Stuart, and Elizabeth Ewen (1992) *Channels of Desire: Mass Images and the Shaping of American Consciousness*. 2nd ed. Minneapolis: University of Minnesota Press.

Fabian, Johannes (1983) *Time and the Other: How Anthropology Makes its Object*. New York: Columbia University Press.

Falk, Richard A. (1995) *On Humane Governance: Toward a New Global Politics*. Cambridge: Polity Press.

Farber, David (1994) "The Dream of Global Desire: The Marlboro Man Goes to Hong Kong," *Borderlines: Studies in American Culture*, 1, 4: 327–340.

Featherstone, Mike (1991) *Consumer Culture and Postmodernism*. London: Sage.

_____. (1995) *Undoing Culture: Globalization, Postmodernism, and Identity*. London: Sage.

Fehrenbach, Heide, and Uta G. Poiger (2000) "Introduction: Americanization Reconsidered," in Heide Fehrenbach and Uta G. Poiger (eds.) *Transactions, Transgressions, Transformations* (pp. xiii-xxxvii). New York — Oxford: Berghahn.

Ferguson, Marjorie, and Peter Golding (eds.) (1997) *Cultural Studies in Question*. London: Sage.

Fish, Stanley E. (1980) *Is There a Text in This Class? The Authority of Interpretive Communities*. Cambridge, MA: Harvard University Press.

Fluck, Winfried (1990) "The Americanization of Literary Studies, *American Studies International*, 28, 2: 9–22.

_____. (1998) "The Humanities in the Age of Expressive Individualism and Cultural Radicalism," *Cultural Critique*, 40: 49–71.

Fluck, Winfried (2000) "Internationalizing American Studies: Do We Need an International American Studies Association and What Should Be Its Goals?," *European Journal of American Culture*, 19, 3: 148–155.

Foner, Eric (1984) "Why Is There No Socialism in the United States?," *History Workshop Journal*, 17, Spring: 57–80.

Foot, Rosemary, MacFarlane, S. Neil, and Michael Mastanduno (2003a) "Introduction," in Rosemary Foot, S. Neil McFarlane, and Michael Mastanduno, *US Hegemony and International Organizations: The United States and Multilateral Institutions* (pp. 1–22). Oxford: Oxford University Press.

_____, _____, and _____. (2003b) "Conclusion," in Rosemary Foot, S. Neil McFarlane, and Michael Mastanduno, *US Hegemony and International Organizations: The United States and Multilateral Institutions* (pp. 265–272). Oxford: Oxford University Press.

Forgacs, David (1993) "Americanisation: The Italian Case 1938–1954," *Borderlines: Studies in American Culture*, 1, 1: 157–169.

Foucault, Michel (1984) *The Foucault Reader*. Harmondsworth: Penguin.

Frank, Thomas (1997) *The Conquest of Cool: Business Culture, Counterculture, and the Rise of Hip Consumerism*. Chicago: University of Chicago Press.

_____. (2000) *One Market Under God: Extreme Capitalism, Market Populism, and the End of Economic Democracy*. New York: Anchor Books.

Franzen, E. (1952) "Europa blickt auf Amerika," *Der Monat* 8, 50: 147.

Fried, Richard M. (1990) *Nightmare in Red: The McCarthy Era in Perspective*. New York: Oxford University Press.

Friedman, Jonathan (1994) *Cultural Identity and Global Process*. London: Sage.

Friedman, Thomas L. (2000) *The Lexus and the Olive Tree: Understanding Globalisation*. New York: Farrar, Straus & Giroux

_____. (2005) *The World is Flat: A Brief History of the*

Twenty-First Century. New York: Farrar, Straus and Giroux.

Frith, Simon (1983) *Sound Effects: Youth, Leisure and the Politics of Rock*. London: Constable.

_____. (1989) "Euro Pop," *Cultural Studies*, 3, 2: 166–172.

Fukuyama, Francis (1989) "The End of History?," *The National Interest*, 16 (Summer): 3–16.

_____. (1992) *The End of History and the Last Man*. New York: Free Press.

_____. (1999) "Second Thoughts: The Last Man in a Bottle," *The National Interest*, 56 (Summer): 16–33.

García Canclini, Néstor (1995) *Hybrid Cultures: Strategies for Entering and Leaving Modernity*. Trans. Christopher L. Chippari and Silvia L. López. Minneapolis: University of Minneapolis Press.

Gardner, Lloyd C. (ed.) (1986) *Redefining the Past: Essays in Diplomatic History in Honor of William Appleman Williams*. Corvallis, Oregon: Oregon State University Press.

Garton Ash, Timothy (1990) *We the People — the Revolution of '89*. London: Penguin/Granta Books.

Gemünden, Gerd (1998) *Framed Visions: Popular Culture, Americanization, and the Contemporary German and Austrian Imagination*. Ann Arbor: The University of Michigan Press.

Gerstle, Gary (1986) "The Politics of Patriotism: Americanization and the Formation of the CIO," *Dissent* 33, 1 (Winter): 84–92.

_____. (1989) *Working-class Americanism: The Politics of Labor in a Textile City, 1914–1960*. Cambridge: Cambridge University Press.

_____. (1994) "The Protean Character of American Liberalism," *American Historical Review*, 99 (October): 1043–1073.

_____. (2001) *American Crucible*. Princeton: Princeton University Press.

Giddens, Anthony (1990) *The Consequences of Modernity*. Cambridge: Polity Press.

Gienow-Hecht, Jessica C.E. (2000) "Shame on US? Academics, Cultural Transfer, and the Cold War — A Critical Review," *Diplomatic History*, 24, 3 (Summer): 465–494.

_____. (2004) "Whose Music Is It Anyway? The Limits of Transnational Culture in the Nineteenth Century," in Rob Kroes (ed.) *Straddling Borders: The American Resonance in Transnational Identities* (pp. 34–50). Amsterdam: VU University Press.

Gill, Stephen (1990) *American Hegemony and the Trilateral Commission*. Cambridge: Cambridge University Press.

Gills, Barry K. (ed.) (2001) *Globalization and the Politics of Resistance*. London: Palgrave.

Gilman, Carolyn (2003) *Lewis and Clark — Across the Divide*. Washington and London: Smithsonian Books.

Gilpin, Robert (2000) *The Challenge of Global Capitalism: The World Economy in the 21st Century*. Princeton, NJ: Princeton University Press.

Giroux, Henry A. (2004) *The Terror of Neoliberalism*. Boulder — London: Paradigm Publishers.

Gitlin, Todd (1995) *The Twilight of Common Dreams: Why America Is Wracked by Culture Wars*. New York: Metropolitan Books — Henry Holt and Company.

Gleason, Philip (1982) "American Identity and Americanization," in William Petersen, Michael Novak, and Philip Gleason (eds.) *Concepts of Identity* (pp.

57–143) Cambridge: The Belknap Press of Harvard University Press.

Goethe, Johann Wolfgang von (1948) "To America," trans. Stephen Spender, in *The Permanent Goethe*, ed. Thomas Mann (p. 655). New York: Dial.

Goldfield, David (2002) "Religion and Politics in the United States," in Matthew Sweney and Michal Peprnik (eds.) *Spirituality and Religion in American Culture*. (pp. 57–62). Olomouc: Univerzita Palckého v Olomouci.

Golding, Peter, and Phil Harris (1997) "Introduction," in Peter Golding and Phil Harris (eds.) *Beyond Cultural Imperialism: Globalization, Communication and the New International Order* (pp. 1–9). London: Sage.

Goldstein, Robert J. (1978) *Political Repression in Modern America*. Cambridge, Mass.: Schenkman.

Gorman, Paul R. (1996) *Left Intellectuals and Popular Culture in Twentieth-Century America*. Chapel Hill and London: The University of North Carolina Press.

Gowan, Peter (1999) *The Global Gamble: Washington's Faustian Bid for Global Dominance*. London: Verso.

_____. (2001) "Neoliberal Cosmopolitanism," *New Left Review* 11 (September): 79–93.

Gramsci, Antonio (1971) "Americanism and Fordism," in Antonio Gramsci, *Prison Notebooks* (pp. 279–318). Ed. and trans. Quentin Hoare and Geoffrey Nowell Smith. New York: International Publishers.

Gray, John (1998) *False Dawn: The Delusions of Global Capitalism*. London: Granta.

Griffith, Robert (1970) *The Politics of Fear: Joseph R. McCarthy and the Senate*. Lexington: University of Kentucky Press.

Gross, Gary (2000) *An All-Consuming Century: Why Commercialism Won in Modern America*. New York: Columbia University Press.

Guyatt, Nicholas (2000) *Another American Century? The United States and the World after 2000*. London: Zed Books.

Hall, John R., and Mary Jo Neitz (1993) *Culture: Sociological Perspectives*. Englewood Cliffs, NJ: Prentice Hall.

Hall, Stuart (1980) "Encoding/Decoding," in Stuart Hall, Dorothy Hobson, Andew Lowe and Paul Willis (eds.) *Culture, Media, Language* (pp. 128–138). London: Hutchinson.

_____. (1981) "Notes on Deconstructing 'the Popular,'" in Raphael Samuel (ed.) *People's History and Socialist Theory* (pp. 227–240). London: Routledge and Kegan Paul.

_____, and Fredric Jameson (1990) "Clinging to the Wreckage," *Marxism Today*. September: 28–31.

_____, and Paddy Whannel (1964) *The Popular Arts*. London: Pantheon Books.

Hamby, Alonzo L. (1968) "Henry A. Wallace, the Liberals, and Soviet-American Relations," *Review of Politics*, 30 (April): 153–169.

Hampden-Turner, Charles, and Fons Trompenaars (1993) *The Seven Cultures of Capitalism*. New York: Doubleday.

Hannerz, Ulf (1992a) "Networks of Americanization," in Rolf Lundén and Erik Åsard (eds.) *Networks of Americanization: Aspects of the American Influence in Sweden* (pp. 9–19). *Studia Anglistica Upsaliensia* 79.Uppsala: Acta Universitatis Upsaliencis.

_____. (1992b) *Cultural Complexity: Studies in the Social*

Organization of Meaning. New York: Columbia University Press.

Hart, John (2003) "The Presidency," in Robert Singh (ed.) *Governing America: The Politics of a Divided Democracy* (pp. 169–188). Oxford: Oxford University Press.

Hartmann, Edward G. (1948) *The Movement to Americanize the Immigrant*. New York: Columbia University Press.

Hartz, Louis (1955) *The Liberal Tradition in America: An Interpretation of American Political Thought since the Revolution*. New York: Harcourt Brace.

Harvey, David (1989) *The Condition of Postmodernity*. Oxford: Basil Blackwell.

_____. (2000) *Spaces of Hope*. Edinburgh: Edinburgh University Press.

_____. (2003) *The New Imperialism*. Oxford: Oxford University Press.

_____. (2005) *A Brief History of Neoliberalism*. Oxford: Oxford University Press.

Haufler, Daniel (1997) "Amerika, hast Du es besser? Zur deutschen Buchkultur nach 1945," in Konrad Jarausch and Hannes Siegrist (eds.) *Amerikanisierung und Sowjetisierung in Deutschland, 1945–1970* (pp. 387–408). Frankfurt: Campus.

Hebdige, Dick (1982) "Towards a Cartography of Taste (1935–1962)," in Bernard Waites, Tony Bennett, and Graham Martin (eds.) *Popular Culture: Past and Present* (pp. 194–218). London: Croom Helm.

_____. (1988) *Hiding in the Light: On Images and Things*. London: Routledge.

Heidegger, Martin (1959) *Introduction to Metaphysics*. Trans. Ralph Manheim. New Haven: Yale University Press.

Held, David (1995a) *Democracy and the Global Order*. Stanford, CA: Stanford University Press.

_____. (1995b) "Democracy and the International Order," in David Held, and Daniele Archibugi (eds.) *Cosmopolitan Democracy: An Agenda for a New World Order* (pp. 96–118). Cambridge: Polity Press.

_____. (2004) *Global Covenant: The Social Democratic Alternative to the Washington Consensus*. Cambridge: Polity Press.

_____, and Anthony McGrew (2002) *Globalization/Anti-Globalization*. Cambridge: Polity Press.

_____, _____, David Goldblatt and Jonathan Perraton (1999) *Global Transformations: Politics, Economics and Culture*. Cambridge: Polity Press.

Henwood, Doug (2005) "The Dollar's Doldrum's," *The Nation*, 280, 19 (May 16): 6, 8.

Herman, Edward S., and Robert W. McChesney (1997) *The Global Media: The New Missionaries of Corporate Capitalism*. London and Washington: Cassell.

Hermand, Jost, and Frank Trommler (1988) *Die Kultur der Weimarer Republik*. Frankfurt am Main: Fischer Taschenbuch Verlag.

Hesmondhalgh, David (2002) *The Cultural Industries*. London: Sage.

Hill, Howard C. (1919) "The Americanization Movement," *American Journal of Sociology*, 24, May: 609–642.

Hobsbawn, Eric, and Terence Ranger (eds.) (1983) *The Invention of Tradition*. Cambridge: Cambridge University Press.

Hofstadter, Richard (1972) *The Age of Reform: From Bryan to FDR*. First pub. 1955. New York: Alfred A. Knopf.

Hoggart, Richard (1957) *The Uses of Literacy*. Harmondsworh: Penguin

Hollinger, David A. (1971) "Ethnic Diversity, Cosmopolitanism and the Emergence of the American Liberal Intelligentsia," *American Quarterly*, 27 (May): 133–151.

Holton, Robert J. (1998) *Globalization and the Nation-State*. New York: St. Martin's Press.

Holtzman, Elizabeth (2006) "The Impeachment of George W. Bush," *The Nation*, 282, 4 (January 30): 11, 13–14, 16, 18.

Hoogvelt, Ankie (2001) *Globalisation and the Postcolonial World: The New Political Economy of Development*. 2nd ed. London: Palgrave.

Hopkins, A.G. (2002) "Introduction: Globalization — An Agenda for Historians," in A.G. Hopkins (ed.) *Globalization in World History* (pp. 1–10). London: Pimlico.

Hornung, Alfred (2002) Contribution to Debate on "Transculturations: American Studies in a Globalizing World — the Globalizing World in American Studies," *Amerikastudien/American Studies*, 47, 1: 110–114.

Huizinga, Johan (1972a) "Men and the Masses in America," in Johan Huizinga, *America: A Dutch Historian's Vision, from Afar and Near* (pp. 1–225), transl. of "Mensch en Menigte in Amerika" (1918) by Herbert H. Rowen. New York: Harper and Row.

_____. (1972b) "Life and Thought in America," in Johan Huizinga, *America: A Dutch Historian's Vision, from Afar and Near* (pp. 227–326), transl. of "Amerika Levend en Denkend" (1927) by Herbert H. Rowen. New York: Harper and Row.

Hunter, James Davidson, and Yoshua Yates (2002) "In the Vanguard of Globalization: The World of American Globalizers," in Peter L. Berger and Samuel P. Huntington (eds.) *Many Globalizations: Cultural Diversity in the Contemporary World* (pp. 323–357). Oxford: Oxford University Press.

Huntington, Samuel P. (1996) *The Clash of Civilizations and the Remaking of World Order*. New York: Simon and Schuster.

_____. (2004) *Who Are We? The Challenges to America's National Identity*. New York: Simon & Schuster.

Hutton, Will (2003) *The World We're In*. London: Abacus.

_____, and Anthony Giddens (2000) "Is Globalisation Americanisation? Will Hutton and Anthony Giddens in Conversation," *Dissent*, 47, 3 (Summer): 58–63.

"In Fact …," *The Nation*, 281, 4 (August 1/8, 2005): 10.

Jacobs, Lawrence R., and Theda Skocpol (eds.) (2005) *Inequality and American Democracy: What we know and what we need to learn*. New York: Russell Sage Foundation.

Jacoby, Russell (1994) *Dogmatic Wisdom: How the Culture Wars Divert Education and Distract America*. New York: Doubleday.

Jameson, Fredric (1979) "Reification and Utopia in Mass Culture," *Social Text* 1, 1: 130–148.

_____. (1991) *Postmodernism or, The Cultural Logic of Late Capitalism*. London: Verso.

_____. (1992) *The Geopolitical Aesthetic*. Bloomington: Indiana University Press.

Jarausch, Konrad H., and Hannes Siegrist (1997) "Amerikanisierung und Sowjetisierung. Eine vergleichende Fragestellung zur deutsch-deutschen

Nachkriegsgeschichte," in Konrad Jarausch and Hannes Siegrist (eds.), *Amerikanisierung und Sowjetisierung in Deutschland, 1945–1970* (pp. 11–46). Frankfurt: Campus.

Jensen, Joli, and John J. Pauly (1997) "Imagining the Audience: Losses and Gains in Cultural Studies," in Marjorie Ferguson and Peter Golding (eds.) *Cultural Studies in Question* (pp. 155–169). London: Sage.

Johnson, Chalmers (2004) *The Sorrows of Empire: Militarism, Secrecy, and the End of the Republic*. New York: Metropolitan Books — Henry Holt and Company.

Johnson, Leslie (1979) *The Cultural Critics: From Matthew Arnold to Raymond Williams*. London, Boston and Henley: Routledge & Kegan Paul.

Joseph, Gilbert M. (1998) "Close Encounters. Toward a New Cultural History of U.S.-Latin American Relations," in Gilbert M. Joseph, Catherine C. Legrand, and Ricardo D. Salvatore (eds.) *Close Encounters of Empire: Writing the Cultural History of U.S.-Latin American Relations* (pp. 3–46). Durham and London: Duke University Press.

Kaes, Anton (1985) "Mass Culture and Modernity: Notes toward a Social History of Early American and German Cinema," in Frank Trommler and Joseph McVeigh (eds.) *America and the Germans: An Assessment of a Three-Hundred-Year History*. vol. 2 (pp. 317–331). Philadelphia: University of Pennsylvania Press.

Kalff, Donald (2004) *Onafhankelijkheid voor Europa: Het Einde van het Amerikaanse Ondernemingsmodel*. Amsterdam — Antwerpen: Business Contact.

Kallen, Horace M. (1915) "Democracy versus the Melting-Pot," *The Nation*, February 18 and 25: 190–194, 217–220.

_____. (1924) *Culture and Democracy in the United States: Studies in the Group Psychology of the American Peoples*. New York: Boni and Liveright.

Kammen, Michael (1993) "The Problem of American Exceptionalism: A Reconsideration," *American Quarterly*, 45: 1 (March): 1–43.

_____. (2000) *American Culture American Tastes: Social Change and the 20ᵗʰ Century*. New York: Alfred A. Knopf.

Kang, Liu (1998) "Is There an Alternative to (Capitalist) Globalization? The Debate about Modernity in China," in Fredric Jameson and Masao Miyoshi (eds.) *The Cultures of Globalization* (pp. 164–188). Durham, NC: Duke University Press.

Kaplan, E. Ann (1987) *Rocking Around the Clock: Music Television, Postmodernism, and Consumer Culture*. London: Methuen.

Kaspi, André (1990) "By Way of Conclusion," in Denis Lacorne, Jacques Rupnik and Marie-France Toinet, *The Rise and Fall of Anti-Americanism: A Century of French Perception* (238–243). London: Macmillan.

Katz, Stephen (2001) "Michel Foucault," in Anthony Elliott and Bryan S. Turner (eds.) *Profiles in Contemporary Social Theory* (pp. 117–127). London: Sage.

Kaufmann, Eric P. (2003) "Race and Multiculturalism," in Robert Singh (ed.) *Governing America: The Politics of a Divided Democracy* (pp. 449–466). Oxford: Oxford University Press.

_____. (2004) *The Rise and Fall of Anglo-America*. Cambridge, MA: Harvard University Press.

Kazin, Michael (1998) *The Populist Persuasion: An American History*. Ithaca, NY: Cornell University Press.

Kellner, Douglas (1999) "Theorizing/Resisting McDonaldization: A Multiperspectivist Approach," in Barry Smart (ed.) *Resisting McDonaldization* (pp. 186–206). London: Sage.

Keohane, Robert O., and Joseph S. Nye (1989) *Power and Interdependence: World Politics in Transition*. 2nd ed. New York: HarperCollins.

King, Desmond (2000) *Making Americans: Immigration, Race, and the Origins of the Diverse Democracy*. Cambridge, MA: Harvard University Press.

_____. (2005) *The Liberty of Strangers: Making the American Nation*. Oxford: Oxford University Press.

Kirk, Russell (1953) *The Conservative Mind: From Burke to Santyana*. Chicago: The University of Chicago Press.

_____. (1957) *The American Cause*. Chicago: The University of Chicago Press.

_____. (1983) Introduction to Albert Jay Nock, *Mr. Jefferson*. Delavan, Wis.: Hallberg.

Kivikuru, Ullamaija (1988) "From Import to Modelling: Finland — An Example of Old Periphery Dependency," *European Journal of Communication* 3: 9–34

Klein, Marcus (1981) *Foreigners: The Making of American Literature 1900–1940*. Chicago: University of Chicago Press.

Korten, David C. (2001) *When Corporations Rule the World*. 2nd. ed. San Francisco: Kumarian Press — Berrett-Koehler Publishers.

Kovács, János Máyás (2002) "Rival Temptations and Passive Resistance: Cultural Globalization in Hungary," in Peter L. Berger and Samuel P. Huntington (eds.) *Many Globalizations: Cultural Diversity in the Contemporary World* (pp. 146–182). Oxford: Oxford University Press.

Kraske, Gary E. (1985) *Missionaries of the Book: The American Library Profession and the Origins of United States Cultural Diplomacy*. Westport, Conn.: Greenwood Press.

Krasner, Stephen (1978) *Defending the National Interest*. Princeton: Princeton University Press.

_____ (ed.) (1983) *International Regimes*. Ithaca, NY: Cornell University Press.

Kroes, Rob (1986) "The Great Satan versus the Evil Empire: Anti-Americanism in the Netherlands," in Rob Kroes and Maarten van Rossem (eds.) *Anti-Americanism in Europe* (pp. 37–50). Amsterdam: Free University Press.

_____. (1991) "Among the Receivers: American Culture Transmitted Abroad," in Rob Kroes (ed.) *Within the U.S. Orbit: Small National Cultures vis-à-vis the United States* (pp. 1–10). Amsterdam: VU University Press.

_____. (1993) "Americanisation: What Are We Talking About?," in Rob Kroes, Robert W. Rydell and Doeko F. Bosscher (eds.) *Cultural Transmissions and Receptions: American Mass Culture in Europe* (pp. 302–320). Amsterdam: VU University Press.

_____. (1996a) *If You've Seen One, You've Seen the Mall: Europeans and American Mass Culture*. Champaign, Ill.: University of Illinois Press.

_____. (1996b) "Advertising: The Commodification of American Icons," in Annemoon van Hemel, Hans Mommaas and Cas Smithuijsen (eds.) *Trading Cul-*

ture: GATT, European Cultural Policies and the Transatlantic Market (pp. 137–147). Amsterdam: Boekman Foundation.

_____. (1999a) "There Are No Borders: American Studies in the Netherlands, America in the World," in Hans Krabbendam and Jaap Verheul (eds.) *Through the Cultural Looking Glass: American Studies in Transcultural Perspective* (pp. 69–88). Amsterdam: VU University Press.

_____. (1999b) "American Empire and Cultural Imperialism," *Diplomatic History*, 23 (Summer): 463–477.

_____. (2000) *Them and Us: Questions of Citizenship in a Globalizing World*. Urbana — Chicago: The University of Illinois Press.

Krugman, Paul (2003) *The Great Unraveling: Losing Our Way in the Twentieth Century*. New York: Norton.

Krul, W.E. (1990) "Moderne Beschavingsgeschiedenis. Johan Huizinga over de Verenigde Staten," in K. van Berkel (ed.) *Amerika in Europese Ogen: Facetten van de Europese Beeldvorming van het Moderne Amerika* (pp. 86–108). 's-Gravenhage: SDU.

Kuisel, Richard F. (1993) *Seducing the French: The Dilemma of Americanization*. Berkeley: University of California Press.

_____. (2000) "The French Cinema and Hollywood: A Case Study of Americanization," in Heide Fehrenbach and Uta G. Poiger (eds.) *Transactions, Transgressions, Transformations* (pp. 208–223). New York — Oxford: Berghahn.

_____. (2003) "Debating Americanization: The Case of France," in Ulrich Beck, Natan Sznaider and Rainer Winter (eds.) *Global America? The Cultural Consequences of Globalization* (pp. 95–113). Liverpool: Liverpool University Press.

Lacorne, Denis, and Jacques Rupnik (1990), "Introduction: France Bewitched by America," in Denis Lacorne, Jacques Rupnik and Marie-France Toinet (eds.), *The Rise and Fall of Anti-Americanism: A Century of French Perception* (1–31). London: Macmillan.

LaFeber, Walter (1999) *Michael Jordan and the New Global Capitalism*. New York — London: W.W. Norton & Company.

_____. (2003) "The United States and Europe in an Age of American Unilateralism," in R. Laurence Moore and Maurizio Vaudagna (eds.) *The American Century in Europe* (pp. 25–46). Ithaca, NY: Cornell University Press.

Lambert, John (1991) "Europe: The Nation-State Dies Hard," *Capital and Class* 43 (Spring): 9–24.

Lamont, Michèle (1989) "The Power-Culture Link in a Comparative Perspective," Graig Calhoun (ed.) Vol. 11 *Culture of Comparative Social Research* (pp. 131–150). Greenwich, CT — London: JAI Press.

Lasch, Christopher (1991) *The True and Only Heaven: Progress and Its Critics*. New York — London: Norton.

Lauck, W. Jett (1926) *Political and Industrial Democracy, 1776–1926*. New York: Funk & Wagnalls.

Leach, William (1993) *Land of Desire: Merchants, Power, and the Rise of a New American Culture*. New York: Pantheon.

Lealand, Geoff (1988) *A Foreign Egg in Our Nest? American Popular Culture in New Zealand*. Wellington: Victoria University Press.

Lears, T. Jackson. (1985) "The Concept of Cultural Hegemony: Problems and Possibilities," *American Historical Review*, 90, 3: 567–593.

Leavis, F.R. (1930) *Mass Civilisation and Minority Culture*. Cambridge: Minority Pamphlets No. 1.

_____. (1972) *Nor Shall My Sword*. London: Chatto & Windus.

_____, and Denys Thompson (1933) *Culture and Environment*. London: Chatto and Windus.

Leavis, Q.D. (1979) *Fiction and the Reading Public*. Orig. 1932. Harmondsworth: Peregrine.

Lechner, Frank J., and John Boli (eds.) (2000) *The Globalization Reader*. Malden, MA: Blackwell.

Leggewie, Claus (2000) *Amerikas Welt: Die USA in unseren Köpfen*. Hamburg: Hoffman und Campe.

Lenz, Günther (1990) "The Radical Imagination: Revisionary Modes of Radical Cultural Criticism in Thirties America," in Steve Ickringill (ed.) *Looking Inward, Looking Outward: From the 1930s through the 1940s* (pp. 94–126). Amsterdam: VU University Press.

_____. (1991) "'Ethnographies': American Culture Studies and Postmodern Anthropology," *Prospects*, 16: 1–40.

_____. (2002) "Transculturations: American Studies in a Globalizing World — the Globalizing World in American Studies," *Amerikastudien/American Studies*, 47, 1: 97–98.

Levine, Lawrence W. (1977) *Black Culture and Black Consciousness: Afro-American Folk Thought from Slavery to Freedom*. Oxford: Oxford University Press.

_____. (1993) *The Unpredictable Past: Explorations in American Cultural History*. Oxford: Oxford University Press.

Lewis, Bernard (1990) "The Roots of Muslim Rage," *The Atlantic Monthly*, September: 52.

Lewis, George H. (1978) "The Sociology of Popular Culture," *Current Sociology*, 26, 3.

Lind, Michael (2003) *Made in Texas: George W. Bush and the Southern Takeover of American Politics*. New York: Basic Books.

Lipset, Seymour M. (1996) *American Exceptionalism: A Double-Edged Sword*. New York — London: Norton.

_____. and Earl Raab (1978) *The Politics of Unreason: Right-Wing Extremism in the United States 1790–1977*. 2nd. ed. Baltimore: Johns Hopkins University Press.

Lovato, Roberto (2004) "Fear of a Brown Planet," *The Nation*, 278, 25 (June 28): 17–18, 20–21.

_____. (2006) "Voices of a New *Movimiento*," *The Nation*, 282, 24 (June 19): 11, 13–14.

Luce, Henry R. (1941) "The American Century," *Life*, 17 February, 61–65.

Lukacs, John (1984) *Outgrowing Democracy: A History of the United States in the Twentieth Century*. New York: Doubleday.

Lukes, Steven (1974) *Power: A Radical View*. London: Macmillan.

Lundén, Rolf (1991) America in Sweden: Visible and Invisible Influence," in Rob Kroes (ed.) *Within the U.S. Orbit: Small National Cultures vis-à-vis the United States* (pp. 140–151). Amsterdam: VU University Press.

Lundestad, Geir (1986) "Empire by Invitation? The United States and Western Europe, 1945–1952," *Journal of Peace Research*, 23: 1–23.

Lynd, Robert S., and Helen Merrell Lynd (1929) *Middletown: A Study in Modern American Culture*. San Diego: Harcourt Brace Jovanich.

_____, and _____. (1937) *Middletown in Transition: A Study in Cultural Conflicts*. New York: Harcourt Brace Jovanich.

Maase, Kaspar (1992) *BRAVO Amerika: Erkundungen zur Jugendkultur der Bundesrepublik in den fünfziger Jahren*. Hamburg: Junius.

_____. (1993) "'Halbstarke' and Hegemony: Meanings of American Mass Culture in the Federal Republic of Germany During the 1950s," in Rob Kroes, Robert W. Rydell and Doeko F. Bosscher (eds.) *Cultural Transmissions and Receptions: American Mass Culture in Europe* (pp. 152–170). Amsterdam: VU University Press.

_____. (1996a) "Amerikanisierung von unten. Demonstrative Vulgarität und kulturelle Hegemonie in der Bundesrepublik der fünfziger Jahre," in Alf Lüdtke, Inge Marßolek, and Adelheid von Saldern (eds.) *Amerikanisierung: Traum and Alptraum im Deutschland des 20. Jahrhunderts* (pp. 291–313). Stuttgart: Steiner.

_____. (1996b) "A Taste of Honey: Adorno's Reading of American Mass Culture," in John Dean and Jean-Paul Gabilliet (eds.) *European Readings of American Popular Culture* (pp. 201–211). Westport, Connecticut: Greenwood Press.

_____. (1999) "Diagnose: Amerikanisierung. Zur Geschichte eines Deutungsmusters," *Transit*, 17: 72–89.

Makinson, David (ed.) (2000) "The Development Debate: Beyond the Washington Consensus," *International Social Science Journal*, 166: 435–548.

Malone, Bill C. (1979) *Southern Music — American Music*. Lexington: The University of Kentucky Press.

Maltby, Richard (1989) "Introduction," in Richard Maltby (ed.) *Dreams for Sale: Popular Culture in the 20th Century* (pp. 8–19). London: Harrap.

Mann, Michael (2003) *Incoherent Empire*. London: Verso.

Marcus, George E., and Michael M.J. Fischer (1986) (eds.) *Anthropology as Cultural Critique: An Experimental Moment in the Human Sciences*. Chicago: University of Chicago Press.

Marcuse, Herbert (1964) *One-Dimensional Man*. London: Routledge.

Martineau, Harriet (1981) *Society in America*. orig. 1837. New Brunswick, NJ: Transaction Books.

Marqusee, Mike (2004) "Patriot Acts [essay review of five books on the Red Scare]," *The Nation*, 279, 20 (December 13): 30–32, 34.

Massey, Doreen (1993) "Power-geometry and a Progressive Sense of Place" in Jon Bird, Barry Curtis, Tim Putnam, George Robertson and Lisa Tucker (eds.) *Mapping the Futures: Local Cultures, Global Change* (pp. 59–69). London: Routledge.

Mathy, Jean-Philippe (1993) *Extrême-Occident: French Intellectuals and America*. Chicago and London: The University of Chicago Press.

Mattelart, Armand, and Michèle Mattelart (1998) *Theories of Communication: A Short Introduction*. London: Sage.

Matthews, F.H. (1970) "The Revolt against Americanism: Cultural Pluralism and Cultural Relativism as an Ideology of Liberation," *Canadian Review of American Studies*, 1, 1 (Spring): 4–31.

Matthews, Jill Julius (1998) "Which America?," in Philip Bell and Roger Bell (eds.) *Americanization and Australia* (pp. 15–31). Sydney: University of New South Wales Press.

McAlister, Melani (2001) *Epic Encounters: Culture, Media and U.S. Interests in the Middle East, 1945–2000*. Berkeley: University of California Press.

McChesney, Robert W. (2000) *Rich Media Poor Democracy: Communication Politics in Dubious Times*. New York: The New Press.

McGerr, Michael (1991) "The Price of the 'New Transnational History,'" *American Historical Review*, 96 (August): 1056–1072.

McGrew, Anthony (1992) "A Global Society?," in Stuart Hall, David Held and Tony McGrew (eds.) *Modernity and Its Futures* (pp. 61–102). Cambridge: Polity Press.

McGuigan, Jim (1992) *Cultural Populism*. London and New York: Routledge.

McKay, George (1997) "Introduction: Americanization and Popular Culture," in George McKay (ed.) *Yankee Go Home [& Take Me With U]: Americanization & Popular Culture* (pp. 11–52). Sheffield: Sheffield Academic Press.

McKenzie, Frederick A. (1902) *The American Invaders*. London: G. Richards.

McLennan, Gregor (1992) "The Enlightenment Project Revisited," in Stuart Hall, David Hall and Tony McGrew (eds.) *Modernity and Its Futures* (pp. 327–377). Cambridge: Polity Press.

Mead, Walter Russell (2001) *Special Providence: American Foreign Policy and How It Changed the World*. New York: Knopf.

Meeus, Tom-Jan (2005) "Ogenschijnlijk dédain van Bush voor rechtsstaat," *NRC Handelsblad*, December 20: 5.

_____. (2006) "Amerikaanse illegaal heeft opeens een naam," *NRC Handelsblad*, April 11: 1, 4.

Menand, Louis (2004) "Patriotic Games: The New Nativism of Samuel P. Huntington," *The New Yorker*, May 10 (http://www.newyorker.com/printable/?critics/040517crbo_books).

Merelman, Richard M. (1984) *Making Something of Ourselves: Culture and Politics in the United States*. Berkeley: University of California Press.

Merriam, Charles (1931) *The Making of Citizens*. Chicago: Chicago University Press.

Merriam-Webster's Collegiate Dictionary (2001) Tenth Ed. Springfield, MA: Merriam-Webster, Incorp.

Mertes, Tom (ed.) (2004) *A Movement of Movements*. London: Verso.

Merton, Robert K. (1968) "Social Structure and Anomie," orig. 1938, revised and expanded, in Robert K. Merton, *Social Theory and Social Structure* (185–214). New York: The Free Press.

Meyer, John W., John Boll, George M. Thomas, and Francisco O. Raminez (1997) "World Society and the Nation-State," *American Journal of Sociology*, 103, 1: 144–181.

Micklethwait, John, and Adrian Wooldridge (2004) *The Right Nation: Conservative Power in America*. New York: The Penguin Press.

Mill, John Stuart. (1963) Essays on *Politics and Culture*, ed. Gertrude Himmelfarb. New York: Anchor Books.

Miller, J. Hillis (1987) "Presidential Address 1986. The Triumph of Theory, the Resistance to Reading, and the Question of Material Base," *PMLA*, 102, 3: 281–291.

Mills, C. Wright (1959) *The Sociological Imagination*. New York: Oxford University Press.

Milner, Helen (1997) *Interests, Institutions and Infor-*

mation: Domestic Politics and International Relations. Princeton: Princeton University Press.

Minganti, Franco (1993) "Rock 'n' Roll in Italy: Was It True Americanisation?," in Rob Kroes, Robert W. Rydell and Doeko F. Bosscher (eds.) Cultural Transmissions and Receptions: American Mass Culture in Europe (pp. 139–151). Amsterdam: VU University Press.

_____. (2000) "Jukebox Boys. Postwar Italian Music and the Culture of Covering," in Heide Fehrenbach and Uta G. Poiger (eds.) Transactions, Transgressions, Transformations (pp. 148–165). New York — Oxford: Berghahn.

Mitchell, Katharyne (1996) "In Whose Interest? Transnational Capital and the Production of Multiculturalism in Canada," in Rob Wilson and Wimal Dissanayake (eds.) Global/Local: Cultural Production and the Transnational Imaginary (pp. 219–251). Durham, NC: Duke University Press.

Miyoshi, Masao (1991) Off Center: Power and Culture Relations between Japan and the United States. Cambridge, MA: Harvard University Press.

_____. (1993) "A Borderless World? From Colonialism to Transnationalism and the Decline of the Nation-State," Critical Inquiry 19 (Summer): 726–751.

Montgomery, Maureen E. (2002) Contribution to Debate on "Transculturations: American Studies in a Globalizing World — the Globalizing World in American Studies," Amerikastudien/American Studies, 47, 1: 115–119.

Moore, R. Laurence (1970) European Socialists and the American Promised Land. New York: Oxford University Press.

Morales, Ed (2006) "The Media Is the Mensaje," The Nation, 282, 19 (May 15): 6–8.

Morin, Edgar (1970). Journal de Californie. Paris: Seuil, 1970.

Morley, David (1992) "Electric Communities and Domestic Rituals: Cultural Consumption and the Production of European Cultural Identities," in Michael Skovman and Kim Christian Schrøder (eds.) Media Cultures: Reappraising Transnational Media (pp. 65–83). London — New York: Routledge.

_____. (1997) "Theoretical Orthodoxies: Textualism, Constructivism and the 'New Ethnography' in Cultural Studies," in Marjorie Ferguson and Peter Golding (eds) Cultural Studies in Question (pp. 121–137). London: Sage.

Morris, Meaghan (1988) "Tooth and Claw: Tales of Survival, and Crocodile Dundee," in The Pirate's Fiancée: Feminism, Reading, Postmodernism (pp. 241–269). London: Verso.

Mosler, David, and Bob Catley (2000) Global America: Imposing Liberalism on a Recalcitrant World. Westport, Conn. — London: Praeger.

Mulhern, Francis (1981) The Moment of Scrutiny. London: Verso.

Murdock, Graham (1997) "Basic Notes: The Conditions of Cultural Practice," in Marjorie Ferguson and Peter Golding (eds.) Cultural Studies in Question (pp. 86–101). London: Sage.

Mutsaers, Lutgard (1990) "Indorock: An Early Euro-rock Style," Popular Music, 9,3: 307–330.

Muwakkil, Salim (2006) "A Shared Vision," The Nation, 282, 24 (June 19): 16.

Nader, Ralph (2004) The Good Fight: Declare Your In-dependence & Close the Democracy Gap. New York: Regan Books.

Nash, George H. (1976) The Conservative Intellectual Movement in America Since 1945. New York: Basic Books.

Nathan, James, and James Oliver (1987) Foreign Policy Making and the American Political System. Boston: Little, Brown.

Nederveen Pieterse, Jan (1994) "Globalisation as Hybridisation," International Sociology, 9: 161–184.

_____. (1995) "Globalization as Hybridization," in Mike Featherstone, Scott Lash and Roland Robertson (eds.) Global Modernities (pp. 45–68). London and Newbury Park, CA: Sage.

_____. (2003) "Hyperpower Exceptionalism: Globalization the American Way," in Ulrich Beck, Natan Sznaider and Rainer Winter (eds.) Global America? The Cultural Consequences of Globalization (pp. 67–94). Liverpool: Liverpool University Press.

Nelson, Elizabeth (1989) The British Counter-Culture, 1966–73: A Study of the Underground Press. London: Macmillan.

The New Oxford Dictionary of English (2001). New York: Oxford University Press.

Nietzsche, Friedrich (1974) The Gay Science. Trans. Walter Jafmann. New York: Vintage Books.

_____ (1986) Human, All Too Human. Trans. R.J. Hollingdale. Cambridge: Cambridge University Press.

Ninkovich, Frank (2001) The United States and Imperialism. Oxford: Blackwell.

Nolan, Mary (1994) Visions of Modernity: American Business and the Modernization of Germany. Oxford: Oxford University Press.

_____. (2003) "Consuming America, Producing Gender," in R. Laurence Moore and Maurizio Vaudagna (eds.) The American Century in Europe (pp. 243–261). Ithaca, NY: Cornell University Press.

_____. (2004) "What Difference Does a Cold War Make? Reflections on the German-American Relationship," in Ruud Janssens and Rob Kroes (eds.) Post–Cold War Europe and Post–Cold War America (pp. 30–44). Amsterdam: VU University Press.

Nye, Joseph S., Jr. (1990) Bound to Lead: The Changing Nature of American Power. New York: Basic Books.

_____. (2002) The Paradox of American Power: Why the World's Only Superpower Can't Go It Alone. Oxford: Oxford University Press.

O'Dell, Tom (1997) Culture Unbound: Americanization and Everyday Life in Sweden. Lund: Nordic Academic Press.

Ohmae, Kenichi (1990) The Borderless World: Power and Strategy in the Interlinked World Economy. New York: Harper Business.

_____. (1995) The End of the Nation-State: The Rise of Regional Economies. New York: Free Press.

Ong, Aihwa (1999) Flexible Citizenship. Durham, NC and London: Duke University Press.

Ong Hing, Bill (1997) To Be an American: Cultural Pluralism and the Rhetoric of Assimilation. New York: New York University Press.

Ory, Pascal (1990) "From Baudelaire to Duhamel: An Unlikely Antipathy," in Denis Lacorne, Jacques Rupnik and Marie-France Toinet (eds.), The Rise and Fall of Anti-Americanism: A Century of French Perception (42–54). London: Macmillan.

Ostrovsky, Sergei (1993) "Americanisation of Culture in Russia: From Jazz 'On the Bones' to Coca-Cola on the Chest," *Borderlines: Studies in American Culture*, 1, 1: 71–84.

Owens, John E. (2003) "Congress: The Coequal Partner," in Robert Singh (ed.) *Governing America: The Politics of a Divided Democracy* (pp. 189–214). Oxford: Oxford University Press.

Pacini Hernandez, Deborah (2001) "Race, Ethnicity and the Production of Latin/o Popular Music," in Andres Gebesmair and Alfred Smudits (eds.) *Global Repertoires: Popular Music Within and Beyond the Transnational Music Industry* (pp. 57–72). Aldershot: Ashgate.

Panitch, Leo (2000) "The New Imperial State," *New Left Review*, 11, 1: 5–20.

Parsons, Talcott (1971) *The System of Modern Societies.* Englewood Cliffs, NJ: Prentice Hall.

Pattison, Robert (1987) *The Triumph of Vulgarity: Rock Music in the Mirror of Romanticism.* New York: Oxford University Press.

Paz, Octavio (1993) "América en plural y en singular," *Vuelta* 194 (January): 11.

Pells, Richard (1997) *Not Like Us: How Europeans Have Loved, Hated, and Transformed American Culture Since World War II.* New York: Basic Books.

_____. (2004) "From Postmodernism to the Movies: The Globalization of American Culture in the 20th Century," in Rob Kroes (ed.) *Straddling Borders: The American Resonance in Transnational Identities* (pp. 51–61). Amsterdam: VU University Press.

Petterson, James (2000) "No More Song and Dance: French Radio Broadcast Quotas, *Chansons*, and Cultural Exception," in Heide Fehrenbach and Uta G. Poiger (eds.) *Transactions, Transgressions, Transformations* (pp. 109–123). New York — Oxford: Berghahn.

Petras, James, and Henry Veltmeyer (2001) *Globalization Unmasked: Imperialism in the 21st Century.* London: Zed Books.

Pfaff, William (1993) *The Wrath of Nations: Civilization and the Furies of Nationalism.* New York: Simon & Schuster.

Pickus, Noah M.J. (1997) *Becoming American/America Becoming.* Final Report of the Duke University Workshop on Immigration and Citizenship. Durham, NC: Terry Sanford Institute of Public Policy, Duke University.

Pinto, Diana (1990) "The French Intelligentsia Rediscovers America," in Denis Lacorne, Jacques Rupnik and Marie-France Toinet (eds.), *The Rise and Fall of Anti-Americanism: A Century of French Perception* (97–107). London: Macmillan.

Piore, Michael, and Charles Sabel (1984) *The Second Industrial Divide: Possibilities for Prosperity.* New York: Basic Books.

Pocha, Jehangir S. (2005) "Letter from Beijing. China's New Left," *The Nation*, 280, 18 (May 9): 22–24.

Portes, Jacques (1990) *Une fascination réticente: Les États-Unis dans l'opinion française, 1870–1914.* Presses Universitaires de Nancy.

Potter, Jonathan, and Margaret Wetherell (1987) *Discourse and Social Psychology: Beyond Attitudes and Behaviour.* London: Sage.

Pratt, Marie Louise (1992) *Imperial Eyes: Travel Writing and Transculturation.* New York: Routledge.

Preston, P.W. (1997) *Political/Cultural Identity: Citizens and Nations in a Global Era.* London: Sage.

Prévos, André J.M. (1997) "The Origins and Evolution of French Rap Music and Hip Hop Culture in the 1980s and 1990s," in George McKay (eds.), *Yankee Go Home [& Take Me With U]: Americanization & Popular Culture* (pp. 146–160). Sheffield: Sheffield Academic Press.

Prucha, Francis Paul (1985) *The Indians in American Society: From the Revolutionary War to the Present.* Berkeley: University of California Press.

Quart, Leonard (1977) "Frank Capra and the Popular Front," *Cinéaste*, Summer: 4–7.

Ragsdale, John W., Jr. (1989) "The Movement to Assimilate the American Indians: A Jurisprudential Study," *University of Missouri-Kansas City Law Review*, 57: 399–436.

Reich, Robert (1991) *The Work of Nations: Preparing Ourselves for Twenty-First Century Capitalism.* New York: Alfred A. Knopf.

Reid, T.R. (2004) *The United States of Europe: The New Superpower and the End of American Supremacy.* London: Penguin.

Rémont, René (1962) *Les États-Unis devant l'opinion française (1815–1852).* Paris: Armand Colin.

Rifkin, Jeremy (2004) *The European Dream: How Europe's Vision of the Future is Quietly Eclipsing the American Dream.* Cambridge: Polity Press.

Rigby, Brian (1991) *Popular Culture in Modern France: A Study of Political Discourse.* London: Routledge.

Ritzer, George (1992) *Sociological Theory.* Third Edition. New York: McGraw-Hill.

_____. (1993) *The McDonaldization of Society.* Thousand Oaks, CA: Pine Forge Press.

_____. (1998) *The McDonaldization Thesis: Explorations and Tensions.* London: Sage.

_____. (2000) *The McDonaldization of Society.* New Century Edition. London: Sage.

_____. (2001) *Explorations in the Sociology of Consumption: Fast Food, Credit Cards and Casinos.* London: Sage.

_____, and Todd Stillman (2003) "Assessing McDonaldization, Americanization and Globalization," in Ulrich Beck, Natan Sznaider and Rainer Winter (eds.) *Global America? The Cultural Consequences of Globalization* (pp. 30–48). Liverpool: Liverpool University Press.

Robertson, Roland (1992) *Globalization: Social Theory and Global Culture.* London: Sage.

_____. (1995) "Glocalization: Time-Space Homogeneity and Heterogeneity," in Mike Featherstone, Scott Lash, and Ronald Robertson (eds.) *Global Modernities* (pp. 25–44). London: Sage.

_____. (2001) "Globalization Theory 2000+: Major Problematics," in George Ritzer and Barry Smart (eds.) *Handbook of Social Theory* (pp. 458–471). London: Sage.

_____. (2003) "Afterword. Rethinking Americanization," in Ulrich Beck, Natan Sznaider and Rainer Winter (eds.) *Global America? The Cultural Consequences of Globalization* (pp. 257–264). Liverpool: Liverpool University Press.

Robinson, William I. (1996) *Promoting Polyarchy: Globalization, US Intervention, and Hegemony.* Cambridge: Cambridge University Press.

Rogin, Michael Paul (1967) *The Intellectuals and Mc-*

Carthy: The Radical Specter. Cambridge, MA: The M.I.T. Press.

Roosevelt, Theodore (1923) "Straight Americanism," in Hermann Hagedorn (ed.) *The Americanism of Theodore Roosevelt: Selections from His Writings and Speeches* (199–210). Boston: Houghton Mifflin.

Roseberry, William (1998) "Social Fields and Cultural Encounters," in Gilbert M. Joseph, Catherine C. Legrand, and Ricardo D. Salvatore (eds.) *Close Encounters of Empire: Writing the Cultural History of U.S.-Latin American Relations* (pp. 515–524). Durham and London: Duke University Press.

Rosenau, James N. (1992) "Governance, Order, and Change in World Politics," in James N. Rosenau and Ernst-Otto Czempiel (eds.) *Governance without Government: Order and Change in World Politics* (pp. 1–29). Cambridge: Cambridge University Press.

Rosenau, Pauline Marie (1991) *Post-Modernism and the Social Sciences: Insights, Inroads, and Intrusions.* Princeton, NJ: Princeton University Press.

Rosenberg, Emily S. (1982) *Spreading the American Dream: American Economic and Cultural Expansion, 1890–1945.* New York: Hill and Wang.

_____. (1998) "Turning to Culture," in Gilbert M. Joseph, Catherine C. Legrand, and Ricardo D. Salvatore (eds.) *Close Encounters of Empire: Writing the Cultural History of U.S.-Latin American Relations* (pp. 479–514). Durham and London: Duke University Press.

Rosendorf, Neal M. (2000) "Social and Cultural Globalization: Concepts, History, and America's Role," in Joseph S. Nye, Jr. and John D. Donahue (eds.) *Governance in a Globalizing World* (pp. 109–134). Washington, D.C.: Brookings Institution Press.

Ross, Edward A. (1914) *The Old World in the New.* London: Fisher Unwin.

Ross, George (2000) "Labor Versus Globalization," *The Annals of the American Academy of Political and Social Science*, 570 (July): 78–91.

Ross, Kristin (1995) *Fast Cars, Clean Bodies: Decolonization and the Reordering of French Culture.* Cambridge, MA: The MIT Press.

Ruggie, John, G. (1994) "At Home Abroad, Abroad at Home: International Liberalisation and Domestic Stability in the New World Order," *Millennium* 24, 3: 507–526.

Rumbaut, Rubén G. (1997) "Assimilation and Its Discontents: Between Rhetoric and Reality," *International Migration Review*, 31, 4 (Winter): 134–155.

Rupert, Mark (1995) *Producing Hegemony: The Politics of Mass Production and American Global Power.* Cambridge: Cambridge University Press.

Sachs, Jeffrey (2000) "New Global Consensus on Helping the Poorest of the Poor," *Global Policy Forum Newsletter*, 18 April.

Said, Edward W. (1978) *Orientalism.* London: Routledge and Kegan Paul.

Salacuse, Jeswald (1991) *Making Global Deals: Negotiations in the Global Marketplace.* Boston: Houghton Mifflin.

Samson, Leon (1933) *Toward a United Front: A Philosophy for American Workers.* New York: Farrar and Rinehart.

Sanchez, George J. (1990) "'Go After the Women': Americanization and the Mexican Immigrant Woman, 1915–1929," in Ellen Carol DuBois and Vickie L. Ruiz (eds.) *Unequal Sisters: A Multicultural Reader in U.S. Women's History* (pp. 250–263). New York and London: Routledge.

Sarkar, Saurav (2006) "What They're Marching For," *The Nation*, 282, 24 (June 19): 18–20.

Sassen, Saskia (1996a) "The Spatial Organization of Information Industries: Implications for the Role of the State," in James H. Mittelman (ed.) *Globalization: Critical Reflections* (pp. 33–52). Boulder — London: Lynne Rienner Publishers.

_____. (1996b) *Losing Control? Sovereignty in an Age of Globalization.* New York: Columbia University Press.

_____. (1998) *Globalization and Its Discontents: Selected Essays.* New York: The Free Press.

_____. (2000) "The State and the New Geography of Power," in Don Kalb, Marco van der Land, Richard Staring, Bart van Steenbergen, and Nico Wilterdink (eds.) *The End of Globalization: Bringing Society Back In* (pp. 49–65). Lanham, MD: Rowan & Littlefield.

Schaefer, Nancy A. (2004) "American-Led Revival Meetings as Ethnic Identity Arenas in Britain," in Simon Coleman and Peter Collins (eds.) *Religion, Identity and Change: Perspectives on Global Transformations* (pp. 119–135). Aldershot: Ashgate.

Schäfer, Hans Dieter (1986) "Bekenntnisse zur neuen Welt: USA-Kult vor dem 2. Weltkrieg," in Willi Bucher and Klaus Pohl (eds.) *Schock und Schöpfung: Jugendästhetik im 20. Jahrhundert* (pp. 383–388). Darmstadt — Neuwied: Hermann Luchterhand Verlag.

Schildt, Axel (1991) "Reise zurück in die Zukunft: Beiträge von intellektuellen USA-Remigranten zur atlantischen *Allianz*, zum westdeutschen Amerikabild, und zur 'Amerikanisierung,' in den fünfziger Jahren," *Exilforschung*, 9: 25–45.

Schinkel, Maarten (2005a) "De man na Alan Greenspan," *NRC Handelsblad*, October 25: 13.

_____. (2005b) "De ramkoers van de Amerikaanse economie," *NRC Handelsblad*, November 18/19: 27–28.

Schlesinger, Arthur M., Jr. (1991a) *The Disuniting of America: Reflections on a Multicultural Society.* Knoxville, Ten.: Whittle Direct Books.

Schlesinger, Philip (1991b) *Media, State and Nation: Political Violence and Collective Identities.* London: Sage.

_____. (1996) "Should We Worry About America?," in Annemoon van Hemel, Hans Mommaas and Cas Smithuijsen (eds.) *Trading Culture: GATT, European Cultural Policies and the Transatlantic Market* (pp. 96–110). Amsterdam: Boekman Foundation.

Schmitt, Carl (1996). *The Concept of the Political*, notes and transl. by George Schwab. Orig. 1932. Chicago and London: The University of Chicago Press.

Scholte, Jan Aart (2000) *Globalization: A Critical Introduction.* New York: St. Martin's Press.

Schou, Søren (1992) "Postwar Americanisation and the Revitalisation of European Culture, " in Michael Skovman and Kim Christian Schrøder (eds.) *Media Cultures: Reappraising Transnational Media* (pp. 142–158). London — New York: Routledge.

Schulte Nordholt, Jan Willem (1986) "Anti-Americanism in European Culture: Its Early Manifestations," in Rob Kroes and Maarten van Rossem (eds.) *Anti-Americanism in Europe* (pp. 7–10). Amsterdam: Free University Press.

Schwartz, Peter, Peter Leyden, and Joel Hyatt (1999) *The Long Boom: A Vision for the Coming Age of Prosperity.* Reading, Mass.: Perseus Publishing.

Seamann, W.R. (1992) "Active Audience Theory: Pointless Populism," *Media, Culture and Society* 14, 2: 301–311.

Sexton, Patricia Cayo (1991) *The War on Labor and the Left: Understanding America's Unique Conservatism.* Boulder: Westview Press.

Shannon, David A. (1955) *The Socialist Party of America: A History.* New York: Macmillan.

Shaw, Martin (1997) "The State of Globalization: Towards a Theory of State Transformation," *Review of International Political Economy*, 4, 3: 497–513.

Shiach, Morag (1989) *Discourse on Popular Culture: Class, Gender and History in Cultural Analysis, 1730 to the Present.* Cambridge: Polity Press.

Siegfried, André (1927) *America Comes of Age.* Trans. H.H. Hemming and Doris Hemming. New York: Harcourt.

Simmel, Georg (1991) "Money in Modern Culture," *Theory, Culture & Society*, 8: 29.

Sinclair, John (1987) *Images Incorporated: Advertising as Industry and Ideology.* London : Croom Helm.

Sinclair, Timothy J. (1994) "Passing Judgment: Credit Rating Processes as Regulatory Mechanisms of Governance in the Emerging World Order," *Review of International Political Economy*, 1, 1 (Spring): 133–159.

Singh, Robert (2003) "Introduction," in Robert Singh (ed.) *Governing America: The Politics of a Divided Democracy* (pp. 1–10). Oxford: Oxford University Press.

Skard, Sigmund (1961) *The American Myth and the European Mind: American Studies in Europe, 1776–1960.* Philadelphia: University of Pennsylvania Press.

Sklair, Leslie (2001) *The Transnational Capitalist Class.* Oxford: Blackwell.

_____. (2002) *Globalization: Capitalism and its Alternatives.* Oxford: Oxford University Press.

Sklar, Robert (1975) *Movie-made America: A Cultural History of American Movies.* New York: Random House.

Slater, David (1999) "Locating the American Century: Themes for a Post-Colonial Perspective," in David Slater and Peter J. Taylor (eds.) *The American Century: Consensus and Coercion in the Projection of American Power* (pp. 17–31). Oxford: Blackwell.

_____, and Peter J. Taylor (1999) "Preface," in David Slater and Peter J. Taylor (eds.) *The American Century: Consensus and Coercion in the Projection of American Power* (pp. xi-xiv) Oxford: Blackwell.

Smith, Clive Stafford (2005) "CIA kan zich niet verstoppen. Tijdperk van Amerikaanse folterkamer nog niet voorbij," *NRC Handelsblad*, December 15: 9.

Smith, Neil (2003) *American Empire: Roosevelt's Geographer and the Prelude to Globalization.* Berkeley: University of California Press.

Smith, Peter H. (2000) *Talons of the Eagle: Dynamics of U.S.-Latin American Relations.* Second. Ed. New York and Oxford: Oxford University Press.

Smith, Rogers M. (1993) "Beyond Tocqueville, Myrdal, and Hartz: The Multiple Traditions in America," *American Political Science Review*, 87, 3 (September): 549–566.

_____. (1997) *Civic Ideals: Conflicting Visions of Citizenship in U.S. History.* New Haven and London: Yale University Press.

Sombart, Werner (1976) *Why Is There No Socialism in the United States?* Orig. 1906. White Plains, NY: International Arts & Sciences Press.

Soros, George (2002) *George Soros on Globalization.* New York: Public Affairs.

Srinivas, Tulasi (2002) "'A Tryst with Destiny': The Indian Case of Cultural Globalization," in Peter L. Berger and Samuel P. Huntington (eds.) *Many Globalizations: Cultural Diversity in the Contemporary World* (pp. 89–116). Oxford: Oxford University Press.

Stead, William T. (1901) *The Americanization of the World, or the Trend of the Twentieth Century.* New York: Horace Markley.

Steger, Manfred B. (2002) *Globalism: The New Market Ideology.* Lanham, MD: Rowan & Littlefield.

Stern, Fritz (1961) *The Politics of Cultural Despair: A Study in the Rise of Germanic Ideology.* Berkeley: University of California Press.

Stiglitz, Joseph (2002) *Globalization and Its Discontents.* London: Penguin.

Stocking, George W., Jr. (ed.) (1974) *A Franz Boas Reader: The Shaping of American Anthropology, 1883–1911.* Chicago and London: Chicago University Press.

Storey, John (1997) *An Introduction to Cultural Theory and Popular Culture.* Second Edition. Hemel Hempstead: Prentice Hall.

_____. (1998) (ed.) *Cultural Theory and Popular Culture. A Reader.* Second Edition. Hemel Hempstead: Prentice Hall.

Strange, Susan (1989) "Toward a Theory of Transnational Empire," in Ernst-Otto Czempiel and James N. Rosenau (eds.) *Global Changes and Theoretical Challenges: Approaches to the World Politics of the 1990s* (pp. 161–176), Lexington, MA — Toronto: Lexington Books.

_____ (1997) "The Future of Global Capitalism; Or, Will Divergence Persist Forever?," in Colin Crouch and Wolfgang Streeck (eds.) (1997) *Political Economy of Modern Capitalism: Mapping Convergence and Diversity* (pp. 182–191). London: Sage.

Strinati, Dominic (1992) "The Taste of America: Americanization and Popular Culture in Britain," in Dominic Strinati and Stephen Wagg (eds.) *Come on Down: Popular Media Culture in Post-War Britain* (pp. 46–81). London and New York: Routledge.

_____. (1995) *An Introduction to Theories of Popular Culture.* London and New York: Routledge.

Sywottek, Arnold (1993) "The Americanization of Everyday Life? Early Trends in Consumer and Leisure-Time Behavior," in Michael Ermarth (eds.) *America and the Shaping of German Society, 1945–1955* (pp. 132–152). Providence — Oxford: Berg.

Taylor, Peter J. (1999) "Locating the American Century: A World-systems Analysis," in David Slater and Peter J. Taylor (eds.), *The American Century: Consensus and Coercion in the Projection of American Power* (pp. 3–16). Oxford: Blackwell.

ter Braak, Menno (1949–1951) "Waarom ik 'Amerika' afwijs." Orig. 1928, in Menno ter Braak. *Verzameld Werk I.* Amsterdam: Van Oorschot.

Therborn, Göran (1995) "Routes to/through Modernity," in Mike Featherstone, Scott Lash, and Ronald Robertson (eds.) *Global Modernities* (pp. 124–139). London: Sage.

Thomas, Caroline (1997) "Globalization and the South," in Caroline Thomas and Peter Wilkin (eds.) *Globalization and the South* (pp. 1–17). New York: St. Martin's Press.

Thomas, William I., and Dorothy S. Thomas (1928) *The Child in America: Behavior Problems and Programs.* New York: Alfred A. Knopf.

Thompson, John B. (1988) "Mass Communication and Modern Culture: Contribution to a Critical Theory of Ideology," *Sociology,* 22, 3: 359–383.

_____. (1995) *Media and Modernity.* Cambridge: Polity Press.

Thompson, Kenneth (1992) "Social Pluralism and Post-Modernity," in Stuart Hall, David Hall and Tony McGrew (eds.) *Modernity and Its Futures* (pp. 221–271). Cambridge: Polity Press.

Thurley, Keith, and Hans Wirdenius (1989) *Towards European Management.* London: Pittman.

Tillett, A.S. (1961) "Some Saint-Simonian Criticism of the United States before 1835," *Romanic Review* 10, 4 (February): 3–16.

Toinet, Marie-France (1990) "Does Anti-Americanism Exist?," in Denis Lacorne, Jacques Rupnik and Marie-France Toinet (eds.), *The Rise and Fall of Anti-Americanism: A Century of French Perception* (219–235). London: Macmillan.

Tomlinson, John (1991) *Cultural Imperialism: A Critical Introduction.* London: Pinter Publishers.

_____. (1997) "Cultural Globalization and Cultural Imperialism," in Ali Mohammadi (ed.) *International Communication and Globalization: A Critical Introduction* (pp. 170–190). London: Sage.

_____. (1999) *Globalization and Culture.* Cambridge: Polity Press.

Trennert, Robert A. (1990) "Educating Indian Girls at Nonreservation Boarding Schools, 1878–1920," in Ellen Carol DuBois and Vickie L. Ruiz (eds.) *Unequal Sisters: A Multicultural Reader in U.S. Women's History* (pp. 224–237). New York and London: Routledge.

Trilling, Lionel (1963) *Matthew Arnold.* London: Unwin Books.

Tunstall, Jeremy (1977) *The Media are American: Anglo-American Media in the World.* London: Constable.

Turner, Bryan S. (1999) *Classical Sociology.* London: Sage.

_____, and Chris Rojek (2001) *Society and Culture: Scarcity and Solidarity.* London: Sage.

UNCTAD (2004a) *World Investment Report 2004: The Shift Towards Services.* New York and Geneva: United Nations.

_____. (2004b) *World Investment Report 2004: The Shift Towards Services. Overview.* New York and Geneva: United Nations.

Utley, Robert M. (1994) *The Lance and the Shield: The Life and Times of Sitting Bull.* New York: Ballantine Books.

van Elteren, Mel (1989) "Dutch Youth under the Spell of Anglo-American Mass Culture, 1945–1965," *Economic and Social History in the Netherlands,* 1: 171–194.

_____. (1991) "The 'Roaring Twenties' in a Cosy Society," in Rob Kroes (ed.) *Within the US Orbit: Small National Cultures vis-à-vis the United States* (pp. 32–66). Amsterdam: VU University Press.

_____. (1992) "Psychology and Sociology of Work within the Anglo-American Orbit," in Hans Loeber (ed.) *Dutch-American Relations 1945–1969: A Partnership. Illusions and Facts* (pp. 153–178, 204–205, 212–214. Assen — Maastricht: Van Gorcum.

_____. (1996a) "Rocking and Rapping in the Dutch Welfare State," in John Dean and Jean-Paul Gabilliet (eds.) *European Readings of American Popular Culture* (pp. 55–68). Westport, Connecticut: Greenwood Press.

_____. (1996b) "Conceptualizing The Impact of U.S. Popular Culture Globally," *Journal of Popular Culture,* 30, 1 (Summer): 47–90.

_____. (1996c) "Gatt and Beyond: World Trade, the Arts and American Popular Culture in Western Europe," *Journal of American Culture,* 19, 3: 59–73.

_____. (1997) "American Life by Proxy: Dutch Youth and Their Sense of Place," in George McKay (ed.) *Yankee Go Home (& Take me with U): Americanization & Popular Culture* (pp. 131–145). Sheffield: Sheffield Academic Press.

_____. (1998) "Dutch Country Music: Between Creative Appropriation and Mere Epigonism," *Popular Music and Society,* 22, 1 (Spring): 89–112.

_____. (1999) "The Subculture of the Beats; A Sociological Revisit," *Journal of American Culture,* 22, 3 (Fall): 71–99.

_____. (2001) "The PCA and Popular Culture Studies at the End of the Millennium: *Quo Vadis?* A View from Europe," *Journal of Popular Culture,* 35, 1 (Summer): 107–143.

_____. (2003). "U.S. Cultural Imperialism Today; Only A Chimera?," *SAIS Review,* a Journal of International Affairs associated with the Paul H. Nitze School of Advanced International Studies of Johns Hopkins University, Washington, DC, 23, 3 (Summer-Fall): 169–188.

_____. (2005) "Teaching Popular Culture in Relation to the Social Sciences: A Critical-Emancipatory View from Europe," in Ray B. Browne (ed.) *Popular Culture Studies Across the Curriculum* (pp. 181–234). Jefferson, NC: McFarland.

_____. (2006) "Imperial Gestures in Portrayals of U.S. Culture as a 'Universal Culture,'" *Amerikastudien/American Studies,* 51, 2: 207–238.

Vaughan, Leslie J. (1991) "Cosmopolitanism, Ethnicity and American Identity: Randolph Bourne's 'Trans-National America,'" *Journal of American Studies,* 25, 3: 443–459.

Volosinov, Valentin (1973) *Marxism and the Philosophy of Language.* London: Seminar Press.

Voss, Kim (1993) *The Making of American Exceptionalism: The Knights of Labor and Class Formation in the Nineteenth Century.* Ithaca, NY: Cornell University Press.

Wagnleiter, Reinhold (1993) "Propagating the American Dream: Cultural Policies as Means of Integration," in Richard P. Horwitz (ed.), *Exporting America* (pp. 305–343). New York & London: Garland Publishing, Inc.

Wallace, Henry A. (1942) "The Price of Free World Victory," in Leland M. Goodrich (ed.) *Documents on American Foreign Relations,* Vol. IV: July 1941— June 1942. Boston World Peace Foundation.

_____. (1943) *The Century of the Common Man.* Russell Lord, ed. New York: Reynal & Hitchcock.

Waterhouse, Richard (1998) "Popular Culture," in Philip Bell and Roger Bell (eds.) *Americanization and Australia* (pp. 45–60). Sydney: University of New South Wales Press.

Watson, James (ed.) (1997) *Golden Arches East: McDonald's In East Asia.* Stanford: Stanford University Press.

Weber, Max (1922) *Gesammelte Aufsätze zur Religionssoziologie*. Tübingen: J.C.B. Mohr.

_____. (1949) *The Methodology of the Social Sciences*. Orig. 1903–1917. Glencoe, IL.: The Free Press.

_____. (1958) *The Protestant Ethic and the Spirit of Capitalism*. Orig. 1904–1905. New York: Scribner's.

_____. (1981) *General Economic History*. Orig. 1927. New Brunswick, NJ: Transaction Books.

Webster, Duncan (1988) *Looka Yonder! The Imaginary American of Populist Culture*. London and New York: Comedia Book — Routledge.

_____. (1989) "Coca-colonization and National Cultures," *Over Here: Reviews in American Studies*, 9, 2: 64–75.

Webster's Third New International Dictionary of the English Language, vol. 1 (1981). Springfield, MA: Merriam.

Weinstein, James (2003) *The Long Detour: The History and Future of the American Left*. Boulder, CO: Westview Press.

Wermuth, Mir (1993) "Weri Man!," in *Kunst en Beleid in Nederland* 6 (78–111). Amsterdam: Boekmanstichting/Van Gennep.

Wetherell, Margaret, and Jonathan Potter (1992) *Mapping the Language of Racism: Discourse and the Language of Exploitation*. Hemel Hempstead: Harvester/Wheatsheaf.

White, Richard (1983) "A Backwater Awash: The Australian Experience of Americanisation," *Theory, Culture & Society*, 1, 3: 108–122.

Wicke, Peter (1990) *Rock Music: Culture, Aesthetics and Sociology*. Cambridge: Cambridge University Press.

Wilk, Richard (1995) "The Local and the Global in the Political Economy of Beauty: From Miss Belize to Miss World," *Review of International Political Economy*, 2, 1: 117–134.

Wilkins, Mira (1974) *The Maturing of Multinational Enterprise: American Business Abroad from 1914 to 1970*. Boston: Harvard University Press.

Williams, Raymond (1977) *Marxism and Literature*. London: Oxford University Press.

Williams, T. Harry (1981) *Huey Long*. New York: Vintage Books.

Williamson, Judith (1986) *Consuming Passions*. London: Marion Boyars.

Wilson, Charles Reagan (1989) "History," in Charles Reagan Wilson and William Ferris (co-eds.), Ann J. Abadie and Mary L. Hart (associate eds.) *Encyclopedia of Southern Culture* (pp. 583–595). Chapel Hill and London: University of North Carolina Press.

Wilson, Edmund (1957) "The United States," in Edmund Wilson, *A Piece of Mind: Reflections at Sixty* (pp. 20–31). London: W.H. Allen.

Wilterdink, Nico (1991) "The Netherlands Between the Greater Powers: Expressions of Resistance to Perceived or Feared Foreign Cultural Domination," in Rob Kroes (ed.) *Within the US Orbit: Small National Cultures vis-à-vis the United States* (pp. 13–31). Amsterdam: VU University Press.

Winock, Michel (1990) "The Cold War," in Denis Lacorne, Jacques Rupnik and Marie-France Toinet (eds.), *The Rise and Fall of Anti-Americanism: A Century of French Perception* (67–76). London: Macmillan.

Wittke, Carl (1952) *Refugees of Revolution: The German Forty-Eighters in America*. Philadelphia: University of Pennsylvania Press.

Wolfe, Alan (1989) *Whose Keeper?: Social Science and Moral Obligation*. Berkeley: University of California Press.

_____. (1992) "Democracy versus Sociology: Boundaries and Their Political Consequences," in Michèle Lamont and Marcel Fournier (eds.) *Cultivating Differences: Symbolic Boundaries and the Making of Inequality* (309–326). Chicago and London: University of Chicago Press.

Wolfley, Jeanette (1991) "Jim Crow, Indian Style: The Disenfrachisement of Native Americans," *American Indian Law Review*, 16, 1: 167–122.

World Bank (2004) *World Development Report, 2004: A Better Investment Climate for Everyone*. New York: Oxford University Press.

Worpole, Ken (1983) *Dockers and Detectives: Popular Reading, Popular Writing*. London: Verso.

Ybarra, Michael J. (2004) *Washington Gone Crazy: Pat McCarran and the Great American Communist Hunt*. Hanover, NH: Steerforth.

Zeitlin, Irving M. (1968) *Ideology and the Development of Sociological Theory*. Englewood Cliffs, NJ: Prentice-Hall.

Zeitlin, Jonathan (2000) "Introduction: Americanization and Its Limits: Reworking US Technology and Management in Post-War Europe and Japan," in Jonathan Zeitlin and Gary Herrigel (eds.) *Americanization and its Limits: Reworking US Technology and Management in Post-war Europe and Japan* (pp. 1–50). Oxford: Oxford University Press.

_____, and Gary Herrigel (eds.) (2000) *Americanization and its Limits: Reworking US Technology and Management in Post-war Europe and Japan*. Oxford: Oxford University Press.

Zimmerman, Peter (1984) *Rock 'n' Roller, Beats und Punks. Rockgeschichte und Sozialization*. Essen: Rigdon Verlag.

Zinn, Howard (2003) *A People's History of the United States. 1492-Present*. New York: HarperCollins.

Index